NEW PSYCHOLOGICAL TESTS AND TESTING RESEARCH

NEW PSYCHOLOGICAL TESTS AND TESTING RESEARCH

LYDIA S. BOYAR

EDITOR

Nova Science Publishers, Inc.

New York

NOTICE TO THE READER

The Publisher has taken reasonable care in the preparation of this book, but makes no expressed or implied warranty of any kind and assumes no responsibility for any errors or omissions. No liability is assumed for incidental or consequential damages in connection with or arising out of information contained in this book. The Publisher shall not be liable for any special, consequential, or exemplary damages resulting, in whole or in part, from the readers' use of, or reliance upon, this material.

Independent verification should be sought for any data, advice or recommendations contained in this book. In addition, no responsibility is assumed by the publisher for any injury and/or damage to persons or property arising from any methods, products, instructions, ideas or otherwise contained in this publication.

This publication is designed to provide accurate and authoritative information with regard to the subject matter covered herein. It is sold with the clear understanding that the Publisher is not engaged in rendering legal or any other professional services. If legal or any other expert assistance is required, the services of a competent person should be sought. FROM A DECLARATION OF PARTICIPANTS JOINTLY ADOPTED BY A COMMITTEE OF THE AMERICAN BAR ASSOCIATION AND A COMMITTEE OF PUBLISHERS.

LIBRARY OF CONGRESS CATALOGING-IN-PUBLICATION DATA

New psychological test and testing research/Lydia S. Boyar, editor.
    p. cm.
  Includes index.
  ISBN-13:978-1-60021-570-4 (hardcover)
  ISBN 978-1-60021-570-4 (hardcover)
  1. Psychological tests. I. Boyar, Lydia S.
BF176.N484 2007
150.28'7—dc22

Published by Nova Science Publishers, Inc. ✦ New York

CONTENTS

PREFACE

Psychological testing has grown exponentially as techological advances have permitted it to and societal complexities have necessitated it's growth. Psychological testing or psychological assessment is a field characterized by the use of samples of behavior in order to infer generalizations about a given individual. By samples of behavior, one means observations over time of an individual performing tasks that have usually been prescribed beforehand. These responses are often compiled into statistical tables that allow the evaluator to compare the behavior of the individual being tested to the responses of a norm group. The broad catagories of psychological evaluation tests include: Norm-referenced, IQ/achievement tests, Neuropsychological tests, Personality tests, Objective tests (Rating scale), Direct observation tests, Psychological evaluations using data mining. This new book presents gathers significant research from around the world.

Chapter 1 - A fundamental challenge in inpatient psychiatry involves accurate diagnosis. This chapter addresses the role of psychological testing on an inpatient service and its contribution to differential diagnosis and treatment planning. Relevant tests include tests of intellectual functioning (with emphasis on the WAIS-III), projective tests (the Rorschach, TAT) and targeted tests of specific disorders and syndromes (e.g., Yale Brown Obsessive Compulsive Scale (YBOCS); Positive and Negative Symptoms Scale (PANSS)). Literature on the relationship between cognitive and projective testing and other measures of psychopathology will be reviewed. An overarching conceptual framework within which to approach differential diagnosis will also be proposed, specifically a hierarchical systems model of mental phenomena. Guidelines for interpreting test results will then be discussed with an emphasis on a step-wise approach to test interpretation. The first step focuses on potential confounds of test results (e.g., perceptual problems, excessive sedation). The second step involves assessment of cognitive function. Cognitive assessment is used to establish the client's level of information processing, to identify mental retardation, and to delineate specific cognitive impairments. The third step involves assessment of axis I pathology such as psychosis, depression, and mania. Information on relevant mental status parameters, such as organization of thought and regulation of affect, is gleaned from both cognitive and projective testing as well as patient history and behavioral observation. Additionally, specific axis I disorders can be assessed with targeted instruments. As the presence of significant mental status changes can confound assessment of character pathology, assessment of axis I pathology must precede assessment of axis II pathology. The fourth step involves evaluation of axis II or character pathology. Projective testing, including the Rorschach and the TAT, can illuminate patterns of self and other representation. Structured clinical interviews and self report questionnaires can also identify specific DSM IV axis II diagnoses and relevant personality traits. Finally, case material will be included to illustrate key points.

Chapter 2 - There exist few brief Japanese measures of coping that have adequate psychometric properties. The purpose of the present study was to develop and test the validity of a brief Likert-type scale measuring three dimensions of coping—cognitive approach, behavioral approach, and avoidance coping—in Japanese people. The developed measure was called the Coping Inventory for the Japanese (CIJ). The items of the preliminary inventory were selected from an initial item pool on the basis of the three dimensions of coping. The CIJ is composed of 15 items that were selected from among the preliminary inventory items on the basis of an item analysis of data derived from 318 college students. As a result of the factor analysis, a three-factor structure was confirmed. Each of the three factors constituted a subscale—the Cognitive Approach Coping Scale, the Behavioral Approach Coping Scale, and the Avoidance Coping Scale. The data supported that each subscale of the CIJ had acceptable internal consistency and test-retest reliability. As expected, the three-factor structure was again identified by a factor analysis of data from 167 college students. Intercorrelations between the subscale scores were significant but weak. The convergent validity of the CIJ was established through correlations between the scores on the CIJ and an existing coping scale that assesses almost the same construct as that assessed by the CIJ. It was found that the subscale scores on the CIJ were correlated in the expected direction with scores for social support, optimism, and self-esteem. In addition, the subscale scores were significantly correlated with the scores for subsequent perceived stress. Therefore, the CIJ has good construct validity.

Chapter 3 - The COPE is a widely used multidimensional self-report instrument intended to measure 15 dimensions of coping. A review of the literature suggested that the factor structure of the COPE is unstable and that the instrument contains many redundant items. Hence, the purpose of this study was to examine the internal structure and intrascale redundancy of the COPE using an Australian sample. The proposed factor structure was not replicated and a high level of intrascale redundancy was found, rather than well conceptualized items. Moreover, 13 of the 60 items failed to show adequate substantive validity. Therefore, findings and conclusions based on the use of the COPE should be critically re-examined as widespread use of this instrument might have contributed to inconsistencies in the coping literature.

Chapter 4 - A computerized neuropsychiatric diagnostic and psychodynamic psychotherapeutic process is described built on a content analysis methodology that has been previously tested and used in many different settings and a variety of circumstances. The potential usefulness of this technological development requires further clinical trials and validation.

Chapter 5 - The short-scale of the Eysenck Personality Questionnaire-revised (EPQR-S; Eysenck and Eysenck, 1992) is a 48-item personality questionnaire primarily designed to measure an individual's level of introversion-extraversion and neuroticism. Although Francis, Brown, and Philipchalk, (1992) have created the Eysenck Personality Questionnaire revised - abbreviated (EPQR-A), an even briefer version of the EPQR-S, the reliability coefficients of the measures have been less than satisfactory (Forrest, Lewis, and Shevlin, 2000). Since brevity and reliability are both extremely important, the goal of the present study was to create a briefer version of the EPQR-S that is more reliable than the EPQR-A. This was achieved by making slight alterations in the item content as well as the response format of the EPQR-S. In study 1, 257 participants completed the EPQR-S once and the EPQ-BV twice. The measures in this version of the questionnaire revealed high internal consistency and test-retest reliability. The measures in the EPQ-BV correlated highly with the corresponding original measures in the EPQR-S. A principal component analysis revealed a solution with factor loadings accurately reflecting the primary measures of the EPQR-S. In study 2, 467 participants completed the EPQ-BV. A confirmatory factor analysis using LISREL 8 (Jöreskog and Sörbom, 1999) with all of the items of the scale as observed variables and introversion-extraversion and neuroticism as latent variables revealed acceptable goodness of fit. These findings are discussed in relation to the psychometric properties of the EPQR-A and the original version of the EPQR-S.

Chapter 6 - A sample of 554 first year undergraduate students attending a university-sector college in Wales (UK) completed the Myers-Briggs Type Indicator (Form G Anglicised) and the Keirsey Temperament Sorter (1978 edition). The underlying continuous scale scores generated by the two instruments are highly correlated and appear to be assessing similar psychological constructs. However, the methods proposed by the two instruments for assigning individuals to discrete psychological types are dissimilar and result in the generation of significantly different type profiles. When compared with each other, the Myers-Briggs Type Indicator tends to generate a significantly higher representation of sensing, thinking, and perceiving, while the Keirsey Temperament Sorter tends to generate a significantly higher representation of intuition, feeling, and judging. The current study points to the relative unreliability of the MBTI and the KTS as comparable type indicators, but also to the relatively strong relationship between the MBTI and the KTS as indicators of personality traits. Comparisons of type categorisations generated by the two instruments may need, therefore, to be treated with caution.

Chapter 7 - Behavioral interventions are becoming increasingly popular in neurorehabilitation settings to treat problem behaviors that interfere with the recovery of patients. Interventions are particularly effective when adequate assessment procedures are utilized to guide the intervention plan. The purpose of this chapter, therefore, is to underscore behavioral assessment methods that are appropriate for use in neurorehabilitation settings, including behavioral interviewing, standardized rating scales and behavioral checklists, behavioral observation, and self-monitoring. Implementation of the aforementioned assessment methods are reviewed in the context of functional assessment, an integral part of behavioral assessment that emphasizes the identification of problem behaviors, problem analysis, intervention planning, and behavioral progress indicators.

Chapter 8 - Health care professionals are now faced with a growing number of patients from different ethnic groups, and from different socio-economical backgrounds. In the field of neuropsychology there is an increasing need for reliable and culturally fair assessment measures. Spanish is the official language in more than 20 countries and the second most spoken language in the world. The purpose of this article was to describe two tests developed and standardized for Spanish-speaking population and to review the main findings with a variety of clinical and experimental populations. The Brief Neuropsychological Test Battery NEUROPSI briefly assesses a wide spectrum of cognitive functions, including orientation, attention, memory, language, visuoperceptual abilities, and executive functions; normative data were collected from 1614 monolingual Spanish-speaking individuals, ages 16 to 85 years. Four age groups were used: (1) 16 to 30 years, (2) 31 to 50 years, (3) 51 to 65 years, and (4) 66 to 85 years. Data also are analyzed and presented within 4 different educational levels that were represented in this sample: (1) illiterates (zero years of school); (2) 1 to 4 years of school; (3) 5 to 9 years of school; and (4) 10 or more years of formal education. The NEUROPSI Attention and Memory was designed to assess orientation, attention and concentration, executive functions, working memory and immediate and delayed verbal and visual memory. Normative data were obtained from a sample of 950 monolingual Spanish Speaking subjects, aged 6 to 85 years. Educational level ranged from 0 to 22 years of education. These instruments may help fill the need for brief, reliable and objective evaluation of a broad range of cognitive functions in Spanish-speaking people.

Chapter 9 - Vascular dementia is an uncertain nosological entity, in which unevenly distributed patterns of cognitive deficits comprising slowing of cognitive processing, and impairment of executive function occur. Nevertheless, its clinical role in the detection of early dementia and its correlations with other cognitive process is still under investigation. Considering the potential role of subcortical frontal circuits in vascular dementia, executive functions and behaviour should be taken into account for a correct definition of the clinical diagnosis. In conclusion, new neuropsychological criteria, based on study of the natural course of vascular cognitive impairment, that focus on early disease are urgently needed. The Ten-Point Clock test (TPCT) can be used to identify early forms of Alzheimer's disease, because it is a reliable, well accepted, and easily administered at the bedside. The TPCT is a valid well-accepted, cross-cultural executive measure, correlated with verbal and semantic fluency, and with left and right recognition

Chapter 10 - The objective of this study was to adapt and validate the child version of the Personality Assessment Questionnaire with12-year-old Sinhala speaking school children in Sri Lanka. Content and consensual validity was determined by the Delphi Process. Criterion validity was determined by the degree of consensus between a clinical psychologist's assessment and respondent's total score on the instrument. Test-retest and internal consistency reliability were determined in two ways - a large group administration and a small group administration. The instrument showed satisfactory content and consensual validity. The cut-off score for the Sinhala version of the Child PAQ was determined as 89, at a sensitivity of 71.1% and specificity of 69.4% (95% confidence interval). The validated version's full scale test-retest and internal consistency reliability were satisfactory. The instrument is best administered in small rather than in large groups of respondents.

Chapter 11 - Identifying factors associated with human performance could provide evidence on which to develop intervention strategies designed to enhance performance. A prospective research methodology that is sensitive to the range of psychological states experienced by individuals performing under stress needs to be developed for such a purpose. Collecting data intrudes on the typical preparation of individuals in such situations. The act of completing a psychological inventory can make participants aware of how they feel. For example, asking a soccer penalty taker how anxious he/she feels before shooting could raise anxiety as the researcher has made the participant sensitive to how anxious they are feeling. What could follow from this is the player, who is likely to have experienced anxiety previously, will make self-regulatory efforts to reduce anxiety. Theoretically, researchers do not wish to change the construct they are seeking to assess, and if such research has damaging effects to participants beyond the benefits of conducting the research, then the study is unethical. Research teams need to consider the research skills of data collectors. The aim of the present chapter is to evaluate issues relevant to selecting psychometric measures used in research that seeks to assess relationships between psychological constructs and performance. The chapter outlines an approach for developing measures that participants are more likely to complete and suggestions for future research.

Chapter 12 - The effects of age on accuracy, consistency, and confidence of visual recognition memory were tested with the Continuous Visual Memory Test (CVMT) in an adult life-span sample (20-88 yrs, n = 83). CVMT delayed recognition was without warning again administered by mail after a mean retention interval of 10 weeks. The participants were also asked to rate how confident they were in each of their judgments at the 10 weeks test. Statistical analyses were done for each of the seven sets of CVMT target items separately and for the total scores. It was demonstrated that older participants are less confident in their memory judgments than younger, independently of memory performance. Further, the analyses revealed that the different target items of CVMT had non-identical psychometric characteristics. In predicting memory performance, an interaction between retention interval and target items from CVMT was found, and memory consistency turned out as a trait associated with type of item, not age group or retention interval.

Chapter 13 - This study investigated the effect of sport expertise level and motor skill requirements on mental rotation ability, by comparing athletes with non-athletes abilities using a well-established mental rotation questionnaire. A total of 496 students (404 athletes and 92 non-athletes), aged from 17 to 32 years, participated in the study and completed the Mental Rotation Test (Vandenberg and Kuse, 1978). The results confirmed the well-established gender effect, men scoring higher than women. However, the results showed that athletes did not score better than non-athletes and they challenged the hypothesis stating that athletes, who usually have to perform spatial body rotations may have greater mental rotation ability than those whose sporting activities do not require a modification of the body's postural organization. There was, therefore, a lack of evidence of any transfer between the ability to perform physical rotations during sporting situations to mental rotations of non-body objects. Finally, no effect related to expertise level was found, suggesting that the general mental rotation ability did not depend on expertise level, by contrast to the motor imagery ability.

PROJECTIVE TESTING

Lisa J. Cohen

Associate Professor of Clinical Psychiatry
Beth Israel Medical Center

Projective tests in American psychology have had a long and checkered career. Many such tests were first developed in the 1920's and 1930's and reached their high point by the middle of the 20th century. At their peak of popularity, projective tests were seen to provide unparalleled access to the hidden motivations, drives, conflicts, and defenses that clinical interview alone might not reveal. Despite the early efforts of several investigators, problems of interpretation were often left up to the discretion of the individual clinician or to popular convention. Thus evidence of inter-rater reliability, construct validity, and discriminant validity were woefully lacking. Because of this overall disregard for psychometric properties, once popular projective tests such as the Rorschach and the Thematic Apperception Test were roundly criticized by psychologists outside the psychoanalytic fold. With the rise of biological psychiatry, neuroscience, and psychopharmacology as well as research-based models of psychotherapy such as cognitive behavioral therapy, psychoanalytic authority was further eclipsed. John Exner's development of the Comprehensive Scoring System for the Rorschach added some much needed psychometric rigor to the best known of projective tests. Nonetheless, Exner's Rorschach system and other projective tests are still widely criticized. But it is worth while to ask: Has the pendulum swung too far in the opposite direction? Are there benefits from projective tests that are not to be found in other formats? For one, projective tests, like neurocognitive tests, directly measure behavior. Unlike interviews or questionnaires which measure the subjects' self report of their own feelings, attitudes, self view or behavior, projective tests can be seen as objective measures of test taking behavior. Thus they are protected from self report bias in a way that distinguishes them from all self-report measures. Secondly projective tests capture a broader range of clinical phenomena than do self report measures, which are necessarily targeted only to the construct measured. Thus projective tests, like cognitive tests, offer tremendous hypothesis-generating potential. This does not preclude the need for sound psychometric properties but rather raises the question of what specific psychometric properties should be established. As with cognitive tests, norms are critically important in projective tests. Ideally, norms should be based on large samples, stratified for age, gender and education and representative of the ethnic distribution of the

United States. Depending on the test, projective tests can tap information processing styles (e.g., attention to detail, organization of thought, precision of information processing), problem solving/coping styles (e.g., impulsivity, frustration tolerance, anger management)or themes related to interpersonal schemas (e.g., trust, dependency, self esteem, views of authority). Interpretation of any such information is dependent upon knowledge of the comparative frequency of such responses. Given the importance of differential diagnosis, comparisons across clinical populations would also be highly useful. Construct validity can also be demonstrated via correlations with related scales. Finally, scoring methods should not neglect face validity; scores should make intuitive sense. In sum, with proper psychometric support, projective tests can uniquely contribute to a psychological test battery.

In: New Psychological Tests and Testing Research
Editor: Lydia S. Boyar, pp. 1-33

ISBN: 978-1-60021-570-4
© 2007 Nova Science Publishers, Inc.

Chapter 1

PSYCHOLOGICAL TESTING IN INPATIENT PSYCHIATRY

Lisa J. Cohen

Associate Professor of Clinical Psychiatry; Beth Israel Medical Center;
1st Ave and 16th St. NY, NY 10003; Ph: 212-420-2316; Lcohen@chpnet.org

ABSTRACT

A fundamental challenge in inpatient psychiatry involves accurate diagnosis. This chapter addresses the role of psychological testing on an inpatient service and its contribution to differential diagnosis and treatment planning. Relevant tests include tests of intellectual functioning (with emphasis on the WAIS-III), projective tests (the Rorschach, TAT) and targeted tests of specific disorders and syndromes (e.g., Yale Brown Obsessive Compulsive Scale (YBOCS); Positive and Negative Symptoms Scale (PANSS)). Literature on the relationship between cognitive and projective testing and other measures of psychopathology will reviewed. An overarching conceptual framework within which to approach differential diagnosis will also be proposed, specifically a hierarchical systems model of mental phenomena. Guidelines for interpreting test results will then be discussed with an emphasis on a step-wise approach to test interpretation. The first step focuses on potential confounds of test results (e.g., perceptual problems, excessive sedation). The second step involves assessment of cognitive function. Cognitive assessment is used to establish the client's level of information processing, to identify mental retardation, and to delineate specific cognitive impairments. The third step involves assessment of axis I pathology such as psychosis, depression, and mania. Information on relevant mental status parameters, such as organization of thought and regulation of affect, is gleaned from both cognitive and projective testing as well as patient history and behavioral observation. Additionally, specific axis I disorders can be assessed with targeted instruments. As the presence of significant mental status changes can confound assessment of character pathology, assessment of axis I pathology must precede assessment of axis II pathology. The fourth step involves evaluation of axis II or character pathology. Projective testing, including the Rorschach and the TAT, can illuminate patterns of self and other representation. Structured clinical interviews and self report questionnaires can also identify specific DSM IV axis II diagnoses and relevant personality traits. Finally, case material will be included to illustrate key points.

INTRODUCTION

Psychological testing can be a highly valuable component of inpatient psychological treatment. Due to the severity and acuity of patients' conditions, accurate diagnosis is critically important. When the diagnostic picture is not readily determined by psychiatric interview, psychological testing can be an extremely useful addition to the treatment plan.

The most common diagnoses seen on inpatient psychiatric units include schizophrenia/schizoaffective disorders, mania, depression and severe personality disorders. Also frequent are organic mental syndromes, substance induced mood or psychotic disorders and mental retardation. For example on a single day on a 30-bed unit in a large, metropolitan hospital,[1] the following diagnoses were present. (Because of comorbid disorders the number of diagnoses exceeds thirty.)

12 patients were diagnosed with schizophrenia or schizoaffective disorder,
4 patients with bipolar mania,
7 with major depressive disorder (3 with psychotic features),
3 patients with severe axis II pathology (3 borderline, 1 Cluster A, and 2 antisocial),
3 with substance induced mood or psychotic disorder,
2 with mental retardation,
1 with mood disorder due to a general medical condition,
3 with dementia, and
1 with psychosis NOS.

For most patients, a thorough clinical interview along with solid collateral information is sufficient to establish the diagnosis. For other patients, however, this is insufficient and the picture remains murky. In these cases, psychological testing can shed light on critical aspects of mental status not readily apparent on clinical interview. In fact, psychological testing on an inpatient unit differs from that in many other settings. For one there is an enormous amount of clinical information already available. The testing clinician can read the chart, speak with the treating clinicians and other members of the interdisciplinary team, and observe the patient over a period of time. If the testing clinician works on the unit, he or she may already know the patient and thus be able to contextualize the test results to a greater extent than in most other settings.

In the following chapter we will discuss psychological testing on the inpatient setting. Specific emphasis will be placed on the importance of differential diagnosis, the relationship between axis I and axis II pathology, and the utility of tests with less reliance on self report, such as cognitive and projective tests. The chapter will be organized into a stepwise approach to psychological testing with Step 1 involving potential confounds to test data, Step 2 the assessment of cognitive function, Step 3 the assessment of axis I pathology, and Step 4 the assessment of axis II pathology. We will also present an overarching conceptual framework within which to approach differential diagnosis. Finally, three case examples will be presented to illustrate the concepts discussed.

---

[1] October 6, 2006 at Beth Israel Medical Center in New York, NY

HIERARCHICAL SYSTEMS MODEL

As a conceptual framework with which to approach inpatient psychological testing, we will use a hierarchical systems model of mental functioning. Such a systems model proposes the mind to be an organic, coherent whole comprised of interacting but distinct parts working in concert (Cohen et al, 1997; von Bertalanffy, 1968). The hierarchical model is similar to that used in studies of neuropsychological function (Siegel, 1999; Goldberg, 2001; Stuss et al, 2001). In this view, those mental functions that a) are most simple, b) form the basis of more complex mental functions, and c) are mediated by evolutionarily older, lower and deeper parts of the brain are considered lower level functions. Higher level functions are likewise a) more complex, b) built upon simpler, lower level functions, and c) mediated by evolutionarily newer, higher, and more anterior parts of the brain. For example, simple arousal and alertness is widely considered a lower level function and is mediated by the reticular activating system, located in the brain stem (Goldberg, 2001; Stuss et al, 2001). In contrast, abstract thinking, widely considered a high level mental function, is a complex function mediated by the prefrontal cortex (Goldberg, 2001; Stuss et al, 2001). Borrowing from the systems model of Sabelli and Carlson-Sabelli (1989), lower level functions can be considered *fundamental*, in that all higher level functions depend upon them. Likewise, higher level functions are considered to have *priority* in that they have greater power to direct the system as a whole (i.e., executive power).

Conceptualizing diverse mental functions as belonging to a single, integrated, and hierarchically organized system has significant implications for differential diagnosis and therefore for psychological testing. In general, the level at which the primary psychopathology occurs determines the diagnosis. Moreover, the pathologies located at lower levels need to be ruled out before considering higher level pathology. For example, a patient may present with demanding and presumptuous interpersonal behavior but also with flight of ideas and expansive affect. In this case, the primary impairment in cognition and affect suggests a more fundamental level of psychopathology than the interpersonal disruptions alone might indicate. Thus a diagnosis of mania must be considered before assuming a diagnosis of narcissistic personality pathology. Likewise, the relationship of lower level pathology to that of higher levels is always a concern with differential diagnosis. This concept is particularly important for psychologists, as their expertise in higher-level psychological functions may tend to bias them towards presumptions of higher-level psychopathology.

Figure 1 gives a schematic overview of the hierarchy of mental functions relevant to psychological testing on an inpatient psychiatric setting. This conceptual schema is meant to be used as a general guideline and not as an exact mapping of psychobiological systems. Moreover, it is recognized that not all psychological functions or brain regions can be seen as falling on a single dimension. Nonetheless, there is general agreement that a broadly hierarchical approach is a useful heuristic tool when considering the relationship among diverse psychological functions (Sabelli and Carlson-Sabelli, 1989, Cohen et al, 1997; Schwartz, 1981).

Cognition	Emotion	Behavior	Brain Areas	Diagnostic Realm
Interpersonal Representations (Self and Others)				Axis II Character Pathology
Complex Cognition	Self Conscious Emotions	Complex Planned Behavior	Prefrontal Cortex	
		Impulse Control	Orbital Frontal Cortex Cortico-Limbic Areas	
	Affect			Major Axis I Disorders
Simple Cognition	Mood	Goal Directed Behavior	Striatal Systems	
		Psychomotor Function		
		Sensory/Perceptual	Primary Sensory Areas	
				Neurology
		Alertness/Arousal	Reticular Activating System	

Figure 1. Schematic Overview of Hierarchical Structure of Psychological Functions As Pertinent to Differential Diagnosis.

As depicted in figure 1, the domain focused upon in inpatient testing is toward the top of the figure. In other words, psychological testing addresses fairly high level, complex psychological functions which are nonetheless built upon lower level, simpler functions. Note also that axis I pathology is identified with mood, affect, cognition and behavior and is located below axis II character pathology. It is a central tenet of this chapter that character pathology, diagnosed on axis II (e.g., narcissistic and borderline pathology), reflects impairment in higher level interpersonal representations, whereas the major axis I disorders (e.g., schizophrenia, bipolar disorder) reflect primary impairment in more fundamental, lower level psychological processes (e.g, mood, affect, cognition). Differentiating between these two classes of pathology, therefore, involves locating the appropriate level of primary pathology.

STEP 1: POSSIBLE CONFOUNDS TO TEST DATA

Step 1 is less about psychological testing per se than ruling out possible confounds to interpretation of the results. Many of these confounds come from levels below or above the level of psychology. Sub-psychological confounds can include sedation or perceptual problems. Supra-psychological confounds can include cultural or societal factors. For example, the patient must first be observed and the records reviewed in order to ensure that there are no significant sensory or perceptual difficulties, such as visual or auditory problems, that would preclude valid test results. Sedation is another factor that should be considered, especially on an inpatient unit where patients may be heavily medicated. If perceptual/sensory impairments can be corrected with glasses or hearing aids, testing can proceed. Otherwise tests which do not rely on the compromised sense modality should be used.

Language can also be a confound when patients are tested in a language other than their native language. While non-native speakers of English can be tested in English, interpretation of results must take language fluency into account. Further, tests with minimal reliance on verbal skills and culturally mediated learning should be included. It is of course preferable if standardized translations are available in the patient's native language, as well as a tester who speaks the patient's native language. This may be more likely in areas where the patient's native language is widely spoken, as with Spanish speakers in the United States. Additionally, features of the testing environment should be considered. While ideal testing situations are generally rare on inpatient settings, distractions such as outside noise should be minimized as much as possible and taken into account when interpreting test results.

Finally, there are numerous possible confounds resulting from differences in cultural background and educational level. To the extent possible, the patient should be considered relative to their cultural and educational norms. Separate norms for subjects with different educational levels are available for some tests (e.g., Boston Naming Test, Trailmaking Test, Stroop) (Mitrushina et al, 2005). Other tests are obviously more dependent on educational exposure than others, for example the Information subtest on the WAIS-III, which includes questions such as "Who wrote Faust?" Simple visual-spatial tests should be less sensitive to educational and cultural background. Although there remains considerable debate about this issue (Lezak et al, 2004), arguably it is virtually impossible to remove the role of cultural bias from psychological testing. Nonetheless, it is incumbent upon the tester to be mindful of these issues.

STEP 2: ASSESSING COGNITION

Because cognition is so central to higher level affective and interpersonal functions and to regulation of complex behavior, it is extremely helpful to thoroughly assess cognition prior to assessing other mental functions. Additionally, numerous cognitive disorders, such as mental retardation, dementia, or learning disability, are frequently found in inpatient psychiatry. Such disorders can either lead to or complicate the emotional and behavioral disturbances that precipitate inpatient admission. Primary cognitive disorders can also produce symptoms that mimic other disorders. For example, it may be difficult at times to distinguish delusional ideation from magical thinking, a failure of logic which is associated with cognitive immaturity (Subbotsky, 2004) and neuropsychological dysfunction (te Wildt and Schultz-Venrath, 2004). Finally, many axis I disorders have considerable cognitive sequelae. Depression results in decreased attention and concentration (Lockwood et al, 2002; Taylor et al, 2006; APA, 1994), psychosis affects executive functions and abstraction (Brickman et al, 2004; Joyce et al, 2005), and autism is characterized by increased focus of interests and impaired social cognition (APA, 1994).

The WAIS-III

The Wechsler Adult Intelligence Scale-3rd edition (WAIS-III; Wechsler, 1997, 2002) is one of the most widely used cognitive tests available, with extensive data supporting multiple aspects of reliability and validity. Due to both its excellent psychometric properties and the comprehensive profile it provides, it is a highly valuable tool on an inpatient setting. The

WAIS-III is comprised of 14 subtests, 4 Index Scores (Verbal Conceptual Index (VCI), Perceptual Organizational Index (POI), Working Memory Index (WMI), and Processing Speed Index (PSI)) and 3 overall intelligent quotients (Full Scale IQ, Verbal IQ and Performance IQ). All indices are standardized with a mean of 100 and a standard deviation of 15. For all subtests, the mean is 10 and the standard deviation 3. The WAIS-III was normed on a sample of 2,450 American adults, stratified according to age, gender, race/ethnicity, educational level and geographical region to match the United States census. Criterion validity was obtained by correlating the four indices and three IQ scores with the Stanford-Binet Intelligence Scale and the Standard Progressive Matrices. Convergent and divergent validity was obtained by correlating the seven composite measures with 17 external measures, grouped according to general cognitive ability, attention, memory, language, spatial processing, executive functions and fine motor speed and dexterity. Although these last data support the discriminative validity of the WAIS-III, the sample sizes involved were often very small, ranging from 103 down to 16.

When interpreting the WAIS it is helpful to move from the general to the particular. The Full Scale, Verbal and Performance IQ's (FSIQ, VIQ, and PIQ) give an overall sense of the patient's cognitive ability. The Index Scores should next be considered to gain a more finely grained understanding of cognitive function. The differences between WAIS scores are also important and the test manual provides normative data on discrepancies between them. It is important next to consider the individual test scores. Particularly on an inpatient setting, the subtests within each index might vary considerably from each other. Thus the amount of inter-test scatter offers critical information. Significant scatter may indicate the intrusion of psychiatric illness into cognitive performance or the presence of a specific neuropsychological deficit. In contrast, individuals with mild and moderate mental retardation tend to show low, flat profiles with little variation across indices (Wechsler, 1997). Intra-test scatter also warrants attention. If a patient answers more difficult questions correctly but misses easier ones, he or she may be functioning below capacity, possibly due to psychopathology. Finally, peaks and troughs of subtest scores should be noted. All of these features can have diagnostic implications, as will be discussed in more detail under Step 3: Assessment of Axis I Pathology.

It is also important to consider the time course of cognitive impairment. While the WAIS-III gives only a cross-sectional assessment, the pattern of scores can give clues as to whether the impairment is acute or longstanding or reflective of a higher level of premorbid functioning. The distinction between crystallized and fluid intelligence is helpful in this regard (Cattell, 1987; Horn and Catell, 1966). Crystallized intelligence refers to learned information or skills that are relatively resilient to age and psychopathology. WAIS tests associated with verbal conceptual abilities, such as Vocabulary and Information, may be seen as reflective of crystallized abilities. Similarly, word knowledge or reading ability is frequently used to measure premorbid IQ and has been found to remain relatively intact in patients with neuro-cognitive and psychiatric disorders (Crawford et al, 1992; Joyce et al, 2005).

Fluid intelligence refers to the ability to reason and solve problems effectively and relates to functions such as attention, learning, memory, and processing speed (Douchemane and Fontaine, 2003: Engle et al, 1999). These skills tend to deteriorate with age and are compromised in many psychiatric illnesses (Lockwood et al, 2002; Taylor et al, 2006; Nebes et al, 2000; Brickman et al, 2004; Joyce et al, 2005). WAIS tests that might be associated with fluid skills include Digit Symbol, Digit Span, and Letter-Number Sequencing. Some tests, such as Arithmetic, may tap both crystallized and fluid processing skills. Reduced fluid skills juxtaposed against higher crystallized knowledge may suggest deterioration from a higher level of functioning. Likewise, lowered crystallized and fluid abilities may suggest longstanding and even lifelong cognitive impairment.

Additional Cognitive Tests

While the WAIS-III gives an excellent overview of overall cognitive function, there are times when more targeted cognitive assessments are indicated. For this a wealth of additional cognitive tests are available. The Mini Mental Status Exam (MMSE) (Folstein, Folstein, and McHugh, 1978) is a widely used screen for dementia while the Dementia Rating Scale (Mattis, 1988) offers a more thorough dementia evaluation. The Wechsler Memory Scale-3rd Edition (WMS-III) (Wechsler, 1997, 2002) provides a comprehensive and well standardized assessment of memory; the Boston Naming Test assesses language (Kaplan et al, 1983); and the Halstead Reitan Battery (Reitan and Wolfson, 1993) and the Luria-Nebraska Neuropsychological Battery (Golden and Freshwater, 2001) offer more comprehensive assessments of neuropsychological function. There are also a number of test manufacturers, such as Psychological Assessment Resources (1-800-331-8378), Pro-Ed (1-800-897-3202), and Harcourt Assessment (formerly the Psychological Corporation) (1-800-211-8378), that publish cognitive tests. Additionally, there are two classic compendia of cognitive tests by Lezak and colleagues (Lezak, Howieson, and Loring, 2004) and by Spreen and Strauss (1998). Finally *The Handbook of Normative Data* by Mitrushina et al (2005) lists norms for a number of tests lacking norms from the test manufacturers.

STEP 3: ASSESSMENT OF AXIS I PATHOLOGY

The assessment of axis I pathology is often the primary goal of inpatient testing. Consistent with the hierarchical model of mental processes mentioned earlier, axis I disorders are conceptualized to reflect disruption at the level of thought, emotion and behavior. Such pathology might involve affective lability or flattening; impaired initiative or impulse control; or significant disorganization of thought.

Because of the wealth of clinical information available on the inpatient unit, we will first focus on tests that address questions not easily answered in the clinical interview. Specifically we will focus upon the WAIS-III and the Rorschach Inkblot Test, both of which provide a rich overview of mental processes. As such, they are particularly useful for either generating clinical hypotheses or confirming provisional diagnoses. Moreover, as these tests measure actual test taking behavior as opposed to self description they are less vulnerable to self-report biases than many questionnaires or interviews. Following this discussion, we will address more targeted tests of specific axis I diagnoses.

Diagnostic Indications of the WAIS-III

While there is little literature that specifically compares WAIS performance across psychiatric diagnoses, there is a large cognitive literature about different psychiatric disorders. Given the excellent validity of the WAIS, it is reasonable to hypothesize that robust neurocognitive findings about various psychiatric diagnoses will be reflected in WAIS performance. Of course, these suggestions must be seen as preliminary and awaiting empirical validation. Nonetheless, examination of WAIS profiles can reveal valuable information to help the clinician form diagnostic hypotheses during the testing process.

Depression

Neurocognitive studies of depression have shown decrements in working memory, processing speed, attention/concentration and psychomotor speed (Lockwood et al, 2002; Taylor et al, 2006; Nebes et al, 2000) and reduced concentration is a diagnostic criterion for major depression in DSM-IV (APA,1994). Thus we would anticipate lower Performance IQ than Verbal IQ in depression along with select decreases in Working Memory and Processing Speed Indices. Among Perceptual Organization Index tests, we would anticipate worse performance on timed (e.g., Block Design) vs. untimed tests (e.g., Matrix Reasoning). Verbal Conceptual scales, such as Vocabulary, Information and Comprehension[2], should be relatively intact.

Psychosis

There is a large literature documenting neurocognitive pathology in schizophrenia and related psychotic disorders. Schizophrenics, and to a lesser extent patients with schizotypal personality disorder and first degree relatives of schizophrenics, demonstrate marked deficits in working memory, executive functions, and attention (Brickman et al, 2004; Joyce et al, 2005).

Further, patients with schizophrenia demonstrate evident deterioration from premorbid IQ (Joyce et al, 2005; Crawford et al, 1992). Thus, as with depressed patients, we would expect lowered performance on the Working Memory Index and Psychomotor Speed Index. In fact, as reported in the WAIS-III manual, a sample of schizophrenics scored best on the VCI (93.3 $\pm$ 16.4) followed by the POI (89.6 $\pm$ 13.9), the WMI (85.0 $\pm$ 15.1) and the PSI (83.4 $\pm$ 11.8). Whereas such deficits in depressed patients may be related to reduced effort and processing speed (Lockwood et al, 2002; Nebes et al, 2000), problems organizing and synthesizing information may be more prominent with schizophrenics. For example, difficulties synthesizing complex details into a whole may lead to lowered Block Design or Object Assembly. Additionally, difficulties maintaining a coherent mode of processing may result in notable intra-test scatter. Further, schizophrenics show a select difficulty with abstraction, such that tests of abstraction abilities, e.g., proverbs, are often used in mental status exams (Sadock and Sadock, 2003). Thus lowered Similarities relative to other VCI scales may be a useful marker of a schizophrenic process.

As language functions in schizophrenics have been shown to be less impaired than memory, attention, executive, motor or visual-spatial functions (Bilder et al, 2000; Brickman

---

[2] Although Comprehension is not included in the VCI, it does load on the Verbal Conceptual factor (Wechsler, 1997).

et al, 2004) Verbal Conceptual tests, such as Vocabulary and Information, may be relatively intact. In the case of significant thought disorder, however, the abstract thought necessary for defining words may be compromised, reducing the Vocabulary score. The duration of illness should also be taken into consideration. While there is robust evidence of significant cognitive impairment even at illness onset (Bilder et al, 2000; Joyce et al, 2005; Brickman et al, 2004), greater duration of illness can result in greater cognitive decline (Bilder et al, 2000).

Negative Symptoms

As the literature has shown a strong relationship between negative symptoms and neurocognitive impairment in schizophrenia (Milev et al, 2005), globally reduced cognitive function in the absence of florid psychotic process may be indicative of prominent negative symptoms. Reduced processing speed, working memory, attention, visuo-spatial skills, problem-solving, and language skills have all been correlated with negative symptoms (Milev et al, 2005). In contrast, strikingly disorganized thought process may be more reflective of positive symptoms and may be thus more responsive to medication (Andreasen, 1985; Buchanan et al, 1998).

Mania

Studies of neurocognition in mania have been mixed and surprisingly sparse compared to similar literature on schizophrenia. Bipolar patients offer a number of difficulties with regard to characterization of their cognitive functioning. There is considerable variety among patients with bipolar disorder, as such patients vary according to level of baseline functioning, degree of depressive, manic or mixed symptomatology, and degree of psychotic process. As all of these factors have a strong impact on cognitive functioning, we can expect significant heterogeneity in cognitive function among bipolar patients, which has been supported by the literature (Dickerson et al, 2004). Overall, bipolar patients have been shown to have general decrements in fluid processing skills, which are less severe than those of schizophrenics (Hobart et al, 1999). In a study comparing demographically matched pairs of bipolar and schizophrenic patients, bipolar patients scored better than schizophrenics in most tests of a large neuropsychological battery. The largest effect sizes were observed with general intellectual functioning (WAIS III full scale IQ), WAIS Vocabulary test, memory and complex attention (Hobart et al, 1999). The same study demonstrated a smaller decline in general intellectual functioning from estimated premorbid IQ in bipolar patients relative to schizophrenics. In addition, although this must be seen as entirely speculative, it is worth considering whether hypomanic patients, particularly those without notable thought disorder, may have elevated attention and psychomotor speed and thus might show elevations on tests within the Psychomotor Speed and Working Memory Indices.

Autism/PDD

Although there is still considerable debate about the assessment of autism spectrum disorders (ASD's), studies have suggested several consistent neurocognitive findings. Deficits in social functioning are characteristic of autism and related disorders and form part of the criteria for diagnosis. Therefore, we should expect relative deficits in scales sensitive to social competence, such as Comprehension and Picture Arrangement. Studies on visual spatial functioning have been inconsistent, suggesting that some patients demonstrate reduced visual-spatial function, while others may show enhanced visual-spatial processing (Caron et al,

2006; Williams et al, 2005). A number of studies have documented elevated Block Design scores in autistic subjects (Caron et al, 2006; Motron, 2004). Thus patients with ASD's may demonstrate either decreased or elevated Perceptual Organizational Index Tests, especially Block Design.

Although patients in the autistic spectrum have demonstrated memory deficits in several studies (Salmond et al, 2005; Minshew and Goldstein, 2001), there is also evidence for superior memory in at least a subgroup of ASD's. Such strengths appear to be restricted to particular types of memory, including memory for factual information (O'Shea et al, 2000), or "rote" memory (Toichi and Kamio, 2002). This is consistent with the diagnostic criteria for autism and Asperger's Syndrome, which include highly focused interests and preoccupations (APA, 1994). This is also consistent with the clinical presentation of ASD's, and especially autistic savants, who can store and process vast amounts of factual information about very specific topics, such as train schedules or calendars (Bodaert et al, 2005). If we extrapolate such findings to the WAIS, we could hypothesize that some individuals falling on the autistic spectrum would have relative strengths on Information and Digit Span (Digits Forward more than Backward), as these tests are sensitive to rote or factual memory.

Learning Disorders

If there is a consistent relative deficit across a particular cognitive domain (e.g., verbal or spatial skills), a learning disorder should be considered. Learning disabilities can have direct implications for school or occupational functioning and may also result in associated problems with frustration tolerance, perseverance, and achievement behavior (Charlton, 1985). As such, test taking behavior can also support diagnosis of an undiagnosed learning disorder. Comments such as "I've never been good at this" or a pattern of giving up easily on tests in which the subject does poorly while persevering on tests of intact skills may also reflect adaptation to long standing but specific cognitive deficits.

The Rorschach Inkblot Test

The Rorschach Inkblot Test is uniquely sensitive to psychotic processes that may not be discernible on clinical interview. Because of the debate surrounding its merits, we will discuss its history and psychometric properties in some detail. First developed by Hermann Rorschach in 1922, the Rorschach Inkblot test has had a long and somewhat controversial history. Rorschach, a psychiatrist with an interest in psychoanalysis, was intrigued by the evocative power of his inkblots. Selecting 10 blots from an initially larger collection, he created the standard stimuli for the Rorschach test, which would later become a cornerstone of psychoanalytic assessment. Of interest, given our focus on the inpatient setting, his work was originally based on comparisons between healthy adults and schizophrenics (Rorschach,1922). Although quite a few scoring systems were developed, spanning from comprehensive assessments (Klopfer et al, 1954; Hertz, 1942; Rapoport et al, 1946; Shafer, 1954; Beck, 1944) to measurements of more specific psychological traits (Blatt and Lerner, 1983; Blatt et al, 1976; Mayman, 1967; Urist, 1977), the extensive claims of Rorschach interpretive power were inadequately grounded in conventional psychometric data. Largely because of this, outside of psychoanalytic circles the Rorschach was vigorously discredited (Meyer, 2003; Meyer and Archer, 2001; Exner, 1993). This problem was greatly minimized in 1974 when John Exner published the Comprehensive Scoring System for the Rorschach. Basing his scoring system on previous comprehensive approaches, Exner finally provided extensive psychometric data to bring the Rorschach up to contemporary standards of psychological test construction. Although distrust of the Rorschach still continues, the Society for Personality Assessment has recently produced a white paper supporting the psychometric properties of the Rorschach (SPA, 2005). Meanwhile, the Comprehensive System has been revised and updated several times (Exner, 1993; Exner 1997).

There is at present a fairly large empirical literature on the Rorschach, the vast majority of studies using Exner's system. Meyer and Archer (2001) applied meta-analytic techniques to compare the reliability and validity of the Rorschach to that of other well known instruments. With regard to general concurrent validity, i.e., the relationship between any subscale and any outcome measure, the Rorschach, MMPI, and the WAIS "obtained generally similar estimates of global validity, falling in the range between .25 and .35." (p. 490). These effect sizes lie in the moderate range and are similar to those found in many other psychological studies. A similar meta-analysis was performed looking at specific subscales (e.g., the Rorschach SCZI, DEPI, and oral dependency scale) and outcome variables, (e.g., thought disturbance, depressive diagnosis, and dependent behavior, respectively). Again concurrent validity of Rorschach scales was comparable to that found in MMPI and IQ scales.

As the authors point out, however, while there is adequate data supporting the overall reliability and validity of Rorschach scales, there is inadequate data evaluating the specific Rorschach scales and summary indices. In fact, in the second meta-analysis, the Rorschach schizophrenia index (SCZI) produced a considerably higher effect size (.44) than did the depression index (DEPI) (.14). This discrepancy may reflect variation in face validity across Exner's scores. For example, measures of disorganized thought process on the Rorschach have clear similarities with disorganized thought process in other contexts. On the other hand, it is a much greater inferential leap to determine depression from scores of reflections or three dimensional vistas, which are included in the DEPI.

The issue of face validity has relevance for clinicians. As discussed by Meyer and Archer (2001), scores that have less intuitively obvious relation to the constructs attributed to them may have weaker evidence of construct validity than scores that bear more obvious relation to their associated constructs.

It should also be noted that there has been criticism of the generalizability of the norms provided by Exner, suggesting they may lead to overestimation of pathology in non-patient adults (Wood et al, 2001). Whereas norms for many tests are drawn from samples representative of the US population, Exner derived his norms from non-patient adults, thereby producing an atypically healthy sample (Meyer and Archer, 2001). Thus there may be difficulties using such data to gauge precise levels of psychopathology. It is therefore recommended that the clinician use the norms as guidelines for test interpretation, rather than as definitive diagnostic criteria.

Despite these caveats, Exner's extensive normative data is a pivotal contribution to the Rorschach literature and provides the best comparative data of individual scores across different clinical groups. In the 1993 edition of the 1st volume of his series on the Comprehensive System (Exner, 1993), Exner presents norms for 700 healthy adults along with those of children of various ages, inpatient schizophrenics, inpatient depressives and several other groups. Although he does not present statistical analyses of these data, he does provide sufficient information (means, standard deviations and n's) to calculate t-tests, such that different patient groups can be compared with the sample of healthy adults. Table 1 lists the means and standard deviations from his samples of normal adults, 10 year old children, inpatient schizophrenics and inpatient depressives, along with the statistical significance of each group's comparisons with the index group of normal adults. Additionally, t-tests were performed to compare inpatient schizophrenics with inpatient depressives. Variables were selected for their significance for the inpatient setting. Data on ten year old children were also included to illustrate response patterns typical of immature minds, which may show parallels with emotionally immature adults as well as individuals with developmental delays or mental retardation. Due to the large sample sizes involved, relatively small differences reach high levels of statistical significance.

Table 1. Comparison of Rorschach Scores Based on Exner's Normative Data

Rorschach Measure	Normal Adults n=700	10 y.o. Children N=120[#]	Inpatient Schizophrenics N=320	Inpatient Depressives N=315
Intellectual Complexity				
R	22.67 + 4.2	20.97 + 1.9[c]	23.44 + 8.7	22.70 + 8.5
W	8.55 + 1.9	9.52 + 0.9[c]	8.79 + 5.1	8.48 + 4.1
Dd	1.23 + 1.7	1.35 + 0.4	4.86 + 5.0[c]	4.28 + 5.3[c]
S	1.47 + 1.2	1.48 + 0.7	2.77 + 2.5[c]	2.51 + 2.3[c]
Thought Organization				
FQxo	16.99 + 3.3	15.80 + 2.0[c]	8.92 + 3.4[c,f]	11.76 + 4.3[c]
FQxu	3.25 + 1.8	2.95 + 0.8[b]	4.89 + 3.2[c]	5.20 + 3.2[c]
FQx-	1.44 + 1.0	1.58 + 1.0[c]	8.95 + 5.3[c,f]	4.70 + 3.4[c]
X-%	0.07 + 0.1	0.08 + 0.1	0.37 + 0.1[c,f]	0.20 + 0.1[c]
Xu%	0.14 + 0.1	0.15 + 0.1	0.20 + 0.1[c,e]	0.22 + 0.1[c]
WSum6	3.28 + 2.9	10.22 + 3.8[c]	44.69 + 35.4[c,f]	18.20 + 13.7
Color (Affective Processing)				
FC	4.09 + 1.9	2.55 + 1.0[c]	1.54 + 1.6[c]	1.58 + 2.0[c]
CF	2.36 + 1.3	3.68 + 1.3[c]	1.24 + 1.4[c,e]	1.58 + 1.4[c]
C	0.08 + 0.3	0.13 + 0.3	0.42 + 0.7[c,f]	0.72 + 1.0[c]
SumColor	6.54 + 2.3	6.37 + 1.5	3.25 + 2.6[c,e]	3.91 + 2.5[c]
WSumC	4.52 + 1.8	5.16 + 1.3[c]	2.63 + 2.2[c,f]	3.45 + 2.2[c]
Shading (Dysphoric Affect)				
SumC'	1.53 + 1.3	0.79 + 0.9[c]	1.50 + 1.6[f]	2.16 + 1.8[c]
SumV	0.26 + 0.6	0.02 + 0.13[c]	0.60 + 1.2[c,f]	1.09 + 1.23[c]
SumY	0.57 + 1.0	0.43 + 0.7	2.12 + 2.6[c]	1.81 + 1.4[c]
Sum Shading	3.39 + 2.2	1.83 + 1.3[c]	4.68 + 4.5[c,f]	5.92 + 3.7[c]
Movement Responses				
M	4.31 + 1.9	3.65 + 1.6[c]	6.00 + 4.3[c,f]	3.57 + 2.2[c]
FM	3.70 + 1.2	5.53 + 1.5[c]	2.41 + 2.4[c,f]	3.12 + 2.8[c]
MQ-	0.03 + 0.2	0.17 + 0.4[c]	2.42 + 2.5[c,f]	0.58 + 0.8[c]
a	6.48 + 2.1	7.15 + 1.4[c]	5.51 + 3.9[c,d]	4.79 + 3.2[c]
p	2.69 + 1.5	3.27 + 0.7[c]	4.25 + 3.3[c,d]	3.66 + 2.5[c]
Content				
H	3.40 + 1.8	2.47 + 1.1[c]	3.17 + 2.4[f]	2.05 + 1.5[c]
A	8.18 + 2.0	8.92 + 1.2[c]	8.21 + 3.5[d]	7.57 + 3.3[b]

[#] n=90 for some Rorschach variables.

[a] p<.05, [b] p<.01, [c] p<.001 compared to Normal Adults.

[d] p<.05, [e] p<.01, [f] p<.001 for schizophrenics vs. depressives.

The first section in table 1 includes measures considered reflective of intellectual effort and ideational complexity. R refers to the number of responses generated. W, Dd, and S refer to the areas of the blots incorporated into the subject's response. W is scored when the subject incorporates the whole blot into the concept, Dd when the subject utilizes an infrequently used area of the blot, and S when the subject incorporates the white space into the response. In comparison with normal adults, 10 year old children have significantly fewer R responses and significantly more W responses, while no such differences are found with the two adult patient groups. This suggests reduced complexity in children's responses, consistent with their developmental level. In contrast, both inpatient groups showed significantly more Dd and S responses than the normal adults, reflecting unconventional modes of attending to features of the blot.

The second section refers to the organization of thought. Because the accuracy of the subject's percepts cannot be objectively determined, Exner estimates accuracy of perception by measuring the frequency of each response within a normative population. Responses listed by at least 2% of the normative sample are coded as having ordinary form quality (Fo). Those that are less commonly perceived but still maintain some visual link to the contours of the blot (as determined either by scoring guidelines or subjectively by the tester) are coded unusual (Fu) and those that are both uncommon and have no visual connection to the blot are coded as having poor form quality (F-). The first five variables listed in this section all refer to form quality. While all groups demonstrate lower form quality than the normal adults, the differences are most dramatic among the schizophrenics, followed by the inpatient depressives and then the children. Thus, schizophrenics demonstrate the most difficulty perceiving ambiguous information in conventional ways. The last variable, WSum6, refers to the number of special scores, which indicate responses with illogical and bizarre reasoning. Thus while form quality may be seen as a measure of reality testing, special scores may be seen as a measure of thought disorder. As is evident in table 1, schizophrenics far exceed the other groups on this measure as well. Of note, schizophrenics score significantly worse than inpatient depressives on most of these measures.

The processing of color is considered reflective of the processing of emotion. FC responses incorporate both form and color into the percept but predominantly rely on form. This suggests an integration of affect and cognition, in which cognition strongly mediates the experience and expression of emotion. FC responses thus reflect healthy and mature emotional functioning. Likewise, in table 1, FC responses are more common in the index group of healthy adults than in all other groups. CF responses also incorporate both color and form but are predominantly dependent on color, suggesting that affect dominates the exercise of cognition. In support of this notion, healthy adults produce more FC responses and fewer CF responses than do 10 year old children. Pure C responses involve color with no form, suggestive of affect wholly unmediated by cognition. These are relatively rare but are nonetheless least common in the index group of healthy adults. Further, the relative paucity of color based responses in both the schizophrenic and depressed patients is consistent with the constricted or blunted affect characteristic of both diagnostic groups.

Responses based on shading or variations in black and white tonality are considered indicative of dysphoric emotion, and thus should be elevated in depressed patients. As presented above, both depressed and schizophrenic inpatients show significantly more shading responses than do normal adults, with depressives also providing more shading scores than schizophrenics. Children, on the other hand, provide significantly fewer shading responses than the index group, probably reflecting their tendency towards simpler and less nuanced responses.

Human movement (M) and animal movement (FM) responses may be reflective of several traits, such as ideational complexity, interpersonal relatedness, and level of mental activation. Children are expected to see more animal movement responses relative to human movement responses than do adults, which is supported by the data above. Similarly, relative to adults, children have less human content (H) and more animal content (A) responses. While schizophrenics show more M responses than either normal adults or depressives, the form quality of these responses (MQ-) is much lower than the other groups. Finally both patient groups show fewer active movement responses (a) and more passive movement responses (p) than do normal adults.

Exner (1986) also compared 84 borderline personality disorder patients to 80 schizophrenic and 76 schizotypal patients (using DSM III diagnoses) on a broad range of scores from the Comprehensive System. Borderlines clearly differed from both schizophrenic and schizotypal patients on color (WSumC, D), achromatic color (sum shading, es), and special scores (Sum6, WSum6), such that borderlines showed increased expression of emotion, including dysphoric emotion, and better organization of thought than either of the other groups. Additionally borderlines had a much higher percentage of extratensive subjects (WSumC - M > 1.5) than either group and 35% of borderlines had CF + C – FC >1. These findings suggest a propensity towards emotion-dominated thought in borderline patients, consistent with their characteristic affective lability and impulsivity. Of note, schizophrenics, but not schizotypals, also showed a high rate of color dominated color responses (CF + C – FC >1). Thus while both borderlines and schizophrenics can demonstrate signs of poorly mediated affect, borderlines demonstrate greater affectivity overall and significantly less thought disorder than do schizophrenics.

In summary, use of the Rorschach can illuminate aspects of patients' mental functioning, such as mood, emotional regulation, mental maturity, and the complexity and organization of thought processes, which might not be accessible through either self report or behavioral observation. Thus, as part of a broad-based, comprehensive assessment, the Rorschach can be highly useful tool in the service of differential diagnosis.

Additional Tests

The value of the WAIS and the Rorschach is in their breadth of focus and hypothesis-generating capacity. Once specific diagnoses are identified, however, more targeted measures of specific axis I disorders may be indicated.

The Structured Clinical Interview for DSM-IV (SCID I) (First et al, 1997)

This is a semi-structured interview that assesses whether the subject meets criteria for a range of DSM-IV axis I disorders. There is an extensive overview section followed by six modules, Mood Episodes, Psychotic and Associated Symptoms, Differential Diagnosis of Psychotic Disorders, Mood Disorders, Alcohol and Other Substance Use Disorders, and Anxiety and Other Disorders. The clinician version (SCID-CV) has been streamlined from the original research versions to focus on the most common diagnoses. While administration of the entire SCID-I is fairly time intensive, separate modules can be selected to evaluate specific diagnoses.

The Positive and Negative Symptoms Scale (PANSS) (Kay et al, 1994)

The PANSS is also a semi-structured interview and assesses schizophrenic symptomatology in considerable detail. Ratings are made only after the completion of the interview. The PANSS consists of three scales totaling 30 items, Positive Symptoms (7 items), Negative Symptoms (7 items) and General Psychopathology, which includes somatic, mood and anxiety symptoms among others (16 items). As ratings depend on clinical judgment, the PANSS is most effective with raters with some clinical and interviewing experience.

The Young Mania Scale (Young et al, 1978)

This is a clinician administered checklist that measures the severity of manic symptoms. There are eleven items ranked on either a 4 point or 8 point scale. While reliability for total scores is strong, there is more variability in reliability for individual items (APA, 2000). Ratings incorporate clinician observations of patients' behavior and thus, while less reliant on self report, ratings are more dependent on inter-rater reliability. Nonetheless, this is a relatively short and easily administered instrument.

The Hamilton Depression Rating Scale (HRSD) (Hamilton, 1980)

The HRSD is a clinician administered questionnaire which rates the severity of depressive symptomatology. The original 17-item version has the strongest psychometric support but a 21 item version is also available. This is a widely used instrument to measure depression and is fairly quick and easy to administer. As with the PANSS and YMS, however, the ratings do depend on some degree of clinical judgment; thus clinical training and experience can influence the outcome.

Yale Brown Obsessive Compulsive Scale (YBOCS) (Goodman et al, 1989)

The YBOCS is a clinician-administered questionnaire that addresses the severity of obsessions, compulsions and related symptoms. The YBOCS symptom checklist assesses for the presence (current or past) of 64 OCD symptoms. The original 10 item scale is comprised of a 5-item scale measuring severity of obsessions, a 5 item scale for severity of compulsions and a 10-item total score. An additional 9 items have been added which assess indecisiveness, pathological doubting, avoidance and other symptoms associated with OCD. The YBOCS is considered the gold standard of OCD research and, like the HRSD and the YMS, it is fairly quick and easy to administer.

The South Oaks Gambling Scale (SOGS) (LeSeur and Blume, 1987)

The SOGS is also a clinician administered questionnaire. The rater asks 26 questions which incorporate 35 items but only 20 items are actually scored. Questions address severity of gambling and gambling related activities (e.g., Have you ever borrowed from someone and not paid them back as a result of your gambling?). As the general clinician may not be as familiar with the details of pathological gambling as with the symptoms of other disorders, this instrument is a useful and informative measure that is relatively easily administered.

For more information, *The Handbook of Psychiatric Outcomes and Measures* (APA, 2000) is an excellent compendium of clinically relevant psychiatric measures.

STEP 4: ASSESSING AXIS II PATHOLOGY

The distinction between axis I and axis II is a controversial and complex topic and merits discussion in some detail. There is even question of the utility of this distinction. Likewise, some authors have conceptualized borderline personality disorder to be a variant of mood disorders (Gunderson et al, 2006). From the perspective of inpatient testing, however, the distinction between the major axis I disorders and the axis II personality disorders is extremely useful. For example, this distinction has implications for the degree of volitional control the patient has over problematic behavior, the utility of behavioral reinforcement contingencies, the effectiveness of medication, and the type of follow up treatment needed. To illustrate, if combative and threatening behavior is deemed to be secondary to mania, the patient will be aggressively medicated, expected to improve rapidly, and outpatient follow up will focus upon adequate monitoring of medication. If the behavior is deemed secondary to personality pathology, verbal and behavioral interventions will be the primary line of treatment, pharmacological treatment will be deemed secondary if even indicated, and outpatient follow up will focus upon psychotherapy or a more intensive behavioral treatment such as Dialectical Behavioral Therapy (DBT) (Linahan, 1993).

To address the assessment of personality pathology on an inpatient setting, it is necessary to first provide a definition. Cloninger (Cloninger et al, 1993; Cloninger, 1994) defined personality to be comprised of both *temperament* and *character*. Temperament refers to in-born, mostly hereditary, information processing biases that are largely impervious to learning, memory and environmental influences. Relevant personality traits include shyness, sensation seeking, introversion, extraversion, and to some extent impulsivity (Cloninger et al, 1993; Cloninger, 1994, 1996; Cohen et al, 2005). In this light, many axis I disorders, such as ADHD, hypomania, or autism spectrum disorders, might be conceptualized as grossly abnormal temperaments. Similarly the emotionality associated with borderline personality disorder could be partly attributable to temperament. Thus in keeping with the hierarchical systems model employed in this chapter, temperament would fall on a level similar to that of axis I pathology.

In contrast, *character* may be considered a higher-order structure than either temperament or the fundamental processes underlying axis I pathology. In Cloninger's definition, character refers to a system of learned concepts. Prototypes of interpersonal relationships are derived from salient experiences in childhood. These create a set of expectations which in turn guide thought, affect and behavior in interpersonal contexts. Thus character is comprised of a system of interpersonal representations.

While it is beyond the scope of this chapter to determine to what extent axis II diagnoses can be attributed to either temperament or character, it is a central tenet of this chapter that character pathology has a critical if not predominant role in axis II personality diagnoses. Thus the evaluation of character pathology has a meaningful, albeit not necessarily isomorphic, relationship with the diagnosis of axis II personality disorders. Moreover, as will be evident below, the diagnostic measures of axis II personality disorders expressly address aspects of interpersonal representations.

The concept of character presented here has a rich history, originating in psychoanalytic literature. The notion of interpersonal representations as a kind of blue-print for psychological functioning was explored and developed in multiple psychoanalytic schools, including Object Relations, Interpersonal Psychology, Relational Psychoanalysis, and Self Psychology (Mitchell, 1988; Kernberg, 1975; Kohut, 1968). The construct was later adopted and refined by empirical psychologists, including attachment theorists, who spoke of internal working models (Main, Kaplan, Cassidy, 1985; Bretherton, 1993) and cognitive therapists, who spoke of schemas and core beliefs (Beck et al, 1990; Young, 1990). While the concepts of character from these different traditions are not identical, we can summarize a number of central, overlapping features.

1. Character is based on a system of interpersonal representations, out of which are abstracted representations of self and other.
2. Fundamental interpersonal representations are laid down in childhood but continue to be elaborated throughout life.
3. Interpersonal representations are conceptual systems derived from memory: a kind of prototypical memory of a routine, comprised of a set of expectations or rules about how events transpire. (e.g., Mother acts like this, I act like this. If I want X, I have to do Y.)
4. Interpersonal representations are higher order mental structures that serve to guide thought, affect and behavior. Thus character influences psychological functions from the top down.
5. While fairly fixed and conservative, they are nonetheless open to modification. Depth psychotherapy works by restructuring core interpersonal representations.

To illustrate, a child with a loving mother will develop a sense of self as worthy, competent, and able to make an impact on others. S/he will develop a representation of others as benign and emotionally responsive. The child will then interact with the world in an optimistic, confident way and consequently tend to elicit consonant responses. Alternatively, a child with a rejecting and critical mother will develop a sense of self as inadequate and unworthy along with a sense of others as cold, rejecting, and unreachable. With concomitant feelings of isolation and anger, the child will tend to see the world and interpret ambiguous situations concordantly, thereby eliciting hostile, critical or distant reactions. Of course, these scenarios should be seen as highly simplified, omitting consideration of extra-familial and post-childhood influences.

Character *pathology* can be defined as any deficit in the content and form of interpersonal representations that impedes flexible adaptation to the environment. Maladaptive content may include malevolent, distant, critical, or coercive views of others or overly dependent, appeasing, or helpless views of self. Such representations are rigid, fixed and unresponsive to new information.

Problems in form refer to the organizational quality of interpersonal representations. Theories of cognitive development stipulate that mental representations develop from a state of relative simplicity to relative complexity (Werner and Kaplan, 1963). These developmental processes include the coordinated processes of integration and differentiation (Piaget, 1954).

Psychoanalytic theorists adapted these concepts to the study of character pathology, such that pathology was considered a failure of development (Blatt and Lerner, 1983; Blatt et al, 1976; Fast, 1985, 1996). Maladaptive representations remain overly global, totalistic, and lacking nuance. There is inadequate integration of disparate elements of self and other, and inadequate differentiation of self from other. For example the classic splitting of a borderline involves a totalistic and global representation of the other as "all bad," a failure to integrate previous, more benign experiences of the other with the current denigrated form, and a failure to differentiate the evaluation of the other from the person's own affective state. Developmentally, this is akin to the psychological processes of a very young child.

We can now consider how this conceptualization of character pathology can be applied to psychological testing on an inpatient unit. As above it is necessary to first delineate the degree to which pathology derives from a more fundamental level of organization, as in the case of mood disorder, psychosis, or low IQ. After this is established, the content and form of interpersonal representations can be evaluated. Of note, this is not meant to imply that axis I and character pathology are mutually exclusive. Patients can certainly have character pathology along with axis I illness. Nonetheless, in the case of a clear axis I disorder, clinicians must be very cautious in interpreting character pathology, especially if the symptomatic behavior is consistent with the axis I disorder, as in the case of negativistic and dependent traits in a patient with major depression. However, if the traits in question are not consistent with the axis I diagnosis, there may well be comorbid axis II pathology. For example if someone with bipolar II disorder has a history of self mutilation, intense dependency, unstable and overly involved relationships and childhood sexual abuse, comorbid borderline pathology is strongly indicated.

Scales for assessing maladaptive form and content of interpersonal representations have been developed for use with the Rorschach (Blatt and Lerner, 1983; Blatt et al, 1976; Mayman, 1967; Urist, 1977). In Exner's system, the quality of interpersonal representations is reflected in the content of scores. The number of human movement responses (M) and associated cooperative (COP) vs. aggressive (AGG) or morbid (MOR) descriptors are informative in this regard as are specific content scores, such as explosions, blood, and sex.

The Thematic Apperception Test (TAT) (Murray, 1943)

The TAT is particularly well suited for eliciting both the content and form of interpersonal representations. Developed by Henry Murray in 1938, the TAT consists of 20 cards with evocative and ambiguous images generally involving one or more people. Typically, only 10 cards are administered at a time. Subjects are instructed to tell a story about what is happening in the picture, what led up to the picture, and what will happen afterwards. Subjects are also asked what the characters are thinking and feeling. The ambiguity of the images allows for personalized responses that reflect the subject's characteristic modes of processing interpersonal stimuli. This is the traditional aim of a projective test. The naturalistic depictions, however, constrain variability, making it easier to identify atypical responses.

Although there have been numerous scales developed to measure the TAT, most of these scales measure targeted personality traits. Such measures include the Self Integration and Self-Other Differentiation Scales (Fast et al, 1996), the Defense Mechanism Manual (DMM)

(Cramer 1988), The Social Cognition and Object Relations Scale (SCORS) (Westen et al, 1990) and the Personal Problem Solving Scale (PPSS) (Ronan et al, 1993). A review of meta-analytic studies comparing the last three scales with other psychological measures suggested comparable reliability and validity (Meyer, 2003). To date, however, there is no comprehensive scoring system similar to Exner's that provides normative data of characteristic responses to each card. Consequently, the TAT is frequently used as a qualitative measure.

Originally, Murray developed a quantifiable scoring system for the TAT (Murray, 1943; Groth-Marnat, 1984). Clearly influenced by Freudian drive theory, Murray proposed personality and behavior to result from the interplay of Needs and Presses. "Needs" refer to motivational forces, such as affiliation, achievement, and aggression. "Presses" refer to the actual or perceived environmental contingencies that impact on the expression of needs, e.g., nurturance, rejection, lack or loss. In Murray's system, subjects' responses to each card were scored on 5-point scales according to the intensity of specific Needs and Presses along with the outcomes of the story and the overall story themes. Unfortunately, adequate reliability and validity were never established. Consequently the scoring system fell out of favor. Thus the field awaits a comprehensive revision of Murray's system which would a) be compatible with contemporary models of personality and b) provide acceptable psychometric properties.

Nonetheless qualitative analysis of the TAT still affords significant information on the content of basic interpersonal schemas despite the inherent limitations in quality control. This is particularly true with psychiatric inpatients, whose TAT stories are often quite dramatic. It must be noted, however, that such qualitative analysis should only be used in conjunction with a much broader test battery and substantial background information about the patient. While the TAT can serve as a useful addition to a test battery, it cannot stand alone.

Themes such as the perceived malevolence, trustworthiness, invasiveness or concern of others or the perceived competence, isolation, dependency or self-reliance of the self can be identified in subjects' stories. In addition, coping and problem solving techniques may also be evident, such as the presence or absence of delayed gratification, long-term planning, and impulse control. Of particular relevance to inpatient psychiatry, themes of violence, hopelessness and suicidality can also appear in TAT protocols. Likewise, Murray's initial descriptions of the cards and the typical themes they elicit can provide guidance for such a qualitative analysis. Table 2 presents this information for select cards as presented in Murray (1943) and Groth-Marnat (1984). Additional commentary is also provided, based upon the author's clinical experience with approximately 150 TAT protocols on inpatient and outpatient psychiatric patients.

The formal properties of interpersonal representations can also be evaluated with the TAT. Are the characters presented as uni-dimensional (an evil person) or as multi-faceted and nuanced? Do they have distinct motivations or are they defined solely in response to each other (e.g., she wants him to stay with her and he just wants to hurt her)? Is the story appropriate to the image or does the subject inject unrelated material? Of course severe incoherence in story structure may indicate psychosis.

Table 2. Murray's Descriptions and Typical Themes for Select TAT Cards

Card Number	Description	Themes
1	A young boy is contemplating a violin which rests on a table in front of him.	Typical stories emerging from this card revolve around a rebellious boy being forced by his parents, or some other significant authority figure, to play the violin, or around a self-motivated boy who is daydreaming about becoming an outstanding violinist. (*Issues of aspiration, self-discipline, and authority are common*)
2	Country Scene: in the foreground is a young woman with books in her hand: in the background a man is working in the fields and an older woman is looking on.	Frequently encountered stories for this card involve a young girl who is leaving the farm to increase her education or to seek opportunities which her present home environment cannot provide. Usually the family is seen as working hard to gain a living from the soil, with an overall emphasis on maintaining the status quo.
3BM	On the floor against a couch is the huddled form of a boy with his head bowed on his right arm. Beside him on the floor is a revolver.	The stories usually revolve around an individual who has been emotionally involved with another person or who is feeling guilty over some past behavior he has committed. (*Suicidal depression is also a frequent theme.*)
4	A woman is clutching the shoulders of a man whose face and body are averted as if he were trying to pull away from her.	Often the woman is seen as the advice giving moral agent who is struggling with the more impulsive and irrational man. In approximately half the stories, the vague picture of a woman in the background is brought into the plot. (*Frequently, the woman is trying to dissuade the man from abandoning her.*)
5	A middle aged woman is standing on the threshold of a half-opened door looking into a room.	The most frequent plot is of a mother who either has caught her child misbehaving or is surprised by an intruder entering her house.
6BM	A short elderly woman stands with her back turned to a tall young man. The latter is looking downward with a perplexed expression.	The picture typically elicits stories of a son who is either presenting sad news to his mother or attempting to prepare her for his departure to some distant location. (*A mother and son concerned about his father or her husband are also common*)
7GF	An older woman is sitting on a sofa close beside a girl, speaking or reading to her. The girl, who holds a doll in her lap, is looking away.	The picture is usually perceived as a mother and her daughter, with the mother advising, consoling, scolding, or instructing the child. Less frequently, there are themes where the mother is reading to the child for pleasure or entertainment.
8BM	An adolescent boy looks straight out of the picture. The barrel of a rifle is visible at one side, and in the background is the dim scene of a surgical operation, like a reverie-image.	Stories revolve around either ambition, in that the young man may have aspirations towards becoming a doctor, or aggression. Frequently the aggressive stories related to fears of becoming harmed or mutilated while in a passive state. Another somewhat less frequent theme centers on a scene in which someone was shot and is now being operated on.
9BM	Four men in overalls are lying on the grass taking it easy.	Stories typically provide some sort of explanation of why the men are there and frequently describe them either as hoboes or as working men who are taking a much-needed rest.
13MF	A young man is standing with downcast head buried in his arm. Behind him is the figure of a woman lying in bed.	The most frequent plot centers on guilt induced by illicit sexual activity. Themes involving the death of the woman on the bed and the resulting grief of the man, who is often depicted as her husband, are somewhat less frequent.
18GF	A woman has her hands squeezed around the throat of another woman whom she appears to be pushing backwards across the banister of a stairway.	Aggressive mother-daughter interactions or sibling relationships are often disclosed in response to this picture.

Descriptions are obtained from Murray (1943) and themes from Groth-Marnat (1983). Italics are drawn from the author's clinical experience with approximately 150 inpatient and outpatient protocols.

Additional Personality Tests

Evaluation of the content and formal qualities of interpersonal representations can give general data about the presence and severity of character pathology. This can be critical when attempting to discern whether target behavior is secondary to an axis I disorder or to character pathology. As mentioned above, however, such information may not directly translate into DSM-IV axis II diagnoses. For this purpose, there are many questionnaires and interviews with well established psychometric properties. While the psychometric data increases confidence in test results, the self-report nature of most of the axis II measures can be a limitation, however. This is especially pertinent for psychiatric inpatients whose insight and reliability as informants are often sub-optimal.

Structured Clinical Interview for DSM-IV Axis II (SCID-II) (First et al,1997)

The SCID II is a widely used semi-structured interview that assesses for the presence of all of the axis II diagnoses in DSM IV as well as two of the diagnoses from Appendix B of the DSM IV (passive aggressive and depressive personality disorder). There is a 119 item questionnaire that can be given as a screening instrument. All items which the subject endorses can be followed up in greater detail in the interview. While the screening questionnaire has no validity scales to check for response bias, it does permit a much less time-intensive evaluation.

Personality Disorder Interview-IV (PDI-IV) (Widiger et al, 1995)

Similar to the SCID-II, the PDI-IV is a semi-structured interview that assesses for the presence of all DSM-IV axis II personality disorders plus passive aggressive (negativistic) and depressive personality disorders from Appendix B. There are two versions of the PDI, one in which the questions are arranged by topic (e.g., Attitudes towards self, Attitudes towards others) and another in which the questions are arranged by diagnosis. There is no screening questionnaire with the PDI-IV.

The Structured Interview for DSM-IV Personality (SIDP-IV) (Pfohl et al, 1997)

The SIDP-IV is also a semi-structured interview which assesses for all DSM-IV axis II personality disorders. The SIDP-IV also includes passive aggressive, depressive and self-defeating personality disorder as well as the criteria for sadistic personality disorder. Similar to the PDI-IV, there are two versions, a thematic version that is arranged into 10 topics (e.g., Interests and Activities, Work Style, Close Relationships, Self-Perception) and a modular version arranged by personality disorder. As with the PDI-IV, there is no screening questionnaire.

The Personality Questionnaire-4 (PDQ-4) (Hyler, 1994)

The PDQ-4 is a self-administered questionnaire that assesses for all of the DSM-IV axis II diagnoses. There are 85 items with two validity scales to measure response bias. The presence or absence of each disorder is calculated along with the two personality disorders in Appendix B. A total score is also calculated, measuring the overall degree of personality disturbance. The Clinical Significance Scale provides a brief interview through which the clinician can probe personality disorders that have been positively identified. Computerized versions are also available.

Millon Clinical Multiaxial Inventory (MCMI-III) (Millon et al, 1997)

This 175-item, true-false, self administered questionnaire assesses for 14 DSM-IV axis II diagnoses. The MCMI III also assesses 10 clinical syndromes, such as dysthymic, anxiety or thought disorder. There are also 4 Correction scales (3 Modifying and 1 Validity scale) and 4 scoring methods, including hand scoring, computerized scoring, optical scanning or a mail-in scoring service.

For more information on personality tests, the *Handbook of Psychiatric Measures* (APA, 2000) and the *Comprehensive Handbook of Psychological Assessment, Volume 2, Personality Assessment* (Hilsenroth et al, 2003) are valuable resources.

CASE EXAMPLES

Three case examples will now be presented to illustrate the concepts discussed in this chapter. The first example involves a fairly straightforward case of mild mental retardation. The second case concerns comorbid diagnoses of schizophrenia and a nonverbal learning disability. The third case addresses the complex interplay between major depression, psychotic thought process, severe character pathology and organic brain disease.

Case 1

Case I involves a 27 year old male who had originally been admitted to medicine with excessively high blood sugar levels. His apparent lack of concern about his poorly regulated diabetes was attributed to a major depressive disorder. However, his presentation on the psychiatric unit, along with his concrete thought process, suggested an additional diagnosis of mental retardation. In order to obtain the appropriate outpatient services for him, an IQ test was requested. The WAIS III scores are presented below.

WAIS III

FSIQ	56	(0.2%)	VCI	61	(0.5%)
VIQ	57	(0.2%)	POI	64	(1.0%)
PIQ	63	(1.0%)	WMI	51	(0.1%)
			PSI	66	(1.0%)

Verbal Subtests	Score	%tile	Performance Subtests	Score	%tile
Vocabulary	3	1	Picture Completion	4	2
Similarities	3	1	Digit Symbol	4	2
Arithmetic	1	<1	Block Design	4	2
Digit Span	3	1	Matrix Reasoning	3	1
Information	3	1	Picture Arrangement	5	5
Comprehension	2	<1	Symbol Search	2	<1
Letter-Number Seq.	2	<1	Object Assembly	5	5

This WAIS III profile is consistent with mild retardation. While there is slight variation across index scores and subtests, the patient performed at or below the 5th percentile for all tests. Further, none of the subtests significantly differ from the mean subtest score. That the Working Memory Index significantly differs from the other three index scores is consistent with his history of depression.

Case 2

Case 2 involves a 31 year old male who was admitted after escalated arguments with his parents. He had an approximately 10 year psychiatric history, although his diagnosis was unclear. Differential diagnoses included bipolar disorder, major depressive disorder with psychotic features, and borderline personality disorder. The WAIS profile is listed below.

WAIS III

FSIQ	93	(32%)	VCI	105	(63%)
VIQ	106	(66%)	POI	76	(5%)
PIQ	77	(6%)	WMI	99	(47%)
			PSI	76	(5%)

Verbal Subtests	Score	%tile	Performance Subtests	Score	%tile
Vocabulary	12	75	Picture Completion	9	37
Similarities	8	25	Digit Symbol-Coding	6	9
Arithmetic	12	75	Block Design	7	16
Digit Span	10	50	Matrix Reasoning	7	16
Information	14	91	Picture Arrangement	5	5
Comprehension	13	84	Symbol Search	4	3
Letter-Number Sequencing	9	37			

Of immediate interest is the significant discrepancy between VIQ and PIQ, which is borne out by the similar contrast between the VCI and WMI vs. the POI and PSI. This dramatic and consistent discrepancy points to a non-verbal learning disorder which presumably predates his 10 year psychiatric history. Nonetheless, among the verbal tests, his relative deficit in Similarities and Letter-Number Sequencing suggests some decrement in fluid intelligence, indicating possible deterioration from a higher level of baseline functioning. His score of 8 on Similarities is in stark contrast to his other VCI scores (Vocabulary = 12, Information = 14, Comprehension = 13) and points to deterioration in the capacity for abstract thinking. This raises the question of a schizophrenic process.

His Rorschach profile is also illuminating. His R (number of responses) of 12 is well below the mean and in fact too low to be considered a valid profile. At least 14 responses are required to yield fully reliable quantitative data. Nonetheless, 8 out of his 12 responses (67%) were pure form responses, 11 out of 12 (92%) had poor form quality, and there were 5 special scores, three of which were quite serious (WSum6=14). Thus his reality testing was extremely poor and there was evidence of thought disorder. Of note, his responses appeared highly perseverative, which lead them to depart from the formal properties of the stimulus blot. His use of color was also interesting. While the predominance of pure form is consistent with affective constriction, color occurred only in color-dominated responses (2 CF-'s), with one form dominated shading response (FC'-). Thus when affect is expressed, it is poorly mediated by cognition and consequently may be explosive. Overall this protocol is consistent with a schizophrenic spectrum disorder. In response to this testing, the diagnosis was changed accordingly, the anti-psychotic medication increased and the patient's affect and relatedness improved noticeably.

It must also be noted that his poor performance on the Rorschach may have been confounded by his difficulty processing visual-spatial stimuli. This is a significant consideration and may have also affected his effort, in that he was less likely to put full effort into cognitive tasks that have traditionally been difficult for him. Nonetheless, taken together, his grossly impaired Rorschach record, his history of poor occupational and social functioning, his long psychiatric history, and his low Similarities score supported the interpretation of psychosis above and beyond the influence of visual-spatial processing deficits. The subsequent improvement of his mental status with increased antipsychotic medication further supported this conclusion.

Case 3

Case 3 is more complex than the previous two cases. This involves a 58 year old woman with a 40 year history of anorexia nervosa. For most of her adulthood she had a fairly high level of functioning, having worked as a grade school teacher and lived in her own apartment. More recently, however, she spent her entire inheritance in the space of two years, lost her apartment, and ended up in a homeless shelter. On admission she was profoundly labile, dysphoric and tearful. In an initial interview she admitted to a childhood history of sexual abuse by a close female relative. Provisional diagnoses included major depressive disorder with psychotic features, anorexia nervosa, and Cluster A personality disorder. The patient also reported a history of seizure disorder and a fall during a seizure 5 years previously that caused a skull fracture. As her abrupt decline in functioning suggested possible organic pathology, an MRI was ordered. An old encephalomalocia in her left inferior temporal lobe cortex and an ischemic lesion in the white matter of the left posterior frontal lobe were identified on MRI. The encephalomalocia was attributed to contusion and therefore may have caused by her fall. For the psychological evaluation, the WAIS III, Rorschach, TAT, several neuropsychological tests, and the MCMI-II were administered. The WAIS results are presented below.

WAIS-III

FSIQ	112	(79%)	VCI	124	(95%)
VIQ	122	(93%)	POI	111	(77%)
PIQ	99	(47%)	WMI	115	(84%)
			PSI	73	(4%)

Verbal Subtests	Score	%tile	Performance Subtests	Score	%tile
Vocabulary	14	91	Picture Arrangement	10	50
Similarities	16	98	Picture Completion	12	75
Information	13	84	Block Design	9	37
Comprehension	11	63	Matrix Reasoning	15	95
Arithmetic	12	75	Digit Symbol	4	3
Digit Span	15	95	Symbol Search	6	9
Letter-Number Seq.	11	63	Object Assembly	9	37

Her WAIS is remarkable for the degree of inter-test scatter. Her subtests range from the 98th percentile (Similarities) to the 3rd percentile (Digit Symbol). Her extremely strong VCI speaks to a very high cognitive baseline. Most of the lowered test scores can be attributed to psychomotor slowing. Likewise, her processing speed index is grossly impaired (PSI = 73, 4%). Moreover, her performance on Matrix Reasoning (15, 95%), which is untimed, was two standard deviations higher than her performance on Block Design (9, 37%), which is time-sensitive. The two tests measure fairly similar visual-spatial functions. There is also evidence of a relative deficit on Letter-Number Sequencing, a test of working memory, although it still falls in the average range (11, 63%). Additionally, her Comprehension score is surprisingly lower than the VCI scores, suggesting a relative deficit in social processing, possibly of longstanding.

The Rorschach is also striking. There were 16 responses, sufficient for a valid protocol. Most notable were the number of special scores (Sum6=8). There were three Deviant Responses, reflective of extraneous commentary, suggesting a difficulty restricting her verbalizations to the task at hand.

> "Maybe it's a bear or a tiger skin, a hide hanging on the wall as a trophy. I hate hunting. That was taken from a living creature while it still needed it. It's a trophy to the inhumanity of many humans."

Additionally there were five special scores indicative of more serious thought disorder (WSum6=21). There was an unusual amount of movement scores, with elephants dancing, fish swimming and a volcano exploding. The large number of movement responses (M+m+FM=13) is puzzling. It could reflect some degree of mania or a habitual focus upon elaborated fantasy, consistent with her suggested Cluster A traits. There was also a considerable number of art, anthropology, geography, and science content scores, which reflect both a high level of education and a tendency to intellectualization (2AB + Art + Ay:R=25%). Also of note was the unusual references to pure human emotion, scored as human experience (Hx=4).

"Something sinister and foreboding. Something to guard against…. It's two projections here and it is black and dark…. They are out to get somebody. They are sharp. There is no friendly intention."

In sum, the complexity of her Rorschach responses (Zsum=45, Blends:R= 35%) is consistent with a high level of premorbid intelligence. The elevated number of special scores points to a loosening of thought process. The predominant use of color, shading and human experience responses suggests high affective reactivity and extremely poor emotional regulation.

In this case, the TAT was particularly revealing. While the Rorschach did not disturb her, she evidenced significant distress at several of the TAT cards. Her themes were predominantly dysphoric with questions of suicidality occurring frequently. A focus on the historical and cultural details of the images was consistent with her Rorschach protocol. Profound difficulties with mother-child relationships were also evident as is illustrated in the responses below.

Card 6BM

She's the mother, he is the son. And he's trying to communicate something important to her but she's looking out the window as an escape from the reality of what she knows her son's pain is. He walks away—he gives up. He has no one to talk to, no friends. Although he is a man, he wanted a mother. It's not that she can't be a mother, it's that she won't – she's very selfish. (What caused the man's pain?) He lost his job because of the emotional damage done to him by this mother. He knows he is basically all alone. I think he's going to kill himself. (Long pause) She'll find a way to escape that, too. And then she'll draw attention to herself, none to her son.

Card 7GF

The woman is the mother and the girl is the daughter. She's not in the least bit interested in the doll she's holding. The mother is really trying—sincerely trying to be a good mother. I think she's holding a book – I'm not sure –but she's reading to the daughter. She bought the child pretty clothes, pretty barrettes for her hair, nice shoes and socks, but the girl …here it is the mother who is the victim. Here is a girl who is emotionally disturbed and unable to respond to the mother. The mother has a lot of love for her daughter but she doesn't know how to reach her. (How does it end?) The daughter is institutionalized and the mother is broken-hearted. That doesn't happen for a number of years, though. I think it's in the 1940's, again because of the clothing, and the help the daughter needed was not available at that time. Had she gotten the help she needed then, it wouldn't be that way.

Her severely personalized and disorganized response to Card 5 is also notable, suggestive of a dissociative response to experiences perceived as traumatic concurrent with an escapist focus on intellectual pursuits.

Card 5

I like everything in this picture except the woman. Her face is one of shock and dismay. I like the interior of the room – there are flowers, the lamp. I want to shut the door on her. The books on the bookshelf are all my favorite books and I want to read them. I don't want to help her, I just want to shut her out. No compassion, and I do shut her out. There aren't any happy pictures? Only depressed ones?

Along with the obvious disturbances in content, the formal quality of the interpersonal representations is also significant. Portrayals of the relationships and the individuals within them are global, unidimensional, and entirely lacking in nuance. Relationships are depriving, frustrating, and hurtful. Characters are either self-involved and withholding or victimized and abandoned. There are no mixed emotions or motivational conflicts; nor is there any complexity in mental states. Moreover, characters' behaviors are solely determined by the relationship to the other ("He lost his job due to the emotional damage done to him by his mother.") Thus the form and content of this patient's interpersonal representations are indicative of significant character pathology.

In order to test for neuropsychological impairment, several tests were administered. The Controlled Oral Word Association (COWA) (Benton 1969, Ruff 1996), a test of verbal fluency associated with left prefrontal function, showed no impairment. The Trailmaking test (Lezak et al, 2004) was also administered. This measures set switching, an executive function mediated by the prefrontal cortex. While her work was neat and accurate, her extreme psychomotor slowing significantly impaired her performance. Thus it is unclear whether slowed performance or executive dysfunction is implicated. On the Bender-Gestalt, a test of visual-spatial function and planning (Brannigan and Decker, 2003), her designs were largely accurate and well placed. When two of the last and most complex designs proved too difficult for her, however, she responded with fairly disorganized scribbles across the right side of the page. Thus when taxed, her problem solving abilities appear to break down.

Finally, the MCMI-II revealed elevations in schizoid, avoidant, and obsessive-compulsive personality disorder scales.

To summarize, this protocol is consistent with significant affective reactivity and lability, profound dysphoric affect, uneven but pronounced cognitive impairment in someone with high premorbid intelligence, and moderate disorganization of thought. There appears to be notable premorbid character pathology with particular disturbance of representations of mother-child relationships. She also has evidence of dissociative and post-traumatic responses. In conclusion, it appears that her current diagnosis involves a major depressive disorder with psychotic features that is complicated by fronto-temporal lesions. Likewise her premorbid character pathology is likely disinhibited by these lesions, rendering her grossly unable to modulate her affect and exercise adequate judgment.

CONCLUSION

In conclusion, psychological testing on an inpatient unit offers unique challenges and opportunities. The dramatic and often quite complex psychopathology of psychiatric inpatients is well captured on test protocols and test findings can provide valuable input to aid in differential diagnosis and treatment planning. In this chapter a hierarchical systems model of mental processes was proposed as a conceptual framework within which to address the critical question of differential diagnosis. A stepwise approach to inpatient psychological testing was then reviewed, starting with an assessment of possible confounds, then moving to the assessment of cognitive function, axis I pathology and axis II pathology. Finally, case examples were provided to illustrate the concepts discussed above.

REFERENCES

Andreasen, N. C. (1985). Positive and negative symptoms in schizophrenia: A critical evaluation. *Schizophrenia Bulletin, 11*, 380-389.

Beck A.T., Freeman A., and Associates. (1990). *Cognitive Therapy of Personality Disorders.* New York: Guilford Press.

Beck, S.J.(1944). *Rorschach's Test I: Basic Processes.* New York: Grune and Stratton.

Benton, A. (1969) Differential behavioral effects in frontal lobe disease. Oral version of word fluency test. *Neuropsychologia, 6*, 53-60.

Beversdorf, D.Q., Smith, B.W., Crucian, G.P., Anderson, J.M., Keillor, J.M., Barrett, A.M., Hughes, J.D., Felopulos, G.J., Bauman, M.L., Nadeau, S.E., Heilman, K.M. (2000) Increased discrimination of "false memories" in autism spectrum disorder. *Proceedings of the National Academy of Sciences of the United States of America, 97*, 8734-7.

Bilder, R.M., Goldman, R.S., Volavka, J., Czobor, P., Hoptman, M., Sheitman, B., Lindenmayer, J.P., Caron, M.J., Mottron, L., Berthiaume, C., Dawson, M. (2006). Cognitive mechanisms, specificity and neuroal underpinnings of visuospatial peaks in autism. *Brain. 129*(7),1789-1802.

Blatt, S.J., Brennis, B., Schimek, J.G., Glick, M. (1976). Normal development and psychopathological impairment of the concept of the object on the Rorschach. *Journal of Abnormal Psychology, 85*, 364-373.

Blatt, S.J. and Lerner, H. (1983). The psychological assessment of object representations. *Journal of Personality Assessment, 47,*7-28.

Boddaert, N., Barthelemy, C., Poline, J.B., Samson, Y., Brunelle, F., Zilbovicius, M. (2005). *British Jouranl of Psychiatry, 187*, 83-86.

Brannigan, G.G., Decker, S.L. (2003). *Bender Visual-Motor Gestalt (Bender-Gestalt II).* Itasca, IL: Riverside Publishing.

Bretherton, I. (1993). From dialogue to internal working models: The co-construction of self in relationships. In C. A. Nelson (Ed.) *Minnesota Symposia on Child Psychology: Vol. 26. Memory and Affect in Development* (pp.237-264.) Hillsdale, NJ: Erlbaum.

Buchanan, R.W., Breier, A., Kirkpatrick, B., Ball, P., Carpenter, W.T. (1998). Positive and negative symptom response to clozapine in schizophrenic patients with and without the deficit syndrome. *American Journal of Psychiatry, 155,*751-760.

Cattell, R. B. (1987). *Intelligence: Its Structure, Growth, and Action.* New York: Elsevier Science Pub. Co.

Charlton, T. (1985). Locus of control as a therapeutic strategy for helping children with behaviour and learning problems. *Maladjustment and Therapeutic Education, 3*(1), 26-32.

Citrome, L., McEvoy, J., Kunz, M., Chakos, M., Cooper, T.B., Horowitz, T.L., Lieberman, J.A. (2002). Neuropsychology of first-episode schizophrenia: Initial characterization and clinical correlates. *American Journal of Psychiatry, 157*, (4): 549-559.

Cloninger, C.R. (1996). Assessment of the impulsive-compulsive spectrum of behavior by the seven-factor model of temperament and character. In J.M. Oldham, E. Hollander, and A.E. Skodol (Eds.) *Impulsivity and Compulsivity,* (pp. 59-95) Washington, DC: American Psychiatric Press.

Cloninger, R.C., Svrakic, D.M., Prsybeck, T.R. (1993). A psychobiological model of temperament and character. *Archives of General Psychiatry, 50,*975-990.

Cloninger, R.C. (1994). Temperament and personality. *Current Opinion in Neurobiology, 25,*189-96.

Cohen, L.J.(2005). The Neurobiology of Antisociality. In C. Stough (Ed.). *Neurobiology of Exceptionality* (pp.107-124). New York: Kluwer Academic/Plenum.

Cohen, L.J., Stein, D., Galynker, I., and Hollander, E. (1997) Towards an integration of psychological and biological models of OCD: Phylogenetic considerations. *CNS Spectrums: International Journal of NeuroPsychiatric Medicine, 2,* 26-44.

Cramer, P. (1988). Threat to gender representations: identity and identification. *Journal of Personality* 66, 335-357.

Crawford, J.R., Besson, J.A., Bremner, M. et al (1992). Estimation of premorbid intelligence in schizophrenia. *British Journal of Psychiatry, 161,* 69-74.

Dickerson, F.B., Boronow, J.J., Stallings, C.R., Origoni, A.E., Cole, S., Yolken, R.H. (2004). Associations between cognitive functioning and employment status of persons with bipolar disorder. *Psychiatric Services, 55,*(2):54-58.

Douchemaine, D., Fontaine, R. (2003). Can fluid intelligence decline with aging be explained by complexity? *Vieillissement et Developpement Adulte: Cognition, Rhymicite et Adaption.* Tours, France: Universite Francois Rabelais (pp.1-4) http://www.univtours. fr/ed/ edsst/comm2003/douchemane.pdf.

Engle, R.W., Tuholski, S.W., Laughlin, J.E., Conway, A.R. (1999). Working memory, short-term memory, and general fluid intelligence: a latent-variable approach. *Journal of Experimental Psychology General, 128,* (3):309-31.

Exner, J.E. (1986). Some Rorschach data comparing schizophrenics with borderline and schizotypal personality disorders. *Journal of Personality Assessment, 50,* (3),455-471.

Exner, J.E. (1997). *The Rorschach: A Comprehensive System. Vol. 1, Basic Foundations and Principles of Interpretation.* (4th edition). Hoboken, NJ: John Wiley and Sons.

Fast, I. (1985). *Event Theory: A Piaget-Freud Integration.* Hillsdale, NJ, Erlbaum, N.J.

Fast, I., Marsden, G., Cohen, L., Heard, H., and Kruse, S.. (1996). The self as subject: A formulation and an assessment strategy. *Psychiatry,59,* 34-47.

First, M., Gibbon, M., Spitzer, R.L., Williams, J.B.W. (1997). *Structured Clinical Interview for DSM-IV Axis II Personality Disorders (SCID II.)* Washington, D.C.: American Psychiatric Press.

First, M.B., Spitzer, R.L., Williams, J.B.W. et al. (1997). *Structured Clinical Interview for DSM-IV – Clinician Version (SCID-CV) (User's Guide and Interview).* Washington D.C.: American Psychiatric Press.

Folstein, M.F., Folstein, S.E., McHugh, P.R. (1975). "Mini-Mental State": A practical method for grading the cognitive state of patients for the clinician. *Journal of Psychiatric Research, 12,* 189-198.

Goldberg, E. (2001). *The Executive Brain: Frontal Lobes and the Civilized Mind.* New York: Oxford.

Golden, C. J., Freshwater, S. M. (2001). Luria-Nebraska Neuropsychological Battery, In W. I. Dorfman and M. Hersen (Eds.).*Understanding Psychological Assessment: Perspectives on Individual Differences*. New York: Kluwer Academic/Plenum Publishers.

Goodman, W.K., Price, L.H., Rasmussen, S.A., Mazure, C., Fleischmann, R.L., Hill, C.L., Heninger, G.R., Charney, D.S. (1989). The Yale Brown Obsessive Compulsive Scale, I: Development, use, and reliability. *Arch Gen Psychiatry, 746,*1006-1011.

Groth-Marnat, G. (1984). *Handbook of Psychological Assessment*. New York: Van Neustrand Reinhold.

Gunderson, J.G., Weinberg, I., Daversa, M.T., Kueppenbender, K.D., Zanarini, M.C., Shea, M.T., Skodol, A.E., Sanislow, C.A., Yen, S., Morey, L.C., Grilo, C.M., McGlashan, T.H., Stout, R.L., Dyck I. (2006) Descriptive and longitudinal observations on the relationship of borderline personality disorder and bipolar disorder. *American Journal of Psychiatry, 163,*(7):1173-8.

Hamilton, A. (1980). Rating depressive patients. *J Clin Psychiatry, 41,*(12):21-24.

M.Hersen, M. J. Hilsenroth, D.L. Segal (Eds.) (2003). *Comprehensive Handbook of Psychological Assessment, Volume 2, Personality Assessment*. Hoboken, NJ: John Wiley and Sons.

Hertz, M.R. (1942). *Frequency Tables for Scoring Rorschach Responses*. Cleveland: Western Reserve University Press.

Horn, J.L. and Cattell, R.B. (1966) Refinement and test of the theory of fluid and crystallized general intelligence *Journal of Educational Psychology, 57,*253-270.

Hyler, E. (1994). *Personality Diagnostic Questionnaire—4*. New York: New York State Psychiatric Institute.

Joyce, E.M., Hutton, S.M., Mutsatsa, S.H., Barnes, T.R.E. (2005). Cognitive heterogeneity in first-episode schizophrenia. *The British Journal of Psychiatry, 187(6),* 516-522.

Kaplan, E., Goodglass, H., Weintraub, S. (1983).*The Boston Naming Test*. Philadelphia: Lea and Febiger.

Kay, S.R., Opler, L.A., Fiszbein, A. (1994). *Positive and Negative Symptoms Scale Manual*. North Tonawanda, NY: Multi Health Systems.

Kernberg, O. (1975) *Borderline Conditions and Pathological Narcissism*. Dunmore, PA: Jason Aronson.

Klopfer, B., Ainsworth, M.D., Klopfer, W.G., and Holt, R.R. (1954). *Developments in the Rorschach Technique. I. Technique and Theory*. Yonkers-on-Hudson, NY: World Book.

Kohut, H. (1968). The psychoanalytic treatment of narcissistic personality disorders: Outline of a systematic approach. *The Psychoanalytic Study of the Child. 23,* 86-113.

LeSeur, H.R., Blume, S.B. (1987). The South Oaks Gambling Screen (SOGS): A new instrument for the identification of pathological gamblers. *American Journal of Psychiatry, 144,*1184-1188.

Lezak, M.D., Howieson, D.B., Loring, D.W. (2004). *Neuropsychological Assessment 4th Edition*. New York: Oxford University Press.

Linahan, M.M. (1993). *Skills Training Manual for Treating Borderline Personality Disorder*. New York: The Guilford Press.

Main, M., Kaplan, N., and Cassidy, J. (1985), Security in infancy, childhood and adulthood: A move to the level of representation. In I. Bretherton and E. Waters (Eds.) Growing points of attachment theory and research. *Monographs of the Society of Research in Child Development, 50*(2-3, Serial No. 209), 66-104.

Marmor, J. (1983). Systems thinking in psychiatry: some theoretical and clinical implications. *American Journal of Psychiatry,140*, 833-838.

Mattis, S. (1988). *Dementia Rating Scale: Professional Manual*. Odessa, FL: Psychological Assessment Resources.

Mayman, M. (1967), Object representations and object relationships in Rorschach responses. *Journal of Projective Techniques and Personality Assessment, 32*, 303-316.

Meyer, G.J. (2003). The reliability and validity of the Rorschach and Thematic Apperception Test (TAT) compared to other psychological and medical procedures: An analysis of systematically gathered evidence. In M.J. Hilsenroth, D.L. Segal, M. Hersen (Eds.), *Comprehensive Handbook of Psychological Assessment, Volume 2, Personality Assessment*. Hoboken, NJ: John Wiley and Sons.

Meyer, G..J, Archer, R.P. (2001). The hard science of Rorschach research: What do we know and where do we go? *Psychological Assessment, 13*, (4) 486-502.

Millon, T., Davis, R., Millon, C. (1997). *MCMI-III Manual, 2nd edition*. Minneapolis, MN: National Computer Systems.

Minshew, N., Goldstein, G. (2001). The pattern of intact and impacted memory functions in autism. *Journal of Child Psychology and Psychiatry, 42*,(8) 1095-1101.

Mitchell, S.A. (1988). *Relational Concepts in Psychoanalysis: An Integration*. Cambridge, Mass: Harvard University Press.

Mitrushina, M., Boone, K.B., Razani, J., D'Elia, L.F. (2005). *Handbook of Normative Data for Neuropsychological Assessment, 2nd Ed*. New York: Oxford University Press, Inc.

Mottron, L. (2004). Matching strategies in cognitive research with individuals with high-functioning autism: Current practices, instrument biases and recommendations. *Journal of Autism and Developmental Disorders, 34*,(1):19-27.

Murray, H.A. (1943). *Thematic Apperception Test Manual*. Cambridge, MA: Harvard University Press.

Pfohl, B., Blum, N., Zimmerman, M. (1997). *Structured Interview for DSM-IV Personality*. Washington, D.C.: American Psychiatric Press.

Piaget, J. (1986/1954) *The Construction of Reality in the Child*. New York, Basic Books.

Rapoport, D., Gill, M., and Schafer, R. (1946). *Diagnostic Psychological Testing. Volumes 1 and 2*. Chicago: Yearbook Publishers.

Reitan, R.M., Wolfson, D. (1993). *The Halstead Reitan Neuropsychological Test Battery: Theory and Clinical Applications (2nd Ed.)* Tucson, Az: Neuropsychology Press.

Ronan, G.F., Colavito, V.A., Hamontree, S.R. (1993). Personal Problem-Solving System for scoring TAT responses: Preliminary validity and reliability data. *Journal of Personality Assessment*, 61, 28-40.

Ruff, R.M., Light, R.H., Parker, S.B. (1996) Benton Controlled Oral Word Association Test: Reliability and updated norms. *Archives of Clinical Neuropsychology,11*,329-338.

Sabelli, H.C., Carlson-Sabellim L. (1989). Biological priority and psychological supremacy: a new integrative paradigm derived from process theory. *American Journal of Psychiatry, 146*, 1541-1551

Sadock, B.J., Sadock, V.A. (2004). *Kaplan and Sadock'S Synopsis of Psychiatry: Behavioral Sciences/Clinical Psychiatry, 9th Edition*. Philadelphia, PA: Lippincott Williams and Wilkins.

Salmond, C.H., Ashburner, J., Connelly, A., Friston, K.J., Gadian, D.G., Vargha-Khadem, F. (2005). The role of the medial temporal lobe in autistic spectrum disorders. *European Journal of Neuroscience, 22*(3):764-72.

Schafer, R. (1954). *Psychoanalytic Interpretation in Rorschach Testing*. New York: Grune and Stratton.

Schwartz, G.E. (1981) A systems analysis of psychobiology and behavior therapy: Implications for behavioral medicine. *Psychotherapy and Psychosomatics, 36,*159-184.

Siegel, D.J. (1999). *The Developing Mind: How Relationship and the Brain Interact to Shape Who We Are*. New York: The Guilford Press.

Society for Personality Assessment. (2005). The status of the Rorschach in clinical and forensic practice: An official statement by the Board of Trustees of the Society for Personality Assessment. *Journal of Personality Assessment, 85,* (2): 219-237.

Spreen, O. and Strauss, E. (1998). *A Compendium of Neuropsychological Tests (2nd Ed.)*. New York: Oxford University Press.

Stuss, D.T., Picton, T.W., Alexander, M.P. (2001). Consciousness, self-awareness, and the frontal lobes. In S.P. Salloway, P.F. Malloy, J.D. Duffy (Eds.) *The Frontal Lobes and Neuropsychiatric Illness*. Washington, D.C.: American Psychiatric Publishing, Inc.

Subbotsky, E. (2004). Magical thinking in judgments of causation: Can anomalous phenomena affect ontological causal beliefs in children and adults? *British Journal of Developmental Psychology, 22,*(1):123-152.

Task Force for the Handbook of Psychiatric Measures (Eds.). (2000). *Handbook of Psychiatric Measures*. Washington, DC: American Psychiatric Association.

Taylor, B.P., Bruder, G.E., Stewart, J.W., McGrath, P.J., Halperin, J., Ehrlichman, H., Quitkin, F.M. (2006). Psychomotor slowing as a predictor of fluoxetine nonresponse in depressed outpatients. *American Journal of Psychiatry, 163,* (1), 73-78.

Toichi, M., Kamio, Y. (2002). Long-term memory and levels-of-processing in autism. *Neuropsychologia, 40,*(7):964-9.

Te Wildt, B.T., Schultz-Venrath, U. (2004). Magical ideation—Defense mechanism or neuropathology? A study with multiple sclerosis patients. *Psychopathology, 37,*141-144.

Urist, J. (1977). The Rorschach test and the assessment of object relations. *Journal of Personality Assessment, 41,* 3-9.

von Bertolanffy, L. (1968) *General Systems Theory*. New York, Braziller.

Wechsler, D. (2002). *WAIS-III, WMS-III Technical Manual—Updated*. San Antonio, TX: Psychological Corporation.

Werner, H., Kaplan, B.(1984/1963). *Symbol Formation*. Hillsdale, NJ: Erlbaum.

Westen, D., Lohr, N., Silk, K.R., Gold, L., Kerber, K. (1990). Object relations and social cognition in borderlines, major depressives, and normals: A Thematic Apperception Test analysis. *Psychological Assessment, 2,* 355-364.

Widiger, T.A., Mangine, S., Corbitt, E.M., Ellis, C.G., Thomas, G.V (1995). *Personality Disorder Interview-IV: A Semi-Structured Interview for the Assessment of Personality Disorders*. Odessa, Fla: Psychological Assessment Resources.

Williams, D.L., Goldstein, G., Carpenter, P.A., Minshew, N.J.(2005) Verbal and spatial memory in autism. *Journal of Autism and Developmental Disorders,35,* (6):747-756.

Wood, J.M., Paso, M.T., Garb, H.N., Lilienfeld, S.O. (2001) The misperceptions of psychopathology: Problems with the norms of the comprehensive system for the Rorschach. *Clinical Psychology: Science and Practice, 8,*(3) 350-373.

Young, J.E. (1990). *Cognitive Therapy For Personality Disorders: A Schema-Focused Approach*. Sarasota, FL: Professional Resource Exchange.

Young, R.C., Biggs, J.T., Ziegler, V.E., Meyer, D.A. (1978). A rating scale for mania: Reliability, validity, and sensitivity. *British Journal of Psychiatry, 133*,429-435.

In: New Psychological Tests and Testing Research
Editor: Lydia S. Boyar, pp. 35-61

ISBN: 978-1-60021-570-4
© 2007 Nova Science Publishers, Inc.

Chapter 2

DEVELOPMENT AND VALIDATION OF THE COPING INVENTORY FOR THE JAPANESE (CIJ)

Katsunori Sumi[1]

Nagoya Institute of Technology, Japan

ABSTRACT

There exist few brief Japanese measures of coping that have adequate psychometric properties. The purpose of the present study was to develop and test the validity of a brief Likert-type scale measuring three dimensions of coping—cognitive approach, behavioral approach, and avoidance coping—in Japanese people. The developed measure was called the Coping Inventory for the Japanese (CIJ). The items of the preliminary inventory were selected from an initial item pool on the basis of the three dimensions of coping. The CIJ is composed of 15 items that were selected from among the preliminary inventory items on the basis of an item analysis of data derived from 318 college students. As a result of the factor analysis, a three-factor structure was confirmed. Each of the three factors constituted a subscale—the Cognitive Approach Coping Scale, the Behavioral Approach Coping Scale, and the Avoidance Coping Scale. The data supported that each subscale of the CIJ had acceptable internal consistency and test-retest reliability. As expected, the three-factor structure was again identified by a factor analysis of data from 167 college students. Intercorrelations between the subscale scores were significant but weak. The convergent validity of the CIJ was established through correlations between the scores on the CIJ and an existing coping scale that assesses almost the same construct as that assessed by the CIJ. It was found that the subscale scores on the CIJ were correlated in the expected direction with scores for social support, optimism, and self-esteem. In addition, the subscale scores were significantly correlated with the scores for subsequent perceived stress. Therefore, the CIJ has good construct validity.

[1] Correspondence concerning this article should be sent to Katsunori Sumi, Ph.D., Nagoya Institute of Technology, Gokiso-cho, Showa-ku, Nagoya 466-8555, Japan. E-mail: sumi@nitech.ac.jp. I thank Akiko M. Sumi and those who kindly volunteered to participate in the study.

INTRODUCTION

Over the past three decades, the subject of stress and coping has been given increasing importance by researchers and practitioners (Carver, 1996; Lazarus, 1999). At present, the concept of coping is one of the important concepts in psychology (Schwarzer and Knoll, 2003). An individual's coping response to a stressful situation can be an essential component in determining the impact that the situation will have on the individual (Clark, Bormann, Cropanzano, and James, 1995; Endler and Parker, 1990).

Coping refers to the cognitive and behavioral efforts to reduce and master the requirements of a specific situation that benefit, harm, pose a challenge or threat to, or result in loss for a person (Lazarus, 1991; Lazarus and Folkman, 1984). In the context of the positive psychology movement, the conceptualization of coping has recently been broadening, and it now also encompasses self-regulated, goal attainment strategies and personal growth (Schwarzer and Knoll, 2003). To understand the construct of coping, it has been pointed out that at least three important features of coping should be considered: (1) Coping need not be a completed "successful" act, but an effort needs to have been made; (2) this effort need not be expressed in actual behavior, but can be directed to cognitions as well; and (3) a cognitive appraisal of the taxing situation is a prerequisite for the initiation of coping attempts (Schwarzer and Schwarzer, 1996).

Despite the rich history of the study of coping, current popularity of the concept, and the importance of the concept to an individual's well-being, there does not exist sufficient coherence in the theory, research, and understanding of coping. The complexity of the coping domain is reflected in the diversity of the existing approaches for the assessment of coping. Moreover, problems involved in the measurement of coping have been pointed out (Moos and Schaefer, 1993; Schwarzer and Schwarzer, 1996).

In this chapter, we provide a report on a new coping inventory developed for the Japanese. Prior to this, existing coping measures including those developed in Japan, some issues in the measurement of coping, and the relationships between coping and relevant factors are outlined.

Existing Measures of Coping

Over the past three decades, numerous attempts have been made to develop measures of coping. In this section, a brief review of the principal features of the coping inventories that are used frequently is conducted. The measures reviewed here include self-report Japanese scales developed in Japan as well as English scales developed in the English speaking world.

Coping Measures Developed in the English-Speaking World

1. Ways of Coping-Revisited

The Ways of Coping-Revisited (WOC-R; Folkman and Lazarus, 1985) has been used in numerous studies on self-reported coping and has played a significant role in advancing coping research (Stone, Greenberg, Kennedy-Moore, and Newman, 1991). In Japanese coping research, the WOC-R and its revised version are the most frequently used inventories (Japanese Institute of Health Psychology, 1996; Kusakabe, Chida, Chin, Matsumoto, Tsutsui,

Ozaki, Ito, Nakamura, Miura, Suzuki, and Sakano, 2000). The WOC-R has been developed in line with the transactional phenomenological stress theory that suggests two main functions of coping: problem solving and emotion regulation (cf. Lazarus, 1991). The WOC-R is a 66-item self-report scale designed to identify the thoughts and actions that an individual has used to cope with a specific stressful encounter. In other words, it treats coping as a response to a specific stressor in a particular situation (Clark et al., 1995). Using a 4-point scale, respondents are asked to indicate the extent to which they used each of the 66 coping responses in dealing with the specific problem. The WOC-R is composed of eight subscales: Problem-Focused Coping, Wishful Thinking, Distancing, Emphasizing the Positive, Self-Blame, Tension-Reduction, Self-Isolation, and Seeking Social Support. Six of the eight subscales assess approach coping and two assess avoidance coping (Moos and Schaefer, 1993). However, a further study found that the scale assesses somewhat different factors (Folkman, Lazarus, Gruen, and DeLongis, 1986).

2. COPE

The COPE (Carver, Scheier, and Weintraub, 1989), which has been used in a number of health-relevant studies originated in part from the literature on coping, including the Lazarus and Folkman (1984) model of coping and the Carver and Scheier (1981, 1990) model of behavioral self-regulation (Carver, 1997; Carver et al., 1989). This measure is conceived as a more fine-grained dispositional measure of individual differences in coping (Schwarzer and Schwarzer, 1996). The COPE is a 60-item scale designed to assess 15 coping strategies. On a 4-point scale, the respondents are instructed to rate how they generally cope with stressful situations. Based on a substantial review of the literature, Carver et al. (1989) identified 15 conceptually distinct subscales: Active Coping, Planning, Suppression of Competing Activities, Restraint Coping, Seeking Instrumental Social Support, Seeking Emotional Social Support, Positive Reinterpretation and Growth, Acceptance, Religion, Focus On and Venting Emotions, Denial, Behavioral Disengagement, Mental Disengagement, Alcohol/Drug Use, and Humor. The first five categories are subdimensions of problem-focused coping and the remaining categories are subdimensions of emotion-focused coping. A factor analysis produced almost the same structure as was hypothesized (Carver et al., 1989). A second-order analysis identified four factors that reflected active coping, seeking support, denial and disengagement, and acceptance and reinterpretation (Carver et al., 1989).

3. Coping Inventory for Stressful Situations

The Coping Inventory for Stressful Situations (CISS; Endler and Parker, 1991), which was initially called the Multidimensional Coping Inventory (Endler and Parker, 1990), was designed to assess dispositional coping styles. The CISS has very good psychometric properties at it was developed in an accurate and rigorous manner (Schwarzer and Schwarzer, 1996). The respondents are asked to rate 48 coping activities on 5-point frequency scale in terms of the extent to which they engage in the activities when they encounter a difficult, stressful, or upsetting situation. Factor analyses yielded three factors: Task-Oriented, Emotion-Oriented, and Avoidance-Oriented Coping. Each subscale has 16 items. The avoidance dimension could be further subdivided into a Distraction Scale and a Social Diversion Scale.

4. Coping Strategy Indicator

The Coping Strategy Indicator (CSI-A; Amirkhan, 1990) is a 33-item scale that treats coping as a situation-specific response. While the CSI-A was intended as a situation-specific measure, there is evidence to suggest that the instrument is effective in identifying more generalized, cross-situational coping tendencies (Amirkhan, 1994). The scale items were selected by eliminating many coping strategies from existing scales as well as from Amirkhan's previous research and choosing only a few; this was done in a step-by-step manner by conducting a series of factor analyses with independent large samples. The CSI-A has exhibited desirable psychometric qualities (Amirkhan, 1994). Respondents are asked to explain a recent stressful encounter and on a 3-point scale, rate the degree to which they engaged in each of the 33 coping options. The scale is designed to measure three coping strategies: Problem-Solving, Seeking Social Support, and Avoidance.

5. Coping Responses Inventory

The Coping Responses Inventory (CRI; Moos, 1992) assesses an individual's approach and avoidance coping skills in response to stressful life circumstances and other challenges. The CRI was developed after constructing several preliminary versions and subscales (e.g., Billings and Moos, 1981, 1984; Moos, Cronkite, Billings, and Finney, 1986). There are two versions: one for adults and the other for youths. For the adult form, the respondents are asked to identify a recent stressful episode and on a 4-point scale, rate the degree of their reliance on each of the 48 coping responses. The measure is composed of eight subscales: Logical Analysis, Positive Reappraisal, Seeking Guidance and Support, Problem Solving, Cognitive Avoidance, Acceptance or Resignation, Seeking Alternative Rewards, and Emotional Discharge. The first four scales are conceptualized as measuring approach coping, and the latter four scales are conceptualized as measuring avoidance coping.

6. Coping Strategies Inventory

The Coping Strategies Inventory (CSI-T; Tobin, Holroyd, Reynolds, and Wigal, 1989) is a 72-item self-report coping scale. Respondents are asked to identify a recent stressful event and using a 5-point scale, rate the degree to which they used the 72 coping strategies. As a result of a hierarchical factor analysis of the CSI-T, a hierarchical model with three levels was reported (Tobin et al., 1989). The hierarchical model was composed of eight primary factors (Problem Solving, Cognitive Restructuring, Emotional Expression, Social Support, Problem Avoidance, Wishful Thinking, Self-Criticism, and Social Withdrawal), four secondary factors (Problem Engagement, Emotion Engagement, Problem Disengagement, and Emotion Disengagement), and two tertiary factors (Engagement and Disengagement). The eight primary factors were dimensions of coping that had been identified in previous empirical research and theoretical writing (Tobin et al., 1989). Moreover, Tobin et al. pointed out that the emergence of the four secondary and two tertiary factors provided empirical support for two theoretical hypotheses concerning the structure of coping: (a) problem-focused and emotion-focused coping (e.g., Lazarus and Folkman, 1984) and (b) engagement or approach coping and disengagement or avoidance coping (e.g., Scheier, Weintraub, and Carver, 1986).

7. Miller Behavioral Style Scale

The Miller Behavioral Style Scale (MBSS; Miller, 1987) is a 32-item scale that assesses coping styles on the basis of an individual's attentional style in stressful situations. The

MBSS consists of four hypothetical stress-evoking situations of an uncontrollable nature. Two of these situations involve physical threat and the remaining two involve ego-threat. Each of the four stress-evoking situations is accompanied by eight coping styles: half of them reflect a "monitoring" attentional style, and the other half reflects a "blunting" attentional style. The monitoring and blunting attentional style correspond to the information-seeking and information-avoiding or distracting styles, respectively. The scores are obtained by adding up the corresponding items to yield a monitoring and a blunting score. From among a total of eight statements, the respondents are asked to choose one or more items that represent their preferred way of responding to each presented situation.

8. Constructive Thinking Inventory

The Constructive Thinking Inventory (CTI; Epstein and Meier, 1989) is a 108-item self-report inventory that measures the constructive and destructive beliefs and thinking patterns that underlie emotional intelligence, coping ability, and physical and emotional well-being. The inventory consists of items that describb common automatic constructive and destructive ways of thinking. The respondents rate each of the items on a 5-point scale. The CTI provides scores on seven scales: a global scale and six more specific scales. The six scales are Emotional Coping, Behavioral Coping, Categorical Thinking, Personal Superstitious Thinking, Esoteric Thinking, and Naive Optimism. The Global Constructive Thinking scale was selected for the purpose of assigning subjects to groups on the basis of their general coping ability (Epstein, 1992).

Coping Measures Developed in Japan

1. Stress Coping Scale

As mentioned above, the inventory used with the greatest frequency in Japanese coping research is the WOC-R and its revised version (Kusakabe et al., 2000). On the other hand, from among the coping inventories developed in Japan, the Stress Coping Scale (SCS; Sakata, 1989) has been used most frequently in coping studies on Japanese people. The SCS is a 58-item self-report scale designed to assess various coping strategies that are frequently utilized by Japanese adults. The respondents are asked to identify an important stressful event and answer whether they engaged in each of the 58 coping strategies. On the basis of the results of factor analyses and the examination of item content, Sakata (1989) classified the 58 coping strategies into 19 categories: Planning, Information Searching, Reexamination, Making an Effort, Heightening Value, Changing Focus, Lessening Value, Disengagement, Resignation, Negligence, Acceptance, Expectancy, Making Oneself Understood, Seeking Support, Distraction, Self-Control, Escape, Aggression, and Rationalization.

2. Coping Scale for College Students

The Coping Scale for College Students (CSCS; Ozeki, 1993; Ozeki, Haraguchi, and Tsuda, 1991, 1994) is a 14-item coping scale and is a part of the 119-item Stress Self-Rating Scale (Ozeki, 1993; Ozeki et al., 1991, 1994), which assesses the stress response, stressor, cognitive appraisal, coping, social support, and humor as a comprehensive stress scale for Japanese college students. In the CSCS, like the SCS, the respondents are asked to think of an important stressful event and then indicate, using a 4-point frequency scale, the extent to which they used each of the 14 coping strategies in dealing with the stressful event. The

CSCS is composed of three subscales: Problem-Focused Coping, Emotion-Focused Coping, and Avoidance-Escape Coping. However, a confirmatory factor analysis extracted two factors: Active Coping and Passive Coping (Ozeki, 1993).

3. Tri-Aaxial Coping Scale

The Tri-Axial Coping Scale 24-item version (TAC-24; Kamimura, Ebihara, Sato, Togazsaki, and Sakano, 1995) was designed as a means to evaluate a person's tendencies to adopt a certain coping style. Each of the scale items that was made to developed corresponded to one of eight quadrants that were created on the basis of three axes: the engagement-avoidance axis, emotion focused-problem focused axis, and cognitive-behavioral axis. On a 5-point scale, the respondents are asked to rate how they generally cope with stressful situations. The TAC-24 is composed of eight subscales: Getting Information, Giving Up, Positive Interpretation, Plan Drafting, Avoidance-Like Thinking, Distractive Recreation, Catharsis, and Evading One's Responsibilities.

4. General Coping Questionnaire

Like the COPE, the General Coping Questionnaire (GCQ; Sasaki and Yamasaki, 2002) is a dispositional measure of coping. The respondents are instructed to think about how they generally cope with stressful situations. The responses to the 32 coping strategies are made on a 5-point frequency scale. The questionnaire has the following four subscales, each having eight items: Emotion Expression, Emotional Support Seeking, Cognitive Reinterpretation, and Problem Solving. The dimensions of the GCQ were supported by an exploratory and confirmatory factor analysis. The first two scales are conceptualized as measuring the emotion-focused coping style, and the latter two scales are conceptualized as measuring the problem-focused coping style (Sasaki and Yamasaki, 2002).

Issues in the Measurement of Coping

Various issues in the measurement of coping have been pointed out (Kato, 2006; Schwarzer and Schwarzer, 1996). In particular, the subsequent conceptual issues complicate the measurement of coping (Schwarzer and Schwarzer, 1996). In this section, some of these issues are reviewed.

Dimensionality of Coping

Many attempts have been made to reduce the large number of possible coping responses to a more parsimonious set of dimensions. As the results of these theoretical or empirical attempts, various dimensions of coping responses have been reported. For example, as mentioned in the previous section, each existing coping measure is composed of various dimensions. In addition, it is possible that the extracted factors from a factor analysis of the measures change from sample to sample or from stressor to stressor (Parker and Endler, 1992). The dimensionality of coping, which involves the conceptualization of coping, seems to be a basic problem in most coping measures.

From among the many conceptualizations of coping dimensions, the most popular is the conceptualization of the problem-focused and emotion-focused dimensions, proposed by Lazarus and Folkman (1984). It has also been suggested that coping strategies can be appropriately classified into two categories— adaptive and maladaptive coping strategies— according to the presumed outcome (Tobin et al., 1989).

Other theorists have proposed that coping responses can be classified into two distinct categories, approach and avoidance coping. (Moos and Schaefer, 1993; Tobin et al., 1989). Moreover, Scheier et al. (1986) attempted to integrate the approach/avoidance and problem-focused /emotion-focused formulation and proposed two coping categories, namely, engagement and disengagement coping.

As mentioned above, Tobin et al. (1989) identified a hierarchical model with three levels by using hierarchical factor analysis. The second-order categories, i.e., problem engagement, emotion engagement, problem disengagement, and emotion disengagement, presented problem and emotion-focused constructs, and the first-order categories, i.e., engagement and disengagement, presented the formulation proposed by Scheier et al. (Tobin et al., 1989).

Moos and Schaefer (1993) pointed out that there are two main conceptual approaches to classifying coping processes: approaches emphasizing the focus of coping and those emphasizing the method of coping. The approaches emphasizing the focus of coping distinguish approaching the problem and making active efforts to resolve it from trying to avoid the problem, and focus mainly on managing the emotions associated with it. The approach emphasizing the method of coping focuses on the cognitive and behavioral efforts to solve the problem. Moos and Schaefer combined the two approaches to develop a more integrated conceptualization of coping processes and proposed four coping categories, i.e., the cognitive approach coping, behavioral approach coping, cognitive avoidance coping, and behavioral avoidance coping.

There is also a conceptual distinction between assimilative and accommodative coping (Schwarzer and Knoll, 2003). The former aims at modifying the environment, while the latter aims at modifying oneself (Brandtstadter, 1992).

Other basic dimensions such as instrumental, attentive, vigilant, or confrontative coping have been proposed in contrast with avoidant, palliative, and emotional coping (Schwarzer and Schwarzer, 1996). The dimensions of the representative coping measures are as mentioned in the preceding section.

Situational and Dispositional Coping

Indeed, there has been various arguments about the differences between dispositional coping styles and situational coping strategies (Carver and Scheier, 1994). Individuals may employ habitual coping strategies across situations or across time points. Alternatively, individuals may choose diverse and adequate coping strategies according to the situation encountered. Lazarus (1991) pointed out that coping responses can change from moment to moment across the stages of a stressful transaction. On the other hand, individuals can develop certain coping styles as habitual strategies for dealing with stressful encounters; these coping styles, in turn, can influence coping responses in new situations (Carver and Scheier, 1994).

This difference in position with regard to the association between coping and situations is naturally associated with the measurements of coping. For example, the WOC-R, CSI-A, CRI, CSI-T, SCS, and CSCS are situation-specific coping measures that treat coping as a response to a particular situation. In contrast, the COPE, CISS, and GCQ are dispositional coping measures (Stone et al., 1991).

Consistency of Coping Across Situations

The consistency of coping responses by an individual across different situations is also one of the issues to which attention should be paid. Different situations may require a person to use different coping responses according to the situation. On the contrary, a person may apply the same coping strategies regardless of the type of situation. Besides, people may tend to choose similar strategies for specific situations. This issue is, not to mention, also closely associated with a differences in perspective, for example, situational coping versus dispositional coping.

Temporal Stability of Coping

One topic that is closely related to the consistency of a coping response across situations is the temporal stability of coping. Situation-specific coping measures are developed under the assumption that coping is temporally stable, whereas dispositional coping measures are based on an assumption pertaining to the relative stability of the coping style that is formed. In spite of the difference in these fundamental premises, higher temporal stability is not desired in coping measures (Schwarzer and Schwarzer, 1996). The reason for this is that in general, individuals are expected to apply coping responses corresponding to each stressful situation. In other words, the same strategies do not necessarily need to be continuously applied over time. In addition, the issue concerning the temporal stability of coping is also a consideration in assessing the reliability of coping measurement.

Variety of Coping Strategies Used

Even if individuals adjust their coping responses to the requirements of each situation, the variety of coping strategies used by individuals is limited. For example, if a specific coping strategy is successful, the person no longer needs to apply other strategies within the same dimensions (Folkman, 1992). This topic is a consideration in assessing the internal consistency of a coping measure, particularly that of a situation-specific coping measure. Owing to the nature of coping, it is difficult to achieve a high level of internal consistency with coping measures (Folkman, 1992; Stone and Neale, 1984).

Confounding of Coping with Its Resources

While coping resources are relatively static antecedents that enable a person to cope, coping is a process that depends on these coping resources (Lazarus and Folkman, 1984; Schwarzer and Schwarzer, 1996). In the elucidation of the coping process, it is necessary to differentiate between coping resources and actual coping. Nevertheless, both constructs may in effect be difficult to disentangle. For example, there are cases in which we can not decide with certainty whether the optimistic view of handling a problem with a person reflects a personality trait such as optimism or whether it is just an effective coping strategy. All the same, in the exploration of coping, attention needs to be paid to discriminating actual coping from coping resources.

Confounding of Cognitive Coping with Cognitive Appraisal

As Lazarus (1991) pointed out, there is some overlap between cognitive coping and cognitive appraisal. Cognitive coping refers to what a person thinks when he/she is trying to manage an emotional encounter, and cognitive appraisal refers to an evaluation of what could be thought or done in that encounter (Lazarus, 1991). It is difficult to distinguish sharply between these two constructs. Lazarus even stated that cognitive coping is a form of appraisal in its own right. Since both constructs can be easily confused, caution is needed when developing a coping measure.

Other Issues in the Measurement of Coping

In relation to the abovementioned confounding between cognitive coping and cognitive appraisal, the need to clarify the differences between coping and its outcomes as well as the difference between coping resources and cognitive appraisal has been pointed out (Lazarus and Folkman, 1984; Schwarzer and Schwarzer, 1996). In addition to this, there are many coping measures that continue to be used without a sufficient assessment of their validity (Amirkhan, 1994). Moreover, as an issue inherent in the retrospective method applied to most self-report coping measures, there is the possibility that a respondent's actual coping responses are distinct from those that the respondent claims to use.

Relationships with Coping-Related Factors

There are a considerable number of factors associated with coping. In this section, some of these factors are reviewed. We also briefly describe the relationships between coping and some such factors. These relationships provide the criteria on the basis of which to assess the construct validity of coping inventories.

Situation

As mentioned earlier, coping refers to the cognitive and behavioral efforts to reduce and master the requirements of a specific situation (Fleming, Baum, and Singer, 1984; Lazarus, 1991; Lazarus and Folkman, 1984). Actual coping is undoubtedly influenced by the situation that needs to be adjusted to. However, an assumed degree of the influence of the situation may differ among views of coping. The view of situational coping may assume a higher degree of the influence of the situation on coping than that assumed by the view of dispositional coping. The association with each dimension of coping may also be affected by the implications of the situation. For example, emotion-focused or avoidance coping may be applied more frequently than problem-focused coping or approach coping in a situation that is evaluated as uncontrollable and difficult to overcome (Terry, 1994).

Social Support

Social support has also been regarded as one of the resources that can be used for a variety of purposes, such as solving a problem, obtaining information, calming down, or feeling relief (Pierce, Sarason, and Sarason, 1996; Schwarzer and Schwarzer, 1996). Regardless of the different conceptualizations, social support enables an individual to engage in personal coping, provides the required assistance, and enable the individual to adopt engagement or approach coping (Pierce et al., 1996). Furthermore, as mentioned above, a dimension with regard to social support is included in many coping measures such as the WOC-R, COPE, CISS, and CSI-T.

Personality

Personality is considered to be linked closely with the coping process (Fleishman, 1984; Hewitt and Flett, 1996; Lazarus and Folkman, 1984). It is assumed that personality does not directly influence specific coping strategies for dealing with stressful events; nevertheless, certain personality traits interact with coping to produce or maintain maladjustment (Hewitt and Flett, 1996).

Some personality traits such as dispositional optimism, hardiness, self-efficacy, and self-esteem have received attention as coping resources. Individuals with high levels of such personality traits may use more engagement or approach coping strategies and less disengagement or avoidance coping strategies than individuals with low levels of such personality traits (Carver et al., 1989; Gentry and Kobasa, 1984; Hewitt and Flett, 1996; Terry, 1994). This is presumably because individuals who possess such personality traits are likely to believe that their own coping strategies will be effective in managing stressful situations and are likely to positively and actively deal with the situation (Carver et al., 1989; Gentry and Kobasa, 1984; Hewitt and Flett, 1996; Terry, 1994).

On the contrary, other personality traits may make the psrson likely to use more disengagement or avoidance coping strategies. Some example of these personality traits are neuroticism, trait anxiety, and Type A behavior pattern (Carver et al., 1989; Endler and Parker, 1990; Gentry and Kobasa, 1984; Hewitt and Flett, 1996; Terry, 1994).

Perceived Stress and Well-Being

With regard to the important role of coping in the stress process, little need be said. In the transactional model of stress (Lazarus and Folkman, 1984), along with cognitive appraisal, coping is a critical process that mediates the person-environment relationship. Psychological stress, not to mention, occurs when a particular person-environment relationship is appraised by the person as taxing or exceeding his or her resources and endangering his or her well-being (Lazarus and Folkman, 1984). Therefore, effective coping is likely to reduce perceived stress and promote well-being.

Purpose of this Study and Procedure of Developing the Inventory

In the previous sections, we provided an outline of the existing coping measures, issues in coping measurement, and the relationships between coping and relevant factors. In the subsequent sections, we will describe the development of a new self-report Likert-type coping inventory, which we called the Coping Inventory for the Japanese (CIJ). The CIJ was developed as a brief measure for the Japanese, while taking into account the issues mentioned above. Such a brief coping measure can reduce the response burden on the participants when the repeated measurement design is used or when a large number of measures are included in the study (Carver, 1997).

The inventory assesses dispositional coping on the basis of three dimensions of coping; cognitive approach, behavioral approach, and avoidance coping. As mentioned in the previous section, theorists and researchers have often proposed various basic dimensions of coping. The CIJ was based on the four categories—cognitive approach, behavioral approach, cognitive avoidance, and behavioral avoidance coping—by Moos and Schaefer (1993) that have been outlined above, the two avoidance categories were combined to minimize the number of inventory items. Cognitive approach coping refers to coping that involves cognitively approaching the problem and making active efforts to resolve it. Behavioral approach coping refers to behavioral efforts at approaching the problem and resolving it. Avoidance coping refers to efforts to try to avoid the problem and focus mainly on managing the emotions associated with it. Hence, the CIJ was assumed to have three subscales, which were termed the Cognitive Approach Coping Scale (CAS), Behavioral Approach Coping Scale (BAS), and Avoidance Coping Scale (AS).

In the procedure to develop the CIJ, first, an item pool to tap the coping responses used by Japanese people was generated. Next, the items that were selected from among the item pool on the basis of the necessary properties of the inventory constituted a preliminary scale. The final scale, on which further analyses were conducted, was composed of items that were evaluated using item analyses. Finally, the reliability and construct validity of the scale were examined.

In examining the construct validity of the CIJ, given the considerations outlined above, we formulated hypotheses about the relationships between the scores on the three subscales of the CIJ and other scales. It was assumed that the scores on the CAS, BAS, and AS would have higher correlations with the scores on coping scales that have been designed to assess the same construct than with the scores on coping scales that have been designed to assess a different construct. The scores on the social support, optimism, and self-esteem scales would be positively correlated with the scores on the CAS and BAS and would be negatively correlated with the scores on the AS. It was also expected that the initial scores on the CAS and BAS subscales of the CIJ would predict a lower level of perceived stress; on the contrary, the initial scores on the AS would predict a higher level of perceived stress.

Creation of Preliminary Inventory

The first step in the development of the coping measure was to obtain suitable questions. For this purpose, we compiled an item pool based on the following: (1) English version of the coping measures, (2) coping measures developed in Japan, (3) the literature in English on coping, (4) the available literature in Japanese, and (5) ideas gathered from graduate students.

Items from the following English version coping measures, which have been used widely were examined: the WOC-R (Lazarus and Folkman, 1984); the COPE (Carver et al., 1989); the MCI (Endler and Parker, 1990); and the CSI-A (Amirkhan, 1990). Items from the following coping inventories developed in Japan were also evaluated: the SCS (Sakata, 1989), the Worker's Coping Behavior Scale (Shoji and Shoji, 1992), the CSCS (Ozeki, 1993; Ozeki et al., 1991, 1994), the TAC-24 (Kamimura et al., 1995), the Coping Scale for Elementary School Children (Otake, Shimai, and Shimada, 1998), the Interpersonal Stress-Coping Inventory (Kato, 2000), and the GCQ (Sasaki and Yamasaki, 2002). We reviewed literature in English such as Folkman and Lazarus (1985); McCrae (1984); Stone and Neale (1984); and Stanton, Parsa, and Austenfeld (2002). We also evaluated literature on coping that was described in some available literature in Japan, for example, Fuse and Kosugi (1996), Kato and Imada (2001), Kusakabe et al. (2000), Koguchi (2002), and Kato (2005),. Moreover, referring to the items and lists on coping responses that Japanese people had actually made (Kikushima, 2002; Wada, Xiao-Qi, and Xiao Lan, 1993, 1996), additional items were generated by graduate students. The list of items thus collected were a wide variety of coping responses.

In the next step, one psychologist and some graduate students reduced the list to 18 items by removing redundant items and items that seemed biased toward certain groups of individuals by combining like items. In the selection of appropriate items, we also took into account the correspondence of the items with the three aspects of coping responses: cognitive approach coping, behavioral approach coping, and avoidance coping.

When the selected 18 coping items were presented to the respondents, the following 5-point frequency scales were used: 1 (*not at all*), 2 (*not much*), 3 (*a little bit*), 4 (*quite a bit*), and 5 (*very much*). When administering this preliminary scale, the following instructions were given:

> Please read each item below and indicate, by circling the appropriate number from 1 to 5 for each of the items, how much you engaged in these types of activities when you recently encountered a difficult, stressful, or upsetting situation.

METHOD

Participants

The participants in this study were Japanese college students who were divided into three groups, Sample A, Sample B, and Sample C.

Sample A
This sample consisted of 119 college students attending a college in a major city. Of the respondents, 26 were women (21.8%) and 93 were men (78.2%). Their mean age was 20.76 years (*SD* = .82), and their age range was 19 to 25 years.

Sample B
Sample B consisted of 199 college students. This sample consisted of 41 women (20.6%) and 158 men (79.4%) whose ages ranged from 18 to 27 years (*M* = 19.22, *SD* = .89). They attended the same college as that attended by the students in Sample A.

Sample C
Sample B consisted of 167 college students. They attended one of two local colleges in their cities. This sample consisted of 113 women (67.7%) and 54 men (32.3%) whose ages ranged from 18 to 21 years (*M* = 19.28, *SD* = .55).

Measures

Coping Responses
Coping responses were assessed by the Japanese version of the Coping Responses Scale (CRS; Billings and Moos, 1981; Sumi, 1999). This scale was used to assess the convergent validity of the CIJ. The CRS consists of 19 items and the participants have to rate the manner

in which they dealt with recent personal crises or stressful life events. The CRS contains factors corresponding to the categories pertaining to three methods of coping: active-cognitive coping, active-behavioral coping, and avoidance coping. Active-cognitive coping refers to attempts to manage one's appraisal of the stressfulness of the event. Active-behavioral coping includes overt behavioral attempts to deal directly with the problem and its effects. Avoidance coping refers to attempts to avoid actively confronting the problem or indirectly reduce emotional tension by behavior such as excessive eating. On comparing each subscale of the CRS with the subscales of the CSJ, it was clear that the subscale items of both the scales were designed to assess almost the same coping responses.

The scale items were selected from a previous inventory and a review of the literature on coping responses in a variety of situation (Billings and Moos, 1981). The active-cognitive coping scale (ACS), active-behavioral coping scale (ABS), and avoidance coping scale (AVS) have 6, 6, and 5 items, respectively. Each item of the Japanese version of the CRS used a 5-point response format ranging from 1 (*I haven't been doing this at all*) to 5 (*I have been doing this a lot*). Higher scores on the subscale indicate a greater use of that particular coping response. Previous studies (Billings and Moos, 1981; Sumi, 1999) have reported acceptable psychometric properties for the scale of the original version of the CRS as well as the Japanese version. In this study, the alpha coefficients for the Japanese version were .62 for the CC, .58 for the BC, and .55 for the AC. Although the indicators of internal consistency in the CRS were low, Billings and Moos concluded that the scale indicated moderate internal homogeneity because the alpha coefficient of the coping responses measure that was minimized to reduce item redundancy within each coping category may have an upper limit.

Social Support

The Japanese version of the 6-item Social Support Questionnaire Short-Form (Sarason, Sarason, Shearin, and Pierce, 1987; Sumi, 1997) was used to measure perceived social support. This scale is a reduced version of the Social Support Questionnaire (Sarason, Levine, Basham, and Sarason, 1983) and consists of two subscales: the Number of Supports Scale (SSQ-N) and Satisfaction with Support Scale (SSQ-S). The SSQ-N assesses the size of a person's support networks, in other words, the number of other people expected to provide available support. The SSQ-S assesses a person's satisfaction with the actual support. The respondents list up to a number of nine supports with regard to all the six items and rate their satisfaction with each support on a 6-point scale with reference to all the items. The SSQ-N scores range from 0 to 54, while the Satisfaction with Support Scale scores range from 6 to 36. The higher the score, the higher is the degree of perceived social support. The original SSQ-N and SSQ-S have well-established and sufficient reliability and validity (Sarason et al., 1987). The Japanese version has been reported to have adequate psychometric properties (Sumi, 1997). For the present sample, the alpha coefficients for the SSQ-N and SSQ-S were .91 and .89, respectively.

Optimism

The personality disposition of optimism was assessed with the Japanese version of the Life Orientation Test (LOT; Scheier and Carver, 1985; Sumi, 1997). The LOT provides a self-report measure of individual differences in global optimism, defined in terms of the favorableness of the person's generalized outcome expectancies. The scale is an 8-item scale (with an additional four fillers) that yields a continuous distribution of scores. Of the eight items, four items are positively worded and the other four are negatively worded. Respondents are asked to indicate the extent to which they agree with each of the items by using the 4-point response format anchored by 0 (*strongly disagree*) to 4 (*strongly agree*). The LOT scores range from 0 to 32, and higher scores indicate more dispositional optimism. Prior work has reported that the LOT has adequate reliability and validity (Scheier and Carver, 1985). Similarly, the Japanese version has been reported to have adequate psychometric properties (Sumi, 1997). The alpha coefficient for the Japanese version in this sample was .78.

Self-Esteem

Self-esteem was assessed with the Japanese version (Yamamoto, Matsui, and Yamanari, 1982) of the Rosenberg Self-Esteem Scale (RSE; Rosenberg, 1965). The RSE is the most widely used measure of global self-esteem (Heatherton and Wyland, 2003). The scale measures an individual's self-worth and self-acceptance. Although the original scale is a 10-item Guttman scale, the Japanese version was modified by using a 5-point Likert scale ranging from 1 (*strongly disagree*) to 5 (*strongly agree*). Half of the 10 items were reverse scored. Since the self-esteem score is the sum of the scores on each item, the range of the scale scores is from 10 to 50. High scores indicate higher self-esteem. The Japanese version has been reported to have adequate psychometric properties (Yamamoto et al., 1982). The alpha coefficient in this sample was .86.

Perceived Stress

The Japanese version of the Perceived Stress Scale (PSS; Cohen, Kamarck,and Mermelstein, 1983; Cohen and Williamson, 1988; Sumi, 1998, in press) was used to measure perceived stress. The PSS used in this study was a 10-item revised version (Cohen, and Williamson, 1988). The scale is a self-report measure that assesses the degree to which situations in one's life are appraised as stressful. Each item of the PSS was designed to tap the degree to which respondents found their lives to be unpredictable, uncontrollable, and overloaded, and it includes many direct queries about the current levels of experienced stress. The respondents have to rate the items on a 5-point frequency scale, ranging from 0 (*never*) to 4 (*very often*), and have to answer the questions on the basis of their life situation in the last month. A total perceived stress score is obtained by reversing the scoring on the positive items and then summing the scores across the ten items. The range of the scale scores is from 0 to 40, and higher scores indicate more perceived stress. Prior work has reported that the original 10-item PSS has adequate reliability and validity (Cohen, and Williamson, 1988). Similarly, the Japanese version has been reported to have adequate psychometric properties (Sumi, 1998, in press). The alpha coefficient for the Japanese version of the PSS in this sample was .79.

Procedure

For the entire sample, anonymous surveys were conducted by the teachers on an extra curricular basis after obtaining the voluntary consent of the students. All the participants and teachers who instructed the participants about the survey were Japanese. The survey sheets as well as all the instructions throughout the survey were in Japanese.

All the participants in the three groups, namely, Sample A, B, and C, completed the set of questionnaires, which included the CIJ, CRS, SSQ-N, SSQ-S, LOT, RSE, and PSS, at Time 1. Moreover, only Sample B completed both the CIJ and PSS again, 3 weeks later, at Time 2. The participants also reported their gender and age.

We labeled the 318 participants from Sample A and Sample B who completed the set of questionnaires at Time 1 as Sample AB. Similarly, we labeled the 485 participants from Sample AB and Sample C as Sample ABC.

Data Analysis

The first analysis was to verify the factor structure of the coping items in Sample AB by using exploratory principal-components analysis with a varimax rotation. Each of the final factors comprised a subscale of the CIJ. After examining the corrected item-total correlation, the internal consistency and temporal stability of each subscale were tested.

The equality of the scale structure between different samples was evaluated by principal-components factor analysis by using the data obtained from Sample C. To assess the construct validity of the inventory, correlations between the scores on the subscales of the CIJ and scores on the CRS, SSQ-N, SSQ-S, LOT, and RSE were examined. In addition, partial correlations between the subscale scores and the PSS scores at Time 2 while controlling for the PSS scores at Time 1 were evaluated for Sample B.

RESULTS

Scale Construction

Factor Analyses

A principal components factor analysis with Sample AB revealed four factors with eigenvalues greater than 1.00. The factors were extracted with eigenvalues of 6.57, 1.36, 1.12, and 1.00, which together explained 55.8% of the variance (see Table 1). The factor analysis with a varimax rotation on 18 items was repeated only for the first four factors. Table 1 shows the results of the analysis. All the four factors had at least one item loading that exceeded .40. Three items have had to be deleted due to double loadings above .40.

Then, a principal components factor analysis, which was conducted for the remaining 15 items, yielded three factors with eigenvalues greater than 1.00. The three factors had eigenvalues of 5.27, 1.23, and 1.06, and accounted for 50.8% of the total variance (see Table 2). The factor analysis with a varimax rotation was repeated only for the three factors. As shown in Table 2, the resultant factor solution yielded identical subscales, which we originally assumed. Each factor was composed of five items. The first, second, and third factors were labeled "Cognitive Approach Coping, " "Avoidance Coping, " and "Behavioral Approach Coping, " respectively.

Table 1. Factor Loadings of the Preliminary 18 items for Sample AB

Items (key terms)	Factor 1	Factor 2	Factor 3	Factor 4
Clarifying the problem	.74	.13	.24	.05
Considering alternatives	.65	.21	.33	.12
Being more objective	.72	.33	.22	-.11
Remembering my experiences	.76	.13	.14	.09
Seeing the positive side	.74	.25	.18	-.21
Preparing myself for the worst	.51	.54	.14	-.01
Doing something to make up	.59	.50	.12	.04
Getting busy with other things	.28	.64	-.06	.10
Eating and drinking more	.11	.51	.23	-.09
Taking it out on other people	.25	.41	.34	.04
Refusing to think about the problem	.13	.76	.15	.02
Going along with fate	.26	.71	.12	.03
Exercising more	.13	.55	.41	.16
Solving the problem steadily	.22	-.04	.71	.02
Making an effort to solve the problem	.28	.15	.51	.12
Seeking advice from others	.26	.18	.55	-.25
Consulting books	.06	.37	.64	.03
Making a plan and following it	.02	.09	.04	.93
Unrotated eigenvalue	6.57	1.36	1.12	1.00
Unrotated % of variance	36.49	7.57	6.23	5.56

Note. $N = 318$. Underlined values are loadings above .40.

Table 2. Factor Loadings of the 15 Items for Sample AB

Items (key terms)	Factor 1	Factor 2	Factor 3
Clarifying the problem	.72	.15	.16
Considering alternatives	.61	.24	.25
Being more objective	.75	.27	.23
Remembering my experiences	.73	.16	.16
Seeing the positive side	.79	.21	.19
Getting busy with other things	.29	.65	-.04
Eating and drinking more	.16	.53	.20
Taking it out on other people	.28	.44	.19
Refusing to think about the problem	.19	.78	.13
Going along with fate	.29	.64	.15
Solving the problem steadily	.16	-.07	.74
Making an effort to solve the problem	.22	.23	.52
Consulting books	.09	.29	.62
Seeking advice from others	.27	.11	.60
Making a plan and following it	-.27	.34	.45
Unrotated eigenvalue	5.27	1.23	1.06
Unrotated % of variance	35.11	8.63	7.09

Note. $N = 318$. Underlined values are loadings above .40.

Item Analyses

Table 3 shows the item means, standard deviations, and corrected item-total correlations for all the items. The analysis of the data from Sample AB revealed that the corrected item-total correlations on each subscale were adequate, ranging from .52 to .65.

Table 3. Item Means and Corrected Item-Total Correlations for Final 15 items for Sample AB

Subscales of CIJ	Items (key terms)	M	SD	CITC
CAS	Clarifying the problem	3.08	1.15	.65
	Considering alternatives	3.63	.95	.58
	Being more objective	3.24	1.09	.63
	Remembering my experiences	3.11	1.17	.62
	Seeing the positive side	3.15	1.08	.52
BAS	Solving the problem steadily	2.42	1.12	.57
	Making an effort to solve the problem	1.94	1.06	.52
	Consulting books	2.77	1.19	.62
	Seeking advice from others	2.31	1.10	.61
	Making a plan and following it	3.03	1.20	.60
AS	Getting busy with other things	2.98	1.15	.64
	Eating and drinking more	2.00	1.02	.58
	Taking it out on other people	.3.30	1.04	.58
	Refusing to think about the problem	2.55	1.27	.60
	Going along with fate	2.39	1.12	.57

Note. $N = 318$. CITC = corrected item-total correlations; CAS = Cognitive Approach Coping Scale; BAS = Behavioral Approach Coping Scale; AS = Avoidance Coping Scale.

Subscale Construction

To construct separate subscales to measure coping with respect to cognitive approach coping, behavioral approach coping, and avoidance coping, on the basis of the results of the item analyses, we summed the five items loading on each factor. Potential scores for the subscales ranged from 5 to 25. Table 4 presents the means and standard deviations for each subscale.

Table 4. Subscale Means, Standard Deviations, Cronbach's Alpha, and Test-Retest Reliability

Subscales of CIJ	M	SD	α	TRR
CAS	16.21	3.28	.68	.46
BAS	12.47	3.11	.73	.25
AS	13.22	3.33	.65	.39

Note. All the statistics except TRR were obtained for Sample AB ($N = 318$). TRR = test-retest reliability coefficients that were obtained for Sample B ($N = 199$). CAS = Cognitive Approach Coping Scale; BAS = Behavioral Approach Coping Scale; AS = Avoidance Coping Scale.

Reliability

Cronbach's alpha and test-retest reliability coefficients of the CAS, BAS, and AS are also presented in Table 4. The alpha coefficients ranged from .65 to .73. The results indicated that the three subscales of the CIJ had acceptable internal consistency.

The test-retest reliability coefficients for Sample B were statistically significant ($ps <$ .001) but low. Therefore, the temporal stability of the CAS, BAS, and AS was rather low.

Construct Validity

Confirmation of Factor Structure

A principal components factor analysis of the 15 items was conducted on the data of Sample C. Three factors were extracted in this analysis with eigenvalues of 2.81, 2.37, and 1.73 (see Table 5). These factors accounted for 46.0% of the total variance. The varimax-rotated factor loadings for the three-factor solution are shown in Table 5. Each factor comprised five items. The first, second, and third factors were Behavioral Approach Coping, Cognitive Approach Coping, and Avoidance Coping, respectively. Although there were differences in term of the eigenvalues between the factors in Sample AB and the factors in Sample C, the factors in Sample AB were consistent with the factors in Sample C. All the inventory items loaded on the same factors across the samples.

Table 5. Factor Loadings of the 15 Items for Sample C

Subscales of CIJ	Items (key terms)	Factor 1	Factor 2	Factor 3
CAS	Clarifying the problem	.04	.67	.25
	Considering alternatives	-.01	.66	.08
	Being more objective	-.07	.64	-.30
	Remembering my experiences	-.06	.69	.10
	Seeing the positive side	.35	.67	-.04
BAS	Solving the problem steadily	.50	.07	.13
	Making an effort to solve the problem	.73	-.10	-.13
	Consulting books	.82	.02	.07
	Seeking advice from others	.66	.04	.22
	Making a plan and following it	.58	-.08	.05
AS	Getting busy with other things	.19	.16	.69
	Eating and drinking more	.10	.13	.50
	Taking it out on other people	.14	.12	.71
	Refusing to think about the problem	-.12	-.17	.63
	Going along with fate	.27	-.12	.57
Unrotated eigenvalue		2.81	2.37	1.73
Unrotated % of variance		18.70	15.77	11.54

Note. N = 167. Underlined values are loadings above .40.

A comparison of the subscale means of Sample AB with those of Sample C revealed no significant differences. Hence, further analyses were conducted with Sample ABC. Table 6 presents the subscale means, standard deviations, and Cronbach's alphas for Sample ABC. The means for Sample ABC approximated the means for Sample AB, which were summarized in Table 4 ($ps > .05$). Compared to Sample AB, the Cronbach's alphas for Sample ABC were slightly low. The correlations between the scores on the subscales were statistically significant but low (see Table 6).

Table 6. Subscale Means, Standard Deviations, Cronbach's Alpha, and Internal Correlations for Sample ABC

Subscales of CIJ	M	SD	α	1.	2.
1. CAS	16.11	3.12	.62		
2. BAS	12.59	2.89	.68	.15**	
3. AS	13.10	3.83	.63	.19**	.12*

Note. N = 485. CAS = Cognitive Approach Coping Scale; BAS = Behavioral Approach Coping Scale; AS = Avoidance Coping Scale.
*$p < .05$, **$p < .01$.

Convergent Validity

Table 7 shows the zero-order correlations between the scores on the subscales of the CIJ and the scores on the CRS. All the correlation coefficients were positive and significant ($ps < .001$). The scores on the subscales of the CIJ were strongly correlated with the scores on the corresponding subscales of the CRS: the correlation coefficients between the CAS and the ACS were $r = .87$, those between the BAS and the ABS were $r = .73$) and those between the AS and the AVS were $r = .68$. On the other hand, the correlations between the scores on the subscales of the CIJ and the non-corresponding subscales of the CRS were weak to modest ($rs = .23$ to $.34$). The results supported the expected convergent validity of the CIJ.

Table 7. Correlations between the Scores on the Subscales of the CIJ and Those of CRS for Sample ABC

Subscales of CIJ	Subscales of CRS		
	ACS	ABS	AVS
CAS	.87	.28	.33
BAS	.23	.73	.30
AS	.34	.26	.68

Note. N = 485. All the correlation coefficients are significant at the .1% alpha level. ACS = Active-Cognitive Coping Scale; ABS = Active-Behavioral Coping Scale; AVS = Avoidance Coping Scale; CAS = Cognitive Approach Coping Scale; BAS = Behavioral Approach Coping Scale; AS = Avoidance Coping Scale.

Correlations with the Relevant Variables

Zero-order correlation coefficients between the scores on the subscale of the CIJ and the relevant variables are presented in Table 8. While the scores on the CAS and BAS were positively correlated with the ratings on both the social support subscales, i.e., the SSQ-N and the SSQ-S (*rs* = .22 to .29, *ps* < .001), the scores on the AS were negatively correlated with the scores on the SSQ-N (*r* = -.10, *p* < .05) and nonsignificantly correlated with the scores on the SSQ-S (*r* = .08). The scores for optimism were positively correlated with the scores on both the CAS and BAS (*rs* = .16 and .20, respectively, *ps* < .01). There was a negative correlation between the scores on the AS and those on the LOT (*r* = -.11, *p* < .05). Significant positive correlations were obtained between the scores on the CAS and the scores for self-esteem, and the BAS and the scores for self-esteem (*rs* = .18 and .09, *ps* < .01 and .09, respectively). However, the scores on the AS were nonsignificantly correlated with the scores on the RSE (*r* = -.04).

Table 8. Correlations of the Subscales of the CIJ with the Four Scales for Sample ABC

Subscales of CIJ	SSQ-N	SSQ-S	LOT	RSE
CAS	.23***	.22***	.16***	.18***
BAS	.29***	.26***	.20***	.09*
AS	-.10*	.08	-.11*	-.04

Note. N = 485. SSQ-N = Number of Supports Scale; SSQ-S = Satisfaction with Support Scale; LOT = Life Orientation Test; RSE = Rosenberg Self-Esteem scale; CAS = Cognitive Approach Coping Scale; BAS = Behavioral Approach Coping Scale; AS = Avoidance Coping Scale. *p < .05, ***p < .001.

To clarify whether the CIJ scores affect the future level of perceived stress, partial correlations between the scores on the subscales of the CIJ and the PSS scores at Time 2, while controlling for the PSS scores at Time 1, were calculated. Table 9 presents the zero-order correlation coefficients between the subscale scores and the scores on the PSS at Time 1 and Time 2 as well as the partial correlation coefficients. As results, the scores on the subscales of the CIJ had stronger relationships with the scores on the PSS at Time 2 (|*r*|s = .21 to .27) than the scores on the PSS at Time 1 (|*r*|s = .07 to .17). It was found that the scores on the subscales of the CIJ were associated with the PSS scores at Time 2, even after controlling for the PSS scores at Time 1. Furthermore, the PSS scores at Time 2 were negatively correlated with the scores on the CAS and BAS (*prs* = -.21 and -.20, respectively, *ps* < .01), and positively correlated with the scores on the AS (*pr* = .23, *p* < .01).

DISCUSSION

The purpose of the present study was to develop a brief inventory that measures three dimensions of dispositional coping in the Japanese; the inventory was named the CIJ. As a result of examining the data from college students, it was found that the CIJ had good reliability and construct validity.

Table 9. Correlations of the Subscales of the CIJ with Those of the PSS for Sample B

| Subscales of CIJ | *r* | | *pr* |
	Time 1 PSS	Time 2 PSS	
CAS	-.17**	-.27***	-.21**
BAS	-.07	-.21**	-.20**
AS	.14*	.27***	.23**

Note. $N = 199$. PSS = Perceived Stress Scale; CAS = Cognitive Approach Coping Scale; BAS = Behavioral Approach Coping Scale; AS = Avoidance Coping Scale.
$*p < .05, **p < .01, ***p < .001$.

From the factor analyses of the data from Sample AB, 3 of the 18 items were deleted and three factors emerged. The reduction of items is rather expedient for the purpose of developing a brief inventory. The emerged factors indicated three coping dimensions; Cognitive Approach Coping, Behavioral Approach Coping, and Avoidance Coping. In addition, the item analysis revealed an adequate quality of each item comprising the inventory. Then, as expected, a brief coping inventory that had three subscales, CAS, BAS, and AS, was constructed

The internal consistency and temporal stability of each subscale were acceptable but low. The inventory as a dispositional coping measure may require higher reliability. However, because of the minimization of item redundancy and the number of items within each dimension of coping, the alpha coefficient may be constrained (Billings and Moos, 1981); therefore, the low degree of internal consistency of the CIJ may be inevitable (see Schwarzer and Schwarzer, 1996). On the other hand, while individuals may employ habitual coping strategies across situations or across time points (Carver and Scheier, 1994), they may select and adopt somewhat different coping strategies depending on the intensity, frequency, or significance of the stressful encounter in their life. Coping strategies that a person has applied just before completing the CIJ may have some effect on the reply to their responses to the inventory (Pearson, Ross, and Dawes, 1992). One of the reasons for the low degree of temporal stability of the CIJ may be the limitations of retrospective questioning.

The results of the factor analysis with Sample C supported the existence of the same dimensions as those supported with Sample AB. Since the same three dimensions were found across different subjects, the hypothesized dimensions of the CIJ were clearly confirmed. The independence of these dimensions—Cognitive Approach Coping, Behavioral Approach Coping, and Avoidance Coping—was also supported by the weak intercorrelations between the subscales scores. Furthermore, these dimensions were confirmed by the relationships to the scores on the CRS (Billings and Moos, 1981; Sumi, 1999), which was considered to measure the same construct as the CIJ (see Table 7). It is indicated that dispositional coping may be composed of the three dimensions. The relationships, needless to say, support that the CIJ possesses adequate convergent validity.

The correlations between the scores on the subscales of the CIJ and the scores on the relevant variables were largely as expected. The relevant variables, namely social support, optimism, and self-esteem were among the coping resources. Such coping resources may facilitate the employment of approach coping strategies (Carver et al;, 1989; Gentry and Kobasa, 1984; Hewitt and Flett, 1996; Terry, 1994). The existence of an available support network may result in successful support-seeking behaviors. On the contrary, the lack of satisfactory support may promote the use of avoidance coping. An optimistic attitude toward life may result in a more favorable appraisal of a stressful situation and the use of approach coping. Higher self-esteem may enable an individual to employ more approach coping and less avoidance coping (Schwarzer and Schwarzer, 1996). Results of the correlation coefficients were found to be in the expected direction.

On the other hand, such coping resources should be separated from coping itself (Schwarzer and Schwarzer, 1996). The results relevant to the correlations between the variable scores supported our hypotheses pertaining to the magnitude of the correlations. The discriminant validity of the CIJ was also supported by the correlation coefficients.

As expected, the CIJ subscale scores served as significant predictors of increases in the degree of subsequent perceived stress. An increase in subsequent perceived stress scores was positively related to the scores for the two kinds of approach coping. On the contrary, a decrease in the subsequent perceived stress scores was related to the avoidance coping scores. The support for the predictive validity of the CIJ suggests the utility of the CIJ in clinical situations.

Nevertheless, several issues related to future research with the CIJ remain. First, certain psychometric properties of the CIJ still need to be evaluated further. It is necessary to examine psychometric properties of the CIJ, including criterion-related validity and construct validity, with variables that were excluded in this study. Second, the participants were all college students. We need further research to evaluate reliability and validity using other groups such as the elderly and clinical samples. The factor structure should be further examined through confirmatory factor analysis with other groups. Third, we should test whether there are gender or age differences in psychometric properties of the CIJ. Fourth, in the present study, only self-report measures were used. The CIJ scores should be compared with observed coping responses. Finally, the influence of Japanese culture on the CIJ itself and associations with other measures also need to be examined in future studies.

The results of the study supported the fact that the psychometric properties of the CIJ are acceptable. This inventory as a brief coping measure is expected to be widely used on account of the recent tendency to use brief measures (Carver, 1997). There has been a recent increase in the use of applied settings to conduct studies on coping, thereby increasing the response burden on participants in the surveys. A reduction of the response burden can lead to researchers obtaining better data from the participants. The CIJ will display its utility as a better coping measure for Japanese respondents in future.

REFERENCES

Amirkhan, J. H. (1990). A factor analytically derived measure of coping: The Coping Strategy Indicator. *Journal of Personality and Social Psychology, 59*, 1066-1074.

Amirkhan, J. H. (1994). Criterion validity of a coping measure. *Journal of Personality Assessment, 62*, 242-261.

Billings, A. G., and Moos, R. H. (1981). The role of coping responses and social resources in attenuating the stress of life events. *Journal of Behavioral Medicine, 4*, 139-157.

Billings, A. G., and Moos, R. H. (1984). Coping, stress, and social resources among adults with unipolar depression. *Journal of Personality and Social Psychology, 46*, 877-891.

Brandtstadter, J. (1992). Personal control over development: Implications of self-efficacy. In R. Schwarzer (Ed.), *Self-efficacy: Thought control of action* (pp. 127-145). Washington, DC: Hemisphere.

Carver, C. S. (1996). Foreword. In M. Zeidner and N. S. Endler (Eds.), *Handbook of coping: Theory, research and applications* (pp. xi-xiii). New York: Wiley.

Carver, C. S. (1997). You want to measure coping but your protocol's too long: Consider the brief COPE. *International Journal of Behavioral Medicine, 4*, 92-100.

Carver, C. S., and Scheier, M. F. (1981). *Attention and self-regulation: A control-theory approach to human behavior.* New York: Springer-Verlag.

Carver, C. S., and Scheier, M. F. (1990). Principal of self-regulation: Action and emotion. In E. T. Higgins and R. M. Sorrentino (Eds.), *Handbook of motivation and cognition: Foundations of social behavior* (Vol. 2, pp. 3-52). New York: Guilford.

Carver, C. S., and Scheier, M. F. (1994). Situational coping and coping dispositions in a stressful transaction. *Journal of Personality and Social Psychology, 66*, 184-195.

Carver, C. S., Scheier, M. F., and Weintraub, J. K. (1989). Assessing coping strategies: A theoretically based approach. *Journal of Personality and Social Psychology, 56*, 267-283.

Clark, K. K., Bormann, C. A., Cropanzano, R. S., and James, K. (1995). Validation evidence for three coping measures. *Journal of Personality Assessment, 65*, 434-455.

Cohen, S., Kamarack, T., and Mermelstein, R. (1983). A Global Measure of Perceived Stress. *Journal of Health and Social Behavior, 24*, 385-396.

Cohen, S., and Williamson, G. M. (1988). Perceived stress in a probability sample of the United States. In S. Spacapan, and S. Oskamp (Eds.), *The social psychology of health* (pp. 31-67). Newbury Park, CA: Sage.

Endler, N. S., and Parker, J. D. (1990). Multidimensional assessment of coping: A critical evaluation. *Journal of Personality and Social Psychology, 58*, 844-854.

Endler, N. S., and Parker, J. D. (1991). *Coping Inventory for Stressful Situations (CISS): Manual.* Toronto, Canada: Multi Health Systems.

Epstein, S. (1992). Coping Ability, Negative Self-Evaluation, and Overgeneralization: Experiment and Theory. *Journal of Personality and Social Psychology, 62*, 826-836.

Epstein, S., and Meier, P. (1989). Constructive thinking: A broad coping variable with specific components. *Journal of Personality and Social Psychology, 57*, 332-352.

Fleishman, J. A. (1984). Personality characteristics and coping patterns. *Journal of Health and Social Behavior, 25*, 229-244.

Fleming, R., Baum, A., and Singer, J. E. (1984). Toward an integrative approach to the study of stress. *Journal of Personality and Social Psychology, 46*, 939-949.

Folkman, S. (1992). Commentary to part three: Improving coping assessment: Reply to Stone and Kennedy-Moore. In H. S. Friedman (Ed.), *Hostility, coping and health.* (pp. 215-223). Washington, DC: American Psychological Association.

Folkman, S., and Lazarus, R. S. (1985). If it changes it must be a process: study of emotion and coping during three stages of a college examination. *Journal of Personality and Social Psychology, 48*, 150-170.

Folkman, S., Lazarus, R. S., Gruen, R. J., and DeLongis, A. (1986). Appraisal, coping, health status, and psychological symptoms. *Journal of Personality and Social Psychology, 50*, 571-579.

Fuse, M., and Kosugi, S. (1996). Shinri-stress ni okeru coping kenkyu no tenbou —Sono gainen no hensen to stress model ni okeru yakuwari— [A review on the study of coping in the stress processes: The transition of concepts and role in the model of psychological stress]. *Waseda Psychological Reports, 29*, 11-20.

Gentry, W. D., and Kobasa, S. C. (1984). Social and psychological resources mediating stress-illness relationships in humans. In W. D. Gentry (Ed.), *Handbook of behavioral medicine* (pp. 87-116). New York: Guilford Press.

Heatherton, T. F., and Wyland, C. L. (2003). Assessing self-esteem. In S. J. Lopez and C. R. Snyder (Eds.), *Positive psychological assessment: A handbook of models and measures* (pp. 393-409). Washington, DC: American Psychological Association.

Hewitt, P. L., and Flett, G. L. (1996). Personality traits and the coping process. In M. Zeidner and N. S. Endler (Eds.), *Handbook of coping: Theory, research and applications* (pp. 410-433). New York: Wiley.

Japanese Institute of Health Psychology (1996). *Stress Coping Inventory, Jiga-taido Scale Manual —Jissi-hou to hyouka-hou—* [no English title]. Tokyo: Jitsumukyoiku- shuppann.

Kamimura, E., Ebihara, Y., Sato, K., Togazsaki, Y., and Sakano, Y. (1995). Taisho-houryaku no sanjigen model no kentou to atarashii shakudo (TAC-24) no sakusei [A validation of three-dimensional model of coping response and the development of the Tri-axial Coping Scale (TAC-24)]. *Bulletin of Counseling and School Psychology, 33*, 41-47.

Kato, T. (2000). Daigaku-sei-you taijin stress coping shakudo no sakusei [Construction of the Interpersonal Stress-Coping Inventory for undergraduates]. *Japanese Journal of Educational Psychology, 48*, 225-234.

Kato, T. (2005). Eigo bunken ni okeru coping shakudo no shiyou joukyou —1990 nen kara 1995 nen— [A review of self-report measures of coping behavior from 1990 to 1995]. *Bulletin of Faculty of Sociology, Toyo University, 43-2*, 5-24.

Kato, T. (2006). Jikohoukoku-shiki niyoru coping sokutei no houhou-ron-teki mondai [A review of methodological issues for self-report measures of coping behavior]. *Japanese Psychological Review, 47*, 225-240.

Kato, T., and Imada, H. (2001). Stress coping no gainen [no English title]. *Journal of the Literary Association of Kwansei Gakuin University, 51*, 37-53.

Kikushima, K. (2002). Daigakusei ha coping wo donoyou ni ninshiki siteiruka? [How to recognize coping in college students]. *Research report, Center for Research, Training and Guidance in Educational Practice, Aich University of Education, No. 5*, 273-280.

Koguchi, T. (2002). Stress coping to koudou-igaku —Kinnen no kenkyu doukou— [no English title]. *Annual reports of Departments of Sociology and Language and Literature (Shizuoka University), 52*, 69-89.

Kusakabe, N., Chida, W., Chin, S., Matsumoto, A., Tsutsui, J., Ozaki, K., Ito, T., Nakamura, N., Miura, M., Suzuki, S., and Sakano, Y. (2000). Coping shakudo no kaihatsu to sono shinrai-sei no kentou ni kansuru tenbou [Review on development of coping scales and their validation]. *Human Science Research (Graduate School of Human Sciences, Waseda University), 9*, 313-328.

Lazarus, R. S. (1991). *Emotion and adaptation*. New York: Oxford University Press.

Lazarus, R. S. (1999). *Stress and emotion: A new synthesis*. New York: Springer.

Lazarus, R. S., and Folkman, S. (1984). *Stress, appraisal, and coping*. New York, Springer.

McCrae, R. R. (1984). Situational determinants of coping responses: Loss, threat, and challenge. *Journal of Personality and Social Psychology, 46*, 919-928.

Miller, S. M. (1987). Monitoring and blunting: validation of a questionnaire to assess styles of information seeking under threat. *Journal of Personality and Social Psychology, 52*, 345-353.

Moos, R. (1992). *Coping Responses Inventory manual.* Palo Alto, CA: Center for Health Care Evaluation, Department of Veterans Affairs and Stanford University Medical Centers.

Moos, R. H., Cronkite, R. C., Billings, A., and Finney, J. W. (1986). *Health and Daily Living Form manual.* Palo Alto, CA: Socila Ecology Laboratory, Stanford University and Department of Veterans Affairs Medical Center.

Moos, R. H., and Schaefer, J. A. (1993). Coping resources and processes: Current concepts and measures. In L. Goldberger, and S. Breznitz (Eds.), *Handbook of stress: Theoretical and clinical aspects* (pp. 234-257). New York: Free Press.

Otake, K., Shimai, T., and Shimada, H. (1998). Shougaku-sei no coping houryaku no jittai to yakuari [The role of emotional and behavioral coping strategies in elementary school children]. *Japanese Journal of Health Psychology, 11*, 37-47.

Ozeki, Y. (1993). Daigaku-sei-you stress jiko-hyouka-shakudo no kaitei —Transactional na bunseki ni mukete [no English title]. *Annual report of Graduate School of Comparative Studies of International Cultures and Societies, Kurume University, 1*, 95-114.

Ozeki, Y., Haraguchi, M., and Tsuda, A. (1991). Daigaku-sei no seikatsu stressor, coping, personality to stress hannou [Life stressor, coping, personality and stress response in university students]. *Japanese Journal of Health Psychology, 4*, 1-9.

Ozeki, Y., Haraguchi, M., and Tsuda, A. (1994). Daigaku-sei no shinri-teki stress katei no kyoubunsankouzou-bunseki [A coveriance structural analysis to the psychological stress process in university students]. *Japanese Journal of Health Psychology, 7*, 20-36.

Parker, J. D. A., and Endler, N. S. (1992). Coping with coping assessment: A critical review. *European Journal of Personality, 6*, 321-344.

Pearson, R. W., Ross, M., and Dawes, R. M. (1992). Personal recall and the limits of retrospective question in surveys. In J. M. Tanur (Ed.), *Questions about questions* (pp. 65-94). New York: Russell Sage Foundation.

Pierce, G. R., Sarason, I. G., and Sarason, B. R. (1996). Coping and social support. In M. Zeidner and N. S. Endler (Eds.), *Handbook of coping: Theory, research and applications* (pp. 434-451). New York: Wiley.

Rosenberg, M. (1965). *Society and the adolescent self image.* Princeton, NJ: Princeton University. Press.

Sakata, S. (1989). Shinri-teki stress ni kansuru ichi-kenkyu —Coping shakudo (SCS) no sakusei no kokoromi— [no English title]. *Gakujutsu Kenkyu. Education; Academic studies (Waseda University, School of Education), 28*, 61-72.

Sarason, I. G., Levine, H. M., Basham, R. B., and Sarason, B. R. (1983). Assessing social support: The Social Support Questionnaire. *Journal of Personality and Social Psychology, 44*, 127-139.

Sarason, I. G., Sarason, B. R., Shearin, E. N., and Pierce, G. (1987). A brief measure of social support: Practical and theoretical implications. *Journal of Social and Personal Relationships, 4*, 497-510.

Sasaki, M., and Yamasaki, K. (2002). Coping shakudo (GCQ) tokusei-ban no sakusei oyobi shinrai-sei/datou-sei no kentou [Development of a dispositional version of the General

Coping Questionnaire (GCQ) and examination of its reliability and validity]. *Japanese Journal of Public Health, No. 5*, 399-408.

Scheier, M. F., and Carver, C. S. (1985). Optimism, coping, and health: Assessment and implications of generalized outcome expectancies. *Health Psychology, 4*, 219-247.

Scheier, M., Weintraub, J., and Carver, C. (1986). Coping with stress: Divergent strategies of optimists and pessimist. *Journal of Personality and Social Psychology, 51*, 1257-1264.

Schwarzer, R., and Knoll, N. (2003). Positive coping: Mastering demands and searching for meaning. In S. J. Lopez and C. R. Snyder (Eds.), *Positive psychological assessment: A handbook of models and measures* (pp. 393-409). Washington, DC: American Psychological Association.

Schwarzer, R., and Schwarzer, C. (1996). A critical survey of coping instruments. In M. Zeidner and N. S. Endler (Eds.), *Handbook of coping: Theory, research and applications* (pp. 107-132). New York: Wiley.

Shoji, M., and Shoji, K. (1992). Shokuba-you coping shakudo no sakusei oyobi sinrai-sei/datou-sei no kentou [Development of a scale for workers' coping behavior: Its reliability and validity]. *Japanese Journal of Industrial Health, 34*, 10-17.

Stanton, A. L., Parsa, A. and Austenfeld, J. L. (2002). The adaptive potential of coping through emotional approach. In C. R. Snyder and S. J. Lopez (Eds.), *Handbook of positive psychology* (pp. 148-158). New York: Oxford University Press.

Stone, A. A., Greenberg, M. A., Kennedy-Moore, E., and Newman, M. G. (1991). Self-report, situational-specific coping questionnaires: What are they measuring? *Journal of Personality and Social Psychology, 61*, 648-658.

Stone, A. A., and Neale, J. M. (1984). New measure of daily coping: Development and preliminary results. *Journal of Personality and Social Psychology, 46*, 892-906.

Sumi, K. (1997). Optimism, social support, and physical and psychological well-being in Japanese women. *Psychological Reports, 81*, 299-306.

Sumi, K. (1998). Type A behavior, social support, stress, and physical and psychological well-being among Japanese women. *Psychological Reports, 83*, 711-717.

Sumi, K. (1999). Taisho, personality to chikaku sareta stress no kankei [Relationship between coping, personality and perceived stress]. *Journal of Educational and Health Science, 44*, 500-506.

Sumi, K. (in press). Chikaku sareta stress shakudo (Perceived Stress Scale) nihongo-ban ni okeru shinrai-sei to datou-sei no kentou [Reliability and validity of the Japanese version of the Perceived Stress Scale]. *Japanese Journal of Health Psychology*.

Terry, D. J. (1994). Determinants of coping: The role of stable and situational factors. *Journal of Personality and Social Psychology, 66*, 895-910.

Tobin, D. L., Holroyd, K. A., Reynolds, R. V., and Wigal, J. K. (1989). The hierarchical factor structure of the Coping Strategies Inventory. *Cognitive Therapy and Research, 13*, 343-361.

Wada, M., Xiao-Qi, Z., and Xiao Lan, G. (1993). Nihon to chugoku no daigakusei no stress to sono taisho-koudou —Shitsuon-koumoku no sakusei— [Stress and its coping behaviors of undergraduates in Japanese and the people's republic of China]. *Bulletin of Tokyo Gakugei University Sect. 1, 44*, 247-262.

Wada, M., Xiao-Qi, Z., and Xiao Lan, G. (1996). Nihon to chugoku no daigakusei no stress to sono taisho-koudou [Coping behavior with stress in Japanese and Chinese undergraduates]. *Bulletin of Tokyo Gakugei University Sect. I, 47,* 7-15.

Yamamoto, M., Matsui, Y., and Yamanari, Y. (1982). Ninchi sareta jiko no sho-sokumen no kouzou [The structure of perceived aspects of self]. *Japanese Journal of Educational Psychology, 30,* 64-68.

In: New Psychological Tests and Testing Research
Editor: Lydia S. Boyar, pp. 63-86

ISBN: 978-1-60021-570-4
© 2007 Nova Science Publishers, Inc.

Chapter 3

MEASURING COPING: EXAMINING THE INTERNAL STRUCTURE OF THE COPE

Kathleen J. Donoghue and Greg E. Dear
Edith Cowan University

ABSTRACT

The COPE is a widely used multidimensional self-report instrument intended to measure 15 dimensions of coping. A review of the literature suggested that the factor structure of the COPE is unstable and that the instrument contains many redundant items. Hence, the purpose of this study was to examine the internal structure and intrascale redundancy of the COPE using an Australian sample. The proposed factor structure was not replicated and a high level of intrascale redundancy was found, rather than well conceptualized items. Moreover, 13 of the 60 items failed to show adequate substantive validity. Therefore, findings and conclusions based on the use of the COPE should be critically re-examined as widespread use of this instrument might have contributed to inconsistencies in the coping literature.

INTRODUCTION

While coping is considered a multidimensional construct, there is no consensus regarding its underlying dimensions (Skinner, Edge, Altman, and Sherwood, 2003) and widely differing conceptualizations have led to a proliferation of coping instruments (e.g., Amirkhan, 1990; Ayers, Sandler, West, and Roosa, 1996; Carver, Scheier, and Weintraub, 1989; Endler and Parker, 1990, 1994; Folkman and Lazarus, 1980, 1985; Pearlin and Schooler, 1978; Stone and Neale, 1984). Research into coping has been hampered by the limited psychometric properties of the available instruments, particularly with respect to the internal validity of multidimensional measures. Many coping instruments have not been evaluated beyond their sample of origin and there is disagreement among researchers regarding appropriate psychometric standards for coping instruments. The sheer number of coping measures in use, together with disagreement surrounding organization of coping strategies into higher-order dimensions, creates problems for the field. Factor structures tend to vary across samples even when the same instrument and methods are used (Steed, 1998; Westman and Shirom, 1995). Hence, integration and aggregation of findings across studies usually necessitates individual analyses of subscales (Compas, Connor-Smith, Saltzman, Harding Thomsen, and Wadsworth, 2001; Skinner et al., 2003).

Some researchers have argued against further use of exploratory factor analysis in the development and evaluation of coping scales (e.g., Ayers et al., 1996; Coyne and Gottlieb, 1996; Steed, 1998; Stone and Kennedy-Moore, 1992; Stone and Neale, 1984; Suls, David, and Harvey, 1996). This is because coping strategies are interrelated in complex ways, with some used to the exclusion of others, some used in conjunction with others, and some strategies employed in a particular sequence (Thoits, 1991). Therefore strategies that reflect a common function or latent variable might not correlate because effective use of one strategy might lead to not using the other strategies because they were not required (Coyne and Gottlieb, 1996; Steed, 1998; Stone and Neale, 1984). Factor analysis to identify latent variables relies on correlated patterns of use.

Furthermore, endorsement of items has different implications for different people in different contexts and might refer to very different kinds of coping efforts (Carpenter, 1992; Coyne and Gottlieb, 1996; Stone and Neale, 1984). When coping items serve multiple functions they are likely to load on multiple factors leading to their deletion from the item pool (Steed, 1998; Stone, Kennedy-Moore, Newman, Greenberg, and Neale, 1992). Hence, constructing and analysing scales using exploratory factor analysis might be of limited value because valid and useful coping strategies could be deleted from measures based on differences between samples or because of items serving multiple functions. Removal of items from scales based on samples drawn from one population might result in a scale that under represents the range of coping required by populations dealing with other problems. Hence, it might be necessary to develop coping instruments that are specifically tailored to certain populations or contexts (Somerfield and McCrae, 2000). The above issues have undoubtedly contributed to the inherent difficulties with interpretation and replication of factor solutions, especially when generic coping measures have been used without reference to a specific stressor.

Similarly, measures of internal consistency are based on the assumption that endorsement of one item contributing to a scale score makes it more likely that a respondent will endorse other items on that scale. However, coping items violate this assumption because effective employment of one strategy reduces the likelihood that other strategies will be employed (as discussed above). This observation has implications for the way measures are scored and highlights the need to pay close attention to the development and psychometric properties of coping instruments.

It is essential that item pools contain multiple items to tap each category, however, when theoretical dimensions have not been identified in advance (i.e., when scales are developed using exploratory factor analysis) it becomes difficult to ensure that sufficient items are present to allow for the emergence of latent causative variables (Skinner et al., 2003). Factor analysis is based on the assumption that latent variables cause people to respond to subsets of items in certain ways rather than others. However, items can load on a factor for reasons that are unrelated to that particular factor (e.g., items might have the same emotional tone) and items that are intended to represent the same category could load onto separate factors due to other commonalities (e.g., cognitive avoidance and behavioral avoidance; Skinner et al.,

2003). Exploratory factor analysis is data driven and can produce factors in which items load together for idiosyncratic reasons. Hence, it is important to adopt a theoretical approach to the construction of coping scales in order that confirmatory factor analysis (CFA) can be employed as a direct test of proposed constructs and models (Ayers et al., 1996; Ayers, Sandler, and Twohey, 1998; Compas et al., 2001; Connor-Smith, Compas, Wadsworth, Harding Thomsen, and Saltzman, 2000; Skinner et al., 2003).

While many of the problems mentioned above (e.g., items failing to correlate) are equally applicable to CFA, this approach has the advantage of testing the adequacy of a theoretical model of latent structure. Hence, CFA is likely to assist in the identification of dimensions that are more replicable and conceptually meaningful than those obtained with exploratory factor analysis (Ayers et al., 1996; Compas et al., 2001). However, like exploratory factor analysis, CFA depends on the assumption that variations in item scores occur due to the influence of latent causal variables. The COPE was developed based on this assumption and claims have been made that the assumption holds because the internal structure is stable.

The COPE

The COPE (Carver et al., 1989) is a widely used multidimensional self-report instrument with 15 subscales to measure different ways of coping. The COPE has been widely adopted on the basis of its "good factorial properties" (Carver and Scheier, 1994, p.186). However, widespread criticism (e.g., Coyne and Gottlieb, 1996; Coyne and Racioppo, 2000; Endler and Parker, 1990, 1994; Parker and Endler, 1992; Steed, 1998; Stone and Neale, 1984) regarding the measurement of coping suggests that further evaluation of the psychometric properties of the COPE is warranted.

The COPE was described by its authors (Carver et al., 1989) as a theoretically-constructed, multidimensional coping scale with 13 subscales each consisting of four items that focused on distinct aspects of coping. Five subscales measured problem-focused coping: Active Coping, Planning, Suppression of Competing Activities, Restraint Coping, and Seeking Social Support for Instrumental Reasons. A further five subscales measured emotion-focused coping: Seeking of Social Support for Emotional Reasons, Positive Reinterpretation and Growth, Acceptance, Denial, and Turning to Religion. Three subscales, described by Carver et al. (p.267) as "less useful" were labelled Focus on and Venting of Emotions, Behavioral Disengagement, and Mental Disengagement. A single item related to the use of alcohol and drugs was included in the original measure for exploratory reasons. This has since been developed into a four-item scale, and a scale assessing the use of humor was also developed following publication of the original validation study, resulting in a 60-item COPE, with 15 subscales (personal correspondence Carver, Scheier, and Weintraub, January 1989; see also footnotes in Carver and Scheier, 1994). Concept definitions for each of the subscales appear in table 1.

Table 1. Concept Definitions

Concept	Definition
Denial	An attempt to reject the reality of the stressful event.
Religion	Increased engagement in religious activities.
Seeking Instrumental Social Support	Seeking assistance, information, or advice about what to do.
Humor	Making jokes about the stressor.
Restraint Coping	Coping passively by holding back one's coping attempts until they can be of use.
Active Coping	Taking action, exerting efforts, to remove or circumvent the stressor.
Alcohol/Drug Use	Turning to the use of alcohol or other drugs as a way of disengaging from the stressor.
Mental Disengagement	Psychological disengagement from *the goal that the stressor is interfering with*, through daydreaming, sleep, or self-distraction.
Planning	Thinking about how to confront the stressor, planning active coping efforts.
Acceptance	Accepting the fact that the stressful event has occurred and is real.
Seeking Emotional Social Support	Getting sympathy or emotional support from someone.
Suppression of Competing Activities	Suppressing attention to other activities in which one might engage, in order to concentrate more completely on dealing with the stressor.
Behavioral Disengagement	Giving up, or withdrawing effort from trying to attain *the goal that the stressor is interfering with*.
Positive Reinterpretation and Growth	Making the best of the situation by growing from it, or viewing it in a more favourable light.
Focus on and Venting of Emotions	An increased awareness of one's emotional distress, and a tendency to ventilate or discharge those feelings.

Factor Analyses of the COPE

Factor analysis conducted by Carver et al. (1989) yielded eleven factors, nine of which were consistent with the instrument's subscales and two that contained eight items each. The subscales for Active Coping and Planning converged, as did Social Support for Instrumental Reasons and Social Support for Emotional Reasons. These subscales were retained separately by Carver et al. on the basis that they were conceptually distinct. Fontaine, Manstead, and Wagner (1993) replicated the factor structure of the COPE but disagreed with separation of the subscales that converged. In the Fontaine et al. study, the Positive Reinterpretation subscale split into two separate factors but otherwise the overall similarities suggested that the factor structure underlying the COPE was stable and in accordance with Carver et al. Using a later version of the COPE with 14 subscales, Cook and Heppner (1997) conducted CFA and found a moderate degree of support for either a 12- or 14-factor model (depending on treatment of the convergent subscales identified above). However this was not the best fit to the data. In fact, Cook and Heppner found that the COPE was better represented by a 3-factor model.

The three factors identified by Cook and Heppner (1997) were similar to those identified in second-order factor analyses of the COPE reported by its authors. Carver et al. (1989) found a 4-factor solution (which they did not label) with three of the emergent factors being identical across their two studies. The first factor related to problem-focused coping by combining Active Coping, Planning, and Suppression of Activities. The second factor combined the two social support subscales with the Venting of Emotions subscale. A third factor, relating to avoidance coping, consisted of the Behavioral and Mental Disengagement subscales, together with Denial, and Turning to Religion. The fourth factor suggested positive reappraisal and consisted of Acceptance, Restraint Coping, and Positive Reinterpretation and Growth. The only difference between the two analyses carried out by Carver et al. was that Turning to Religion failed to load on any factor in one of their analyses.

Deisinger, Cassisi, and Whitaker (1996) performed a replication of the second-order factor analysis carried out by Carver et al. (1989) but with the inclusion of the two newer subscales (i.e., Humor, Alcohol/Drugs). They found support for a 5-factor model, with the fifth factor (labelled Hedonistic Escapism) consisting of the two newer subscales. The other four factors were identical to those found by Carver et al. with the exception of Restraint Coping, which loaded in with the problem-solving factor. Following removal of redundant items, other researchers have also found a 4-factor model underlying the COPE (e.g., Eisenberg, Fabes, and Murphy, 1995; Phelps and Jarvis, 1994; Washburn-Ormachea, Hillman, and Sawilowsky, 2004). However, these factor solutions differed considerably across studies despite similarly labelled factors, and various subscales were eliminated for their inability to load clearly on any factor.

Lyne and Roger (2000) were highly critical of the factor analyses carried out by Carver et al. (1989) suggesting that seven factor analytic conventions were ignored and that Carver et al.'s validation of the COPE failed to confirm the 13-factor model purported to underlie the instrument. Lyne and Roger attempted to replicate the findings of Carver et al. but were unable to do so, even when they used radial parcel analysis (Cattell and Barrett, 1975, cited in Lyne and Roger, 2000) to force the structure into 13 groups of four items. Lyne and Roger used rigorous factor analytic techniques and found that many of the COPE items failed to load neatly on their intended factors. Whereas Carver et al. reported only two items with double loadings, Lyne and Roger found that anywhere from nine to 17 items had double loadings in the various solutions that their analyses yielded. Lyne and Roger concluded that the factor structure underlying the COPE was highly unstable.

Following removal of 16 redundant items, Lyne and Roger (2000) found the COPE was best conceptualized in terms of three underlying factors. A number of other studies have also identified various 3-factor models underlying the COPE (e.g., Hien and Miele, 2003; Laurent, Catanzaro, and Callan, 1997; Park and Levenson, 2002; Stowell, Kiecolt-Glaser, and Glaser, 2001). Using CFA and following removal of seven redundant items, Hasking and Oei (2002) found some support for both a 14-factor primary structure and a 3-factor higher-order structure with data from a community sample but found that it was impossible to produce any interpretable structure with an alcohol-dependent sample. Wade et al. (2001) found a 6-factor model underlying the COPE. Due to the various range of items included in factor analyses of the COPE it is difficult to compare individual findings, however, taken together the above studies fail to provide support for Carver and Scheier's (1994) claim that the COPE has good factorial properties. In fact, the internal structure of the COPE appears to be very unstable across samples.

Weak Loadings

In the initial analysis (Carver et al., 1989) five items had weak loadings (< .30) on their intended factors. Of particular concern were two items from the Positive Reinterpretation subscale (i.e., "I learn something from the experience," .23; "I try to grow as a person as a result of the experience," .19) and two from the Mental Disengagement subscale (i.e., I daydream about things other than this," .28; "I sleep more than usual," .23). Fontaine et al. (1993) eliminated three items (i.e., "I turn to work or other substitute activities to take my mind off things", "I act as though it hasn't happened," and "I slept more than usual") that failed to load above .40. If a similar cut-off point had been adopted by Carver et al. (1989) ten items would have been deleted. Moreover, only one of them ("I sleep more than usual") would have been the same as in the Fontaine et al. study. Carver et al. (1993) found that three of the subscales (i.e., Active Coping, Denial, and Mental Disengagement) each contained an item that consistently reduced that subscale's reliability. Hence, they dropped these items from their analysis. In order to overcome apparent shortcomings, the COPE has been modified by selecting items with the highest reported loadings (e.g., Begley, 1998; Brissette, Scheier, and Carver, 2002) or items that were more clearly worded (e.g., Carver et al., 1993).

Item Redundancy

Some subscales of the COPE (e.g., Humor, and Alcohol/Drug Use) have questionable content validity in that some items appear to be semantic variations of each other rather than conceptually distinct items. For example, "I kid around about it" versus "I make jokes about it," and "I use alcohol or drugs to help me get through it" versus "I use alcohol or drugs to make myself feel better". Livneh, Livneh, Maron, and Kaplan (1996) questioned the similarity of items from the Denial subscale (i.e., "I act as though it hasn't even happened yet" and "I pretend that it hasn't really happened") and the Planning subscale (i.e., "I try to come up with a strategy about what to do" and "I make a plan of action"). Lyne and Roger (2000) questioned the inclusion of redundant items in the Religion, Alcohol/Drug Use, and Seeking of Emotional Support subscales and found it necessary to remove 16 redundant items. Hence, the COPE appears to contain many items that are redundant, highlighting the need for scrutiny of this measure at the item level because intrascale content redundancy might have seriously undermined the use of factor analysis in its development and validation. Items that are merely paraphrases of each other are certain to be highly correlated and to load together irrespective of their relationship to external criteria (Kline, 1994).

The Present Study

The current research examined the internal structure of the COPE using an Australian community sample to determine whether the factor structure was consistent with that proposed by its authors. The purpose of the present research was twofold. First, factor analysis was carried out specifically to explore the influence of item redundancy on emergent structure. The purpose of the second study was to explore the substantive validity (Anderson and Gerbing, 1991) of the instrument. While examination of the substantive validity of coping instruments has not been reported in the literature, it is an informative methodology that overcomes the limitations inherent in factor analysing coping data. A measure that has poor substantive validity lacks construct validity and will not perform well in factor analysis (Anderson and Gerbing, 1991). Examination of the substantive validity of coping instruments is useful prior to the more rigorous and costly test of CFA.

STUDY ONE

Participants

Second year psychology students at Edith Cowan University in Western Australia completed the COPE inventory and each student recruited three additional participants from the local community. Participation was voluntary and no inducements were offered. This resulted in a sample of 413 respondents with a mean age of 32 (*SD* 12.79) and an age range of 16 to 76. Sixty-two percent of the participants were female and 90% were Caucasian. Table 2 provides complete demographic information.

Table 2. Demographic Breakdown of Participants in Study One

Variable	Category	N	%
Sex	Male	156	37.9
	Female	256	62.1
Age	18 - 20	89	21.7
	21 - 25	80	19.5
	26 - 30	54	13.1
	31 - 35	52	12.7
	36 - 40	23	5.5
	41 and over	113	27.5
Place of Birth	Australia	279	67.8
	Other	133	32.2
Race	Aboriginal	3	0.7
	Caucasian	373	90.8
	Asian	15	3.6
	Other	20	4.9
Student	Yes	150	32.0
	No	263	63.7
Employment status	Full time paid work	157	38.0
	Part time paid work	62	15.0
	Full time student	124	30.0
	Social security benefits	43	10.5
	No income or benefits	27	6.5
Relationship status	Married	140	34.0
	De facto	55	13.4
	Not living together	110	26.8
	Separated/divorced	27	6.6
	Single/not in a relationship	79	19.2

Instrument

The COPE (Carver et al., 1989) contains 15 subscales (representing different ways of coping) with four items in each. Concept definitions for the subscales are listed in table 1. The COPE is preceded by two paragraphs instructing participants on how to complete the questionnaire. The COPE can be administered in either a situational or a dispositional form. To obtain a dispositional measure items are framed in terms of "what the person usually does when under stress", whilst to measure situational coping items are framed in terms of "what the person did, or is doing" in a specific coping situation or a specified period of time (Carver et al., 1989, p. 270). In the present study the COPE was administered in its dispositional form, which is scored on a 4-point Likert-type scale, with scores ranging from 1 (*I usually don't do this at all*) to 4 (*I usually do this a great deal*). Items are summed to produce scale scores with higher scores reflecting greater use of a particular coping strategy.

The COPE consists of 13 original subscales (see table 1) plus two subscales (i.e., Alcohol/Drug Use; Humor) which were developed subsequent to the validation study reported by Carver et al. (1989). Based on findings from Stanton, Danoff-Burg, Cameron, and Ellis (1994), the Focus on and Venting of Emotions subscale (e.g., "I get upset and let my emotions out") was dropped by Carver and Scheier (1994) as it was confounded with distress levels (outcome). However, as this subscale has frequently been used by researchers it was retained for the purposes of the present analysis. Hence, the full 60-item version of the COPE was used in the present studies.

Carver et al. (1989) reported alphas for the situational form of the COPE between .68 and .91, with the exception of the Mental Disengagement subscale. Alpha reliabilities for the dispositional form of the COPE ranged from .45 to .92, with six of the subscales having alphas less than .70, but only one below .60 (i.e., Mental Disengagement, .45). Carver et al. reported test-retest reliabilities for the dispositional form of the COPE ranging from .42 to .89 at six weeks, and from .46 to .86 at eight weeks. However, several of the subscales were not developed at the time of these studies.

Procedure

Participants were instructed to read the cover page prior to completing the inventory in their own time. Informed consent and demographic data were collected with the questionnaire. Each participant was provided with an envelope to ensure confidentiality and students collected and returned the envelopes to the university.

Results

In an attempt to replicate the internal structure found by Carver et al. (1989), Principal Axis factor analysis with oblique rotation (Oblimin with Kaiser normalization) was carried out on the 60 COPE variables using SPSS (version 11.5). The correlation matrix revealed a considerable number of correlations exceeding .30. The Bartlett's test was significant and the KMO measure of sampling adequacy was .87 indicating suitability for factor analysis. In order to replicate the findings of Carver et al., the number of factors to extract was set to 15.

The factor solution obtained by Carver et al. (1989) was not replicated. Three of the extracted factors were consistent with the COPE's subscales, however, items loaded on the remaining twelve factors in ways that did not correspond to the instrument's proposed structure. Two items from the Mental Disengagement subscale failed to load above .30 on any factor and a further 12 items were considered complex variables as they had loadings above .20 on more than one factor. Whilst .30 is the usual convention for determining complexity of variables, the more stringent cut off point of .20 was adopted in the present analysis because the highest factor loading for many of the complex variables was low. For example, the highest loading for item 51 from the Behavioral Disengagement scale was .32, however, it also loaded on two other factors at .26 and .24. Hence, taking into account only those loadings above .30 seemed inappropriate as it failed to capture the complexity of some variables.

Factor one contained all items from the Active Coping and the Planning subscales, however, six of the nine items in this factor also had loadings on other factors. The four Behavioral Disengagement factors formed factor two although one of the items also loaded on two other factors. Factor three contained the eight social support items although two of the Venting of Emotions items also had secondary loadings in this factor. Factors four, five and six were consistent with the COPE subscales for Religion, Humor, and Alcohol/Drug Use respectively. The items that formed these subscales loaded purely into their factors with no secondary loadings.

Factor seven contained the Acceptance items, two of which also had secondary loadings on other factors. Factor eight contained the Venting of Emotions items with two of these items also loading on other factors. The four items from the Restraint Coping scale, together with a Suppression of Competing Activities item, formed Factor nine, and an Active Coping item also had a secondary loading in this factor. Factor 10 contained two of the Mental Disengagement items together with a Suppression of Competing Activities item. Factor 11 contained two of the Positive Reinterpretation and Growth items. Factor 12 contained all four denial items together with secondary loadings for an Acceptance item and a Behavioral Disengagement item. The only item that loaded purely on Factor 13 was a Positive Reinterpretation item. Three of the Suppression of Competing Activities items loaded into Factor 14 but one had an equally high loading on Factor 15 which contained only secondary loadings of complex variables.

As the present analysis failed to replicate the 15 factor model proposed by Carver et al. (1989) the actual internal structure of the data was explored. Three items were found to have low communalities (<.20), indicating that they were unrelated to other items on the instrument. Two of these items were from the Mental Disengagement subscale and the other was from Suppression of Competing Activities. The scree plot suggested that the COPE data was represented by approximately seven factors at most, so the analysis was repeated setting the number of factors to extract at seven.

Seven factors accounted for 49% of the variance in the solution. Factor loadings for the COPE subscales, together with percentages of variance, and estimates of internal consistency (Cronbach's alpha) are reported in table 3. Factor one consisted of eleven items including all items from Active Coping, and Planning, and the three Suppression of Competing Activities items that were included in the analysis. All the items loaded purely on this factor except for one of the Active Coping items which had a secondary loading on Factor 7. Factor one was labelled Problem Engagement and accounted for 16.2% of the variance.

Table 3. Subscales from the COPE with Factor Loadings obtained in Study One

Item No.	COPE Subscale	F1	F2	F3	F4	F5	F6	F7
32	Planning	.74	…	…	…	…	…	…
56	Planning	.70	…	…	…	…	…	…
47	Active Coping	.63	…	…	…	…	…	…
19	Planning	.63	…	…	…	…	…	…
25	Active Coping	.62	…	…	…	…	…	…
39	Planning	.62	…	…	…	…	…	…
33	Suppression of Competing Activities	.58	…	…	…	…	…	…
5	Active Coping	.55	…	…	…	…	…	…
58*	Active Coping	.53	…	…	…	…	…	-.26
42	Suppression of Competing Activities	.51	…	…	…	…	…	…
55	Suppression of Competing Activities	.47	…	…	…	…	…	…
40	Denial	…	.63	…	…	…	…	…
37	Behavioral Disengagement	…	.60	…	…	…	…	…
24	Behavioral Disengagement	…	.58	…	…	…	…	…
51	Behavioral Disengagement	…	.53	…	…	…	…	…
9	Behavioral Disengagement	…	.52	…	…	…	…	…
57	Denial	…	.49	…	…	…	…	…
27	Denial	…	.46	…	…	…	…	…
6	Denial	…	.44	…	…	…	…	…
1**	Positive Reinterpretation	…	.30	…	…	…	…	.29
43**	Mental Disengagement	…	.23	…	…	…	…	…
52	Social Support (Emotional)	…	…	-.91	…	…	…	…
11	Social Support (Emotional)	…	…	-.84	…	…	…	…
23	Social Support (Emotional)	…	…	-.79	…	…	…	…
34	Social Support (Emotional)	…	…	-.77	…	…	…	…
14	Social Support (Instrumental)	…	…	-.71	…	…	…	…
4	Social Support (Instrumental)	…	…	-.70	…	…	…	…

Table 3. (Continued).

Item No.	COPE Subscale	F1	F2	F3	F4	F5	F6	F7
45	Social Support (Instrumental)	...	...	-.68	...	...	...	...
28	Venting of Emotions	...	...	-.63	...	...	...	...
30	Social Support (Instrumental)	...	...	-.62	...	...	...	...
46*	Venting of Emotions	...	.28	-.55	...	...	...	...
3*	Venting of Emotions	...	.20	-.50	...	.22	...	...
17*	Venting of Emotions	...	.29	-.30	...	...	...	...
18	Religion	...	...	...	.96	...	...	...
7	Religion	...	...	...	.91	...	...	...
60	Religion	...	...	...	.88	...	...	...
48	Religion	...	...	...	.86	...	...	...
50	Humor	...	...	...	...	-.84	...	...
20	Humor	...	...	...	...	-.83	...	...
36	Humor	...	...	...	...	-.82	...	...
8	Humor	...	...	...	...	-.69	...	...
29**	Positive Reinterpretation	.21	...	...	...	-.30	...	-.26
16**	Mental Disengagement	...	.24	...	...	-.26	...	...
53	Alcohol/Drug Use	...	...	...	...	...	.96	...
26	Alcohol/Drug Use	...	...	...	...	...	.96	...
35	Alcohol/Drug Use	...	...	...	...	...	.95	...
12	Alcohol/Drug Use	...	...	...	...	...	.92	...
54	Acceptance	...	...	...	...	...	...	-.67
21	Acceptance	...	...	...	...	...	...	-.54
13	Acceptance	...	...	...	...	...	...	-.50
44*	Acceptance	...	.22	...	...	...	...	-.48
22	Restraint Coping	...	...	...	...	...	...	-.46
41*	Restraint Coping	.21	...	...	...	...	...	-.46
49*	Restraint Coping	.23	...	...	...	...	...	-.43
10	Restraint Coping	...	...	...	...	...	...	.32
38*	Positive Reinterpretation	...	...	...	...	-.31	...	-.37

Table 3. (Continued).

Item No.	COPE Subscale	F1	F2	F3	F4	F5	F6	F7
59*	Positive Reinterpretation	.23	...	.24	...	...	...	-.34
2	Mental Disengagement	Not included in analysis as initial extracted communality .19						
15	Suppression of Competing Activities	Not included in analysis as initial extracted communality .19						
31	Mental Disengagement	Not included in analysis as initial extracted communality .16						
% of Variance		16.2	9.2	7.1	6.0	4.5	3.5	2.5
Cronbach's alpha		.88	.78	.92	.93	.89	.96	.67
Label		Problem Engagement	Problem Disengagement	Social Support and Venting	Religion	Humor	Alcohol and Drug Use	Accommodation

Factor loadings <.20 have been suppressed to aid interpretation.

* complex variables (loadings >.20 on more than one factor)

** failure to load >.30 on any factor or not included in analysis as initial extracted communality <.20

Factor two accounted for 9.2% of the variance and consisted of the Behavioral Disengagement items and the Denial items, all of which loaded purely onto this factor, which was labelled Problem Disengagement. Factor three accounted for 7.1% of the variance in the solution. It contained all items from both Social Support scales, together with the Venting of Emotions items and was labelled Social Support and Venting. Three of the four Venting items also had secondary loadings on Factor 2, and one also had a further loading on Factor 5.

Factors four, five, and six were consistent with the COPE scales for Religion, Humor, and Alcohol/Drug Use accounting for 6.0%, 4.5%, and 3.5% of the variance respectively. Item 29 from the Positive Reinterpretation subscale and item 16 from the Mental Disengagement scale had their highest loadings on the factor relating to Humor, however, these were both complex variables with similar loadings on other factors.

Factor seven accounted for 2.5% of the variance and included the subscales for Acceptance, and Restraint Coping, together with two of the Positive Reinterpretation items. Two of the Restraint items, two of the Positive Reinterpretation items, and one of the Acceptance items were complex variables with secondary loadings above .20 on other factors. This factor was labeled Accommodation as the items seemed to be related to acceptance and accommodation of the stressful event.

Three items were removed from analysis due to low communalities, however, a further four items failed to load on any factor. The two Mental Disengagement items that were retained for analysis failed to load above .30 on any factor and two of the Positive Reinterpretation items were complex variables whose highest loading of .30 was very close to secondary loadings (.29, .26) on other factors. Nine additional items had complex loadings. Hence, 16 (27%) of the 60 COPE items failed to perform adequately in the present factor analysis.

Discussion

The present study failed to replicate the factor solution obtained by Carver et al. (1989). Findings did not support the notion that there are 15 distinct coping domains underlying the instrument. Only three of the emergent factors were consistent with subscales from the COPE. Exploratory factor analysis suggested that the internal structure of the COPE consists of no more than seven factors, which accounted for 49% of variance in the solution. Findings from the present analysis were similar to Carver et al.'s (1989) second-order analysis of the COPE.

Only three of the COPE's subscales emerged cleanly in both factor analyses carried out in the present study. These were Humor, Alcohol/Drug Use, and Religion. The subscales for Humor and Alcohol/Drug Use were developed subsequent to validation of the COPE. Hence, they were not included in Carver et al.'s (1989) second-order analyses. The Religion subscale emerged as a factor in its own right in the second-order analysis carried out by Carver et al. when the situational form of the COPE was used but loaded with the denial and disengagement items when the dispositional form was used. The dispositional form of the COPE was used in the present study, however, the religion subscale still formed a unique factor. Hence, turning to religion might reflect a respondent's religious beliefs more so than some latent variable that is reflected in the higher-order structure.

These three scales (and others to a lesser extent) appear to contain a high level of redundancy. The Alcohol/Drug Use scale, for example, consists of the following four items: "I use alcohol or drugs to make myself feel better", "I try to lose myself for a while by drinking alcohol or taking drugs", "I drink alcohol or take drugs, in order to think about it less", and "I use alcohol or drugs to help me get through it". Furthermore, items on these subscales are highly correlated. For example, the items that form the Religion subscale had Corrected Item – Total Correlations ranging from .87 to .92 and loadings of between .92 and .96 on their factor. Hence, the emergence of these three scales as distinct dimensions of coping with high internal consistency is likely to be an artefact of redundancy. It is likely that someone responding to a subscale consisting of redundant items will respond to more of these items because they are repetitions of the same question, not because this strategy was employed more frequently. Therefore, it is not yet clear how these constructs might relate to the other coping constructs under examination.

The remaining four factors that emerged were consistent with Carver et al.'s (1989) second-order analyses of the COPE. The items from the Active Coping, Planning, and Suppression of Competing Activities formed a single factor suggesting an underlying problem-engagement dimension. Suppression of Competing Activities can be seen as complimentary to Active Coping and Planning strategies. A second factor consisted primarily of Denial and Behavioral Disengagement items reflecting a problem-disengagement dimension. These items all related to a reduction of efforts to deal with the stressor, however, the Mental Disengagement items did not load in this factor as they did for Carver et al. Two of the Mental Disengagement items were not included due to low communalities (<.20) and the remaining items failed to load above .30 on any factor. The failure of the Mental Disengagement scale is consistent with prior studies in which these items have consistently been problematic, with internal consistencies as low as .36 in some studies (e.g., Knee, 1998; Zuckerman, Kieffer, and Knee, 1998). Furthermore, the Mental Disengagement subscale had weak loadings (<.30) and unsatisfactory internal consistency (alpha = .45) in the validation studies carried out by Carver et al.

The social support items from both subscales loaded with the Venting of Emotions items to form a single factor. It is reasonable to expect that items related to the expression of emotions would load with social support items as it is often within the social context that such expression occurs. Nonetheless, the items from the Venting of Emotions subscale may be problematic as three of the four also had loadings on at least one other factor.

The final factor seemed to be about accommodating to the stressor as it consisted of the Acceptance, Restraint, and Positive Reinterpretation and Growth subscales. Two of the Restraint items and two of the Positive Reinterpretation items had complex loadings and a Restraint item was found to reduce the internal consistency of this factor. Hence, some of the items included in this factor might be ambiguous and poor indicators of accommodating to the stressor.

Findings from the present analysis suggest that many of the subscales from the COPE consist of inter-related items that could be indicators of higher-order coping dimensions, however, the items fail to distinguish between 15 different types of coping as proposed by Carver et al. (1989). The subscales from the COPE tended to form factors more consistent with higher-order factor analyses carried out on the COPE.

Just over a quarter of the COPE items failed to perform adequately in the present analyses. Three items were initially removed due to low communalities (<.20) which indicated the items were unrelated to other items contained in the instrument. Four additional items failed to load above .30 on any factor and a further nine items were complex variables, loading above .20 on more than one factor. These 16 items would appear to be weak indicators of their respective subscales. The various items might serve different functions for different people and given different samples these items are likely to load more highly on different factors. These weak items could be partly responsible for the variety of different factor solutions that have emerged in factor analytic studies of the COPE (e.g., Cook and Heppner, 1997; Deisinger et al., 1996; Eisenberg et al., 1995; Hien and Miele, 2003; Laurent et al., 1997; Lyne and Roger, 2000; Park and Levenson, 2002; Phelps and Jarvis, 1994; Stowell et al., 2001; Washburn-Ormachea et al., 2004).

Findings from the present analysis indicate that the COPE does not measure 15 distinct ways of coping and provides further support for Lyne and Roger's (2000) assertion that the internal structure of the COPE appears to be unstable. Furthermore, the few subscales that did emerge cleanly in both factor analyses are those that appear to consist of redundant items (i.e., a single item repeated four times with minor variations). Hence, their emergence as factors is likely to be an artefact of this redundancy revealing nothing substantive about the constructs under examination. Substantive validity analysis was, therefore, carried out in a second study in order to obtain another perspective on the COPE items.

STUDY TWO

Participants

Twenty-six first-year psychology students at Edith Cowan University in Western Australia participated on a voluntary basis. This sample consisted mostly of young, female, Australian students. Complete demographic information is provided in table 4.

Table 4. Demographic Breakdown of Participants in Study Two

Variable	Category	n	%
Sex	Male	4	15.4
	Female	22	84.6
Place of Birth	Australia	19	73.1
	Other	7	26.9
Age	< 18	2	7.7
	18 - 20	16	61.5
	21 - 25	3	11.5
	26 - 30	3	11.5
	31 - 35	1	3.9
	36 - 40	1	3.9
Employment status	Full time paid work	1	3.8
	Part time paid work	10	38.5
	Full time student	11	42.3
	Social security benefits	4	15.4
Relationship status	De facto	4	15.4
	Not living together	9	34.6
	Single/not in a relationship	13	50.0

Instrument

Analysis of substantive validity (or item validity) involves independent assessments as to whether each item is a reliable indicator of the domain it is intended to represent and only that domain (Anderson and Gerbing, 1991). Tests of substantive validity utilize small samples of participants who are given the task of assigning items into their respective domains using a pen and paper item-sort task. Coefficients are calculated to determine the degree to which participants are able to identify the appropriate subscale for each item and substantive validity exists when items are correctly allocated to their intended subscales or domains.

The questionnaire instructed participants to label 60 items with one of 15 categories or concept definitions provided, according to where they thought the item belonged. The items were from the COPE and the categories were their corresponding subscale domains. The questionnaire referred to the investigation of coping behaviors but did not identify the items or concepts as belonging to a particular instrument.

Procedure

Participants read an Information Letter and signed the Informed Consent statement before proceeding to the main questionnaire, which was preceded by a paragraph instructing participants on what was required and providing an example. Participants then labelled each of the 60 items with one of the 15 concept definitions, and provided demographic information. The task took approximately 10 to 15 minutes.

Results

Substantive validity coefficients (C_{sv}) were calculated to reflect the extent to which an item was assigned to its intended domain more than to any other domain (Anderson and Gerbing, 1991). The following formula was used:

$$C_{sv} = (n_c - n_o)/N$$

where n_c represents the number of respondents assigning an item to its intended domain, n_o represents the number of times an item is assigned to the alternative domain that received the largest number of assignments, and N represents the total number of respondents. C_{sv} values range from -1 to +1, with higher values indicating greater substantive validity. A large negative value indicates that an item had substantive validity but for a domain other than the one for which the researcher intended (Anderson and Gerbing, 1991).

Following Anderson and Gerbing (1991), C_{sv} values above .55 were considered significant and of *high validity*, whilst C_{sv} values between .30 and .55 represented *moderate validity*. Items with either high or moderate positive C_{sv} values were deemed worthy of retention in the instrument provided that no more than 30% of respondents had assigned the item incorrectly. Items that were found to tap into more than one domain were considered *ambiguous*. Those with C_{sv} values below .30 (including negative values) were considered *useless* as they are the most problematic in subsequent CFA (Anderson and Gerbing, 1991).

Low substantive validity coefficients indicate the existence of either problematic items or problematic concept definitions.

Of the 60 COPE items, 47 (78.7%) had acceptable C_{sv} values, with 46 of these items reflecting high substantive validity (>.55), and one item close to this cut-off, with a C_{sv} value of .54. Of the remaining 13 items, eight were found to be ambiguous, and a further five were found to be useless. Therefore, 21.3% of the COPE items were found to be lacking in substantive validity.

Problematic items were identified from eight of the subscales. Responses to the Mental Disengagement subscale were especially problematic with three of the four items found to be ambiguous, leaving only one item to represent this subscale. The ambiguity of these variables was demonstrated by the broad range of responses to the items, which participants assigned to seven different categories. Fifteen percent of responses to the Mental Disengagement items were assigned to Behavioral Disengagement and a further 10% were assigned to Denial.

Two items from the Active Coping subscale were found to be useless. "I do what has to be done, one step at a time" had a negative C_{sv} of .15 indicating it had higher substantive validity for a domain other than its intended one. Sixteen (61%) respondents incorrectly assigned this item, with 14 (54%) respondents perceiving this item to indicate Planning rather than Active Coping. Thirteen respondents (50%) indicated that "I concentrate my efforts on doing something about it" was also suggestive of Planning. An item from the Planning scale ("I think hard about how I might best handle the problem") was found to be ambiguous as seven (27%) respondents allocated this item to Active Coping.

Three of the eight social support items were found to be ambiguous. Four participants viewed "talking to someone who could do something concrete about the problem" as Active Coping or Planning efforts. Two items from the Emotional Social Support subscale were rated as Instrumental Social Support by 31% of participants.

The substantive validity analysis also identified two problematic items within the Suppression of Competing Activities subscale. "I focus on dealing with this problem and, if necessary let other things slide a little" was incorrectly assigned by eight (31%) respondents. Six participants (23%) rated this item as indicative of Active Coping, whilst two (8%) viewed it as reflecting Restraint Coping. "I keep myself from getting distracted by other thoughts or activities" was found to be a useless item with 15 people (58%) incorrectly assigning it. Five participants (19%) thought this item reflected Active Coping, whilst another five thought it referred to Mental Disengagement.

Two other useless items were identified. "I restrain myself from doing anything too quickly" was incorrectly assigned by 12 (46%) respondents. Eight (31%) respondents viewed this as a Planning item rather than a Restraint item. Finally, 14 (54%) respondents failed to identify "I reduce the amount of effort I'm putting into solving the problem" as a Behavioral Disengagement strategy. Six participants categorized this item as Mental Disengagement, whilst five saw it as Restraint Coping.

Seven of the COPE's subscales showed high substantive validity for all four items. These scales were: Positive Reinterpretation and Growth, Turning to Religion, Acceptance, Focus on and Venting of Emotions, Denial, Alcohol/Drug Use, and Humor. Further information (including C_{sv} values) is available upon request.

Discussion

The item-sort task used in this study showed that 13 (21.3%) of the 60 COPE items lacked substantive validity. The Mental Disengagement scale was especially problematic with three of the four items lacking substantive validity. This finding confirms the inherent weakness of this subscale, which had weak loadings (<.30) and unsatisfactory internal consistency (alpha = .45) in the validation studies carried out by Carver et al. (1989). Furthermore, in reviewing studies that used the COPE the Mental Disengagement subscale was consistently found to be problematic, with internal consistencies as low as .36 in some studies (e.g., Knee, 1998; Zuckerman, Kieffer, and Knee, 1998). Whilst Carver et al. (p.271) argued that lower reliabilities for the Mental Disengagement subscale were not entirely unexpected due to this scale being "more of a multiple-act criterion" than the others, data from the item-sort task clearly suggest that the items are unrelated and ambiguous. Hence the failure of this subscale to perform adequately in factor analysis.

In the validation study carried out by Carver et al. (1989), and the replication by Fontaine et al. (1993), the subscales for Active Coping and Planning converged to form a single factor. In second-order factor analysis (e.g., Carver et al., 1989; Deisinger et al., 1996) and other studies (e.g., Eisenberg et al., 1995; Laurent et al., 1997; Lyne and Roger, 2000) items from the Active Coping and Planning subscales have also tended to form a single factor (together with other items) that generally indicates an underlying problem-focused dimension. Findings from the item-sort task indicate that respondents might have difficulty making the distinction between acting (Active Coping) and forming intentions to act (Planning). The two might not be distinct in people's behavior. Alternatively, it might be that these particular items are poorly worded. The phrase "one step at a time" is strongly indicative of planning, even though the item is about "do[ing] what has to be done". The other problematic Active Coping item used the word "concentrate", which is highly indicative of mental activity, to describe efforts at "doing something". Alternative wording of items would need to be tested to determine whether the items or the constructs are problematic.

Consistent with findings of Carver et al. (1989), participants had some difficulty in distinguishing between Social Support for Instrumental Reasons and Social Support for Emotional Reasons. In the present analysis, the concept definitions clearly make the distinction between these two subscales, however, the two items concerned ("I discuss my feelings with someone" and "I talk to someone about how I feel") might be too vague to clearly articulate this distinction. Alternatively, such a distinction might not be valid in terms of actual behavior. Considering that one is likely to obtain emotional support when seeking instrumental support and vice-versa, the distinction between seeking social support for instrumental versus emotional reasons might not reflect the reality of people's behavior.

In summary, 13 of the 60 COPE variables failed to show adequate substantive validity indicating that these items are poor indicators of the various coping strategies they are supposed to represent or that the constructs themselves are poorly defined. Many of the activities that make up the COPE items can be carried out for reasons other than those intended by the questionnaire. The above findings suggest that some of the theoretical distinctions among the coping strategies proposed by Carver et al. (1989) might not reflect distinctions in terms of people's actual coping behavior. Furthermore, the seven scales which showed high substantive validity are those which appear to contain semantic variations rather than conceptually distinct items (i.e., Alcohol/Drug Use; Humor). The high substantive validity of these items is probably due to the similarity of the items, as well as the fact that many of these subscales measure constructs that are quite distinct from other aspects of coping measured by the instrument.

GENERAL DISCUSSION

The current research examined the internal structure of the COPE to determine whether the factor structure was consistent with that proposed by its authors (Carver et al., 1989). The first study was intended to explore the influence of item redundancy on emergent factor structure, whilst the second study used an item-sort task to explore the substantive validity of the instrument. A replication of the factor analysis carried out by Carver et al. failed to support the 15-factor model proposed to underlie the COPE. The factor structure produced in the present analysis was more parsimonious than that proposed by the COPE's authors with seven factors emerging. Other researchers who have factor analysed data obtained with the COPE have found various different 3-factor models (e.g., Cook and Heppner, 1997; Hien and Miele, 2003; Laurent et al., 1997; Lyne and Roger, 2000; Park and Levenson, 2002; Stowell et al., 2001), 4-factor models (e.g., Eisenberg et al., 1995; Phelps and Jarvis, 1994; Washburn-Ormachea et al., 2004), and a 6-factor model (i.e., Wade et al., 2001). Factor solutions differed considerably across the above studies in spite of similarly labelled factors, and various subscales were eliminated for their failure to load clearly on any factor. Findings from the present studies, taken together with those studies identified above, suggest that the internal structure of the COPE is unstable across samples.

Examination of factor loadings and inter-item correlations revealed that emergent factor structure was strongly influenced by the level of item redundancy present in the instrument. Items from several of the subscales (e.g., Humor, Religion, and Alcohol/Drug Use) were very highly correlated producing factors on which the items loaded very highly and purely on their respective factors. As the majority of items on these scales appear to be semantic variations rather than clearly distinct items they would be expected to load together irrespective of their relationship to external criteria. If redundant items were removed from these subscales there would only be one item to represent each construct. Hence, the relationship of these constructs to latent causative variables and higher-order dimensions of coping is not yet clear as clearly distinct items would need to be developed in order to explore such relationships.

Item redundancy also has consequences in terms of scoring because items from the COPE are summed to produce scale scores with higher scores reflecting greater use of a coping strategy. It is likely that someone responding to a subscale consisting of redundant items will respond to more of these items because they are repetitions of the same question, not because this strategy was employed more frequently. For example, it appears that subscales for religious coping, the use of alcohol and drugs, and denial all contain redundant items. Hence, a person's scores on this instrument might be inflated in terms of these subscales leading to erroneous conclusions about the coping strategies they employ. Studies that have relied on data from the COPE should be critically re-examined as measurement error due to intrascale redundancy renders findings suspect.

Given that coping subscales generally struggle to reach adequate levels of internal consistency, Cronbach's alphas for the seven factors emerging in the present analysis would appear to be relatively high, ranging from .74 to .96 (see table 3). The three subscales that formed their own pure factors (i.e., Humor, Religion, and Drug/Alcohol Use) had alphas of .89, .93, and .96 respectively, which are very high given the small number of items per scale. High internal consistency estimates produced by the COPE might be misleading as estimates of internal consistency are inflated by the inclusion of redundant items.

The other four factors which emerged in the present factor analysis were similar to those found by Carver et al. (1989) in their higher-order factor analyses of the COPE. The various subscales tended to converge forming a problem-engagement factor primarily consisting of Active Coping, Planning, and Suppression of Competing Activities items, a problem-disengagement factor consisting of Behavioral Disengagement and Denial items, an accommodation factor consisting of Acceptance, Positive Reinterpretation and Growth, and Restraint items, and a social support/emotional expression factor consisting of the Social Support (both types) and Venting of Emotions items. The emergent constructs are consistent with those found throughout the coping literature. The items formed interpretable factors, however, the items included in the item pool might not be the best indicators of these constructs because the items were intended to represent 15 narrower constructs, rather than these four broader domains of coping. The failure of items to load purely on one factor might be an indication that the items are not ideal markers for the constructs.

Ten of the COPE items loaded on more than one factor and two failed to load on any factor, which is consistent with findings from the item-sort task in which 13 of the 60 COPE variables failed to show adequate substantive validity. It is also consistent with the fact that in reviewed studies factor solutions differed considerably across studies (e.g., Cook and Heppner, 1997; Eisenberg et al., 1995; Hien and Miele, 2003; Laurent et al., 1997; Lyne and Roger, 2000; Park and Levenson, 2002; Phelps and Jarvis, 1994; Stowell et al., 2001; Wade et al., 2001; Washburn-Ormachea et al., 2004).

Similar to Stone and Neale (1984) the present study included a sorting methodology that did not necessitate administration of the instrument. Consistent with the findings of Stone and Neale, the item-sort task demonstrated that items from the COPE served different functions for different people. Stone and Neale allowed participants to classify coping items into as many categories as they saw fit and they found that items could often represent more than one coping strategy. Coping strategies often have different implications for different people under different conditions and might refer to very different kinds of coping efforts (Carpenter, 1992; Coyne and Gottlieb, 1996; Stone and Neale, 1984). Consequently, when a person selects a certain item, he or she might be doing so for reasons other than those intended by the instrument. When coping items serve multiple functions they are likely to load on multiple factors leading to their deletion from the item pool (Steed, 1998; Stone et al., 1992). Furthermore, Stone and Neale argued that endeavours to identify pure items representative of coping strategies was likely to produce item pools that poorly assess a given construct. For this reason, Stone and Neale rejected a checklist methodology and developed an alternative method for assessing coping that focuses on the intentions of the respondent rather than the test developer.

The intention-based approach developed by Stone and Neale (1984) produces shorter instrumentation because it requires only one item to assess each category of coping. Hence, Stone and Neale found it was ideal for daily assessment purposes overcoming the bias of retrospective accounts. Stone and Neale's instrument presented respondents with one-sentence descriptions of coping strategies and had respondents indicate whether they did anything that fit the categories. Positive responses were followed with an open-ended request for a description of actual thoughts or behaviors carried out. Respondents were also provided with the opportunity to include coping strategies that did not correspond to any of the categories provided. Hence, respondents could report on coping strategies that might be important in a given domain but which otherwise might not be captured due to the limitations imposed by the constructs and item pools of a particular instrument.

Stone and Neale (1984) also had respondents rate stressful events on situational parameters that included controllability, desirability, impact, anticipation, meaningfulness, chronicity, novelty, and stressfulness of the problem event. Pearlin and Schooler (1978) indicated that for efficacious coping a match was required between the specific characteristics of a stressful event and the selection of coping strategies. Hence, the methodology adopted by Stone and Neale not only overcomes the limitations inherent in many coping instruments (e.g., limitation of item pools, ambiguity of items) but it also allows for examination of the efficacy of coping because it collects information pertaining to the situational parameters of the stressful event. Hence, the methodology adopted by Stone and Neale appears to offer a way to measure coping that overcomes many of the drawbacks associated with the use of coping checklists, however, the limitations imposed by the need to analyze qualitative data (i.e., time and cost factors, smaller sample sizes) might deter researchers from adopting this approach when targeting large numbers of people.

CONCLUSION

A review of the literature suggested that the factor structure of the COPE was unstable and that the instrument contained a high level of item redundancy. Supporting this notion, the current factor analysis failed to replicate the proposed factor structure of the COPE and emergent factor structure appeared to be strongly influenced by a high level of intrascale redundancy. In the item-sort task, thirteen of the 60 COPE items failed to show adequate substantive validity. Findings from the current study support Lyne and Roger's (2000) assertion that the factor structure underlying the COPE is unstable. Hence, the COPE appears to lack content validity. This raises serious questions regarding the usefulness of information obtained using this instrument and highlights the need to confirm findings using alternatives to current measures. The methodology adopted by Stone and Neale (1984) overcomes many of the limitations inherent in the use of a checklist methodology to assess coping. Findings and conclusions based on the use of the COPE should be critically re-examined as widespread use of this instrument might have contributed to inconsistencies in the coping literature.

The arguments of Stone and Neale (1984) and Steed (1998) that, unlike trait assessment, coping strategies might be reflected by endorsement of only one or two items on a scale means that other coping instruments developed along traditional psychometric lines might also be problematic. Hence, considerable caution should be exercised when interpreting results that have used similar measures of coping. The need for more research examining the psychometric properties of coping instruments is clear. Sorting tasks such as those used by Stone and Neale, and the present analysis of substantive validity, are informative methods for examining coping instruments.

REFERENCES

Anderson, J.C. and Gerbing, D.W. (1991). Predicting the performance of measures in a confirmatory factor analysis with a pretest assessment of their substantive validities. *Journal of Applied Psychology, 76,* 732-740.

Amirkhan, J.H. (1990). A factor analytically derived measure of coping: The Coping Strategy Indicator. *Journal of Personality and Social Psychology, 59,* 1066-1074.

Ayers, T.S., Sandler, I.N., and Twohey, J.L. (1998). Conceptualization and measurement of coping in children and adolescents. In T.H. Ollendick and R.J. Prinz (Eds.), *Advances in Clinical Child Psychology* (Vol. 26, pp. 243-301). New York: Plenum.

Ayers, T.S., Sandler, I.N., West, S.G., and Roosa, M.W. (1996). A dispositional and situational assessment of children's coping: Testing alternative models of coping. *Journal of Personality, 64,* 923-958.

Begley, T.M. (1998). Coping strategies as predictors of employee distress and turnover after an organizational consolidation: A longitudinal analysis. *Journal of Occupational and Organizational Psychology, 71,* 305-321.

Brissette, I., Scheier, M.F., and Carver, C.S. (2002). The role of optimism in social network development, coping, and psychological adjustment during a life transition. *Journal of Personality and Social Psychology, 82,* 102-111.

Carpenter, B.N. (1992). Issues and advances in coping research. In B.N. Carpenter (Ed.), *Personal Coping: Theory, Research, and Application* (pp. 1-13). Connecticut: Praeger.

Carver, C.S., Pozo, C., Harris, S.D., Noriega, V., Scheier, M.F., Robinson, D.S., et al. (1993). How coping mediates the effect of optimism on distress: a study of women with early stage breast cancer. *Journal of Personality and Social Psychology, 65,* 375-390.

Carver, C.S., and Scheier, M.F. (1994). Situational coping and coping dispositions in a stressful transaction. *Journal of Personality and Social Psychology, 66,* 184-195.

Carver, C.S., Scheier, M.F., and Weintraub, J. K. (1989). Assessing coping strategies: a theoretically based approach. *Journal of Personality and Social Psychology, 56,* 267-283.

Compas, B.E., Connor-Smith, J.K., Saltzman, H., Harding Thomsen, A., and Wadsworth, M.E. (2001). Coping with stress during childhood and adolescence: problems, progress, and potential in theory and research. *Psychological Bulletin, 127,* 87-127.

Connor-Smith, J.K., Compas, B.E., Wadsworth, M.E., Harding Thomsen, A., and Saltzman, H. (2000). Responses to stress in adolescence: Measurement of coping and involuntary stress response. *Journal of Consulting and Clinical Psychology, 68,* 976-992.

Cook, S.W., and Heppner, P.P. (1997). A psychometric study of three coping measures. *Educational and Psychological Measurement, 57,* 906-923.

Coyne, J.C., and Gottlieb, B.H. (1996). The mismeasure of coping by checklist. *Journal of Personality, 64,* 959-991.

Coyne, J.C., and Racioppo, M.W. (2000). Never the twain shall meet? Closing the gap between coping research and clinical intervention research. *American Psychologist, 55,* 655-664.

Deisinger, J.A., Cassisi, J.E., and Whitaker, S.L. (1996). Relationships between coping style and PAI profiles in a community sample. *Journal of Clinical Psychology, 52,* 303-310.

Eisenberg, N., Fabes, R.A., and Murphy, B.C. (1995). Relations of shyness and low sociability to regulation and emotionality. *Journal of Personality and Social Psychology, 68*, 505-517.

Endler, N.S., and Parker, J.D. (1990). Multidimensional assessment of coping: a critical evaluation. *Journal of Personality and Social Psychology, 58*, 844-854.

Endler, N.S., and Parker, J.D. (1994). Assessment of multidimensional coping: task, emotion, and avoidance strategies. *Psychological Assessment, 6*, 50-60.

Folkman, S., and Lazarus, R.S. (1980). An analysis of coping in a middle-aged community sample. *Journal of Health and Social Behavior, 21*, 219-239.

Folkman, S., and Lazarus, R.S. (1985). If it changes it must be a process: study of emotion and coping during three stages of a college examination. *Journal of Personality and Social Psychology, 48*, 150-170.

Fontaine, K.R., Manstead, A.S.R., and Wagner, H. (1993). Optimism, perceived control over stress, and coping. *European Journal of Personality, 7*, 267-281.

Hasking, P.A., and Oei, T.P.S. (2002). Confirmatory factor analysis of the COPE questionnaire on community drinkers and an alcohol-dependent sample. *Journal of Studies on Alcohol, 63*, 631-640.

Hien, D.A., and Miele, G.M. (2003). Emotion-focused coping as a mediator of maternal cocaine abuse and antisocial behavior. *Psychology of Addictive Behaviors, 17*, 49-55.

Kline, P. (1994). *An easy guide to factor analysis.* New York: Routledge.

Knee, C.R. (1998). Implicit theories of relationships: assessment and prediction of romantic relationship initiation, coping, and longevity. *Journal of Personality and Social Psychology, 74*, 360-370.

Laurent, J., Catanzaro, S.J., and Callan, M.K. (1997). Stress, alcohol-related expectancies and coping preferences: a replication with adolescents of the Cooper et al. (1992) model. *Journal of Studies on Alcohol, 58*, 644-651.

Livneh, H., Livneh, C.L., Maron, S., and Kaplan, J. (1996). A multidimensional approach to the study of the structure of coping with stress. *The Journal of Psychology, 130*, 501-512.

Lyne, K., and Roger, D. (2000). A psychometric re-assessment of the COPE questionnaire. *Personality and Individual Differences, 29*, 321-335.

Park, C.L., and Levenson, M.R. (2002). Drinking to cope among college students: prevalence, problems and coping processes. *Journal of Studies on Alcohol, 63*, 486-497.

Parker, J.D., and Endler, N.S. (1992). Coping with coping assessment: a critical review. *European Journal of Personality, 6*, 321-344.

Pearlin, L.I., and Schooler, C. (1978). The structure of coping. *Journal of Health and Social Behavior, 19*, 2-21.

Phelps, S.B., and Jarvis, P.A. (1994). Coping in adolescence: empirical evidence for a theoretically based approach to assessing coping. *Journal of Youth and Adolescence, 23*, 359-372.

Skinner, E.A., Edge, K., Altman, J., and Sherwood, H. (2003). Searching for the structure of coping: A review and critique of category systems for classifying ways of coping. *Psychological Bulletin, 129*, 216-269.

Somerfield, M.R., and McCrae, R.R. (2000). Stress and coping research: methodological challenges, theoretical advances, and clinical applications. *American Psychologist, 55*, 620-625.

Stanton, A.L., Danoff-Burg, S., Cameron, C.L., and Ellis, A.P. (1994). Coping through emotional approach: problems of conceptualization and confounding. *Journal of Personality and Social Psychology, 66*, 350-362.

Steed, L.G. (1998). A critique of coping scales. *Australian Psychologist, 33*, 193-202.

Stone, A.A., and Kennedy-Moore, E. (1992). Commentary to part three: Assessing situational coping: conceptual and methodological considerations. In H.S. Friedman (Ed.) *Hostility, Coping, and Health* (pp. 203-214). Washington: American Psychological Association.

Stone, A.A., Kennedy-Moore, E., Newman, M.G., Greenberg, M., and Neale, J.M. (1992). Conceptual and methodological issues in current coping assessments. In B. N. Carpenter (Ed.) *Personal Coping: Theory, Research, and Application* (pp. 15-29). Connecticut: Praeger.

Stone, A.A., and Neale, J.M. (1984). New measurement of daily coping: development and preliminary results. *Journal of Personality and Social Psychology, 46*, 892-906.

Stowell, J.R., Kiecolt-Glaser, J.K., and Glaser, R. (2001). Perceived stress and cellular immunity: when coping counts. *Journal of Behavioral Medicine, 24*, 323-339.

Suls, J., David, J.P., and Harvey, J.H. (1996). Personality and coping: three generations of research. *Journal of Personality, 64*, 711-735.

Thoits, P. A. (1991). Gender differences in coping with emotional distress. In J. Eckenrode (Ed.) *The Social Context of Coping* (pp. 107-133). New York: Plenum.

Wade, S.L., Borawski, E.A., Taylor, H.G., Drotar, D., Yeates, K.O., and Stancin, T. (2001). The relationship of caregiver coping to family outcomes during the initial year following pediatric traumatic injury.

Washburn-Ormachea, J.M., Hillman, S.B., and Sawilowsky, S.S. (2004). Gender and gender-role orientation differences on adolescents' coping with peer stressors. *Journal of Youth and Adolescence, 33*, 31-40.

Westman, M., and Shirom, A. (1995). Dimensions of coping behavior: a proposed conceptual framework. *Anxiety, Stress, and Coping, 8*, 87-100.

Zuckerman, M., Kieffer, S.C., and Knee, C.R. (1998). Consequences of self-handicapping: effects on coping, academic performance, and adjustment. *Journal of Personality and Social Psychology, 74*, 1619-1628.

In: New Psychological Tests and Testing Research
Editor: Lydia S. Boyar, pp. 87-104

ISBN: 978-1-60021-570-4
© 2007 Nova Science Publishers, Inc.

Chapter 4

COMPUTERIZED PSYCHODYNAMIC PSYCHOTHERAPY

Louis A. Gottschalk[1] *and Robert J. Bechtel[2]*

[1] Department of Psychiatry and Human Behavior;
School of Medicine; University of California, Irvine; Irvine, CA 92697
[2] GB Software LLC; 4607 Perham Road; Corona del Mar, CA 92625

ABSTRACT

A computerized neuropsychiatric diagnostic and psychodynamic psychotherapeutic process is described built on a content analysis methodology that has been previously tested and used in many different settings and a variety of circumstances. The potential usefulness of this technological development requires further clinical trials and validation.

INTRODUCTION

The computerization of psychotherapy involving a health provider and a patient is a challenge that was introduced and pioneered in 1966 by the publication of Eliza (Weizenbaum, 1966). A computer program capable of providing psychotherapy to the diversity of personalities likely to test and use such a program, a program at the same time prepared to adapt to the wide variety of mental conflicts and disorders for which an individual might seek treatment, is far from being accomplished at this time.

Not all mental or physical disorders are capable of being changed or remedied. Which are responsive to treatment and which are not are issues and matters that are worth determining.

Therapy aims to modify and relieve distress, discomfort, and pain in addition to arriving at a diagnostic evaluation and classification. Psychotherapy attempts to achieve such a goal through empathic listening by a well-trained and licensed specialist (for example, psychiatrist, neurologist, psychologist, psychiatric social worker) who uses various verbal techniques, taught by different theoretically based schools, which need not be reviewed here. Other therapeutic procedures directed at mental disorders include neuropsychopharmacology, electroshock and other cerebral electromedical procedures, and cerebral neurosurgical approaches. Moreover, various religiously based methods, guided meditation, worship of statues, religious confession and absolution, the influence of rocks, special stones, jewelry, and photographs and pictures are claimed to have therapeutic value.

METHODS AND PROCEDURES

The computerized diagnostic and therapeutic program described here is not capable of substituting for the expertise of a medical doctor (or other professional person) who is qualified to know what to do with an individual who has a potentially dangerous medical or neuropsychiatric illness. When the possibility of a serious medical disorder (such as, cancer, cardiovascular problem, cerebral vascular stroke, congestive heart failure, infection) or serious mental disorder (potentially suicidal, homicidal, gravely disabled mentally or intoxicated from alcohol or some drug of abuse) is discovered, the subject should be immediately advised to consult a physician and/or appropriate professional specialist.

Under ordinary circumstances, a clinician has several options in obtaining objective and valid clinical evaluations. For example, precision and accuracy may be avoided and impressionistic reactions may be relied on. Some clinicians feel they are able to do competent clinical work with an impressionistic approach. Another clinician can spend considerable time and care in the diagnostic and therapeutic evaluation of patients with the goal of assessing accurately and precisely the magnitude of diverse medical and psychopathological processes within and across patients at different times.

Another diagnostic approach is to use various observer psychiatric rating scales, such as, the Brief Psychiatric Rating Scale, the Hamilton Anxiety or Depression Rating scales or various self-report measures, such as, various adjective checklists. Although such measures are widely used in many clinical research projects, their use carries with them a false sense of security since quite often no inter-rater reliability tests are done with the rating scales, the assumption being that anybody can follow the instructions for rating and no measurement errors are likely to occur. With rating scales, however, raters vary widely on how much of the range of ratings they use with the same subjects. Some raters characteristically select the lower range of the ratings, whereas others habitually chose the higher range of the ratings. With self-report measures, the assumption is the self-raters are all, indeed, in good and equivalent contact with themselves and are not likely to be falsifying, consciously or unconsciously, their self-evaluations, though it is true that the self-rating comes directly from the individual being evaluated.

These kinds of measurement errors in observer rating scales and self-report scales, usually disregarded by researchers and clinicians, are minimized in the measurement method of content analysis of verbal behavior. The individuals being rated are usually not aware what speech content or form is being analyzed, and they have difficulty covering up, even if they have some notions about such matters. Furthermore, the unstructured approach customarily used to elicit speech avoids the questionnaire or cross-examining method, and allows the

* Corresponding Author: Louis A. Gottschalk; +1.949.824.4171 (voice); +1.949.824.1589 (fax); lgottsch@uci.edu

subject to elaborate and use free-will to the extent desired by the self on choice of topics on which to verbalize. Emotions, self-reflections, doubts, and defensive maneuvers are recorded, and these all contribute to the content analysis scores eventually recorded and calculated.

In previous research, we have made some progress along this pathway that will be summarized here. Initially, there was the creation, development, and validation of the measurement of the magnitude of psychobiological states and traits from the content analysis of verbal behavior by human scoring (Gottschalk and Gleser, 1969; Gottschalk, Winget, and Gleser, 1969). In these and subsequent reports (Gottschalk, 1979; Gottschalk, Lolas and Viney, 1986; Koch and Schofer, 1986; Gottschalk, 1995, 1999, 2000), the objective measurement from the content analysis of verbal behavior was validated for the content analysis scales for the following categories:

Anxiety Scale. The type of anxiety that this scale measures is what is sometimes labeled free anxiety in contrast to bound anxiety, which manifests itself in psychological mechanisms of conversion and hypochondriacal symptoms. Some aspects of this anxiety scale are registered by other phenomena, such as, displacements (verbalizing about others or the environment manifesting fearful behavior or activities) or denials (asserting without being asked that one was not scared or anxious). The Anxiety Scale is classified into six subtypes: *death, mutilation, separation, guilt, shame, and diffuse or nonspecific anxiety.* Fear of death is assessed using content items dealing directly with death and destruction. Mutilation anxiety is manifested by allusions to fear of injury. Separation anxiety refers to fear of separation, abandonment, or loss. Guilt anxiety is defined through verbal references to adverse self-criticism, abuse, self-condemnation, moral self-disapproval. Shame anxiety is identified by expressions of self-ridicule, feelings of inadequacy, embarrassment, humiliation or exposure of personal shortcomings. Diffuse or nonspecific anxiety is identified by such references as "nervous" or "jittery" or "rattled."

Hostility Scales. The hostility scales are designed to measure three types of hostility of a transient rather than a sustained affect. Hostility scores derived from several lengthy verbal texts from an individual will provide a trait-like measure.

Hostility Directed Outward Scale measures the intensity of adversely critical, angry, aggressive, assaultive, asocial impulses and drives towards objects outside oneself.

Hostility Directed Inward Scale measures degrees of self-hate and self-criticism, and to some extent feelings of anxious depression and masochism.

Ambivalent Hostility Scale measures not only some aspects of hostility directed inward, but at the same time it measures some features of hostility directed outwards.

All three hostility scales assign higher weights to scorable verbal statements communicating hostility that, by inference, are likely to be strongly experienced by the speaker; whereas completely repressed hostility is not scored.

Social Alienation-Personal Disorganization Scale. This scale was originally designed to measure the relative degree of personal disorganization, social withdrawal or feelings of isolation of schizophrenic persons. The common denominators of the schizophrenic syndrome are considered to be disturbances in the coherence and logicalness of thinking process and deficiencies in human relationships, especially those manifesting in alienation, avoidance, and antagonism. Another principal characteristic of the concept of the schizophrenic syndrome is that it is a syndrome that is quantifiably describable, that is, there are relative degrees of severity of schizophrenia. In some schizophrenic individuals this severity can fluctuate considerably from day to day. This concept of schizophrenia, in fact, holds that these principal characteristics and features of schizophrenia—social alienation and personal disorganization—occur to mild degrees and to a varying extent in nonschizophrenic individuals, but not in such a continuous and/or extreme fashion in schizophrenia itself (Gleser, Winget, Seligman, and Rauh, 1979; Gottschalk and Gleser, 1969; Winget, Seligman, Rauh, and Gleser, 1979).

Cognitive and Intellectual Impairment Scale. The Cognitive Impairment scale is designed to measure transient and reversible changes in cognitive and intellectual impairment as well as permanent and irreversible changes, all due principally to brain dysfunction and minimally to emotional changes in the individual.

Depression Scale. The Depression scale provides dimensions that are compatible with the concept that there are a number of potentially relevant subcategories of constructs of depression that have significant statistical relationships with different underlying pathogenic processes (Gottschalk, 1966). Thus, in addition to providing a total depression score, it has a broad range of phenomenological subscales. These are: *Hopelessness, Self-Accusation, Psychomotor Retardation, Somatic Concerns, Death and Mutilation Depression, Separation Depression, and Hostility Outward*.

Hope Scale. The Hope Scale is designed to measure the intensity of the optimism that a favorable outcome is likely to occur, not only in one's personal earthly activities, but also in cosmic phenomena and as well as spiritual or imaginary events. A high hope score is intended to be of predictive value with respect to human survival, the preservation or enhancement of health, or the welfare or constructive achievement of the self or others (Gottschalk, 1974; Gottschalk, Bechtel, Buchman, and Ray, 2004).

Human Relations Scale. The Human Relations Scale measures the relative inclination an individual has to care about and be interested in helping others. It is a scale that measures the degrees of altruism a person has.

Achievement Strivings Scale. The Achievement Strivings Scale aims to assess the achievement motivation of an individual. It notes the relative degrees of motivation one has mentally and physically and it records and measures various kinds of deterrents and blockages to such achievement-orientations.

Dependency Strivings and Frustrated Dependency Scales. These scales focus on verbal references to dependency wishes and frustrated dependency.

Health/Sickness Scale. The Health/Sickness Scale measures the relative preoccupations of a person with health and heathfulness versus sickness and ill health.

Quality of Life Scale. The Quality of Life Scale measures the relative quality of life an individual reveals based on the content analysis of what they say or write. A review of the criteria on which this scale is based is available in Gottschalk, Bechtel, Buchman, and Ray (2003b). It is derived from content analysis scores from the Human Relations Scale, the Hope Scale, the Social Alienation-Personal Disorganization Scale, the Depression Scale, and the Health/Sickness Scale.

Scoring Norms

Norms (mean scores and standard deviations from the mean) have been established for most, though not all, of the scales. The norms are derived from human-assigned scores. The norms have been shown to vary with age (adult/child, with a cutoff at > 18 years), gender, and (for some scales) ethnicity.

Norms for the various scales, by age and gender, are given in table 1 below. On samples where information is not available about subject age and gender, the adult male norms are used for comparison.

The content analysis approach to the measurement of psychobiological dimensions includes the strengths of both the self-report approach and the observer rating scale approach, and minimizes the weaknesses of both in terms of measurement errors. Of particular interest in the current setting is that content analysis is particularly well suited for use in dialogue systems, which typifies psychotherapy.

To address training and performance obstacles to wider use of the content analysis scales, we developed and tested software capable of reliably scoring computer-readable transcriptions of verbal (speech) samples on the Gottschalk-Gleser scales (Gottschalk and Bechtel, 1982, 1995). Computer scoring was accomplished over a number of years (Gottschalk, Hausmann, and Brown, 1975; Bechtel, 1982; Gottschalk and Bechtel, 1982, 1989, 1998-2002; Gottschalk, Bechtel, Maguire, Katz, Levinson, Harrington, Nakamura, and Franklin, 2002; Gottschalk, Bechtel, Maguire, Harrington, Levinson, Franklin, and Caracamo, 2000; Gottschalk and Gottschalk, 2002; Gottschalk, DeFrancisco, and Bechtel, 2002; Gottschalk, Lolas, and Viney, 1986; Reynolds, 2001: Lavid, Grayden, Gottschalk, and Bechtel, 2001; Maguire, Gottschalk, Riley, Franklin, Bechtel, and Ashurst, 1999). In operation, the program (called PCAD, for Psychiatric Content Analysis and Diagnosis) assigns scores on the user-selected scales to each clause in the input sample, then, at the user's option, reports score summaries for each scored scale with comparisons to established norms for the subject's demographic group, provides an analysis of the score profile, and suggests possible diagnoses drawn from the Diagnostic and Statistical Manual of Mental Disorders, Fourth Edition (DSM-IV) (American Psychiatric Association, 1994). In addition, computerized scoring of these content analysis scales during conversational interactions was achieved (Gottschalk, Bechtel, Buchman, and Ray, 2003, 2004).

A quick review of the steps the PCAD program takes in the process of measuring the relative magnitude of diverse neuropsychobiological states and traits would be helpful at this point.

The software system relies on a reasonably sized dictionary (approximately 200,000 words) marked with associated parts of speech, and a collection of (mostly American) English idiomatic and slang expressions. Some of the words and all of the idioms have been manually identified as possible indicators of semantic content relevant to one or more of the scales. Syntactic information such as part of speech and number is extracted from the dictionary and used by a parser that outputs an analysis of the structure of each input clause.

Table 1. Norms for the Gottschalk-Gleser Content Analysis Scales

Scale	Male Adult		Male Child		Female Adult		Female Child	
	Mean	S.D.	Mean	S.D.	Mean	S.D.	Mean	S.D.
Anxiety Total	1.48	0.70	2.05	0.89	1.48	0.70	2.05	0.89
Death Anxiety (1)	0.30	0.51	0.55	0.45	0.18	0.34	0.63	0.42
Mutilation Anxiety (2)	0.36	0.55	0.79	0.63	0.28	0.51	0.92	0.67
Separation Anxiety (3)	0.30	0.46	1.18	0.78	0.42	0.52	1.16	0.55
Guilt Anxiety (4)	0.31	0.49	0.41	0.22	0.31	0.47	0.43	0.32
Shame Anxiety (5)	0.42	0.57	0.95	0.69	0.70	0.70	0.80	0.59
Diffuse Anxiety (6)	0.35	0.46	0.55	0.27	0.45	0.63	0.69	0.45
Hostility Outward Total	0.97	0.50	1.15	0.58	0.97	0.50	1.15	0.58
Hostility Outward Overt	0.70	0.36	0.80	0.48	0.70	0.36	0.80	0.48
Hostility Outward Covert	0.67	0.46	0.86	0.48	0.67	0.46	0.86	0.48
Hostility Inward	0.60	0.35	0.74	0.54	0.60	0.35	0.74	0.54
Ambivalent Hostility	0.58	0.43	0.68	0.38	0.58	0.43	0.68	0.38
Social Alienate-Personal Disorganize	-2.89	2.70	-1.15	4.75	-2.89	2.70	-1.15	4.75
Cognitive Impairment	0.81	0.47	2.51	1.80	0.81	0.47	2.51	1.80
Hope	0.74	1.03	0.05	1.25	0.74	1.03	0.05	1.25
Depression Total	5.48	1.87	6.16	2.82	5.39	1.53	6.37	2.37
Dep - Hopelessness (I)	0.90	0.31	0.98	0.54	1.05	0.38	1.15	0.53
Dep - Self-Accusation (II)	1.03	0.58	1.11	0.86	1.41	0.76	1.25	0.75
Dep - Guilt	0.37	0.21	0.47	0.18	0.41	0.18	0.50	0.53
Dep - Shame	0.79	0.53	0.83	0.80	1.18	0.78	0.85	0.83
Dep - Hostile Inward	0.64	0.38	0.77	0.45	0.75	0.33	0.72	0.30
Dep - Psychomotor Retardation (III)	0.35	0.10	0.41	0.16	0.41	0.19	0.42	0.28
Dep - Somatic Concerns (IV)	0.34	0.10	0.54	0.32	0.46	0.17	0.51	0.33
Dep - Death/Mutilation (V)	0.93	0.65	0.88	0.78	0.57	0.40	0.86	0.79
Dep - Death	0.65	0.50	0.52	0.33	0.48	0.28	0.56	0.35
Dep - Mutilation	0.70	0.50	0.84	0.70	0.46	0.35	0.75	0.70
Dep - Separation (VI)	0.86	0.63	1.02	0.75	0.71	0.35	0.94	0.43
Dep - Hostility Outward (VII)	1.06	0.56	1.23	0.62	0.77	0.33	1.19	0.46
Dep - Hostility Out Overt	0.72	0.36	0.89	0.49	0.69	0.31	0.88	0.45
Dep - Hostility Out Covert	0.81	0.51	0.84	0.60	0.50	0.19	0.80	0.39

Table 1. (Continued).

Scale	Male Adult		Male Child		Female Adult		Female Child	
	Mean	S.D.	Mean	S.D.	Mean	S.D.	Mean	S.D.
Health/Sickness	0.65	0.40	0.65	0.40	1.40	1.10	1.40	1.10
Health	0.43	0.34	0.43	0.34	0.94	1.09	0.96	1.09
Sickness	0.22	0.24	0.22	0.24	0.46	0.34	0.46	0.34
Human Relations	0.99	0.76	1.78	0.61	1.40	0.95	1.78	0.61
Achievement Strivings	1.11	1.17	1.11	1.17	1.11	1.17	1.11	1.17
Achievement - Support	1.84	0.99	1.84	0.99	1.84	0.99	1.84	0.99
Achievement - Deterrents	0.74	0.54	0.74	0.54	0.74	0.54	0.74	0.54
Dependency Strivings	0.54	0.42	0.54	0.42	0.54	0.42	0.54	0.42
Frustrated Dependency Strivings	0.11	0.18	0.11	0.18	0.11	0.18	0.11	0.18
Quality of Life	-1.67	3.71	-1.67	3.71	-1.67	3.71	-1.67	3.71

When a word or phrase in an input is found in the dictionary as a possible marker of an item from a scale, a partial score is added to a list of scoring candidates. This list of candidates is then examined by a set of scale-dependent procedures that consider the clause structure as well as the scoring candidates to decide the validity of each potential score. For example, the speaker must be the recipient of an action or affect described in a clause for the clause to be scoreable on the Hostility Inward scale, while the speaker must not be the recipient on the Hostility Outward scale. Candidate scores approved by this process are emitted as content analysis scores applicable to the input clause, together with weighting as defined by the scale. Scores for individual clauses are aggregated to provide an overall score for the sample.

A scoring summary is prepared for each active scale. The summary gives tallies of the number of occurrences of the various tags, a word count, and a single score based on scale-specific tag weightings that is used to characterize the verbal sample on each scale. The human scorer of content analysis can distinguish semantic messages being communicated in context across several grammatical clauses; whereas, the software program analyzes the meaning conveyed by context only within each grammatical clause. Thus, computer scoring may miss some aspects of the meaning being conveyed when two or more clauses are required to discern the meaning communicated in context across several grammatical clauses (e.g., "I was very frightened by the situation. It was new to me. I don't think I could become accustomed to that.") Thus, computer scoring may miss some aspects of the meaning being conveyed when two or more clauses are required to discern the meaning. For this reason, the software system does not always precisely match scores assigned by trained human scorers. Since the tagging dictionary was developed manually, occasional errors occur. Some tagging categories require judgments that we have been unable to capture in programmatic form. For example, on the Social Alienation/Personal Disorganization (Schizophrenic) scale, a clause is to be tagged if it contains "Obviously erroneous or fallacious remarks or conclusions; illogical or bizarre statements." To accommodate these differences, the score produced by the software is adjusted to create a "human equivalent" score, with the adjustment derived from a human and computer scoring of a set of 71 samples maintained as a standard.

We have developed regression formulas enabling us to convert computer-derived content analysis scores into human-equivalent scores by scoring large numbers of verbal samples both manually using human experts in scoring and automatically using the computer program. These computer-to-human conversions provide some correction for the problem of missed scores. Since the norms we have obtained for the content analysis scale scores from adults and children are based on human expert scorers, the machine-derived scores may be compared to the human-derived norms whenever it is desirable to determine how many standard deviations from our norms any newly obtained content analysis scores may be.

Not all of the scales have conversion formulae, so not all have human equivalent scores. No conversion to human-equivalent has been established for the following scales:

- Health/Sickness
- Human Relations
- Achievement Strivings
- Dependency Strivings and Frustrated Dependency Strivings
- Quality of Life

The computer-to-human conversion factors are calculated separately for each scale and subscale. The factors are given in table 2 below.

Table 2. Computer-Human Conversion Factors

Scale/Subscale	Multiplier (slope)	Offset (y-intercept)
Death Anxiety	0.92	0.16
Mutilation Anxiety	0.58	0.23
Separation Anxiety	0.46	0.24
Guilt Anxiety	0.91	0.12
Shame Anxiety	0.85	0.29
Diffuse Anxiety	0.85	0.09
Total Anxiety	0.88	0.32
Hostility Outward Overt	0.37	0.62
Hostility Outward Covert	0.27	0.39
Hostility Outward Total	0.27	0.78
Hostility Inward	0.54	0.49
Ambivalent Hostility	0.20	0.58
Social Alienation/Personal Disorganization	0.86	-0.03
Cognitive Impairment	0.75	0.02
Health	0.37	0.20
Hopelessness	0.26	0.23
Guilt Depression	0.91	0.12
Shame Depression	0.85	0.29
Hostility Directed Inward	0.54	0.49
Self-Accusation	0.89	0.41
Psychomotor Retardation	0.15	0.25
Somatic Concerns	0.77	0.33
Death Depression	0.92	0.16
Mutilation Depression	0.58	0.23
Death and Mutilation Depression	0.67	0.34
Separation Depression	0.46	0.24
Hostility Outward Overt	0.37	0.62
Hostility Outward Covert	0.27	0.39
Hostility Outward	0.27	0.78
Total Depression	0.77	1.33

For those scales (above) with established computer-human conversion factors, the human-equivalent score is used for testing against norms. For scales with no established conversion from computer-generated scores to human-equivalents, the computer-generated score is used directly for comparison to the mean.

Example Calculation

Given a computer-generated score (C), the human equivalent (E) is calculated by multiplying the computer-generated score by the multiplier for the scale or subscale, then adding the offset for the scale or subscale. For example, a computer-generated total anxiety score of 0.54 would be converted as follows: $E = mC + b$; $E = 0.88C + 0.32$; $E = (0.88 * 0.54)$

+ 0.32; E = 0.48 + 0.32; E = 0.80. So, a computer-generated score of 0.54 for total anxiety has a human equivalent score of 0.80.

The norm for total anxiety is 1.48, with a standard deviation of 0.70. The human-equivalent score (0.80) is within one standard deviation of the mean, and thus would be considered to fall within the normal range.

The summaries also indicate to what extent the verbal sample score deviates from the norms that have been obtained for each scale (in terms of standard deviations). PCAD uses the distance of a sample score from the mean for a scale to generate commentary and candidate diagnoses for consideration.

- A score that lies within one standard deviation of the mean is considered "in the normal range."
- A score that is more than one but less than two standard deviations from the mean is "slightly high."
- Between two and three standard deviations, scores are described as "moderately high," and
- Above three standard deviations are described as "very high."

On most scales, PCAD reports only deviations above the mean. Exceptions are Hope, Human Relations, Achievement Strivings, and Quality of Life. For these scales, deviations below the mean are reported as "slightly/moderately/very low."

Finally, the system proposes possible neuropsychiatric diagnoses that the user might consider in evaluating the patient or subject.

Thus, the software system generates four distinct classes of output: (1) an interlinear listing of each grammatical clause and the scores assigned to it; (2) a scoring summary for each content analysis scale, including a comparison to established norms for each scale; (3) an analysis or interpretation, in textual form, of the scale scores; and (4) possible neuropsychiatric diagnostic classifications taken from DSM-IV that a clinician might consider in evaluating the subject or patient.

We have adapted the PCAD software to create an initial implementation of a therapeutic agent, called THERAPIST.

THERAPIST begins by presenting a form that the subject can fill out to provide necessary identifying data. The identifying data collected includes: 1. Name; 2. Occupation; 3. Age, 4.Gender; 5. Marital status; 6. Education; 7. Ethnic background; 8. Religion and degree of religious activity (active/inactive); 9. Height; 10. Weight; 11. Number of daughters; 12. Number of sons; 13. Number of brothers; 14. Number of sisters; 15. Mother's age (or age at death, if deceased); 16. Father's age (or age at death, if deceased). 17. Description of mother's health; 18. Description of father's health; 19. Description of medical illnesses; 20. Description of accidents or injuries; 21. Description of mental illnesses; 22. Description of other health issues; 23. Description of medications taken (name and amount).

In order to obtain an initial understanding of the participant's complaints and worries, the computer programs requests that the participant summarize in 100 words or more these complaints, worries, and symptoms. We plan to incorporate introductory comments such as the following to inform potential participants about the nature and goals of this computerized program for psychodynamic psychotherapy.

"Welcome to this program designed to help you understand yourself better. It is organized to compare and contrast your mental and physical status with other people of your sex and age range—children and adult—who are capable of writing about themselves to a computer program and sharing their feelings and attitudes and life problems with an objective artificial intelligence software program that has been intensively researched, scientifically validated, and widely published over many years (www.gb-software.com). The responses and information supplied by participants are regarded as absolutely private and confidential and are not available to anyone other than the participant identifiable only through a password."

The longer and more detailed this initial communication is the more reliable will be the computer program's understanding of the nature and scope of the problems. THERAPIST uses the PCAD capability to analyze the semantic content, that is, the meanings, of the verbal text supplied by the participant and to compare the scores obtained from this initial content analysis with the normal scores typically obtained on the Gottschalk-Gleser content analysis scales.

On the basis of the scores obtained from this initial evaluation, the computer program makes responses appropriate to these scores. For example, if all the content analysis scores are not significantly different from the norms for all of these Content Analysis Scales, THERAPIST tells the participant he/she, on the basis of this initial verbal communication, is normal in every respect. If there turns out to be some deviation from the norms—that is, one, two or three standard deviations from the established norm on any of the content analysis scales, THERAPIST communicates this information to the participant in some polite and objective way and, on some occasions, asks the participant for more information or to elaborate on some relevant theme in his/her initial verbal communication.

The following are a number of examples of content analysis outcomes and the corresponding THERAPIST responses that they trigger.

- No standard deviations from all the norms. "You certainly are in happy frame of mind today. I am wondering what is going on in your life that is making you so comfortable and relaxed?"
- One standard deviation above the norm for total anxiety only. "I have the feeling that something is worrying you. Would you care to tell me about it?"
- Two standard deviations about the norm for total anxiety only. "I get the impression that something is making you feel moderately anxious. Could you elaborate on what is the matter?"
- Three standard deviations above the norm for total anxiety only. "Wow! You're certainly very scared about the matter. Tell me more about it."
- One, two or three standard deviations above the norm for hostility outward (overt or covert). "You are angry and want to retaliate. Please expand and fill out the details so I can better understand how I might help you."
- One, two or three standard deviations above the norm for hostility inward only. "You are quite self-critical. How come?"
- One, two or three standard deviations above the norm for ambivalent hostility only. "You are telling me that people or something is against you. Maybe hurting you or destroying you."

- One two or three standard deviations above the norm for total depression only. "You seem depressed. How long has your depressed condition been going on and what seems to have precipitated it? Have you consulted a physician, especially a psychiatrist? I strongly recommend that you do so as soon as possible, preferably immediately. If you have had any suicidal or homicidal ideas or impulses, you should consult a psychiatrist as soon as possible. Trying to solve such serious problems by a computer program is not possible."

- One, two or three standard deviations above the norm for the Social Alienation-Personal Disorganization Scale. "I wonder whether you ever hear voices or see things that other people do not. Or whether you feel people are talking or thinking bad things about you. Or whether you actually feel a bit disorganized. In any event tell me more about these matters. Have you consulted a physician, especially a psychiatrist? I strongly recommend that you do so as soon as possible, preferably immediately. If you have had any suicidal or homicidal ideas or impulses, you should consult a psychiatrist as soon as possible. Trying to solve such serious problems by a computer program is not possible."

- One, two or three standard deviations above the norm for the Cognitive and Intellectual Impairment Scale only. "Do you have some trouble with your recent memories, for example, where you put some things or where you are or the names of family members or friends? Or do you feel you are just as sharp intellectually as you ever have been?"

- One, two or three standard deviations below the norm for the Hope Scale only. "Do you feel as positive and optimistic as ever? Are people giving you the help or support to which you are accustomed? Or you feel downright hopeless? Please tell me more about your level of hopefulness."

- One, two or three standard deviations below the norm for the Human Relations Scale only. "From what you have communicated to me, I have the impression that the quality of your relationships with others is not going so well. Could you give me more details so that I could understand the bases for the difficulties you are having? I am hoping I can help you."

- One, two or three standard deviations below the norm on the Achievement Strivings Scale. "I believe you are telling me that you are having some problems in achieving some of your aims and goals. Would you tell me more about these problems so that I understand them better and so I can be of possible usefulness in helping you satisfy some of your achievement strivings."

- One, two or three standard deviations above the norms on the Health and Health/Sickness Scale. "I gather from your messages to me that you are troubled by some kind of illness which interferes with your health and well-being. Can you tell me more about the trouble you are having? Do you have a family practitioner, internist, or medical specialist? If not, I recommend that you obtain such a physician right away."

- One, two or three standard deviations above the norms for Dependency and Dependency Frustration Scales. "I think you have communicated to me that there are some shortcomings in the satisfaction of your dependency needs. Could you tell me more about your normal dependency and the frustrations you are having of your dependent needs."

- One, two or three standard deviations below the norms on the Quality of Life Scale. "I get the impression from your messages to me that the quality of your life is not very good. So that I can understand your life situation better, would you tell me more about what is going on in your life in this respect."
- One, two or three standard deviations above the norms for the Total Anxiety Scale and the Depression Scale or some abnormal score in other Content Scale, such as the Quality of Life Scale or the Human Relations Scale or one of the Hostility Scales. "It sounds to me that you may have a depression with some anxiety or maybe occasional panic states. Have you been getting some professional help for this disorder or have you been suffering in silence? Tell me more about your self."
- One, two or three standard deviations above the norms on the Social Alienation-Personal Disorganization and other relevant Content Analysis Scales, such as, the Hostility Scales, the Anxiety Scales, the Human Relations Scale, the Achievement Strivings Scale, the Health/Sickness Scales. "I gather from what you tell me that you have been experiencing some very uncomfortable mental symptoms. Can you tell me more about your self? And have you been getting some professional help for your condition?"
- One, two or three standard deviations above the norms for the Cognitive and Intellectual Impairment Scale as well as any other Content Analysis Scale or Scales. "I wonder whether you are having any problems focusing your attention or experiencing some troubles with your memory. If so, how long have you had these symptoms? And are you getting any professional help for these difficulties? Tell me more about your self."
- One, two or three standard deviations above the norms for two or more Content Analysis Scales. "These are matters we need to talk about more. There must have been a number of stressors in your life that bring on such mental strain. I believe we should consider communicating regularly--maybe daily or weekly--to help me understand the tough times you have gone through. I believe that communicating with someone else about these events will help relieve the inner pressures you are experiencing. Also, I wonder whether your family doctor is prescribing some medications for you that might relieve some of your symptoms. And if so, what are they? Can you give me the names of the drugs, how often you take them and what the doses are?"

At this point, we have the beginning of a fruitful conversation between THERAPIST and the participant who, at will, can share more information with THERAPIST, which THERAPIST is likely to respond to in a supportive and sometimes inquiring manner.

The computer program has an excellent memory, and it will keep track of the participant's identification, present and past history, family history, mental and physical status, and it will keep a good and reliable record of all the preceding communications between the participant and itself. On some occasions where appropriate, THERAPIST may well refer to some of the information retained in its memory and remind the participant about these past intercommunications.

THERAPIST will always be interested in responding to verbal communications from the participant on a regular basis. Like any psychodynamic psychotherapist, THERAPIST is ready to work with the participant on any ramifications of the initial problems that were shared or new ones.

THERAPIST has the ability to help understand and analyze dreams if the participant recalls them and can free-associate about details in the dreams.

We have faced several interesting challenges in adapting the PCAD software to the interactivity required by THERAPIST. While PCAD is useful in a psychiatry or psychology research setting, for example in exploring the writings of the Unabomber for evidence of psychopathology (Gottschalk and Gottschalk, 1999), or in predicting the outcome of psychiatric commitment hearings (Lavid *et al*, 2002), it is strongly oriented to the analysis of samples that are larger than many conversational utterances. For reliable results, the recommended minimum input sample length is 80 words. The focus is usually on overall scale scores, aggregated over all the clauses in a sample, because at that level the established norms can be used for comparison purposes.

At least two earlier efforts have been made to apply the PCAD scoring software in interaction settings. In the first (Gottschalk *et al*, 2003), the software was used to analyze utterances in dialogues among medical personnel and families of patients in a surgical intensive care unit. The problem of short utterances was addressed by aggregating utterances by speaker, enabling calculation of both a per-utterance and cumulative sample score for each speaker. The second interaction application was in a commercial web-based system that generates responses to subject entries, similar in spirit to the original Eliza (Weizenbaum, 1966), but with the (pre-written) response determined by the content analysis scores on the various scales (Journal Genie, 2004).

We are aware that having to type into a computer, at this point in the English language and with fairly good spelling, presents some constraints to our goals. The goals of THERAPIST are to read what the patient writes, decide whether what the patient says has any adverse neuropsychiatric characteristics, has any normal neuropsychiatric dimensions, has any positive and healthy features, decides what the various combinations of these dimensions are with respect to one individual, aims to alleviate the discomfort and disabilities currently involving this individual to any extent possible, and invite the individual to share his mental and emotional experiences through the medium of verbal behavior.

The detection and measurement capability of our existing verbal sample scoring software supplies a useful starting point for our goal of therapeutic support, but it is only a small fraction of what would be needed to attempt psychotherapy. We are in the process of adding entity recognition and tracking to the core content analysis results to better establish the context in which emotions and mental processes of interest appear. For example, if hostility outward is consistently detected with respect to a particular individual, interaction may be guided to examine that relationship in greater depth.

Before a dialogue system such as THERAPIST can respond to mental processes and emotions, it must detect them. Psychiatry and psychology have long experience in the definition, detection, and measurement of these phenomena, both in characterizing the people in whom they occur, their associated behaviors, their diagnostic classification, and in selecting and measuring the efficacy of therapeutic interventions. Our use of the Gottschalk-Gleser content analysis scales provides a means of detecting meaningful psychobiological content in linguistic behaviors, and such information provides cues and guidelines for psychotherapeutic interaction. .

Additional work will be needed in a variety of areas before we can offer readily and easily usable computerized software that can provide diagnostic medical and neuropsychiatric information that can serve as a basis for psychotherapeutic involvement. Systematic responses by THERAPIST will need greater flexibility than has been available in our current text template approach. On the dialogue level, we need to incorporate the medical and neuropsychiatric assessment within a user model, and create a model of the psychotherapy process that can be used to drive a dialogue move engine, such as, TrindiKit (Larsson and Traum, 2000). The need for interacting functionality at so many levels suggests that psychotherapy offers a fertile ground for further work in dialogue research.

To enhance the relationship between the subject (computer software user) and the computer software program (derived in part from PCAD—psychiatric content analysis and diagnosis), we are changing the name THERAPIST to the name FRIEND, which we hope to some extent will be valid.

The question is certainly fair to ask how effective computerized psychotherapy can be. There is considerable published research on the efficacy of psychotherapy. Rosenzweig (1936) was a pioneer in pointing out that there were implicit common factors in diverse methods of psychotherapy. Luborsky (1995), in a creative and clever paper, observed more precisely that there were common factors across different psychotherapies—such as, the attention of a therapist who has a convincing allegiance to the beneficial values of the therapy being provided, the scheduled opportunity to articulate and verbalize one's personal life history and experiences, and the recurring occasions to share private mental conflicts and symptoms. Luborsky, with regards to the issue of the relative outcomes of psychotherapies, repeated Rosenzweig's quote from *Alice in Wonderland:* "everybody has won, so all shall have prizes" which was the "Dodo bird's verdict" after judging the race. The "Dodo bird verdict" has become commonly used in clinical research examining the differential effects of various psychotherapies and/or belief systems. No one has systematically tested the efficacy of computerized psychotherapy, but that activity should be soon forthcoming. A more recent publication by Luborsky and his collaborators (Luborsky, Rosenthal, Diguer, Andrusyna, Berman, Levitt, Seligman, and Krauseet, 2002), examines17 meta-analyses of comparisons of active treatments with each other, in contrast to the more usual comparisons of active treatment with controls, a paper which addresses relevant questions possibly raised by any readers of this article.

CONCLUSIONS

A computerized neuropsychiatric diagnostic and psychodynamic psychotherapeutic procedure is described. The scientific foundations and published pertinent research on which this methodology is based are cited and reviewed, including some previous clinical trials.

The potential diagnostic and therapeutic usefulness of this unique computerized technological achievement are suggested as a therapeutic adjuvant or instrument. Its limitations are noted, especially with respect to use with persons who have disabling medical disorders and who are experiencing suicidal and/or homicidal ideation.

Further development and testing of this computer software are in process.

REFERENCES

American Psychiatric Association. (1994) *Diagnostic and Statistical Manual. Fourth Edition.* American Psychiatric Press.

Bechtel R. (1997) Developments in computer science with applications in text analysis. In Carl W. Roberts (Ed.) *Text Analysis for the Social Sciences. Methods for Drawing Statistical Inferences from Texts and Transcripts.* Mahway, New Jersey: Lawrence Erlbaum Associates, 239-250.

Bechtel RJ and Gottschalk LA. (2004) Detection of neuropsychiatric states of interest in text. *AAAI Fall Symposium on Dialogue Systems for Health Communication.* American Association for Artificial Intelligence.

Gleser GC, Winget C, Seligman, Rauh JL. (1979) Evaluation of psychotherapy in with adolescents using content analysis of verbal samples. In: LA Gottschalk (Ed.) *The Content Analysis of Verbal Samples: Further Studies.* (pp. 213-233) New York: Spectrum.

Gottschalk LA. (1966) Depressions—psychodynamic considerations. In: JE Cole and JR Wittenborn (Eds.) *Pharmacotherapy of Depressions* (pp. 30-46). Springfield, Ill. Charles C Thomas.

Gottschalk LA. (1974) A hope scale applicable to verbal samples. *Archives of General Psychiatry.* 30:779-785.

Gottschalk LA. (Ed.) (1979) *The Content Analysis of Verbal Behavior. Further Studies.* New York: Spectrum Publications.

Gottschalk LA. (1995) *Content Analysis of Verbal Behavior. New Findings and Clinical Applications.* Hillsdale, New Jersey: Lawrence Erlbaum Publisher.

Gottschalk LA. (1997) The unobstrusive measurement of psychological states and traits. In: Carl W. Roberts (Ed.). *Text Analysis for the Social Sciences. Methods for Drawing Statistical Inferences from Texts and Transcripts.* Mahway, New Jersey: Lawrence Erlbaum Associates, pp. 117-130.

Gottschalk LA. (1999) The application of a computerized measurement of the content analysis of natural language to the assessment of the effects of psychoactive.drugs. *Methods and Findings in Experimental and Clinical Pharmacology.* 21: 133-138.

Gottschalk LA. (2000) The application of computerized content analysis of natural language in psychotherapy research now and in the future. *American Journal of Psychotherapy.* 54:305-311.

Gottschalk LA and Bechtel RJ. (1982) The measurement of anxiety through the computer analysis of verbal samples. *Comprehensive Psychiatry*: 23:4 (July/August).

Gottschalk LA and Bechtel RJ. (1989) Artificial intelligence and the computerization of the content analysis of natural language. *Artificial Intelligence in Medicine.* 1:131-111.

Gottschalk LA and Bechtel R. (1995) Computerized measurement of the content analysis of natural language for use in biomedical and neuropsychiatric research, *Computer Methods and Programs in Biomedicine*: 47:123-130.

Gottschalk LA and Bechtel RJ. (2003) *PCAD 2000—Psychiatric Content Analysis and Diagnosis.* Corona del Mar, CA: GB Software (4607 Perham Road; Corona del Mar, CA 92625).

Gottschalk LA, Bechtel RJ, Buchman TA, Ray SE. (2003) Computerized content analysis of conversational interactions. *CIN: Computers, Informatics, Nursing.* 21:249-258.

Gottschalk LA, Bechtel RJ, Buchman TA, Ray SE. (2003b) A computerized measure of quality of life derived from the content analysis of natural language. *Research Communications in Biological Psychology and Psychiatry.* 27:3-14.

Gottschalk LA, Bechtel RJ, Buchman TA, Ray SE. (2004) Measurement of hope and associated neuropsychiatric dimensions by the computerized content analysis of speech and verbal texts. In: Jacklin Elliott (Ed.) *Interdisciplinary Perspectives on Hope.* Nova Science Publishers. (pp.205-220).

Gottschalk LA, Bechtel RJ, Maguire GA, Harrington DE, Levinson D, Franklin DL, Caracamo D. (2000) Computerized measurement of cognitive impairment and associated neuropsychiatric dimensions. *Comprehensive Psychiatry.* 41:326-333.

Gottschalk LA, Bechtel RJ, Maguire GA, Katz M, Levinson DM, Harrington DE, Nakamura K, Franklin DL. (2002) Computerized detection of cognitive impairment and associated neuropsychiatric dimensions from the content analysis of verbal samples. *American Journal of Drug and Alcohol Abuse.* 28:653-668.

Gottschalk LA, DeFrancisco D, Bechtel RJ. (2002) Computerized content analysis of some adolescent writings of Napoleon Bonaparte. A test of the validity of the method. *Journal of Nervous and Mental Disease.* 190:542-548.

Gottschalk LA, Fronczek J, Abel L, Buchsbaum MS, Fallon JH. (2001) The neurobiology of anxiety, anxiety-displacement, and anxiety denial. *Psychotherapy and Psychosomatics.* 70:17-24.

Gottschalk LA and Gleser GC. (1969) *The Measurement of Psychological States Through the Content Analysis of Verbal Behavior.* Berkeley, Los Angeles: California: The University of California Press.

Gottschalk LA and Gottschalk LH. (1999) Computerized content analysis of the Unabomber's writings. *American Journal of Forensic Psychiatry.* 20:5-31.

Gottschalk, LA, Hausmann, C, Brown, JS. (1975) A computerized scoring system for use with content analysis scales. *Comprehensive Psychiatry.* 16:77-90.

Gottschalk LA, Holcombe R, Jackson D, Bechtel RJ. (2003) The effects of anticancer chemotherapeutic drugs upon cognitive function and other neuropsychiatric dimensions in breast cancer patients. *Methods and Findings in Experimental and Clinical Pharmacology.* 25:117-122.

Gottschalk LA, Lolas F, Viney LL. (Eds.). (1986) *Content Analysis of Verbal Behavior. Significance in Clinical Medicine and Psychiatry.* Berlin, Heidelberg, New York, Tokyo: Springer-Verlag.

Gottschalk LA, Winget CN, Gleser GC. (1969) *Manual of Instructions for Using the Gottschalk-Gleser Content Analysis Scales: Anxiety, Hostility, Social Alienation-Personal Disorganization.* Los Angeles, Berkeley, University of California Press.

Guinn C and Hubal R. (2003) Extracting emotional information from the text of spoken dialog. *Proceedings of the International Conference on User Modeling Workshop, Assessing and Adapting to User Attitudes and Affect: Why, When and How?*, June 22, 2003, Pittsburgh, PA. Journal Genie website. (2004) http://www.journalgenie.com/.

Koch U and Schofer G (Hrsg.). (1986) *Sprachinhaltsanalyse in der psychosomatiscshen und psychiatrischen Forschung. Grundlagen und Anwendungsstudien mit den Affektskalen von Gottschalk und Gleser.* Weinheim und Munchen: Psychologie Verlags Union.

Larsson S and Traum D. (2000) Information state and dialogue management in the TRINDI dialogue move engine toolkit. In *Natural Language Engineering* Special Issue on Best Practice in Spoken Language Dialogue Systems Engineering, pp. 323-340. Cambridge University Press, U.K.

Lavid NR, Grayden TJ, Gottschalk LA, Bechtel RJ. (2002) Computerized assessment of the enforced hospitalization and medication from notes of hospitalized psychiatric inpatients. *American Journal of Forensic Psychiatry*. 23:55-69.

Liu H, Lieberman H, and Selker T. (2003) A model of textual affect sensing using real-world knowledge. *Proceedings of the 2003 International Conference on Intelligent User Interfaces*, IUI 2003, pp.125-132. January 12-15, 2003, Miami, FL.

Luborsky L. (1995) Are common factors across different psychotherapies the main explanation for the Dodo bird verdict that "Everyone has won so all shall have prizes"? *Clinical Psychology: Science and Practice*, 2:106-109.

Luborsky L, Rosenthal R, Diguer L, Andrusyna TP, Berman JS, Levitt JT, Seligman DA, Krause ED. (2002) The Dodo bird verdict is alive and well—mostly. *Clinical Psychology: Science and Practice*. 9:2-12.

Madden S. (1999) WebEvaluator: deducing emotion and personality from web pages. http://www.cs.berkeley.edu/~madden/WebEvaluator/WebEvaluator.htm.

Maguire GA, Gottschalk LA, Riley GD, Franklin DL, Bechtel RJ, Ashurst J. (1999) Stuttering: Neuropsychiatric features measured by the content analysis of speech and the effect of risperidone on stuttering severity. *Comprehensive Psychiatry*. 40:308-314.

Reynolds WM. (2001) Psychiatric Content Analysis and Diagnosis (PCAD 2000). Barbara S. Plake, James C. Impara, Linda L. Murphy (Eds.) *The Fourteenth Mental Measurements Yearbook*. The University of Nebraska Press.

Rosenzweig S. (1936) Some implicit common factors in diverse methods of psychotherapy. *American Journal of Orthopsychiatry*. 6:412-415, 1936.

Subasic P. (2000) Affect analysis of text using fuzzy semantic typing. *The Sixth ACM SIGKDD International Conference on Knowledge Discovery and Data Mining*. Boston, August 20-23.

Weizenbaum J. (1966) ELIZA - A computer program for the study of natural language communication between man and machine. *Communications of the ACM*, 9:36-45.

Winget C, Seligman R, Rauh RL, Gleser GC. (1979) Social alienation-personal disorganization assessment in disturbed and normal adolescents. *Journal of Nervous and Mental Disease*. 167:282-287.

Zhe Z and Boucouvalas AC. (2002) Text-to-emotion engine for real time Internet communication." *International Symposium on Communication Systems, Networks and DSPs*, pp. 164-168. 15-17 July 2002, Staffordshire University, UK.

In: New Psychological Tests and Testing Research
Editor: Lydia S. Boyar, pp. 105-120

ISBN: 978-1-60021-570-4
© 2007 Nova Science Publishers, Inc.

Chapter 5

THE PSYCHOMETRIC PROPERTIES OF THE EYSENCK PERSONALITY QUESTIONNAIRE-BRIEF VERSION

*Toru Sato**
Shippensburg University
Shippensburg, Pennsylvania, USA

ABSTRACT

The short-scale of the Eysenck Personality Questionnaire-revised (EPQR-S; Eysenck and Eysenck, 1992) is a 48-item personality questionnaire primarily designed to measure an individual's level of introversion-extraversion and neuroticism. Although Francis, Brown, and Philipchalk, (1992) have created the Eysenck Personality Questionnaire revised - abbreviated (EPQR-A), an even briefer version of the EPQR-S, the reliability coefficients of the measures have been less than satisfactory (Forrest, Lewis, and Shevlin, 2000). Since brevity and reliability are both extremely important, the goal of the present study was to create a briefer version of the EPQR-S that is more reliable than the EPQR-A. This was achieved by making slight alterations in the item content as well as the response format of the EPQR-S. In study 1, 257 participants completed the EPQR-S once and the EPQ-BV twice. The measures in this version of the questionnaire revealed high internal consistency and test-retest reliability. The measures in the EPQ-BV correlated highly with the corresponding original measures in the EPQR-S. A principal component analysis revealed a solution with factor loadings accurately reflecting the primary measures of the EPQR-S. In study 2, 467 participants completed the EPQ-BV. A confirmatory factor analysis using LISREL 8 (Jöreskog and Sörbom, 1999) with all of the items of the scale as observed variables and introversion-extraversion and neuroticism as latent variables revealed acceptable goodness of fit. These findings are discussed in relation to the psychometric properties of the EPQR-A and the original version of the EPQR-S.

Key words: Personality, Introversion-Extraversion, Neuroticism, Assessment.

---

* Correspondence concerning this book chapter should be addressed to: Toru Sato, Department of Psychology, 213 Franklin Science Center, Shippensburg University, Shippensburg, Pennsylvania 17257-2299, USA

According to Eysenck (1990), there are three central "supertraits" that are essential in understanding individual differences in personality. These personality traits are introversion-extraversion, neuroticism, and psychoticism. Compared to introverted individuals, extraverted individuals naturally have a lower arousal level. This makes extraverted individuals seek stimulation to raise their arousal level. In contrast, the naturally high arousal level of introverted individuals makes them avoid stimulation as much as possible. This is considered to be why introverts tend to like quiet activities while extraverts tend to like stimulating activities (Eysenck, 1984). The second personality dimension in Eysenck's (1990) theory is labeled neuroticism (or sometimes referred to as emotional stability). Individuals who are high in neuroticism tend to have a highly reactive autonomic nervous system, making them emotionally unstable. In contrast, the autonomic nervous system of individuals who are low in neuroticism are not highly reactive, making them more emotionally stable (Eysenck, 1990). Third and last personality trait dimension in Eysenck's (1990) theory is psychoticism. Individuals high in psychoticism tend to disregard common sense and behave impulsively and aggressively (Eysenck, Barrett, Wilson, and Jackson, 1992). Though psychoticism is considered to be the third trait dimension in Eysenck's theory, most interest in his work on personality traits has focused on the introversion-extraversion and the neuroticism dimensions (e.g., Fink and Neubauer, 2004; Geen, 1984; Ramirez-Maestre, Martinez, and Zarazaga, 2004).

Eysenck (1952) attributes much of the individual differences in the dimension of introversion-extraversion to a neurological system known and the ascending reticular activating system (ARAS). The ARAS, located in the reticular formation, a central part of the brain stem, functions in part to excite the cerebral cortex in reaction to sensory stimuli. Eysenck (1990) suggested that introverted individuals tend to have a more active ARAS than extraverted individuals. This makes the highly introverted individuals have higher capacity for excitation and lower capacity for inhibition compared to extraverted people. According to this theory, the introvert's higher level of arousal is caused by allowing more sensory information to be processed in their system (compared to extraverts). Research has found that, when compared to extraverts, introverts tend to have larger pupil size prior to specific visual stimulation (Frith 1977; Stelmack and Mandelzys, 1975). Introverts also have greater electrodermal skin conductance response to sound than extraverts (Crider and Lunn, 1971). Due to this interesting characteristic of introverted individuals, they are easily overaroused in situations with high levels of stimulation (Eysenck, 1990). In fact, the average arousal level of introverted people is naturally higher than those of extraverts. Research by Wilson (1990), for example, revealed that introverts naturally have a higher skin conductance level than extraverts. This naturally high level of arousal makes the introverted individuals shy away from situations and places with high levels of stimulation. Since they are too aroused most of the time, they are motivated to find places with less stimulation to calm themselves down. If they cannot find places with less stimulation, they tend to react to high levels of stimulation by minimizing the amount of sensory input entering their system. For instance, research has shown that, compared to extraverts, introverts are known to be faster pupil constrictors in response to light (Holmes, 1967).

In comparison, since extraverted individuals tend to have a less active ARAS than introverted individuals, extraverted individuals have low capacity for excitation and high capacity for inhibition. Extraverts are assumed to have this characteristic because, compared to introverts, they allow much less sensory information into their system. Consistent with this theory, studies has revealed that extraverts have a higher sensory threshold than introverts (Eysenck, 1967). This characteristic of extraverts tends to make them typically underaroused in many situations. Compared to introverts, extraverts have been found to have lower levels of waking cortical arousal according to EEG readings (Frigon, 1976; Marton, 1972). Research has also suggested that extraverts have lower standing electrodermal skin conductance levels than introverts (Desjardins, 1976; Fowles, Roberts, and Nagel, 1977). Because they are typically underaroused, extraverts generally tend to welcome higher levels of stimulation. For example, extraverts are also known to be faster pupil dilators in reaction to visual information than introverts (Holmes, 1967). In addition, extraverts have been found to feel more comfortable than introverts in situations with high levels of stimulation (e.g., Geen, 1984; Zuckerman, 1998). In his research study, Geen (1984) found that when extraverts and introverts were given a choice of various intensities of noise to be exposed to, extraverts chose a higher level of intensity of noise than their introverted counterparts.

Eysenck (1990) suggested that individuals who are high in neuroticism tend to have a highly reactive autonomic nervous system, making them emotionally unstable. More specifically, he attributed the cause of high neuroticism to greater responsivity of the sympathetic nervous system (Eysenck, 1990). In contrast, the autonomic nervous system of individuals who are low in neuroticism have a less responsive sympathetic nervous system and thus are not as emotionally reactive as the individuals with high levels of neuroticism. Although there is more support for Eysenck's (1997) theory on introversion-extraversion than his theory on neuroticism, there has been some research supporting the theory behind neuroticism as a personality dimension. For example, Harvey and Hirschmann, (1980) exposed introverted and extraverted individuals with high and low levels of neuroticism to slides of photographs depicting people who died violently. They studied the heart rates and the orienting responses of these individuals after exposing them to the slides. The results revealed that initial heart rate accelerative responses, indicative of responsivity of the sympathetic nervous system, were evidenced in introverted individuals with high levels of neuroticism. In contrast, initial decelerative responses, indicative of orienting, were evidenced in extraverted individuals with low levels of neuroticism. These findings are consistent with both the theory on introversion-extraversion as well as the theory on neuroticism developed by Eysenck (1990). The higher emotional responsivity of individuals high in neuroticism is assumed to make these individuals more emotionally unstable than the less neurotic individuals (Eysenck, 1990).

Perhaps partly due to the fact that it is the most recently developed personality dimension among the three "supertraits", the third personality dimension in Eysenck's (1990) theory, known as psychoticism, has received the least amount of attention among researchers. Individuals high in psychoticism tend to disregard common sense and behave impulsively and, in some cases, aggressively toward others (Eysenck, 1990). Eysenck (1990) speculates that perhaps neurotransmitters such as monoamine oxidase (MAO) and hormones such as testosterone may be related to this personality dimension. Though psychoticism is considered to be the third trait dimension in Eysenck's theory, most interest in this work has focused on the introversion-extraversion and the neuroticism dimensions (e.g., Fink and Neubauer, 2004; Geen, 1984; Ramirez-Maestre, Martinez, and Zarazaga, 2004).

For many years, researchers have continued to carefully develop questionnaires designed to measure individuals on these personality traits (Eysenck, 1952, 1959; Eysenck and Eysenck, 1964, 1975, 1992; Francis, Brown, and Philipchalk, 1992). These researchers have extended their efforts as far as embedding a "lie scale" into the questionnaire. Since the creation of the original version, many efforts have been made to revise and improve this personality test (Eysenck, 1952, 1959; Eysenck and Eysenck, 1964, 1975, 1992). These revisions have typically caused the questionnaire to include increasingly more items and longer to administer. The early Maudsley Medical Questionnaire (MMQ) contained 40 items (Eysenck, 1952). After this, a revised version known as the Maudsley Personality Inventory (MPI), an instrument containing 48 items, was developed (Eysenck, 1959). Five years later, the Eysenck Personality Inventory (EPI) consisting of 57 items (Eysenck and Eysenck, 1964a) was introduced and 11 years after this, Eysenck and Eysenck, (1975) introduced the Eysenck Personality Questionnaire (EPQ), a questionnaire containing 90 items. In 1985, further revisions were made and the Revised Eysenck Personality Questionnaire (EPQR) was created (Eysenck, Eysenck, and Barrett, 1985). This instrument consisted of 100 items (Eysenck, Eysenck, and Barrett, 1985). More recently, the Eysenck Personality Profiler-short containing 180 items (Eysenck, Wilson, and Jackson, 1999) and the Eysenck Personality Profiler containing 420 items (Eysenck and Wilson, 1999) were developed. This gradual increase in length has primarily increased the reliability of the measures. There are, however, some disadvantages of longer personality tests. A 420 item or even an 180 item questionnaire may not be practical to use in elaborate research projects that consist of additional experimental procedures that are time consuming.

Because of the impractical nature of longer questionnaires, researchers have developed a series of shorter instruments measuring these personality dimensions. In 1958, Eysenck developed two short indices of introversion-extraversion and neuroticism, each containing only 6 items, based on the Maudsley Personality Inventory (Eysenck, 1958). A few years later, Eysenck and Eysenck (1964) developed another pair of 6-item scales to measure introversion-extraversion and neuroticism, based on the Eysenck Personality Inventory. Due to the extremely short nature of these scales, however, their reliability estimates have been compromised (Francis, Brown, and Philipchalk, 1992). More recently, however, researchers have attempted to create a version neither too short nor too long for increased reliability and practicality (Eysenck and Eysenck, 1975, 1992). This version is known as the short-scale of the Eysenck Personality Questionnaire-revised (EPQR-S; Eysenck and Eysenck, 1992). The EPQR-S is a 48-item personality questionnaire primarily designed to measure an individual's level of introversion-extraversion, neuroticism, and psychoticism. Around the same time, Francis, Brown, and Philipchalk, (1992) created the Eysenck Personality Questionnaire revised - abbreviated (EPQR-A), a very brief version of the EPQR-S. Although the brevity of this scale makes it very useful, some researchers have found that the reliability coefficients of the measures (especially the psychoticism and the lie scales) have been less than satisfactory (Forrest, Lewis, and Shevlin, 2000; Shevlin, Bailey, and Adamson, 2002). Furthermore, because the original version was created in Great Britain, some of the items in the EPQR-S and EPQR-A are more suitable for a British population than for an American population. Since this measure is also administered in the United States, it would be very useful to reword some of these items so that it is suitable for both American and British populations.

STUDY 1

Since brevity, reliability, and item content are all extremely important factors in the development of a questionnaire, the goal of the present research project was to create a briefer version of the EPQR-S that is both suitable to an American population and more reliable than the EPQR-A. To create this new briefer version (EPQ-BV), a number of adjustments were made. First, the psychoticism measure, which is both rarely used (e.g., Fink and Neubauer, 2004; Geen, 1984; Ramirez-Maestre et al., 2004) and associated with various psychometric problems (Ferrando, 2003; Forrest et al., 2000), was removed from the scale. Furthermore, since the lie scale can be replaced by embedding items from other scales measuring social desirability if necessary (e.g., Crowne and Marlowe, 1960), this scale was eliminated for the sake of brevity as well. In addition, the response format was changed from a "yes-no" response format to a five-point Likert scale in order to increase the reliability of the measures. Lastly, because one of the items for the introversion-extraversion measure included an expression rarely used in the United States, it was slightly reworded (see Method section). With the exception of the one wording change mentioned above, the remaining items of the EPQ-BV were identical to the introversion-extraversion and neuroticism scales of the original EPQR-S (Eysenck and Eysenck, 1992). The purpose of Study 1 was to examine the concurrent validity, internal consistency, test-retest reliability and factor structure of the EPQ-BV.

METHOD

Participants

Participants were recruited from undergraduate psychology classes and received extra credit for their participation. A total of 289 (119 male, 166 female, 4 unspecified) undergraduate university students participated in this study. Of the 289 participants, we obtained data that was complete and suitable for analysis from 257 (88 male, 166 female, 3 unspecified) of them (see procedure section for details). The mean age of the 257 participants was 20.1 and the ages ranged from 18 to 29.

Measures

Eysenck Personality Questionnaire Revised-Short Form

The Eysenck Personality Questionnaire Revised-Short form is a questionnaire that consists of three measures corresponding to the three personality traits in Eysenck's (1990) theory and a lie scale (Eysenck and Eysenck, 1992). All four measures consist of 12 items. There are 2 reversed items in the introversion-extraversion measure, 7 reversed items in the psychoticism measure, and 9 reversed items in the lie scale. There are no reversed items in the neuroticism measure. The response format for all items is dichotomous ("yes" or "no"). With the exception of the psychoticism measure, all measures have good internal consistency and test-retest reliability (see Eysenck and Eysenck, 1992).

Eysenck Personality Questionnaire-Brief Version

The Eysenck Personality Questionnaire-Brief Version is a newly revised version of the EPQR-S to measure individuals on two primary personality traits in Eysenck's (1990) theory. It consists of two measures, one for introversion-extraversion and one for neuroticism. The psychoticism and lie scales were not included in the EPQ-BV for the sake of brevity.

In addition to the changes mentioned above, the response format the EPQ-BV was changed from a "yes" or "no" format to a five-point Likert scale format ranging from "not at all" (1), "slightly" (2), "moderately" (3), "very much" (4), to "extremely" (5) to increase internal consistency. Lastly, because one of the items for the introversion-extraversion measure included an expression rarely used in the United States, it was slightly reworded. The word "bustle" in the item "Do you like plenty of bustle and excitement around you?" is a term rarely used in United States. Therefore, this item "Do you like plenty of bustle and excitement around you?" was changed to "Do you like plenty of action and excitement around you?" With the exception of this one wording change, the remaining items were identical to the introversion-extraversion and neuroticism scales of the original EPQR-S (Eysenck and Eysenck, 1992). The final version of the EPQ-BV consisted of twenty-four items (12 introversion-extraversion and 12 neuroticism). Past work on the EPQ-BV has suggested that it has a relatively robust factor structure (Sato. 2005) and high internal consistency (Sato, 2004). The coefficient alphas were .92 for the introversion-extraversion measure and .90 for the neuroticism measure. The test-retest reliability levels of the EPQ-BV with time intervals of 2-4 weeks were .92 for both the introversion-extraversion and neuroticism scales (see Sato, 2005 for details).

Procedure

The entire data collection process continued for five weeks. The questionnaires were completed in three sessions two weeks apart from each other. In the first session, participants were randomly divided into two groups. In the first group, 144 undergraduate university students completed the EPQR-S. In the second group, 145 undergraduate university students completed the EPQ-BV. In the second session, 138 of the undergraduate university students who completed the EPQR-S in the first session completed the EPQ-BV. In addition, 131 of the undergraduate university students who completed the EPQ-BV in the first session completed the EPQR-S. In the third and final session, 261 of the participants who completed the questionnaires in both session 1 and 2 completed the EPQ-BV once again.

When participants arrived at each session, they read and signed an informed consent form. After the signed informed consent forms were collected the experimenter said, "Please complete this questionnaire by circling the answer corresponding to how characteristic these items are of you. Please do not spend too much time thinking about each item. Just write down the first thing that comes to mind." All participants were thanked for their participation and fully debriefed after the third session. Of the 261 participants with complete data, four participants scored 6 or higher on the lie scale of the EPQR-S. The data of these participants were omitted in all subsequent analyses.

RESULTS

Psychometric Properties and Correlations

An examination of the order effect of the questionnaires administered in the first two sessions using t-tests did not yield any significant effects. The coefficient alphas for the introversion-extraversion, neuroticism, psychoticism, and lie scales in the EPQR-S were .79, .78, 58, and .72 respectively. The coefficient alphas for the introversion-extraversion and neuroticism scales in the EPQ-BV administered in the first two sessions were .92 and .91 respectively. The corresponding alpha levels for the introversion-extraversion and neuroticism scales of the EPQ-BV in the third session were .91 and .90 respectively. The test-retest reliability values of the two scales of the EPQ-BV used in the present study were .93 for introversion-extraversion and .91 for the neuroticism measure. Consistent with most research concerning the introversion-extraversion and neuroticism measures (e.g., Eysenck, Eysenck, and Barrett, 1985; Francis, 1993), t-tests revealed that there were no significant sex differences on the introversion-extraversion scale but women scored higher than men on the neuroticism scale on both the EPQR-S, $t(252) = 4.35$, $p < .01$, and the EPQ-BV, $t(252) = 4.42$, $p < .01$. Means and standard deviations of the four measures by sex are presented in table 1.

Table 1. Means and Standard Deviations by Sex for EPQ-BV and EPQR-S

Variable	Male (M)	Male (SD)	Female (M)	Female (SD)
1. Extraversion EPQ-BV	42.58	9.11	42.09	8.97
2. Neuroticism EPQ-BV	26.93	9.96	30.54	9.38*
3. Extraversion EPQR-S	8.72	3.41	8.62	3.28
4. Neuroticism EPQR-S	4.47	3.42	6.15	3.17*

*Significant sex difference at $p < .01$
Note: N = 88 (male), 166 (female).

To test the concurrent validity of the new measures in the EPQ-BV, the correlations between the new measures and the corresponding original measures were examined. The results of the correlation analyses are reported in table 2. The measures of the EPQ-BV correlated highly (.89 and .90) with the corresponding measures in the original EPQR-S. The correlations between introversion-extraversion and neuroticism ranged between -.24 and -.28

Table 2. Correlations between the measures of the EPQ-BV and EPQR-S.

Variable	1	2	3	4
1. Extraversion EPQ-BV	1.00	-.25*	.90*	-.28*
2. Neuroticism EPQ-BV		1.00	-.24*	.89*
3. Extraversion EPQR-S			1.00	-.26
4. Neuroticism EPQR-S				1.00

*$p < .001$
Note: N = 269.

Principal Component Analysis

A principal component analysis on all items in the EPQ-BV administered in session three was conducted. An examination of the scree plot of eigenvalues revealed that the curve leveled off after the first two factors. These two factors (both with eigenvalues above four) were retained, and an oblique rotation factor analysis restricted to two factors was conducted. The two factors combined accounted for approximately 53.4% of the total variance. Factor loadings generated by these analyses are presented in table 3. All of the 24 items loaded above .50 on one of the two factors.

Table 3. Factor Loadings for the Principal Component Analysis on EPQ-BV

Items	Item #	Factor 1 Extraversion	Factor 2 Neuroticism
Are you a talkative person?	1	.741	-.013
Are you rather lively?	3	.813	.068
Do you enjoy meeting new people?	5	.619	.247
Can you usually let yourself go and enjoy yourself at a lively party?	7	.757	.242
Do you usually take the initiative in making new friends?	9	.732	.125
Can you easily get some life into a rather dull party?	11	.838	-.133
Do you tend to keep in the background on social occasions?	13	.606	-.288
Do you like mixing with people?	15	.689	-.249
Do you like to plenty of action and excitement around you?	17	.741	-.102
Are you mostly quiet when you are with other people?	19	.653	-.211
Do other people think of you as being very lively?	21	.772	-.045
Can you get a party going?	23	.854	-.147
Does you mood often go up and down?	2	-.110	.741
Do you ever feel miserable for no reason?	4	-.083	.667
Are you an irritable person?	6	-.118	.655
Are your feelings easily hurt?	8	-.146	.644
Do you often feel "fed-up"?	10	-.110	.689
Would you call yourself a nervous person?	12	-.187	.761
Are you a worrier?	14	-.231	.762
Would you call yourself tense or "highly-strung"?	16	-.050	.721
Do you worry too long after an embarrassing experience?	18	-.244	.514
Do you suffer from nerves?	20	-.171	.775
Do you often feel lonely?	22	-.226	.627
Are you often troubled about feelings of guilt	24	-.098	.720

Note: N = 261.

The first factor accounted for approximately 32.3 percent of the variance. All twelve of the items loading on this factor were the items intended to measure introversion-extraversion. The factor loadings for all of the items in this factor were .60 or above (see table 3). As expected, all items for the neuroticism measure loaded lower than .30 and higher than -.30 on this first factor. Furthermore, the reworded introversion-extraversion item, "Do you like plenty of action and excitement around you?" also loaded highly on this factor (factor loading of .74). The second factor accounted for approximately 21.1 percent of the variance. It consisted of all twelve items intended to measure neuroticism. Factor loadings for all of the items in this factor were .51 or above (see table 3). As expected, all items for the introversion-extraversion measure loaded lower than .30 and higher than -.30 on this second factor.

DISCUSSION

The coefficient alphas for the introversion-extraversion and neuroticism scales in the EPQ-BV were higher than those of the original EPQR-S in the present study. These values were also higher than values reported for the EPQR-S and the EPQR-A in the past (Eysenck and Eysenck, 1992; Francis et al., 1992). The coefficient alphas for the introversion-extraversion and neuroticism scales of the EPQR-S are typically in the .78-.87 and .79-.83 range, respectively (Eysenck and Eysenck, 1992; Francis et al., 1992). Depending on the population sampled, the coefficient alphas for the introversion-extraversion and neuroticism scales of the EPQR-A are .74-.84 and .73-.77, respectively (Francis et al., 1992). The test-retest reliability values of the two scales of the EPQ-BV (.93 for introversion-extraversion and .91 for neuroticism) are comparable to other measures of introversion-extraversion and neuroticism such as the EPQR-S (Eysenck and Eysenck, 1992).

The introversion-extraversion scale of the EPQ-BV correlated highly with the introversion-extraversion measure in the original EPQR-S. Likewise, the neuroticism scale of the EPQ-BV correlated highly with the neuroticism measure in the original EPQR-S. These correlations are comparable to the correlations reported with the measures in the EPQR-A (Francis et al., 1992). In the study conducted by Francis and his colleagues (1992), the correlations between the EPQR-S and the EPQR-A for introversion-extraversion and neuroticism ranged between .92-.95 and .92-.94, respectively. Perhaps the two-four week time lag in between the two questionnaires contributed to the slightly lower correlations in the present study. The correlations between introversion-extraversion and neuroticism were comparable to the correlations typically reported with the measures in the EPQR-S and the EPQR-A. Though there has been much variability, the correlations between introversion-extraversion and neuroticism typically range between -.01 and -.37 (e.g., Aluja, Garcia, and Garcia, 2003; Eysenck and Eysenck, 1992; Francis et al., 1992; Shevlin, Bailey, and Adamson, 2002).

To examine its factor structure, a principal component analysis was conducted on the EPQ-BV. The results revealed a two-factor solution accounting for a total of 53.4% of the variance with factor loadings accurately reflecting the primary measures of the EPQR-S (introversion-extraversion and neuroticism). These findings suggest that the EPQ-BV is a short, practical, and most importantly, reliable instrument for measuring individual differences in the two central personality dimensions of Eysenck's (1952) theory.

STUDY 2

Since the results of the principal component factor analysis in Study 1 revealed a factor solution consistent with the two measures of the EPQ-BV, the next step was to test this factor structure using confirmatory factor analysis with a larger sample. In order to conduct this analysis, we used structural equation models with the computer program LISREL 8 (Jöreskog and Sörbom, 1999). Considering the structure of the EPQ-BV, all of the items of the scale were entered as observed variables and introversion-extraversion and neuroticism were entered as latent variables. Each observed variable (i.e., questionnaire item) was entered as loading onto the corresponding latent variables (i.e., introversion-extraversion or neuroticism). Confirmatory factor analysis yields estimated parameters for loadings of items on specified factors, the error variances associated with the loadings, and the correlations among the factors.

Although LISREL 8 outputs reveal a vast number of goodness of fit indices, we used six different goodness of fit indices to examine how well the data derived from this instrument fits Eysenck's (1990) theoretical model. This decision was based on the following suggestions about goodness of fit indices. Although the χ^2 goodness of fit index is one of the most widely used tests, it assumes that the variables are normally distributed and has the tendency to reject satisfactory models when large sample sizes are used. After careful examination, Hoyle and Panter (1995) suggest the goodness of fit index (GFI), comparative fit index (CFI), incremental fit index (IFI), standardized root mean square residual (SRMR) as reliable goodness of fit indices across sample-size and violation / nonviolation of distributional assumptions. Various researchers also suggest the root mean square error of approximation (RMSEA) as a reliable goodness of fit index that is less sensitive to violations of distributional assumptions (Jöreskog and Sörbom, 1996; Raykov, 1998; Steiger, 1990). The findings of an extensive Monte Carlo study conducted by Hu and Bentler (1998, 1999) suggested that the SRMR and a set of alternatives that include the CFI are reliable indices to distinguish true and untrue models most accurately across sample-size and violation / nonviolation of distributional assumptions. Due to these reports by statisticians in the field, the χ^2, GFI, CFI, IFI, SRMR, and RMSEA will be used to assess the goodness of fit of the EPQ-BV to Eysenck's (1990) model.

Although confirmatory factor analysis has never been conducted on the EPQ-BV, various researchers have conducted confirmatory factor analysis with the EPQR-S and EPQR-A. For instance, Aluja, Garcia, and Garcia (2003) conducted a confirmatory factor analysis on the EPQR-S and found that the GFI for their data was .85. They also reported a CFI of .73, and an RMSEA of .05 (Aluja, Garcia, and Garcia, 2003). In another research project examining the factor structure of the EPQR-A, Forrest, Lewis, and Shevlin (2000) found that the RMSEA for the EPQR-A was .0479. A confirmatory factor analysis in a different study on the EPQR-A yielded an RMSEA of .062 and SRMR of .092 (Shevlin, Bailey, and Adamson, 2002). Despite the fact that there seems to be a fairly wide range of indices suggesting different levels of fit, the goodness of fit indices for the EPQ-BV were expected to be in a similar range to those reported above.

METHOD

Participants

Participants were recruited from undergraduate psychology classes and received extra credit for their participation. A total of 467 undergraduate university students (224 male, 238 female, 5 unspecified) participated in the study. The mean age of the participants was 20.3 and the ages ranged from 18 to 28.

Measures

Eysenck Personality Questionnaire-Brief Version (EPQ-BV: Sato, 2005). The Eysenck Personality Questionnaire-Brief Version is a 24 item questionnaire (12 introversion-extraversion and 12 neuroticism) that measures degrees of introversion-extraversion and neuroticism. Participants respond to the questions using a 5-point Likert-type scale with responses ranging from *not at all* (1), *slightly* (2), *moderately* (3), *very much* (4), to *extremely* (5). The higher the score the more extraverted that person was and the lower the score the more introverted the person was. Details regarding the item content and psychometric properties of this measure are discussed in the Method and Results sections of Study 1.

Procedure

Participants reported to a research laboratory room in groups of 15-25 individuals. When they arrived they read and signed an informed consent form. After the signed informed consent forms were collected the experimenter said, "Please complete this questionnaire by circling the answer corresponding to how characteristic these items are of you. Please do not spend too much time thinking about each item. Just write down the first thing that comes to mind." The participants then completed the Eysenck Personality Questionnaire-Brief Version (EPQ-BV: Sato, 2005). After the EPQ-BV was completed, the researchers debriefed the participants and thanked them for participating.

RESULTS

The coefficient alphas for the introversion-extraversion and neuroticism scales in the EPQ-BV were .93 and .91 respectively. These figures are comparable to the results in Study 1 and slightly higher than those reported for the original EPQR-S (Eysenck and Eysenck, 1992) and the EPQR-A (Francis et al., 1992).

In order to confirm the factor structure of the EPQ-BV generated in Study 1, a confirmatory factor analysis using LISREL 8 (Jöreskog and Sörbom, 1999) with all of the items of the scale as observed variables and introversion-extraversion and neuroticism as latent variables was conducted. LISREL 8 outputs reveal a vast number of goodness of fit indices. As explained earlier, however, the $\ulcorner^2$, GFI, CFI, IFI, SRMR, and RMSEA will be used to assess the goodness of fit of the EPQ-BV to Eysenck's (1990) model of personality.

The χ^2 test revealed a $\chi^2(1249) = 2513$, $p < .10$, suggesting good fit for the model. Since the χ^2 goodness of fit index assumes that the variables are normally distributed and the items in the EPQ-BV are not all normally distributed, results using this test should be taken with caution. The goodness of fit index (GFI) measures how much the model fits the data compared to having no model at all. The GFI for this analysis was .85. The following were the results of the other goodness of fit indices, both the comparative fit index (CFI) and incremental fit index (IFI) were .80, the root mean square error of approximation (RMSEA) was .051, and the standardized root mean square residual (SRMR) was .052. All items revealed maximum likelihood estimates with t-values above 1.96 (i.e., $p < .05$). Factor loadings generated by this analysis are presented in table 4. Consistent with the findings in Study 1 as well as other research examining the correlations between introversion-extraversion and neuroticism (Eysenck and Eysenck, 1992; Francis et al., 1992; Forrest et al., 2000; Shevlin et al., 2002), factor correlations in the present confirmatory factor analysis indicated that the introversion-extraversion measure correlated negatively with neuroticism (r = -.26).

Table 4. Factor Loadings for Confirmatory Factor Analysis on EPQ-BV

Items	Item#	Extraversion	Neuroticism
Are you a talkative person?	1	.641*	-
Are you rather lively?	3	.693*	-
Do you enjoy meeting new people?	5	.615*	-
Can you usually let yourself go and enjoy yourself at a lively party?	7	.593*	-
Do you usually take the initiative in making new friends?	9	.638*	-
Can you easily get some life into a rather dull party?	11	.702*	-
Do you tend to keep in the background on social occasions?	13	.637*	-
Do you like mixing with people?	15	.665*	-
Do you like to plenty of action and excitement around you?	17	.649*	-
Are you mostly quiet when you are with other people?	19	.647*	-
Do other people think of you as being very lively?	21	.632*	-
Can you get a party going?	23	694*	-
Does you mood often go up and down?	2	-	.681*
Do you ever feel miserable for no reason?	4	-	.643*
Are you an irritable person?	6	-	.637*
Are your feelings easily hurt?	8	-	.629*
Do you often feel "fed-up"?	10	-	.641*
Would you call yourself a nervous person?	12	-	.686*
Are you a worrier?	14	-	.672*
Would you call yourself tense or "highly-strung"?	16	-	.594*
Do you worry too long after an embarrassing experience?	18	-	.506*
Do you suffer from nerves?	20	-	.658*
Do you often feel lonely?	22	-	.616*
Are you often troubled about feelings of guilt	24	-	.609*

*$p < .05$
Note: N = 467.

DISCUSSION

As was found in Study 1, the coefficient alphas for the introversion-extraversion (.93) and neuroticism scales (.91) in the EPQ-BV were slightly higher than those of the original EPQR-S (Eysenck and Eysenck, 1992) and the EPQR-A (Francis et al., 1992). The coefficient alphas for the introversion-extraversion and neuroticism scales of the EPQR-S are typically in the .78-.87 and .79-.83 range, respectively (Eysenck and Eysenck, 1992; Francis et al., 1992). Depending on the population sampled, the coefficient alphas for the introversion-extraversion and neuroticism scales of the EPQR-A are .74-.84 and .73-.77, respectively (Francis et al., 1992). In Study 1, a principal component analysis was conducted on the EPQ-BV. This revealed that the EPQ-BV has a relatively robust factor structure. In Study 2, we tested the model generated by the principal component analysis in Study 1 using confirmatory factor analysis, a method of analysis based on structural equations. As a general guideline, a GFI, CFI, IFI of .90 or above indicates excellent fit and .80 or above suggests adequate fit. An RMSEA and SRMR of .05 or below indicates excellent fit and .08 or below suggests adequate fit. In the present analysis, the GFI was .85, the CFI and IFI were .80, the RMSEA was .051, and the SRMR was .052. Therefore, all of the goodness of fit indices revealed in the present confirmatory factor analysis suggested that the data was an adequate fit to the model.

The results of Study 2 seem comparable to findings of confirmatory factor analyses using structural equations conducted on the EPQR-S and EPQR-A. For example, Aluja, Garcia, and Garcia (2003) conducted a confirmatory factor analysis on the EPQR-S and found that the GFI for their data was .85. They also reported a CFI of .73, and an RMSEA of .05 (Aluja, Garcia, and Garcia, 2003). The findings using confirmatory factor analysis on the EPQR-A seem to vary more. For instance, Forrest, Lewis, and Shevlin (2000) found that their data on the EPQR-A revealed an RMSEA of .0479. In another research study examining the factor structure of the EPQR-A, a confirmatory factor analysis yielded an RMSEA of .062 and SRMR of .092 (Shevlin, Bailey, and Adamson, 2002). Some of these results with the EPQR-S and the EPQR-A indicate more satisfactory fit and some less satisfactory fit than the ones for the EPQ-BV in the present study. Overall, the general findings of the confirmatory factor analysis in Study 2 seem at least comparable with if not slightly better than the majority of the findings using similar analyses on the EPQR-S and the EPQR-A.

GENERAL DISCUSSION

The findings of Study 1 revealed that the EPQ-BV has higher internal consistency than the EPQR-S or the EPQR-A and test-retest reliability that is comparable to the EPQR-S or the EPQR-A. The findings of Study 2 revealed that, though not excellent, the goodness of fit indices of the confirmatory factor analysis revealed that the two-factor model, consisting of all of the items corresponding to the two central "supertraits" in Eysenck's (1990) theory of personality, seems to adequately fit the data. The findings of the confirmatory factor analysis in Study 2 seem to be at least comparable with if not better than the findings using similar analyses on the EPQR-S and the EPQR-A.

The EPQ-BV consists of the most commonly used measures of the original EPQR-S (introversion-extraversion and neuroticism) with only half of the number of items (24 items) in the EPQR-S. The EPQ-BV takes, on average, less than five minutes to complete, has high internal consistency, test-retest reliability, and a relatively robust factor structure. Perhaps this briefer version may serve as a suitable alternative for use in elaborate research that consists of additional experimental procedures that are time consuming.

Although there are countless future considerations for this line of research, three seem to be especially worth noting. Firstly, further replication using a wider range of samples may be necessary to examine the applicability of this measure to other populations. Secondly, since the results of the confirmatory factor analysis indicated that the fit between the data and the model was adequate but not excellent, future work revising this questionnaire may improve how well this questionnaire is able to produce data that fits the theoretical model proposed by Eysenck (1990). Thirdly, another important step for these new measures is to examine their criterion validity. For instance, examining individuals who score high and low on the introversion-extraversion scale in response to varying levels of sensory stimulation may be useful in examining the criterion validity of the introversion-extraversion measure. To examine the criterion validity of the of neuroticism measure, it may be useful to compare physiological changes associated with emotional reactions in response to stress among individuals with high and low levels of neuroticism. Despite the necessity for further research, it is my hope that the EPQ-BV will continue to develop and serve many researchers as a useful tool to examine the correlates of introversion-extraversion and neuroticism as individual difference variables.

REFERENCES

Aluja, A., Garcia, O., and Garcia, L. (2003). A psychometric analysis of the revised Eysenck Personality Questionnaire short-scale. *Personality and Individual Differences, 35*, 449-460.

Crider, A., and Lunn, R. (1971). Electrodermal lability as a personality dimension. *Journal of Experimental Research in Personality, 5*, 145-150.

Crowne, D. P., and Marlowe, D. (1960). A new scale of social desirability independent of psychopathology. *Journal of Consulting Psychology, 24*, 355-360.

Desjardins, E. C. (1976). *The effects of denotative and connotative linguistic meaning and word concreteness on the habituation of the skin conductance response: Extraversion and neuroticism as subject variables.* Unpublished Doctoral Dissertation: University of Ottawa, Canada.

Eysenck, H. J. (1952). *The scientific study of personality.* London: Routledge.

Eysenck, H. J. (1959). *Manual of the Maudsley Personality Inventory.* London: University of London Press.

Eysenck, H. J. (1984). The place of individual differences in a scientific psychology. *Annals of Theoretical Psychology, 1*, 233-2286.

Eysenck, H. J. (1990). Biological dimensions of personality. In L. A. Pervin (Ed.), *Handbook of Personality: Theory and research* (pp. 244-276). New York: Guilford Press.

Eysenck, H. J. (1997). Personality and experimental psychology: The unification of psychology and the possibility of a paradigm. *Journal of Personality and Social Psychology, 73*, 1224-1237.

Eysenck, H. J., Barrett, P., Wilson, G., and Jackson, C. (1992). Primary trait measurement of the 21 components of the PEN system. *European Journal of Psychological Assessments, 8*, 109-117.

Eysenck, H. J., and Eysenck, S. B. G. (1964). *Manual of the Eysenck Personality Questionnaire.* London: University of London Press.

Eysenck, H. J., and Eysenck, S. B. G. (1975). *Manual of the Eysenck Personality Questionnaire.* London: Hodder and Stoughton.

Eysenck, H. J., and Eysenck, S. B. G. (1992). *Manual for the Eysenck Personality Questionnaire -revised.* San Diego, CA: Educational and Industrial Testing Service.

Eysenck, S. B. G., Eysenck, H. J., and Barrett, P. (1985). A revised version of the psychoticism scale. *Personality and Individual Differences, 6*, 21-29.

Eysenck, H. J., and Wilson, G. (1999). *The Eysenck Personality Profiler* (2nd. Ed.). Guildford: Psi-Press.

Eysenck, H. J., Wilson, G., and Jackson, C. (1999). *The Eysenck Personality Profiler (short)* (2nd. Ed.). Guildford: Psi-Press.

Ferrando, P. J. (2003). The accuracy of the E, N, and P trait estimates: An empirical study using the EPQ-R. *Personality and Individual Differences, 34*, 665-679.

Fink, A., and Neubauer, A. C. (2004). Extraversion and cortical activation: Effects of task complexity. *Personality and Individual Differences, 36*, 333-347.

Forrest, S., Lewis, C. A., and Shevlin, M. (2000). Examining the factor structure and differential functioning of the Eysenck personality questionnaire revised - abbreviated. *Personality and Individual Differences, 29*, 579-588.

Fowles, D. C. Roberts, R., and Nagel, K. (1997). The influence of introversion/extraversion on the skin conductance response to stress and stimulus intensity. *Journal of Research in Personality, 11*, 129-146.

Francis, L. J. (1993). The dual nature of the Eysenckian neuroticism scales: A question of sex differences. *Personality and Individual Differences, 15*, 43-59.

Francis, L. J., Brown, L. B., and Philipchalk, R. (1992). The development of an abbreviated form of the revised Eysenck Personality Questionnaire (EPQR-A): Its use among students in England, Canada, the USA, and Australia. *Personality and Individual Differences, 13*, 443-449.

Frigon, J. (1976). Extraversion, neuroticism and strength of the nervous system. *British Journal of Psychology, 61*, 467-474.

Frith, C. D. (1977, August). Habituation of pupil size and light responses to sound. Paper presented at the 1977 annual convention of the American Psychological Association, San Francisco, CA, USA.

Geen, R. G. (1984). Preferred stimulation levels in introverts and extraverts: Effects on arousal and performance. *Journal of Personality and Social Psychology, 46*, 1303-1312

Harvey, F., and Hirschmann, R. (1980). The influence of extraversion and neuroticism on heart rate responses to aversive visual stimuli. *Personality and Individual Difference, 1*, 97-100.

Holmes, D. S. (1967). Pupillary response, conditioning and personality. *Journal of Personality and Social Psychology, 5*, 95-103.

Hoyle, R. H., and Panter, A. T. (1995). Writing about structural equation models. In R. H. Hoyle (Ed.), *Structural equation modeling: Concepts, issues and applications* (pp. 158-176). Thousand Oaks, CA: Sage Publications.

Hu, L., and Bentler, P. M. (1998). Fit indices in covariance structure modeling: Sensitivity to underparameterized model misspecification. *Psychological Methods, 3*, 424-453.

Hu, L., and Bentler, P. M. (1999). Cutoff criteria for fit indexes in covariance structure analysis: Conventional criteria versus new alternatives. *Structural Equation Modeling, 6*, 1-55.

Jöreskog, K. G., and Sörbom, D. (1996). *LISREL 8: Users reference guide.* Chicago, Illinois: Scientific Software International, Inc.

Jöreskog, K. G., and Sörbom, D. (1999). *LISREL 8.3* [Computer program]. Chicago, Illinois: Scientific Software International, Inc.

Marton, M. L. (1972). The theory of individual differences in neo-behaviourism and in the typology of higher nervous activity. In V. D. Nebylitsyn and J. A. Gray (Eds.), *Biological basis of individual behaviour* (pp. 221-235). New York: Academic Press.

Ramirez-Maestre, C., Martinez, A. E. L., and Zarazaga, R. E. (2004). Personality characteristics as differential variables of the pain experience. *Journal of Behavioral Medicine, 27*, 147-165.

Raykov, T. (1998). On the use of confirmatory factor analysis in personality research. *Personality and Individual Differences, 24*, 291–293.

Sato, T. (2004, June). *The Eysenck Personality Questionnaire: A briefer and more reliable version*. Paper presented at the 2004 annual convention of the Canadian Psychological Association, St. John's, Newfoundland, Canada.

Sato, T. (2005). The Eysenck Personality Questionnaire-Brief Version: Factor structure and reliability. *The Journal of Psychology, 139*, 545-552.

Shevlin, M., Bailey, F., and Adamson, G. (2002). Examining the factor structure and sources of differential functioning of the Eysenck Personality Questionnaire Revised - Abbreviated. *Personality and Individual Differences, 32*, 479-487.

Steiger, J. H. (1990). Structural model evaluation and modification: An interval estimation approach. *Multivariate Behavioral Research, 25*, 173-180.

Stelmack, R. M., and Mandelzys, N. (1975). Extraversion and papillary response to affective and taboo words. *Psychophysiology, 12*, 536-540.

Wilson, G. (1990). Personality, time of day and arousal. *Personality and Individual Differences, 11*, 153-168.

Zuckerman, M. (1998). Psychobiological theories of Personality. In D. F. Barone, M. Hersen, and V. B. Van Hesselt (Eds.), *Advanced personality* (pp. 123-154). New York: Plenum Press.

In: New Psychological Tests and Testing Research
Editor: Lydia S. Boyar, pp. 121-140

ISBN: 978-1-60021-570-4
© 2007 Nova Science Publishers, Inc.

Chapter 6

TWO DIFFERENT OPERATIONALISATIONS OF PSYCHOLOGICAL TYPE: COMPARING THE MYERS-BRIGGS TYPE INDICATOR AND THE KEIRSEY TEMPERAMENT SORTER

*Leslie J. Francis[1], Mandy Robbins[2]
and Charlotte L Craig[3]*

[1] University of Wales Bangor, Bangor, UK
[2] University of Wales Bangor, Bangor, UK
[3] University of Wales Bangor, Bangor, UK

ABSTRACT

A sample of 554 first year undergraduate students attending a university-sector college in Wales (UK) completed the Myers-Briggs Type Indicator (Form G Anglicised) and the Keirsey Temperament Sorter (1978 edition). The underlying continuous scale scores generated by the two instruments are highly correlated and appear to be assessing similar psychological constructs. However, the methods proposed by the two instruments for assigning individuals to discrete psychological types are dissimilar and result in the generation of significantly different type profiles. When compared with each other, the Myers-Briggs Type Indicator tends to generate a significantly higher representation of sensing, thinking, and perceiving, while the Keirsey Temperament Sorter tends to generate a significantly higher representation of intuition, feeling, and judging. The current study points to the relative unreliability of the MBTI and the KTS as comparable type indicators, but also to the relatively strong relationship between the MBTI and the KTS as indicators of personality traits. Comparisons of type categorisations generated by the two instruments may need, therefore, to be treated with caution.

INTRODUCTION

Psychological type is a system for understanding and identifying the basic elements of the human psyche, as proposed by Carl Gustav Jung in his important work *Psychological Types* (1971: first published 1921). Jung recognised that, in order to comprehend the human psyche, it is helpful to attempt to categorise different psychological patterns and features. Classifying human traits and types provides a basis for understanding and explaining individual differences in psychological profile. Jung's theory of psychological types is intended to be a constructive method of recognising and appreciating differences between individual people and understanding the importance of opposites within the human psyche.

Jung's Theory of Psychological Types

Jung's theory develops a long-standing and ancient tradition of categorising people and he acknowledges his debt to previous typologies (see, for example, Jung 1971, p. 510), finding examples and descriptions in medicine, philosophy, theology, poetry, and biography. Nevertheless, he is critical of the way in which 'the ancients' held an 'almost entirely biological valuation' of others, while 'the medieval man' held a 'metaphysical valuation' (p. 8). In contrast to these preceding typologies, Jung seeks to formulate a 'personal valuation... which alone can form the basis of objective psychology' (p. 8). Therefore, Jung proposes a typology that is neither biologically, spiritually, nor morally based; rather his type theory is psychologically based. Jung is concerned with those differences of personality that form a 'fundamental contrast, sometimes quite clear, sometimes obscured, but always apparent when one is dealing with individuals whose personality is any way pronounced' (p. 331). These differences are more than 'idiosyncrasies of character peculiar to individuals' (pp 330-331) or 'isolated individual instances' (p. 331) but quintessential paradigms of the psyche. Shamdasani (2003) argues that in Jung's formulation:

> the personal equation was principally conditioned not by biographical experiences, but by an innate disposition – that is, one's type. Thus if one's psychology constituted one's subjective confession, as Jung held, this was not because it consisted in the transformation of details of one's biography into theoretical terms: rather it designated the fact that one was constrained to view the world from a particular mindset.
>
> (Shamdasani 2003, p.75)

In Jung's theory, type preferences are not founded in experience, age, class, race, or culture. Rather, it is Jung's view that psychological type has a biological foundation. He bases this proposition on the observation that two children of the same family, although treated identically, may display strikingly different attitudes (p. 332). While Jung acknowledges that external factors (such as parental treatment) may influence a child's type preferences, he considers this to be a manipulation and falsification of the true type of the child. A 'normal' child will display attitudes and behaviours consistent with his or her biologically grounded psychological type.

Jung argued that there are three major indices of the psyche which divide the human race. These are the orientations (extraversion *or* introversion), the perceiving processes (sensing *or* intuition), and the judging processes (thinking *or* feeling). Subsequent to Jung's writing, other type theorists (see for example, Myers and McCaulley 1985) have proposed a fourth index, that is, the attitudes towards the outer world (judging *or* perceiving). The indices are dichotomous and, although everyone is capable of using both aspects of the psyche identified by each of the four indices, it is believed that one aspect will always be preferred, and consequently developed, over the other.

The orientations are concerned with the ways in which people gather psychological energy. Extraverts (E) draw their energy from the outer world of events, people and things, and focus their attention on that outer world. Introverts (I) draw their energy from the inner world of thoughts and reflections, and focus their attention on that inner world.

The perceiving processes are concerned with the ways in which people receive and process information. Sensing types (S) focus on perceptions received through the five senses, and are concerned with facts, details, and practical realities in the here and now. Intuitive types (N) focus on perceptions received through intuition, and are concerned with inspirations, meanings, and possibilities for the future.

The judging processes are concerned with the ways in which people make decisions and judgements. Thinking types (T) make judgements based on objective, impersonal logic, and tend to value truthfulness and fairness. Feeling types (F) make judgements based on subjective, personal values, and tend to value harmony and compassion.

The attitudes toward the outer world are concerned with which process (Judging T/F or Perceiving S/N) is preferred for dealing with the outside world. Judging types (J) are orderly, decisive, and organised, as they judge stimuli from the outer world in order to reach conclusions and make decisions swiftly. Perceiving types (P) are open, spontaneous, and flexible, as they perceive stimuli from the outer world in order to continue gathering information as long as possible before reaching conclusions and making decisions.

These four dichotomous indices combine to produce 16 discrete psychological types from which it is possible to define an individual's dominant and auxiliary functions and whether these functions are introverted or extraverted. The dominant function is the function that is most preferred and the auxiliary function is the second preferred function, which may be consciously used when the dominant function is insufficient or inappropriate. Each of the perceiving processes (sensing and intuition) and each of the judging processes (thinking and feeling) can be extraverted (used in the outer world) or introverted (used in the inner world). Whichever of the two perceiving processes is extraverted, the other is introverted. Likewise, whichever of the two judging processes is extraverted, the other is introverted. Judging types extravert their judging function (that is, thinking or feeling) and perceiving types extravert their perceiving function (that is, sensing or intuition). Introverts employ their dominant function in their inner world and use their auxiliary function in their outer world. In contrast, extraverts employ their dominant function in their outer world and use their auxiliary function in their inner world.

Operationalisations of Psychological Type Theory

Jung's theory of psychological types is 'his only work to have given rise to a continued outpouring of experimental studies, by means of questionnaires and statistical tests' (Shamdasani 2003, p.74). In particular, a number of type theorists have attempted to operationalise psychological type theory through the development of type indicators. These type indicators include the Gray-Wheelwright Jungian Type Survey (Gray and Wheelwright 1946), the Keirsey Temperament Sorter (Keirsey and Bates 1978), the Singer-Loomis Inventory of Personality (Loomis 1982), the Myers-Briggs Type Indicator (Myers and McCaulley 1985), the Personal Style Inventory (Ware, Yokomoto and Morris 1985), the Type Differentiation Indicator (Mitchell 1991), the Cambridge Type Inventory (Rawling 1992), the PET Check (Cranton and Knoop 1995), the Jung Type Indicator (Budd,1997), the Personal Preferences Self-Description Questionnaire (Kier, Melancon and Thompson 1998), and the Francis Psychological Type Scales (Francis 2005). The most popular of these type indicators are generally acknowledged to be the Myers-Briggs Type Indicator (MBTI: see, for example, Myers, McCaulley, Quenk and Hammer 1998) and the Keirsey Temperament Sorter (KTS: see, for example, Kelly and Jugovic 2001).

Both the KTS and the MBTI are frequently used to profile the type preferences of groups. For example, in recent years the MBTI has been used to profile the type preferences of nursing assistants (Daub, Friedman, Cresci and Keyser 2000), dental students (Sandow, Jones and Moody 2000), and male Anglican clergy (Francis, Payne and Jones 2001). In recent years the KTS has been used to profile the type preferences of hospital employees (Calabrese 2000), patients suffering from manic-depression (Burge and Lester 2000), and A-level religious studies students (Fearn, Francis and Wilcox 2001).

The KTS and the MBTI have also been frequently used to show how dichotomous types differ. For example, in recent years the MBTI has been used in studies to investigate how dichotomous types differ in terms of personality disorders (Coolidge, Segal, Hook, Yamazaki and Ellett 2001), career indecision (Gaffner and Hazler 2002), and mystical orientation (Francis 2002). In recent years the KTS has been used in studies to investigate how dichotomous types differ in terms of grade-influencing activities (Lawrence and Taylor 2000), depression (Lester 2000), and learning styles (Harrison and Lester 2000).

Both the MBTI and the KTS derive type from continuous scale scores and use forced-choice format questionnaires. Form G of the MBTI (Myers and McCaulley 1985) relies on the generation of eight continuous scores, comprising scales of extraversion (19 items), introversion (19 items), sensing (24 items), intuition (16 items), thinking (20 items), feeling (13 items), judging (20 items), and perceiving (24 items). Form G of the MBTI contains126 items, although only 94 of these items are scored for type; the remaining 32 items are used for research purposes. The MBTI (Form G) uses item weightings, based on Myers' prediction ratio, and has separate male and female weights in respect of scoring feeling and thinking. It contains phrase-pair and word-pair items with a choice of two or three responses.

The first edition of the KTS (Keirsey and Bates 1978) distinguishes between the four dichotomous indices of psychological type through the use of four scales: EI (10 items), SN (20 items), TF (20 items), and JP (20 items). Overall, the KTS contains 70 items consisting of phrase-pair and word-pair items with a choice of two responses. The KTS does not employ item weightings.

There are two main ways in which the reliability of the continuous scores of these two instruments has been assessed. First, the reliability of both the MBTI continuous scores and the KTS continuous scores has been assessed in terms of internal consistency reliability. Second, the reliability of the MBTI continuous scores has been assessed in terms of test-retest reliability.

Reliability of MBTI Continuous Scores

The internal consistency reliability of the MBTI has been investigated by Stricker and Ross (1963), Tzeng, Ware, Outcalt and Boyer (1985), Cowan (1989), Harvey and Murry (1994), Saggino and Kline (1995), Harvey (1996), Tsuzuki and Matsui (1997), Francis and Jones (1999), Barbuto and Plummer (2000), and Boozer, Forte, Maddox and Jackson (2000). For example, in four samples of high school students and undergraduates, Stricker and Ross (1963) reported alpha coefficients of .78, .83, .76 and .78 for EI, .77, .74, .75 and .80 for SN, .64, .70, .74 and .71 for TF, and .78, .81, .84 and .81 for JP. According to Harvey (1996), the data on a mixed sample of 1,676 respondents reported by Harvey and Murry (1994) demonstrated alpha coefficients of .84 for EI, .87 for SN, .85 for TF, and .86 for JP. Harvey (1996), pooling data from three studies generating around 2,400 respondents, calculated alpha coefficients of .86 for EI, .87 for SN, .85 for TF, and .87 for JP. In a mixed sample of 1,798 individuals, Saggino and Kline (1995) reported alpha coefficients of .74 for EI, .78 for SN, .67 for TF (male), .56 for TF (female), and .78 for JP. In a sample of 88 students, Tsuzuki and Matsui (1997) reported alpha coefficients of .81 for EI, .78 for SN, .77 for TF, and .81 for JP. In a sample of 429 participants attending 24 courses concerned with personality and spirituality Francis and Jones (1999) reported on each of the eight continuous scales, finding of 0.80 for extraversion, 0.79 for introversion, 0.87 for sensing, 0.82 for intuition, 0.79 for thinking, 0.72 for feeling, 0.85 for judging, and 0.86 for perceiving. In a sample of 157 continuing education students, Barbuto and Plummer (2000) reported alpha coefficients of .81 for EI, .81 for SN, .73 for TF, and .80 for JP. In a sample of 1,117 members of the Association for Psychological Type, Boozer, Forte, Maddox and Jackson (2000) reported alpha coefficients of .90 for EI, .87 for SN, .86 for TF, and .81 for JP. From the studies surveyed it may be concluded that the MBTI indices are generally internally consistent, in that they tend to achieve Cronbach (1951) alpha coefficients around the level deemed satisfactory by Kline (2000) or by DeVellis (2003) of 0.70 and 0.65 respectively.

Test-retest reliability concerned with continuous scores on the MBTI has been reported by many studies, including Stricker and Ross (1964), Levy, Murphy and Carlson (1972), Steele and Kelly (1976), Carskadon (1977, 1979, 1982), Howes and Carskadon (1979), Levy and Padilla (1982), Levy and Ridley (1987), McCarley and Carskadon (1983), Johnson (1992), Bents and Wierschke (1996), Salter, Evans and Forney (1997), and Tsuzuki and Matsui (1997). For example, Stricker and Ross (1964) reported test-retest reliabilities of continuous scores across a fourteen month interval of .73 for EI, .69 for SN, .69 for JP and .48 for TF. Levy, Murphy and Carlson (1972) reported test-retest reliabilities of continuous scores across a two month interval for three separate samples of .80, .83 and .73 for EI, .69, .78 and .69 for SN, .73, .82 and .43 for TF, and .80, .82 and .69 for JP. Steele and Kelly (1976) reported test-retest reliabilities of continuous scale scores across a one week period of .89 for EI, .86 for TF, and .88 for SN. Carskadon (1977) reported test-retest reliabilities of continuous scores across an eight week interval. For females test-retest correlations ranged from .73 to .78 on the four scales, while for males they ranged from .56 to .79. Howes and Carskadon (1979) reported test-retest reliabilities of continuous scores across a five week interval. They found reliabilities of .82 for EI, .87 for SN, .78 for TF and .81 for JP. Carskadon (1979) reported test-retest reliabilities of continuous scores across a seven week interval. For males and females respectively he found the following reliabilities: EI, .79 and .86; SN, .84 and .87; TF, .48 and .87; JP, .63 and .80. Carskadon (1982) reported test-retest reliabilities of continuous scores across a five week interval. For males and females respectively he found the following reliabilities: EI, .77 and .89; SN, .93 and .85; TF, .91 and .56; JP, .87 and .89. Levy and Padilla (1982) reported test-retest reliabilities of continuous scores on two samples. In one sample across a two month interval they found reliabilities of .83 for EI, .78 for SN, .82 for TF, and .82 for JP. In the second sample across a two week interval they found reliabilities of .85 for EI, .87 for SN, .79 for TF, and .89 for JP. McCarley and Carskadon (1983) reported test-retest reliabilities of continuous scores across a five week period ranging from .77 for TF to .89 for JP. Johnson (1992) reported test-retest reliabilities of continuous scores over a thirty month interval of .70 for EI, .83 for SN, .62 for TF, and .82 for JP. Bents and Wierschke (1996) reported test-retest reliabilities of continuous scores across a six week period of .89 for EI, .80 for SN, .87 for TF, and .91 for JP. Salter, Evans and Forney (1997) reported test-retest reliabilities of continuous scores over a twenty month period of .77 for EI, .75 for SN, .69 for TF, and .77 for JP. Tsuzuki and Matsui (1997) reported test-retest reliabilities of continuous scores over a three month period for male respondents of .79 for EI, .84 for SN, .48 for TF, and .63 for JP.

Reliability of KTS Continuous Scores

The KTS has been found to achieve satisfactory internal consistency in a study by Waskel and Coleman (1991). Using a sample of 331 university students in the USA, they found that the KTS indices achieved Cronbach alpha coefficients of 0.74 (EI), 0.89 (SN), 0.87 (TF), and 0.88 (JP). More recently, Fearn, Francis and Wilcox (2001), in a study among 367 university students in the UK, found that the KTS indices achieved Cronbach alpha coefficients of 0.68 (EI), 0.73 (SN), 0.74 (TF), and 0.82 (JP). In both of these studies the lowest scores were achieved by the EI index which may be attributed to the smaller number of items measuring this index (10 items, compared to 20 for each of the other three indices). From the studies surveyed it may be concluded that the KTS indices are generally internally consistent, in that they tend to achieve Cronbach (1951) alpha coefficients around the level deemed satisfactory by Kline (2000) or by DeVellis (2003) of 0.70 and 0.65 respectively. Currently no published data have been identified on the test-retest reliability of the continuous scale scores of the KTS.

Key Differences between the MBTI and the KTS

The continuous scores of the MBTI and the KTS are transformed into type indicators in different ways. The MBTI (Form G) assigns type preferences according to Myers' prediction ratio, which is intended to prevent a bias in favour of any particular type (Myers and McCaulley 1985). By basing this prediction ratio on samples drawn from the general population, it was hoped to correct for differences in type frequency. Responses for each type were calculated and averaged by the proportion of that type responding in a particular manner. This resulted in item weightings on Form G of the MBTI, in order to ensure no types were overrepresented and to account for sex differences. In contrast, the KTS assumes parity of items on each of its scales, and, therefore, does not employ item weightings.

A further key difference between the MBTI and the KTS is the way in which people are assigned to types. The MBTI assigns all people who complete the type indicator to type categories, even if their continuous scale scores achieve an equal balance on the two opposite components proposed by an index. For example, someone who achieves an equal balance on the EI index is assigned to the introvert type category. This is done in order to ensure that people are more likely to be assigned to the less well-represented types categories. The MBTI assigns people who record equal scores on both opposing scales to introversion, intuition, feeling, and perceiving. By contrast, the KTS assigns people who achieve an equal balance on an index to a neutral category.

Reliability of the MBTI as a Type Sorter

There are a number of studies which have explored the test-retest reliability of the MBTI as a type sorter. Currently no published data have been identified on the test-retest reliability of the KTS as a type sorter. Data regarding the test-retest of the MBTI as a type sorter are reported, for example, by Levy, Murphy and Carlson (1972), Howes and Carskadon (1979), McCarley and Carskadon (1983), Johnson (1992), Silberman, Freeman and Lester (1992), Bents and Wierschke (1996) and Tsuzuki and Matsui (1997). The proportion of subjects classified with identical categorisations at the retest varies considerably from one study to another. For example, Levy, Murphy and Carlson (1972), in a study among 433 undergraduates, found that after a two month period 53% were assigned the same type on both occasions, while 35% differed on one of the four scales, 10% on two scales, and the remaining 2% on three scales. Howes and Carskadon (1979), in a study among 117 undergraduates, found that after a five week period 49% were assigned the same type on both occasions, while 38% differed on one scale, and the remaining 14% differed on two scales. McCarley and Carskadon (1983) found that after a five week period 47% of their subjects retained their specific dichotomous type preferences across all four scales. Johnson (1992) in a study among 74 adults found that after a thirty month interval 66% were assigned the same type on both occasions, while 19% differed on one of the four scales, 12% on two scales, and 3% on three scales or more. Silberman, Freeman and Lester (1992), administered the MBTI to 161 dental students before the beginning of their first year of study and again near the end of their fourth year. They found that 24% were assigned the same type on both occasions, while the remaining 76% differed on at least one of the four scales. This study fails to report on the number of scales on which differences occurred. Bents and Wierschke (1996) administered the MBTI to 40 adults twice over a six week period. They found that 68% were assigned the same type on both occasions, while 25% differed on one scale, and the remaining 8% differed on two scales. Tsuzuki and Matsui (1997) administered the MBTI to 88 students twice over a three month period. They found that 33% were assigned the same type on both occasions, while 48% differed on one scale, 16% differed on two scales and 3% differed on three scales.

The Relationship between the MBTI and the KTS

There are three studies which have investigated the way in which the MBTI and the KTS are related (Quinn, Lewis and Fischer 1992; Tucker and Gillespie 1993; Kelly and Jugovic 2001). These studies have employed two methods of assessing the relationship between these two operationalisations of Jungian psychological theory. The first method assesses to what extent the type designations produced by the KTS and the MBTI match. For example Tucker and Gillespie (1993) conducted a study among 103 psychology students, each of whom completed the MBTI, the KTS, and an online edition of the KTS. They found that 62% of participants achieved matches on all four indices between types as assessed by the KTS and by the MBTI. In addition, it was found that 50% of participants achieved matches on all four indices between types as assessed by an online edition of the KTS and by the MBTI (Tucker and Gillespie 1993). A further study by Kelly and Jugovic (2001) found that 35% of 203 college students achieved matches on all four indices of type as assessed by an online edition of the KTS (1995 edition; Keirsey 1998) and by the MBTI.

The second method of assessing the relationship between the KTS and the MBTI examines correlations between the scales of these two models. Quinn, Lewis and Fischer (1992) administered the KTS and the MBTI Form G to 191 business administration students. They report that the Pearson correlation between the MBTI and the KTS on extraversion was .73; on introversion, .73, on sensing, .67; on intuition, .66; on thinking, .54; on feeling, .74, on judging, .62; and on perceiving, .62. Tucker and Gillespie (1993) also report on the Pearson correlation between the MBTI and the two versions of the KTS used in their study. They report that the Pearson correlation between the KTS (paper and pencil version) and the MBTI was .76 on the EI index, .84 on the SN index, .68 on the TF index, and .73 on the JP index. They also report that the Pearson correlation between the KTS (online version) and the MBTI was .85 on the EI index, .83 on the SN index, .86 on the TF index, and .84 on the JP index. Kelly and Jugovic (2001) also report on the Pearson correlation between the MBTI and an online edition of the KTS (1995 edition; Keirsey 1998), distinguishing between male and female participants. Among 92 male college students they found correlations of .75 on the EI index, .62 on the SN index, .63 on the TF index, and .60 on the JP index. Among 111 female participants they found correlations of .68 on the EI index, .65 on the SN index, .78 on the TF index, and .61 on the JP index.

Aims of the Current Study

The current study aims to build on previous research concerning the relationship between the MBTI and the KTS in three ways. First, the previous studies by Quinn, Lewis and Fischer (1992), Tucker and Gillespie (1993), and Kelly and Jugovic (2001) have used small samples (191, 103, 203) respectively. Although these sample sizes are quite substantial in comparison with some of the empirical studies within the psychological type literature, the distribution of the number of participants across 16 psychological type cells leads to unacceptably small numbers in some cells. The current study, therefore, aims to use a larger sample. Second, previous studies by Quinn, Lewis and Fischer (1992), Tucker and Gillespie (1993), and Kelly and Jugovic (2001) have failed to distinguish between raw and weighted KTS scores. The MBTI weights type categories in order to ensure all participants are assigned to a type preference, while the KTS does not weight type categories, allowing participants to be assigned to a neutral type preference. The current study, therefore, aims to distinguish between raw and weighted KTS scores. Third, previous studies by Quinn, Lewis and Fischer (1992), Tucker and Gillespie (1993), and Kelly and Jugovic (2001) have not attempted to determine if there are significant *differences* in the way in which the KTS and the MBTI assign psychological type preferences. Therefore, the current study will look at statistically significant *differences* between these two instruments.

METHOD

Sample

A sample of 554 first year undergraduate students attending a university-sector college in Wales (UK), specialising in teacher education and liberal arts subjects, participated in the project as part of their induction programme into the life of a research active academic community. The sample comprised 129 males and 425 females. The majority of the participants (78.9%) were aged 18 or 19 years, 10.7% were aged 20 or 21, 5.3% were aged 22-30, and the remaining 5.1% were over the age of 30.

Instruments

Personality was assessed using two different inventories: Anglicised Form G of the Myers-Briggs Type Indicator (MBTI: Myers and McCaulley 1985) and the Keirsey Temperament Sorter (KTS: Keirsey and Bates 1978). The MBTI Form G is a forced-choice format, pencil and paper questionnaire that contains 126 items. The MBTI Form G uses gender weighting on one of the indices, TF. The KTS is a forced-choice format, pencil and paper questionnaire that contains 70 items.

Procedure

As part of an intensive introduction to psychometric assessment, the students were invited to complete a battery of tests. Participation was voluntary, but none of the students who attended the induction sessions declined to take part.

RESULTS

Table 1 presents the internal consistency reliabilities of the eight scales of the MBTI and the eight scales of the KTS in terms of the alpha coefficient (Cronbach 1951). Since the two opposite pairs of each of the two processes and the two attitudes of the KTS are computed from precisely the same set of dichotomous items, the alpha coefficient for the two opposite pairs are also generally identical. Since the scale scores of the MBTI are not calculated in the same way, being based on a different set of items and weightings, the alpha coefficient for the two opposite pairs are independent of each other.

Table 1. Internal reliability of MBTI scales and KTS scales, and correlations between the two instruments

	MBTI alpha	KTS alpha	Comparison Pearson correlation
Extraversion	0.8059	0.6883	0.7616
Introversion	0.7997	0.6883	0.7551
Sensing	0.7815	0.7647	0.7035
Intuition	0.6812	0.7647	0.6830
Thinking	0.7215	0.7519	0.6476
Feeling	0.5854	0.7519	0.6141
Judging	0.7938	0.8358	0.7601
Perceiving	0.8044	0.8358	0.7660

Objective cut-off points for the acceptability of satisfactory internal reliability are difficult to define. Kline (2000) suggests that the alpha coefficient should reach a threshold of 0.70, while DeVellis (2003) accepts a slightly lower threshold of 0.65. All of the KTS scales pass DeVellis' threshold and six of them also pass Kline's threshold. The two lower alpha coefficients are associated with extraversion and introversion. Since the reliability of a scale is associated with the length of the scale, it is important to note that orientation is assessed in the KTS by 10 items, while the processes and the attitude toward the outer world are assessed in the KTS by 20 items each. Seven of the eight MBTI scales pass DeVellis' threshold and six of them also pass Kline's threshold. The lowest alpha coefficient is associated with feeling and the second lowest is associated with intuition. In terms of internal reliability, it could be argued that the poorer measurement of feeling renders the MBTI as the less adequate of the two instruments.

Table 1 also presents the Pearson correlation coefficients between the scales of the two instruments. Given what is already known about the internal reliability of the scales these correlations are acceptable, confirming that the indices are accessing highly similar constructs. The lowest correlation occurs between the two indices of feeling, which is consistent with the poorer internal reliability of the MBTI index of feeling.

Table 2 presents the proportional splits between the four pairs of opposite types as defined by the MBTI and by the KTS. In this table the KTS scores have been calculated in two ways. First, the raw scores have been calculated according to the Keirsey and Bates (1978) formula which assigns individuals who record equal scores on both opposing scales to a third neutral category. According to this model 9.2% of the respondents occupy the middle territory between extraversion and introversion, 9.0% between sensing and intuition, 7.0% between thinking and feeling, and 6.1% between judging and perceiving. Second, the weighted scores have been calculated according to the principle established by the MBTI which assigns individuals who record equal scores on both opposing scales to introversion, intuition, feeling, and perceiving. Using the second method of calculation as a basis for comparing the two instruments, the KTS tends to assign more individuals to extraversion, intuition, feeling, and judging, while the MBTI tends to assign more individuals to introversion, sensing, thinking, perceiving.

Table 2. Type distribution within the sample by MBTI and KTS

Psychological type categories	MBTI %	KTS raw %	KTS weighted %
orientation			
extraversion	67.0	71.3	71.3
introversion	33.0	19.5	28.7
not assigned		9.2	
perceiving process			
sensing	60.8	53.1	53.1
intuition	39.2	37.9	46.9
not assigned		9.0	
judging process			
thinking	28.9	22.6	22.6
feeling	71.1	70.4	77.4
not assigned		7.0	
attitude toward the outer world			
judging	50.5	68.8	68.8
perceiving	49.5	25.1	31.2
not assigned		6.1	

Table 3 presents the proportions of type clarification agreement between the MBTI and the KTS, using both KTS raw scores and KTS weighted scores. The use of weighted scores improves the fit between the two instruments.

Table 3. Proportions of type clarification agreement between MBTI and KTS, using KTS raw scores and KTS weighted scores

Psychological type categories	KTS raw %	KTS weighted %
dichotomous types		
extraversion-introversion	77.4	81.6
sensing-intuition	71.7	75.3
thinking-feeling	75.3	79.6
judging-perceiving	70.4	75.3
sixteen types		
all four letters	31.9	39.2
three of four letters	70.7	77.3
two of four letters	93.3	96.1
one of four letters	98.7	99.3
no agreement	1.3	0.7

The scientific literature concerned with psychological type has developed a distinctive method of presenting full type profiles through a standard 'type table', providing information about the sixteen types, the dichotomous preferences, the pairs and temperaments, the Jungian types, and the dominant types. Type tables are included in the present analysis in order to facilitate comparability with the wider scientific literature concerned with psychological type. Table 4 presents the type distribution for the current sample as assessed by the MBTI.

Table 4. MBTI Type Distribution for First Year Undergraduate Students $N = 554$ + = 1% of N

The Sixteen Complete Types				Dichotomous Preferences		
ISTJ	ISFJ	INFJ	INTJ	E	$n = 371$	(67.0%)
$n = 25$	$n = 57$	$n = 18$	$n = 4$	I	$n = 183$	(33.0%)
(4.5%)	(10.3%)	(3.2%)	(0.7%)			
				S	$n = 337$	(60.8%)
				N	$n = 217$	(39.2%)
				T	$n = 160$	(28.9%)
				F	$n = 394$	(71.1%)
				J	$n = 280$	(50.5%)
				P	$n = 274$	(49.5%)
ISTP	ISFP	INFP	INTP	Pairs and Temperaments		
$n = 11$	$n = 23$	$n = 32$	$n = 13$			
(2.0%)	(4.2%)	(5.8%)	(2.3%)	IJ	$n = 104$	(18.8%)
				IP	$n = 79$	(14.3%)
				EP	$n = 195$	(35.2%)
				EJ	$n = 176$	(31.8%)
				ST	$n = 108$	(19.5%)
				SF	$n = 229$	(41.3%)
				NF	$n = 165$	(29.8%)
ESTP	ESFP	ENFP	ENTP	NT	$n = 52$	(9.4%)
$n = 33$	$n = 60$	$n = 75$	$n = 27$			
(6.0%)	(10.8%)	13.5%)	(4.9%)	SJ	$n = 210$	(37.9%)
				SP	$n = 127$	(22.9%)
				NP	$n = 147$	(26.5%)
				NJ	$n = 70$	(12.6%)
				TJ	$n = 76$	(13.7%)
				TP	$n = 84$	(15.2%)
				FP	$n = 190$	(34.3%)
ESTJ	ESFJ	ENFJ	ENTJ	FJ	$n = 204$	(36.8%)
$n = 39$	$n = 89$	$n = 40$	$n = 8$			
(7.0%)	(16.1%)	(7.2%)	(1.4%)	IN	$n = 67$	(12.1%)
				EN	$n = 150$	(27.1%)
				IS	$n = 116$	(20.9%)
				ES	$n = 221$	(39.9%)
				ET	$n = 107$	(19.3%)
				EF	$n = 264$	(47.7%)
				IF	$n = 130$	(23.5%)
				IT	$n = 53$	(9.6%)

Jungian Types (E)			Jungian Types (I)			Dominant Types			
	n	%		n	%		n	%	Francis, Robbins and Craig
E-TJ	47	8.5	I-TP	24	4.3	Dt. T	71	12.8	
E-FJ	129	23.3	I-FP	55	9.9	Dt. F	184	33.2	MBTI types of first year
ES-P	93	16.8	IS-J	82	14.8	Dt. S	175	31.6	
EN-P	102	18.4	IN-J	22	4.0	Dt. N	124	22.4	undergraduate students

Table 5. KTS Type Distribution for First Year Undergraduate Students and SRTT Comparison with MBTI Type Distribution for First Year Undergraduate Students

N = 554 += 1% of N I = Selection Ratio Index *p<.05 **p<.01 ***p<.001

The Sixteen Complete Types

ISTJ	ISFJ	INFJ	INTJ
n = 23	n = 53	n = 30	n = 6
(4.2%)	(9.6%)	(5.4%)	(1.1%)
I = 0.92	I = 0.93	I = 1.67	I = 1.5
ISTP	**ISFP**	**INFP**	**INTP**
n = 4	n = 7	n = 34	n = 2
(0.7%)	(1.3%)	(6.1%)	(0.4%)
I = 0.36	I = 0.30**	I = 1.06	I = 0.15**
ESTP	**ESFP**	**ENFP**	**ENTP**
n = 5	n = 27	n = 85	n = 9
(0.9%)	(4.9%)	(15.3%)	(1.6%)
I = 0.15***	I = 0.45***	I = 1.13	I = 0.33**
ESTJ	**ESFJ**	**ENFJ**	**ENTJ**
n = 61	n = 114	n = 79	n = 15

Dichotomous Pref

E	395	(71.3%)	I = 1.06
I	159	(28.7%)	I = 0.87
S	294	(53.1%)	**I = 0.87
N	260	(46.9%)	**I = 1.20
T	125	(22.6%)	*I = 0.78
F	429	(77.4%)	*I = 1.09
J	381	(68.8%)	***I = 1.36
P	173	(31.2%)	***I = 0.63

Pairs and Temperaments

IJ	112	(20.2%)	I = 1.08
IP	47	(8.5%)	**I = 0.59
EP	126	(22.7%)	***I = 0.65
EJ	269	(48.6%)	***I = 1.53
ST	93	(16.8%)	I = 0.82
SF	201	(36.3%)	I = 0.64
NF	228	(41.2%)	***I = 1.83
NT	32	(5.8%)	*I = 3.13
SJ	251	(45.3%)	*I = 1.20
SP	43	(7.8%)	***I = 0.34
NP	130	(23.5%)	I = 0.88
NJ	130	(23.5%)	***I = 1.86
TJ	105	(19.0%)	*I = 1.38
TP	20	(3.6%)	***I = 0.24
FP	153	27.6%	*I = 0.81
FJ	276	49.8%	***I = 1.35

Table 5. (Continued).

(11.0%)	(20.6%)	(14.3%)	(2.7%)		n		I = 1.07
I = 1.56*	I = 1.28	I = 1.98***	I = 1.88	IN	72	(13.0%)	I = 1.07
				EN	188	(33.9%)	*I = 1.25
				IS	87	(15.7%)	I = 0.75
				ES	207	(37.4%)	I = 0.94
				ET	90	(16.2%)	I = 0.84
				EF	305	(55.1%)	*I = 1.16
				IF	124	(22.4%)	I = 0.95
				IT	35	(6.3%)	*I = 0.66

Jungian Types (E)				Jungian Types (I)				Dominant Ty				
	n	%	index		n	%	index		n	%	index	
E-TJ	76	13.7	1.62**	I-TP	6	1.1	0.25***	Dt. T	82	14.8	1.15	*Francis, Robbins and Craig*
E-FJ	193	34.8	1.50***	I-FP	41	7.4	0.75	Dt. F	234	42.2	1.27**	*KTS types of first year*
ES-P	32	5.8	0.34***	IS-J	76	13.7	0.93	Dt. S	108	19.5	0.62***	
EN-P	94	17.0	0.91	IN-J	36	6.5	1.64	Dt. N	130	23.5	1.05	*Undergraduate students*

Table 5 presents the type distribution for the current sample as assessed by the KTS (using score weightings). Table 5 also presents the self-selection ratio index as a means of making comparisons between different samples. The self-selection ratio index makes use of the chi-square analysis in order to assess the statistical significance of these comparisons. Table 5 demonstrates that among the KTS type distribution participants with preferences for the following types are overrepresented: intuition ($\chi^2 = 6.81$, $df = 1$, $p < .01$), feeling ($\chi^2 = 5.79$, $df = 1$, $p < .05$), judging ($\chi^2 = 38.25$, $df = 1$, $p < .001$), EJ ($\chi^2 = 32.48$, $df = 1$, $p < .001$), NF ($\chi^2 = 15.65$, $df = 1$, $p < .001$), NT ($\chi^2 = 5.15$, $df = 1$, $p < .05$), SJ ($\chi^2 = 6.25$, $df = 1$, $p < .05$), NJ ($\chi^2 = 21.97$, $df = 1$, $p < .001$), FJ ($\chi^2 = 19.06$, $df = 1$, $p < .001$), EN ($\chi^2 = 6.15$, $df = 1$, $p < .05$), EF ($\chi^2 = 6.07$, $df = 1$, $p < .05$), ESTJ ($\chi^2 = 5.32$, $df = 1$, $p < .05$), ENFJ ($\chi^2 = 14.32$, $df = 1$, $p < .001$), ETJ ($\chi^2 = 7.69$, $df = 1$, $p < .01$), EFJ ($\chi^2 = 17.93$, $df = 1$, $p < .001$), and dominant feeling ($\chi^2 = 9.60$, $df = 1$, $p < .01$). Table 5 also demonstrates that among the KTS type distribution participants with preferences for the following types are underrepresented: sensing ($\chi^2 = 6.81$, $df = 1$, $p < .01$), thinking ($\chi^2 = 5.79$, $df = 1$, $p < .05$), perceiving ($\chi^2 = 38.25$, $df = 1$, $p < .001$), IP ($\chi^2 = 9.17$, $df = 1$, $p < .01$), EP ($\chi^2 = 20.88$, $df = 1$, $p < .001$), SP ($\chi^2 = 49.03$, $df = 1$, $p < .001$), TP ($\chi^2 = 43.46$, $df = 1$, $p < .001$), FP ($\chi^2 = 5.78$, $df = 1$, $p < .05$), IT ($\chi^2 = 4.00$, $df = 1$, $p < .05$), ISFP ($\chi^2 = 8.77$, $df = 1$, $p < .01$), INTP ($\chi^2 = 8.18$, $df = 1$, $p < .01$), ESTP ($\chi^2 = 21.36$, $df = 1$, $p < .001$), ESFP ($\chi^2 = 13.58$, $df = 1$, $p < .001$), ENTP ($\chi^2 = 9.30$, $df = 1$, $p < .01$), ESP ($\chi^2 = 33.55$, $df = 1$, $p < .001$), ITP ($\chi^2 = 11.10$, $df = 1$, $p < .001$), and dominant sensing ($\chi^2 = 21.30$, $df = 1$, $p < .001$).

CONCLUSION

Four features of these data are worth further comment.

First, the current study has confirmed previous research which has found high correlations between the continuous scale scores proposed by the MBTI and the KTS (Quinn, Lewis and Fischer 1992; Tucker and Gillespie 1993; Kelly and Jugovic 2001). The current study has shown there to be Pearson correlations in excess of .60 for all of the eight psychological type scales, which would account for over 36% of the variance in common. In addition, the current study has shown there to be Pearson correlations in excess of .70 for five of the eight psychological type scales, which would account for over half of the variance in common. The weakest correlations between the continuous scale scores of the two instruments are between the intuition scales, the thinking scales, and the feeling scales; this finding may be attributable to the weaker internal reliability of these three scales, as measured by the MBTI.

Second, 31% of participants achieved matches on all four indices of type as assessed by the MBTI and the KTS, when the KTS raw scores were used. However, when the KTS scores were weighted, following the MBTI paradigm, 39% of participants achieved matches on all four indices of type. This suggests that the MBTI and the KTS are more likely to assign participants to the same type categories when they follow the same model of assigning all participants to a type category, employing weightings towards introversion, intuition, feeling, and perceiving.

Third, in the current study, when the KTS weighted scores were used, 39% of participants achieved matches on all four indices of type as assessed by the MBTI and the

KTS. On the one hand, it could be argued that the KTS and the MBTI are assessing different constructs as they assign less than two out of five participants to the same type category. On the other hand, this result is comparable with the test-retest data available for the MBTI. Studies using the MBTI over time have found that the instrument assigned the same type on both occasions for 49% of participants (Howes and Carskadon 1979), 53% of participants (Levy, Murphy and Carlson 1972), 47% of participants (McCarley and Carskadon 1983), 24% of participants (Silberman, Freeman and Lester 1992), 68% of participants (Bents and Wierschke 1996), and 33% of participants (Tsuzuki and Matsui 1997). These studies suggest that the MBTI is a relatively unreliable instrument over time when considered as a type indicator. It seems to be the case that the ability of the MBTI and the KTS to assign individuals to the same psychological types when the two instruments are administered at the same time is not inferior to the ability of the two administrations of the MBTI separated by a period of time.

Fourth, there are significant differences between the type distribution of the MBTI and the KTS on three of the four dichotomous indices. The KTS is significantly more likely to categorise participants as intuitive, feeling, and judging.

From these findings two main conclusions may be drawn. On the one hand, the current study points to the relative unreliability of the MBTI and the KTS as comparable *type indicators*. In other words, there are significant differences between the way in which these instruments sort individuals into discrete categories. On the other hand, the current study points to the relatively strong relationship between the MBTI and the KTS as *indicators of personality traits*. In other words, the KTS and the MBTI continuous scales are highly correlated, suggesting that they grade individuals on the four continua assessing orientations, perceiving functions, judging functions, and attitudes toward the outer world in a similar fashion. This finding is supported by Francis and Jones' (1999, p. 113) review of literature concerning the reliability of the MBTI, from which they concluded that 'the empirical evidence points to the relative unreliability of the MBTI as a *type indicator*. In other words, it is a relatively unstable instrument when employed to sort individuals into discrete categories. Problems often arise in respect of those individuals who record low preference scores. On the other hand, the empirical evidence points to the relative reliability of the MBTI as an indicator of personality traits'. This finding is also supported by a more recent study by Arnau, Green, Rosen, Gleaves and Melancon (2003, p. 233) which employed taxometric analysis of three operationalisations of psychological type: the Singer-Loomis Type Deployment Inventory (Singer, Loomis, Kirkhart and Kirkhart 1996), the Personal Preferences Self-Description Questionnaire (Thompson 1996), and the MBTI. They conclude that psychological type preferences in these three operationalisations 'appear to manifest as continuous dimensions'. These findings support the conclusion that psychological type operationalisations, such as the MBTI and the KTS, are best employed as measures of continuous traits, rather than dichotomous types.

However, these conclusions have been based on a study which employed the 1978 edition of the KTS and the 1985 edition of the MBTI. In 1995 a revised edition of the KTS was published, which included a number of significant changes to the original wording of the items (Keirsey 1998). In 1998 a revised edition of the MBTI (Step 1) was published which also included a number of significant changes to the original wording of the items as well as to the weighting system employed (Myers, McCaulley, Quenk and Hammer 1998). Replication studies need to use the 1995 edition of the KTS and the 1998 edition of the MBTI in order to check whether the revised instruments function in relation to each other in a similar way to that demonstrated by the earlier editions of these instruments.

This study has examined the scale properties of two operationalisations of Jungian type theory, the MBTI and the KTS, among undergraduate students. The data support the comparability of the MBTI and the KTS continuous scales, but fail to support the comparability of the MBTI and the KTS as analogous type indicators. Further research is now needed using recent versions of the KTS and the MBTI.

REFERENCES

Arnau, R.C., Green, B.A., Rosen, D.H., Gleaves, D.H. and Melancon, J.G. (2003). 'Are Jungian preferences really categorical?: An empirical investigation using taxometric analysis'. *Personality and Individual Differences*, 34, 233-251.

Barburto, J.E. and Plummer, B.A. (2000). 'Mental boundaries and Jung's psychological types: a profile analysis'. *Journal of Psychological Type*, 54, 17-21.

Bents, R. and Wierschke, A. (1996). 'Test-retest reliability of the Myers-Briggs Typenindikator'. *Journal of Psychological Type*, 36, 42-46.

Boozer, R.W., Forte, M., Maddox, E. N. and Jackson, W.T. (2000). 'An exploration of the perceived psychological type of the office politician'. *Journal of Psychological Type*, 55, 5-13.

Budd, R.J. (1997). *Manual for Jung Type Indicator*. Bedford, UK: Psytech International.

Burge, M., and Lester, D. (2000). 'Manic-depressives and Jungian dimensions of personality'. *Psychological Reports*, 87, 596.

Calabrese, K.R. (2000). 'Interpersonal conflict and sarcasm in the workplace'. *Genetic, Social and General Psychology Monographs*, 126 (4), 459-494.

Carskadon, T.G. (1977). 'Test-retest reliabilities of continuous scores on the Myers-Briggs Type Indicator'. *Psychological Reports*, 41, 1011-1012.

Carskadon, T.G. (1979). 'Test-retest reliabilities of continuous scores on form G of the Myers-Briggs Type Indicator'. *Research in Psychological Type*, 2, 83-84.

Carskadon, T.G. (1982). 'Sex differences in test-retest reliabilities on form G of the Myers-Briggs Type Indicator'. *Research in Psychological Type*, 5, 78-79.

Coolidge, F.L., Segal, D.L., Hook, J.N., Yamazaki, T.G. and Ellett, J.A. (2001). 'An empirical investigation of Jung's psychological types and personality disorder features'. *Journal of Psychological Type*, 58, 33-36.

Cowan, D.A. (1989). 'An alternative to the dichotomous interpretation of Jung's psychological functions: developing more sensitive measurement technology'. *Journal of Personality Assessment*, 53, 459-471.

Cranton, P. and Knoop, R. (1995). 'Assessing Jung's psychological types: The PET Type Check'. *Genetic, Social and General Psychology Monographs*, 1231, 249-274.

Cronbach, L.J. (1951). 'Coefficient alpha and the internal structure of tests'. *Psychometrika*, 16, 297-334.

Daub, C., Friedman, S.M., Cresci, K. and Keyser, R. (2000). 'Frequencies of MBTI types among nursing assistants providing care to nursing home eligible individuals'. *Journal of Psychological Type*, 54, 12-16.

DeVellis, R.F. (2003). *Scale development: theory and applications.* Thousand Oaks, CA: Sage.

Fearn, M., Francis, L.J. and Wilcox, C. (2001). 'Attitude towards Christianity and psychological type: a survey among religious studies students'. *Pastoral Psychology,* 49 (5), 341-348.

Francis, L.J. (2002). 'Psychological type and mystical orientation: anticipating individual differences within congregational life'. *Sciences Pastorales,* 21 (1), 77-93.

Francis, L.J. (2005). *Faith and Psychology: personality, religion and the individual.* London: Darton Longman and Todd Ltd.

Francis, L.J. and Jones, S.H. (1999). 'The scale properties of the MBTI Form G (Anglicised) among adult churchgoers'. *Pastoral Sciences Journal,* 18, 107-126.

Francis, L.J., Payne, V.J. and Jones, S.H. (2001). 'Psychological types of male Anglican clergy in Wales'. *Journal of Psychological Type,* 56, 19-23.

Gaffner, D.C. and Hazler, R.J. (2002). 'Factors related to indecisiveness and career indecision in undecided college students'. *Journal of College Student Development,* 43 (3), 317-325.

Gray, H. and Wheelwright, J.B. (1946). 'Jung's psychological types, their frequency of occurrence'. *Journal of General Psychology,* 34, 3-17.

Harrison, C. and Lester, D. (2000). 'Learning style and personality type in high school students'. *Psychological Reports,* 87, 1022.

Harvey, R.J. (1996). 'Reliability and validity'. In *MBTI Applications: a decade of research on the Myers-Briggs Type Indicator,* A.L. Hammer (ed.), pp 5-29, Palo Alto, CA: Consulting Psychologists Press.

Harvey, R.J. and Murry, W.D. (1994). 'Scoring the Myers-Briggs Type Indicator: empirical comparison of preference score versus latent-trait methods'. *Journal of Personality Assessment,* 62, 116-129.

Howes, R.J. and Carskadon, T.G. (1979). 'Test-retest reliabilities of the Myers-Briggs Type Indicator as a function of mood changes'. *Research in Psychological Type,* 2, 67-72.

Johnson, D.A. (1992). 'Test-retest reliabilities of the Myers-Briggs Type Indicator and the type differentiation indicator over a 30-month period'. *Journal of Psychological Type,* 24, 54-58.

Jung, C.G. (1971). *Psychological Types: the collected works, volume 6.* London: Routledge and Kegan Paul.

Keirsey, D. (1998). *Please understand me II: temperament, character, intelligence.* Del Mar, CA: Prometheus Nemesis.

Keirsey, D. and Bates, M.B. (1978). *Please Understand Me: character and temperament types.* Del Mar, CA: Prometheus Nemesis.

Kelly, K.R. and Jugovic, H. (2001). 'Concurrent validity of the online version of the Keirsey Temperament Sorter II'. *Journal of Career Assessment,* 9 (1), 49-59.

Kier, F.J., Melancon, J.G. and Thompson, B. (1998). 'Reliability and validity of scores on the Personal Preferences Self-Description Questionnaire (PPSDQ)'. *Educational and Psychological Measurement,* 58, 612-622.

Kline, P. (2000). *Handbook of Psychological Testing.* London: Routledge.

Lawrence, R. and Taylor, L.W. (2000). 'Student personality type versus grading procedures in intermediate accounting courses'. *Journal of Education for Business,* 76, 28-35.

Lester, D. (2000). 'Psychache, depression and personality'. *Psychological Reports,* 87, 940.

Levy, N., Murphy, C. and Carlson, R. (1972). 'Personality types among Negro college students'. *Educational and Psychological Measurement*, 32, 641-653.

Levy, N. and Padilla, A. (1982). 'A Spanish translation of the Myers-Briggs Type Indicator Form G'. *Psychological Reports*, 51, 109-110.

Levy, N. and Ridley, S.E. (1987). 'Stability of Jungian personality types within a college population over a decade'. *Psychological Reports*, 60, 419-422.

Loomis, M. (1982). 'A new perspective for Jung's typology: the Singer-Loomis Inventory of Personality'. *Journal of Analytical Psychology*, 27, 59-69.

McCarley, N.G. and Carskadon, T.G. (1983). 'Test-retest reliabilities of scales and subscales of the Myers-Briggs Type Indicator and of criteria for clinical interpretive hypotheses involving them'. *Research in Psychological Type*, 6, 24-36.

Mitchell, W.D. (1991). 'A test of type theory using the TDI'. *Journal of Psychological Type*, 22, 15-26.

Myers, I.B. and McCaulley, M.H. (1985). *Manual: a guide to the development and use of the Myers-Briggs Type Indicator*. Palo Alto, CA: Consulting Psychologists Press.

Myers, I.B., McCaulley, M.H., Quenk, N.L. and Hammer, A.L. (1998). *Manual: a guide to the development and use of the Myers-Briggs Type Indicator*. Palo Alto, CA: Consulting Psychologists Press.

Quinn, M.T., Lewis, R.J. and Fischer, K.L. (1992). 'A cross-correlation of the Myers-Briggs and the Keirsey instruments'. *Journal of College Student Development*, 33, 279-280.

Rawling, K. (1992). *Preliminary manual: The Cambridge Type Indicator; Research Edition*. Cambridge, UK: Rawling Associates.

Saggino, A. and Kline, P. (1995). 'Item factor analysis of the Italian version of the Myers-Briggs Type Indicator'. *Personality and Individual Differences*, 19, 243-249.

Salter, D.W., Evans, N.J. and Forney, D.S. (1997). 'Test-retest of the Myers-Briggs Type Indicator: an examination of dominant functioning'. *Educational and Psychological Measurement*, 57, 590-597.

Sandow, P.L., Jones, C.A. and Moody, R.A. (2000). 'Psychological type and dentistry'. *Journal of Psychological Type*, 55, 26-42.

Shamdasani, S. (2003). *Jung and the Making of Modern Psychology*. Cambridge, UK: Cambridge University Press.

Silberman, S.L., Freeman, I. and Lester, G.R. (1992). 'A longitudinal study of dental students' personality type preferences'. *Journal of Dental Education*, 56, 384-388.

Singer, J., Loomis, M., Kirkhart, E. and Kirkhart, L. (1996). *The Singer-Loomis Type Deployment Inventory - version 4.1*. Gresham, OR: Moving Boundaries.

Steele, R.S. and Kelly, T.J. (1976). 'Eysenck personality questionnaire and Jungian Myers-Briggs Type Indicator correlation of extraversion-introversion'. *Journal of Consulting and Clinical Psychology*, 44, 690-691.

Stricker, L.J. and Ross, J. (1963). 'Intercorrelations and reliability of the Myers-Briggs Type Indicator Scales'. *Psychological Reports*, 12, 287-293.

Stricker, L.J. and Ross, J. (1964). 'An assessment of some structural properties of the Jungian personality typology'. *Journal of Abnormal and Social Psychology*, 68, 62-71.

Thompson, B. (1996). *Personal Preferences Self-Description Questionnaire*. College Station, TX: Psychometrics Group.

Tsuzuki, Y. and Matsui, T. (1997). 'Test-retest reliabilities of a Japanese translation of the Myers-Briggs Type Indicator'. *Psychological Reports*, 81, 349-350.

Tucker, I.F. and Gillespie, B.V. (1993). 'Correlations among three measures of personality type'. *Perceptual and Motor Skills*, 77 (2), 650.

Tzeng, O.C.S., Ware, R., Outcalt, D. and Boyer, S.L. (1985). 'Assessment of the Myers-Briggs Type Inventory items'. *Psychological Documents*, 15, 17-18.

Ware, R., Yokomoto, C. and Morris, B.B. (1985). 'A preliminary study to assess validity of the personal style inventory'. *Psychological Reports*, 56, 903-910.

Waskel, S.A. and Coleman, J. (1991). 'Correlations of temperament types, intensity of crisis at midlife with scores on a death scale'. *Psychological Reports*, 68, 1187-1190.

In: New Psychological Tests and Testing Research
Editor: Lydia S. Boyar, pp. 141-156

ISBN: 978-1-60021-570-4
© 2007 Nova Science Publishers, Inc.

Chapter 7

BEHAVIOR ASSESSMENT IN NEUROREHABILITATION

Gordon Teichner[1], Sari A. Newman[1] and Brad Donohue[2]*

[1] Private Practice
[2]University of Nevada, Las Vegas

ABSTRACT

Behavioral interventions are becoming increasingly popular in neurorehabilitation settings to treat problem behaviors that interfere with the recovery of patients. Interventions are particularly effective when adequate assessment procedures are utilized to guide the intervention plan. The purpose of this chapter, therefore, is to underscore behavioral assessment methods that are appropriate for use in neurorehabilitation settings, including behavioral interviewing, standardized rating scales and behavioral checklists, behavioral observation, and self-monitoring. Implementation of the aforementioned assessment methods are reviewed in the context of functional assessment, an integral part of behavioral assessment that emphasizes the identification of problem behaviors, problem analysis, intervention planning, and behavioral progress indicators.

Keywords: Behavior Assessment, Behavior Analysis, Neurorehabilitation, Rehabilitation, Functional Assessment.

HISTORY OF BEHAVIORAL ASSESSMENT

Behavior assessment, which is the objective assessment of human behavior, has its roots in Pavlov and Watsons' work in classical conditioning, and the application of operant conditioning to human behavior by other pioneers, such as Azrin and Lindsley. The advent of behavioral therapies in the late 1950s paved the way for the utilization of behavioral

---

* Please address all correspondence to: Gordon Teichner, Ph.D.; 1270 Chrismill Ln., Mount Pleasant, C 29464; (843) 849-9913; (843) 881-6878 – fax; email: teichnerg@hotmail.com

assessment procedures in the early 1960s. Early assessment methods focused on observation of behavioral patterns that were relevant to the individual's functioning. Staats' *Complex Human Behavior* in 1963, and Kanfer and Saslow's *Behavioral Analysis* in 1965, helped to generate widespread interest in behavioral assessment, and within a decade, several handbooks were published to assist clinicians in their assessment of human behavior. For instance, Hersen and Bellack's *Behavioral Assessment* was published in 1976, and marked the emergence of scientific journals specific to behavioral assessment (e.g., *Behavioral Assessment, Journal of Psychopathology and Behavioral Assessment*). During the 1970s, most clinicians who utilized behavioral assessment procedures espoused its original tenets, as these individuals rejected mentalistic and self-report procedures, and instead relied upon observation of overt behavior and functional analysis. However, by the early 1980s there did not appear to be a consistent set of methods, as the practice of behavioral assessment became more diversified. Indeed, observation, which is the hallmark of behavioral assessment, was indicated in less than 15% of articles published in popular behavioral assessment journals in the early to mid-1980s (Fernandez-Ballesteros, 1988). This growing diversity was accompanied by a steady increase in the number of journal articles that were published on the topic of behavioral assessment. Indeed, the term "behavioral assessment" appeared in less than 50 articles per year up to 1980, but exceeded 200 articles in 1983 (Fernandez-Ballestros, 1993). In the late 1980s, the "watering down" of behavioral assessment continued to occur, as standardized questionnaires measuring molar traits were present in more than 75% of articles published in *Behavior Therapy* from 1988 to 1991 (Haynes and Uchigakiuchi, 1993). Moreover, Fernanez-Ballestros, Zamarron, and Huici (1992) reviewed the *Dictionary of Behavioral Assessment Techniques* by Bellack and Hersen (1988), and found only 34% of the instruments included objective observational and physiological assessment procedures. Indeed, 66% of the instruments were based on self-report, structured interviews, or rating scales by others, and these trends have continued into the present. As demonstrated below, these historical events have influenced the method of behavior assessment as applied to rehabilitation, including the use of functional behavioral analysis, neurobehavioral assessment, and objective ratings of behavior.

BEHAVIORAL ASSESSMENT

Behavioral assessment is distinct from other psychological assessment methods in its reliance on objective behavior, and exclusion of trait assumptions. A fundamental assumption of behavioral assessment is that behavior is situation specific. Along these lines, the initiation and maintenance of behavior is a dynamic process that must be assessed across various environments (e.g., cafeteria, chemical dependency unit, cigarette break), and across time (e.g., first day of hospitalization, week before discharge). As Nelson and Hayes (1979) assert, behavioral assessment involves the measurement of target behaviors and their controlling variables so that the environment may be strategically altered to influence behavior in a desirable manner. Controlling variables include stimuli that precede, co-occur, and follow, the behavior of interest, and an examination of their relationship is often referred to as the ABCs of functional assessment (i.e., Antecedent-Behavior-Consequence). An extension of this model, SORKC, reflects antecedent stimuli (S), factors inherent to the organism (O), the target response (R), contingency relationships (K), and consequences (C). This acronym is particularly relevant to functional assessment in neurorehabilitation settings because it emphasizes the importance of factors that are inherent to the organism (i.e., disease, stroke, trauma). Both the ABC and SORKC models are pertinent to functional assessment, which specifically includes identification of problem behavior(s), problem analysis, intervention planning, and utilization of behavioral progress indicators.

Problem Identification

The first step in understanding problem behaviors evinced by patients in neurorehabilitative settings is to systematically identify the behaviors of greatest concern. This process is best accomplished using multi-method assessment procedures; first identifying problems broadly, and becoming more specific as the process unfolds (Donohue, Ammerman, and Zelis, 1998). Target behaviors should be pertinent to the rehabilitation process, and often include basic hygiene, physical activity, exercises in mental processing, medication compliance, failure to attempt full effort during rehabilitative exercises, poor execution in daily living skills, and social inappropriateness. Behavioral methods that may be used to identify problem behaviors include interviews of problem behavior, examination of patient records, behavioral checklists and rating scales, direct observation, and self-monitoring procedures.

Interviews
Problem identification usually begins with the implementation of unstructured behavioral interviews involving the patient, and/or relevant others. These interviews are typically conducted in professional offices, or rehabilitation settings. Initial interviews are focused on identifying, and perhaps broadly understanding, problem behaviors that may be interfering with the patient's rehabilitation so that other appropriate assessment instruments can be determined. A systematic analysis of problem behavior is unnecessary during the initial stage of interviewing. Rather, the assessor should attempt to clearly define problem behaviors that are initially identified. For instance, if a nurse reported that a stroke victim had "no social etiquette," it would probably suffice to learn that this patient grabs the breasts of female staff members, spits on other patients, and kisses visitors without consent. Later, interviews become more focused on factors that maintain these problem behaviors, including stimuli that are associated with the onset and occurrence/non-occurrence of problem behavior, as well as stimuli that precede and follow problem behaviors.

Examination of Patient Records
Examining patient records (i.e., medical charts, psychiatric reports) provide relevant background information that is essential to later treatment planning. The examination of patient records may include an assessment of (a) *developmental history,* including age of mother at birth, medical problems and substance use that may have been present during the pregnancy, length of term, birth weight, birth complications, APGAR scores, achievement of developmental milestones, history of possible language, sensory, or perceptual, problems, history of childhood learning, attentional, behavioral problems, change in lateral dominance; (b) *medical history* focused primarily on seizures, head injury, loss of consciousness, illness

(e.g., hypertension, diabetes, cancer), CVA, coronary dysfunction, toxic exposure, respiratory problems, vascular complications, hospitalizations, operations, results of neurodiagnostic studies (e.g., SPECT, MRI, CT), lab results; (c) past and present use of *medications,* onset, duration, dose, response, and compliance to medications; (d) *psychiatric history* (e.g., depression, anxiety, psychotic behavior), psychiatric hospitalizations, response to psychological interventions, substance use history (i.e., alcohol, illicit drugs, prescription medications, tobacco, caffeine); (e) *family history* including social, vocational, neurological, psychiatric, medical, educational history of relevant family members; (f) *educational history,* such as highest level achieved, grades in school, results from standardized academic tests, special educational placements; (g) *legal history* of offenses, arrests, time spent in jail, DUIs, involvement in litigation; (h) *vocational history,* including.a chronical of the patient's work history, job responsibilities, time in recent jobs, disciplinary actions; and (i) *social history,* particularly social skills, family constellation and quality of relationships, social supports, transportation, resources in community, interests/hobbies, and daily routine. Of course, subsequent interviewing should be performed, as needed, particularly since records are often incomplete or inadequate.

Standardized Rating Scales and Problem Behavior Checklists

There are a number of rating scales and problem checklists that are particularly relevant for use in rehabilitation settings. An excellent measure to assess basic skills is the Functional Independence Measure (FIM; Hamilton, Granger, Sherwin, Zielezny, and Tashman, 1987). The measure consists of 18 items that assess the patient's degree of assistance required (1= Total Assistance, 7=Complete Independence). A total score is derived by summing item scores, and subscales may be used to evaluate specific behavior domains, including eating, grooming, bathing, dressing (upper body), dressing (lower body), toileting, bladder management, bowel management, transfers (regarding bed, chair, wheelchair, toilet, tub, shower), locomotion (walking or wheelchair, stairs), comprehension, expression, social interaction, problem solving, and memory. An expanded version of the FIM has also been developed to address problems specific to individuals with brain-injuries, i.e., Functional Assessment Measure (FAM; Ditunno, 1992; Hall, Hamilton, Gordon, and Zasler, 1993). The FAM offers 12 additional items focusing on cognitive, communicative, and psychosocial functions (see table 1 for FIM + FAM items). Increasingly, neurorehabilitation specialists are using the combined 30-item instrument. The FIM, FAM, and FIM+FAM have excellent test-retest reliability, interrater reliability, concurrent validity, content validity, and construct validity (see for example, Ditunno, 1992; Dodds, Martin, Stolov and Deyo, 1993; Granger and Hamilton, 1992; Hamilton, Laughlin, Granger, and Kayton, 1991; McPherson, Pentland, Cudmore, and Prescott, 1996; Whitneck, 1988).

The Barthel Index was originally published in 1965, was the first measure of disability used in most general medical rehabilitation settings (Mahoney and Barthel, 1965), and is comprised of the ten activities of daily living (see table 2). The Barthel Index was developed to assess functional independence before and after rehabilitation treatment, and to estimate the extent of nursing care necessary. This assessment tool is usually administered by a medical professional who has knowledge of the patient's day-to-day abilities. Items are rated on an ordinal scale, which assesses the patient's degree of dependence. A total score is derived by summing items ranging from 0 to 100; 5-point increments are used. The Modified Barthel Index is a revised version of this instrument (Granger, 1982). The latter version yields two subscale scores (Self-Care, Mobility), and offers a more extensive scoring system. Intra- and inter-rater reliability, internal consistency, and both construct and concurrent validity are good (e.g., Granger, Greer, Liset, Coulombe, and O'Brien, 1975; Kane and Kane, 1981; Loewan and Anderson, 1988; Mattison, Aitken, and Prescott, 1992).

Table 1. FIM+FAM item loadings (FAM loadings in italics)

Subscale	Item
Self-care	Eating, Grooming, Bathing, Dressing (upper body), Dressing (lower body), Toileting, *Swallowing*, Bladder management, Bowel management
Mobility	Transfer to chair, Transfer to toilet, Transfer to bath/shower, *Transfer to car*, Walking/wheelchair, Stairs, *Community access*
Psychological	
Adjustment	Social interaction, *Emotional Status, Adjustment to limitation, Employability*
Communication	Comprehension, Expression, *Reading, Writing, Speech intelligibility*
Cognitive	Problem Solving, Memory, *Orientation, Attention, Safety judgemen* function

Table 2. The Barthel Index

Subscale	Rating (points)	Level of Independence (Circle for each and sum below)
Feeding	(0, 5, 10)	10-Independent; 5- Some help necessary; 0-unable to independently
Wheelchair Transfer	(0, 5, 10, 15)	15-Independent in transfer, or does not require wheelchair; 10-Needs help, requires supervision; 5-Needs great deal of help to get out of chair or bed; 0-Bedridden, bedrest
Personal Care	(0, 5)	5-Can wash face and hands, comb hair, brush teeth, shave; 0-unable
Toilet Transfer	(0, 5, 10)	10-Patient can do it and redress; 5-Patient needs assistance; 0-Unable to perform/catheter/bedpan
Bathing	(0,5)	5-Able to use tub, shower, or complete sponge bath; 0-Requires assistance in bathing
Walking on Level Surface	(0, 5, 10, 15)	15-Able to walk 50 yards without help; 10-Requires help or supervision of another person to walk 50 yards; 5-Unable to walk but able to propel wheelchair; 0-Unable to walk or propel wheelchair
Stairs	(0, 5, 10)	10-Can go up and down stairs without assistance or supervision. Able to use device; 5-Needs help pr supervision, but can perform; 0-Unable
Dressing/undressing	(0, 5, 10)	10-Able to remove and put on all clothing including shoes; 5-Needs help to put on or remove clothing in a reasonable time; 0-Unable
Continence of bowel	(0, 5, 10)	10-Patient controls bowels. No accidents. Can use bedpan at bed rest; 5-Occasionally incontinent; 0-Incontinent, no bowel control
Control of bladder	(0, 5, 10)	10-Controls bladder day and night. Able to use bedpan at bed rest; 5-Occasional accidents, needs help to void; 0-Unable to control bladder, frequently incontinent. Needs catheter.
Date / time: _____		
Total Score: _____		

The PULSES Profile was first developed by Moskowitz and McCann (1957), and has since been revised (Granger, Albrecht, and Hamilton, 1979). Functional ratings in six domains are made using an ordinal scale, ranging from 1 (highest function) to 4 (least independence). Scores are summed to obtain a total score ranging from 6 to 24. A score greater than 12 indicates Severe Disability (Granger et al., 1979), and this scale can be used to monitor a patient's rehabilitative progress (Granger and Greer, 1976; Marshall, Heisel, and Grinnell, 1999). The PULSES Profile is comprised of the following domains: (P) physical condition, which includes cardiovascular, pulmonary, gastrointestinal, urological, and endocrine diseases; (U) upper limb function, including shoulders, cervical, and dorsal spine; (L) lower limb function, including pelvis, lower dorsal, and lumbosacral spine; (S) sensory functions relating to speech, vision, and hearing; (E) excretory functions (i.e., bowel and bladder control); (S) support factors including cognitive functions, emotional adaptability, family support, and financial means. Psychometric properties of this instrument have consistently been demonstrated, including test-retest reliability, interrater reliability, construct validity, criterion validity, and predictive validity (see, for example, Cole, Finch, Gowland, and Mayo, 1994; Granger, Sherwood, and Greer, 1977; Granger and Greer, 1976; Marshall et al., 1999). This measure is appropriate for assessing level of disability, tracking behavioral change, and predicting patient discharge disposition. The PULSES Profile is presented in table 3.

Table 3. The PULSES Profile

Subscale	Level of Functioning (Circle for each and insert below)
(P) Physical Condition	1 - No gross abnormalities for age; 2 - Minor abnormalities that do not require frequent medical/nursing assistance; 3-Moderately severe abnormalities requiring frequent nursing/medical supervision yet still able to ambulate; 4- Severe abnormalities requiring continuous nursing/medical supervision or confining patient to bed or wheelchair
(U) Upper Extremities	1 - No gross abnormalities for age; 2 - Minor abnormalities with adequate range of motion and function; 3 - Moderately severe abnormalities but able to perform daily needs to a limited extent; 4 - Severe abnormalities requiring continual care
(L) Lower Extremities	1 - No gross abnormalities for age; 2 - Minor abnormalities with fairly good range of motion and function; 3 - Moderately severe abnormalities permitting limited ambulation; 4- Severe abnormalities confining individual to bed or wheelchair
(S) Sensory	1- No gross abnormalities for age; 2 - Minor deviations that do not cause any appreciable functional impairment; 3 - Moderate deviations that cause appreciable functional impairment; 4 - Severe impairments causing complete loss of hearing, vision, or speech
(E) Excretory Function	1- Complete control; 2 - Occasional stress incontinence or nocturia; 3 - Occasional stress incontinence or nocturia; 4- Total incontinence, either bowel or bladder
(S) Mental and Emotional Status	1- No gross deviations for age; 2 - Minor deviations in mood, temperment, and personality not impairment social adjustment; 3 - Moderately severe variations requiring some supervision; 4 - Severe variations requiring complete supervision

Profile

P	U	L	S	E	S	Score (6-24)

Date / time: _____

The Level of Rehabilitation Scale-III (Formations, 1992) may be utilized to rate functioning across Activities and Daily Living, Mobility, Communication, and Cognitive Ability. Ratings of Activities and Daily Living are obtained for dressing, grooming, washing/bathing, toileting, and feeding. Mobility ratings are obtained for wheelchair management and ambulation. Communication ratings are obtained for auditory comprehension, oral expression, reading comprehension, written expression, an alternate communication, and Cognitive Abilities assessed include attention, orientation, problem solving, sequencing, short-term memory, and long-term memory. Functions are rated by rehabilitation clinicians utilizing a Likert-scale (1 = unable to perform any aspect of the activity, 5= no rehabilitation is necessary). The LORS-III is applicable for patients who are receiving inpatient rehabilitative care. Adequate psychometrically properties of this instrument have been demonstrated for earlier versions of the LORS (e.g., Carey and Posavac, 1978; 1982), while psychometric evaluations of the LORS-III are limited.

The Disability Rating Scale (Rappaport et al., 1982) objectively assesses disability from the emerging stages of post-injury to long-term follow-up. It serves as a global measure of outcome, including a broad range of items from a variety of functional domains. It is more useful in evaluating outcomes following neurosurgery than it is for acute rehabilitation interventions (Pender and Fleminger, 1999), especially in the initial months following injury. Psychometric properties are adequate (Clifton et al., 1992), and administration and scoring are considerably shorter than similar measures (e.g., FIM).

A number of scales have been developed to assess patients who are in various stages of coma, or who are minimally responsive. Examples include the Coma Recovery Scale (Giacino, Kezmarsky, DeLuca, and Cicerone, 1991), Rancho Los Amigos Scale: Levels of Cognitive Functioning (Hagen, Malkmus, Durham, and Bowman, 1979), the Sensory Modality Assessment and Rehabilitation Technique (SMART; see Gill-Thwaites and Munday, 1999), Glascow Coma Scale (Teasdale and Jennett, 1974), Galveston Orientation and Amnesia Test (Levin, O'Donnell, and Grossman, 1979), and the Western NeuroSensory Stimulation Profile (Ansell and Keenan, 1989). Most of these scales attempt to quantify the patient's level of awareness and responsiveness by objectively assessing motor, sensory, and communicative functions. Level of awareness and responsiveness can be measured over time by comparing the total score obtained on one of these respective measures. Results have been correlated with prognosis (e.g., see Giacino et al., 1991).

Other clinical domains that may be assessed utilizing behavior rating scales include depression (e.g., Beck Depression Inventory, Beck, 1978; Geriatric Depression Scale, Brink et al., 1982; Yesavage et al., 1983), personality (e.g., NEO-Five Factor, MMPI-2, Hathaway et al., 1989), aggression (e.g., Overt Aggression Scale, Yudofsky et. al., 1986), internalizing and externalizing problem behaviors in children (e.g., Child Behavior Checklist, Achenbach, 1991), activities of daily living and independent activities of daily living (see Carswell et al., 1993; Kovar and Lawton, 1994), activities for elderly patients (e.g., The Activities Checklist;

Arbuckle, Gold, Chaikelson, and Lapidus, 1994), vocational readiness (e.g., Work Personality Profile, Brown, 1988; Vocational Adaptivity Scale, Thomas, 1984), and psychosocial outcome (e.g., Katz Adjustment Scale, Katz and Lyerly, 1963; Mayo-Portland Adaptability Inventory, Lezak, 1987). Reviews of these measures are offered by several authors (see for example, Clifton et al., 1992; Lezak, 1995; McNeil and Greenwood, 1999; Neal, 1998; Pender and Fleminger, 1999; Spreen and Strauss, 1998; Tuner-Stokes, 1999).

Behavioral Observation

Self-report measures provide valuable information, but are limited in that these procedures are potentially biased due to social desireability and distortions in memory, among other things. Therefore, these measures are often complemented with the inclusion of behavioral observation procedures, which have traditionally been the hallmark of behavioral assessment. Behavioral observation procedures range in complexity from casual observation of non-specified behaviors (the observational method typically utilized to initially identify problem behaviors) to highly structured observations of molecular behaviors that are clearly defined. Scheduling the time and settings of observation, as well as specifying the behavior that is to be observed, will increase reliability, whereas a varying these observation procedures may provide unique information that might otherwise be overlooked. Behavior of most patients is influenced by the presence of the rater. However, with the passage of time response reactivity dissipates, particularly if the rater is inconspicuous.

An informal observation of the patient in her/his home and/or rehabilitation setting should occur prior to implementing formal observation procedures. Informal observation should be focused on (a) problem behaviors that are elicited from patient records, interviews, rating scales and problem checklists, as well as (b) factors that are thought to influence the maintenance of problem behaviors (e.g., antecedent and consequent stimuli, associated events). Informal observation should always include aspects of motor functioning (e.g., tremor, cogwheeling, balance, gait), sensory and perceptual abilities, attention (e.g., vigilance, distraction), language (e.g., receptive/expressive abilities, production fluency, paraphasias, articulatory agility), thought content, affect (i.e., flat, labile), social skills, and adaptation strategies.

Observation codes that target a broad range of behavior (e.g., tantrums) may be appropriate initially to gain a global understanding of presenting problems. However, target behaviors may need to be specified later to reliably monitor progress in treatment (e.g., yelling, kicking, punching). Assessors will need to determine the number of behaviors to be monitored, the duration of monitoring intervals, and method of recording. The times of observation are relevant to the expected occurrence of presenting problems. For instance, if a patient refuses to walk to the cafeteria for breakfast despite urging to do so by staff, than observations must occur shortly before, during, and after breakfast. Methods of recording observational data vary, and include dichotomous ratings (e.g., presence/absence, appropriate/inappropriate), Likert-scale ratings (e.g., 0=poor, 1=satisfactory, 2=excellent), and qualitative statements (e.g., yells at nurse after being told to put out cigarette, nurse walks away). It is also possible to record by-products of target behavior (e.g., monitoring the number of exercise classes attended will assist in understanding compliance to a weight reduction program). Observation is usually best accomplished in the patient's natural environment. However, when environmental observation is not possible (e.g., behavior of interest does not occur in the presence of others, expense necessary to obtain sufficient sampling of target behaviors is extensive), analog observation is an option. Analog observation involves observation of behavior in environments that are structured to maximize observational efficiency (e.g., encouraging a patient to attempt to change his medication prescription with an actor who is trained to portray a physician who refuses to change the medication). As might be inferred, the primary disadvantage of analog observation is generalizing observed behavior patterns to the patient's natural environment.

Self-Monitoring

In this procedure, target behaviors, and associated factors, are recorded by the patient during specified times or events (e.g., lunchtime, times during the day when the problem behavior occurs). Self-monitoring procedures are usually not utilized to identify problem behaviors, but rather to monitor behaviors that have already been identified, as well as to identify associated events and stimuli of these problems (i.e., how often, and in what stimulus contexts, the problem behavior occurs). The frequency and duration of target behaviors and corresponding times of occurrence are typically recorded, as well as antecedent, concurrent, and consequent stimuli. Feelings and thoughts are often monitored in relation to target behaviors to assist in gathering subjective information from the patient, including corresponding severity ratings (e.g., 1=completely unhappy, 5=completely happy).

Self-monitoring strategies have consistently been found to yield improvements in target behavior (see Becker and Heimberg, 1988). However, these apparent improvements may be due to biases associated with social desireability, particularly when legal sanctions are involved. The accuracy of self-monitoring procedures may also be influenced by the failure of patients to record data as scheduled, and omissions and distortions of recalled information due to limitations in memory. When the validity of self-report data is questionable, significant others may be utilized to monitor the patient's behavior.

Problem Analysis

Once broad diagnostic problem areas have been sufficiently identified, the task switches to the analysis of specific, operationally defined behaviors. Descriptive functional analysis is the process of initially examining the data so that hypotheses may be formulated about the function of problem behaviors. In this method, the identified problem areas are specified into objective, observable, and measureable behaviors. For instance, if interview data indicated that a patient "often gets frustrated," this information could be easily specified by recording the behaviors that occur when the patient is "frustrated" (e.g., walks away, cries). To assist in the organization of data, problem behaviors may be grouped together, according to related themes (e.g., use of cocaine and alcohol might be recorded within the domain of "substance abuse"; swearing and kicking staff members might be clustered together as "aggressive behaviors"). After identified problem behaviors are listed, antecedent and consequent stimuli may be written to the left and right of these behaviors, respectively. For instance, if the problem behavior was "yelling," antecedent stimuli (e.g., instructions to do rehabilitation exercises) would be listed to the left of "yelling," and consequences (rubbing the patient's back, talking softly) would be listed to the right of "yelling." Thus, there would essentially be three columns in this organizational structure (i.e., antecedent stimuli, the target behavior, consequences). Recording data in this manner will permit a critical analysis of the ABC relationship, which in turn will facilitate confirmation/disconfirmation of conceptual hypotheses that are relevant to the development and maintenance of problem behavior [e.g., Mary spits out her food (target behavior) because she does not like the taste or texture of the food (antecedent), and because she gets attention that is otherwise absent (consequence)]. The aforementioned format may also demonstrate additional assessment needs (i.e., problem behaviors that need greater specification, antecedent and consequent stimuli that were not recognized or assessed).

The last stage of problem analysis, experimental functional analysis, involves the experimental manipulation of environmental events and stimuli so that variables may be identified that maintain problem behaviors. For instance, if a patient refused to participate in a computer exercise, and instead watched television, it could be hypothesized that television viewing interfered with the patient's compliance to perform the computer exercise. A reversal design could be utilized to verify the validity of this hypothesis (i.e., permit television access, do not permit television access, permit television assess). If computer practice occurred only during the no television access phase, television access would appear to interfere with the patient's computer practice. Although experimental functional analysis is an excellent method to examine functional hypotheses of problem behavior, this procedure is rarely used in non-research settings due obvious costs and difficulties required to conduct the analyses.

Intervention Plan

After problem behaviors are sufficiently identified, and the functions of these behaviors are sufficiently understood by the assessor, a conceptualization of the development and maintenance of relevant problem behaviors should be provided to the patient and/or others who are involved in the patient's recovery. It is important to disseminate assessment findings for several reasons. By having a clear understanding of the presenting problems, patients are more apt to recognize, and take action to prevent, contributing problem behaviors. This process also provides opportunities to discount unreasonable expectations for behavioral intervention which often lead to an overly critical environment.

After the assessment results are reviewed and conceptualized, the intervention plan may be implemented. It is helpful to begin this process by modifying each behavior that was identified to be problematic into a goal statement that reflects the alternative behavior that is desired (e.g., eating with hands to eating with utensils). When multiple problem behaviors are present, it will be necessary to prioritize the behaviors that are to be targeted during intervention. In this endeavor, the patient, and others when the patient is not capable, should be asked to rank which behaviors are of greatest concern. As might be expected, higher ranked behaviors should be emphasized in therapy (see Donohue and Azrin, 2001).

The patient, and/or relevant others, should also be included in the selection of interventions to be utilized. For each problem behavior that is identified, the patient should be offered at least a couple of empirically-supported interventions from which to choose. For instance, time out, positive practice, and behavioral contracting might be presented as therapy options to the parent of a patient who is frequently noncompliant. A brief rationale (i.e., less than 5 mins.) should be provided for each treatment, including a statement of the intervention's efficacy, an uncomplicated overview of its components, and discussion of expected pros and cons involved in its implementation.

Assessment of Behavioral Progress Indicators

To evaluate the effects of intervention, it will be necessary to monitor the accomplishment of goal oriented behaviors throughout the patient's rehabilitation. Measures that indicated significant problems before the initiation of intervention should be re-administered at the completion of treatment, and ideally at a follow-up examination. However, some behavioral measures that are quick to implement, and representative of primary target behaviors, should be administered more frequently (i.e., once per month). Satisfaction ratings (i.e., 0=completely unhappy, 100=completely happy) that are completed by the patient, are becoming increasingly popular in the evaluation of intervention, particularly since these measures have been found to closely correspond to results obtained from measures of objective behavior and standardized rating scales, and they are quickly administered (Azrin, Donohue, Teichner, Howell, and Decato, 2001).

REFERENCES

Achenbach, T.M. (1991). *Manual for the Child Behavior Checklist/4-18 and 1991 Profile.* Burlington, VT: University of Vermont, Department of Psychiatry.

Ansell, B.J., and Keenan, M.A. (1989). The Western Neuro Sensory Stimulation for assessing slow to recovery head injured patients. *Archives of Physical Medicine and Rehabilitation, 70,* 104-108.

Arbuckle, T.Y., Gold, D.P., Chaikelson, J.S., and Lapidus, S. (1994). Measurement of activity in the elderly: TheActivities Checklist. *Canadian Journal onAging,* 13, 550-565.

Azrin, N.H., Donohue, B., Teichner, G.T., Howell, J.., and Decato, L. (2001). A Controlled Evaluation, and Description, of Individual-Cognitive and Family-Behavioral Therapies in Dually-Diagnosed Conduct-Disordered and Substance-Dependent Youth. *Journal of Child and Adolescent Substance Abuse,11,* 1-43.

Beck, A.T. (1978; Beck, A.T., and Steer, R.A., 1993). *Beck Depression Inventory Manual.* San Antonio, TX: Psychological Corporation.

Becker, R.E., and Heimberg, R.G. (1988). Assessment of social skills. In A. Bellack and M. Hersen (Eds.). Behavioral Assessment: A Practical Handbook (3rd Edition). Boston: Allyn and Bacon.

Brink, T.L., Yesavage, J.A., Lum, O., Heersema, P.H., Adey, M., and Rose, T.S. (1982). Screening test for geriatric depression. *Clinical Gerontologist, 1,* 37-43.

Brown, C. D. (1988). A study of the predictive validity of the Work Personality Profile. *Vocational Evaluation and Work Adjustment Bulletin, 21,* 89-94.

Cantini, E., Gluck, M. and McLean, A. (1992). Psychotropic-absent behavioural improvement following severe traumatic brain injury. Brain Injury, 6(2), 193-97.

Carswell, A., Carson, L., Dulberg, C.,.Walop, W. et al. (1993). The Functional Performance Measure (FPM) for persons with Alzheimer disease. *Canadian Journal of Rehabilitation, 7,* 53-55.

Clifton, G.L., Hayes, R.L., Levin, H.S., Michel, M.E., and Choi, S.C. (1992). Outcome measures for clinical trials involving traumatically brain-injured patients: report of a conference. *Neurosurgery, 31,* 975-978.

Cole, B., Finch, E., Gowland, C., and Mayo, N. (1994). *Physical rehabilitation outcome measures.* Toronto: Canadian Physiotherapy Association.

Corrigan, P., Yudofsky, S., and Silver, J. (1993). Pharmacological and behavioral treatments for aggressive psychiatric inpatients. *Hospital and Community Psychiatry, 44(2),* 125-133.

Delis, D.C., Kramer, J.H., Kaplan, E., and Ober, B.A. (1987). *California Verbal Learning Test: Adult Version Manual.* San Antonio, TX: The Psychological Corporation.

Ditunno, J.R. (1992). Functional assessment measures in CNS trauma. *Journal of Neurotrauma, 9 (Suppl.1):* S301-S305.

Dodds, T.A., Martin, D.P., Stolov, W.C., and Deyo, R.A. (1993). A validation of the Functional Independence Measure and its performance among rehabilitation inpatients. *Archives of Physical Medicine and Rehabilitation, 74,* 531-536.

Donohue, B., Ammerman, R., and Zellis, K. (1998). Child Abuse and Neglect. In T. S. Watson and F.M. Gresham (Eds.). Handbook of Child Behavior Therapy. New York: Plenum Press.

Donohue, B., and Azrin, N.H. (2001). Family Behavior Therapy. In E. Wagner and H. Waldron (Eds.). Innovations in Adolescent Substance Abuse Intervention. Tarrytown, NY: Pergamon Press.

Eames, P. and Wood, R. (1985). Rehabilitation after severe brain injury: A follow-up study of a behavioiur modification approach. *Journal of Neurology, Neurosurgery and Psychiatry, 48,* 613-619.

Fernandez-Ballestros, R. (1988). *Que escriben los evaluadores conductuales?* Unpublished Manuscript, Madrid: Universidad Autonoma de Madrid.

Fernandez-Ballestros, R. (1993). Behavioral assessment: Dying, vanishing or still running. *European Journal of Psychological Assessment, 9,* 159-174.

Fernandez-Ballestros, R., and Zamarron, M.D., and Huici, C. (1992). *Datos bibliograficos recientes sobre evaluacion conductual.* Unpublished manuscript, Autonoma Universidad de Madrid.

Folstein, M.F., Folstein, S.E., and McHugh, P.R. (1975). "Mini-mental State". A practical method for grading the cognitive state of patients for the clinician. *Journal of Psychiatric Research, 12,* 189-198.

Formations (1992). *Level of Rehabilitation Scale (LORS-III) Reference Manual.* Chicago: Formations in Health Care.

Gauthier, L., DeHaut, F., and Joanette, Y. (1989). The Bells Test: A quantitative and qualitative test for visual neglect. *International Journal of Clinical Neuropsychology, 11,* 49-54.

Geanger, C.V., Greer, D.S., Liset, E., Coulombe, J., and O'Brien, E. (1975). Measurement of outcomes of care for patients. *Stroke, 6,* 34-41.

Giacino, J.T., Kezmarsky, M.A., DeLuca, J., and Cicerone, K.D. (1991). Monitoring recovery to predict outcome in minimally-responsive patients. *Archives of Physical Medicine and Rehabilitation, 72,* 897-901.

Gill-Thwaites, H., and Munday, R. (1999). The Sensory modality assessment and rehabilitation technique (SMART): A comprehensive and integrated assessment and treatment protocol for the vegetative state and minimally responsive patient. *Neuropsychological Rehabilitation, 9,* 305-320.

Golden, C.J., Purisch, A.D., and Hammeke, T.A. (1985). *Luria Nebraska Neuropsychological attery: Forms I and II.* Los Angeles: Western Psychological Services.

Granger, C.V. (1982). Health accounting: Functional assessment of the long-term patient. In F.J. Kottke, G.K. Stillwell, and J. F. Lehmann (Eds.), *Krusen's handbook of physical medicine and rehabilitation 3rd ed.,* pp.-253-274, Philadelphia: Saunders.

Granger, C., Albrecht, G., and Hamilton, B. (1979). Outcome of comprehensive medical rehabilitation: Measurement by PULSES profile and the Barthel index. *Archives of Physical Medicine and Rehabilitation, 60,* 145-154.

Granger, C., and Greer, D. Functional status measurement and medical rehabilitation outcomes. *Archives of Physical Medicine and Rehabilitation, 57,* 103-109.

Granger, C.V., and Hamilton, B.B. (1992). UDS report: The Uniform data System for Medical Rehabilitation report for first admissions for 1990. *American Journal of Physical Medicine and Rehabiltiation, 71,* 108-113.

Granger, C., Sherwood, C., and Greer, D. Functional status measures in a comprehensive stroke care program. *Archives of Physical Medicine and Rehabilitation, 58,* 555-561.

Hagen, C., Malkmus, D., Durham, P., and Bowman, K. (1979). Levels of cognitive functioning. *In Rehabilitation of the head injured adult. Comprehensive physical management.* Downey, CA: Professional Staff Association of Rancho Los Amigos Hospital.

Hall, K.M., Hamilton, B.B., Gordon, W.A., Zasler, N.D. (1993). Characteristics and comparisons of functional assessment indices: Disability Rating Scales, Functional Independence Measure and Functional Assessment Measure. *Journal of Head Trauma Rehabilitiation,* 60-71.

Hamilton, B.B., Granger, C.V., Sherwin, F.S., Zielezny, M., and Tashman, J.S. (1987). A uniform national data system for medical rehabilitation. In M. Fuhrer (Ed.), *Rehabilitation Outcomes: Analysis and measurement.* Baltimore: Paul H. Brookes, 137-147.

Hamilton, B.B., Laughlin, J.A., Granger, C.V., and Kayton, R.M. (1991). Interrater agreement of the seven level Functional Independence Measure (FIM) [abstract]. *Archives of Physical Medicine and Rehabilitation, 72,* 790.

Hansen, N.K. (1999). Essential readings in rehabilitation outcomes measurement. *The Journal of Head Trauma Rehabilitation, 14,* 428.

Hathaway, S.R., McKinley, J.C., with Butcher, J.N., Dahlstrom, W.G., Graham, J.R., Tellegen, A., and Kaemmer, B. (1989). *Minnesota Multiphasic Personality Inventory 2: Manual for Administration and Scoring.* Minneapolis: University of Minnesota Press.

Haynes, S.N., and Uchigakiuchi, P. (1993). Incorporating personality measures in behavioral assessment: Nuts in a fruitcake or raisins in a Mai Tai? *Behavior Modification, 17,* 72-91.

Heaton, R.K., Chelune, G.J., Talley, J.L., Kay, G.G., and Curtis, G. (1993). *Wisconsin Card Sorting Test (WCST) Manual Revised and Expanded.* Odessa, Fl: Psychological Assessment Resources.

Hersen, and Bellack (Eds.) (1976). *Behavioral Assessment.* New York: Pergamon Press.

Hersen, M., and Bellack, A. (1988). *Dictionary of behavioral assessment techniques.* New York: Pergamon Press.

Hoenig, H., Nusbaum, N., and Brummel-Smith, K. (1977). Geriatric rehabilitation: State of the art. *Journal of the American Geriatric Society, 45(11),* 1371-1381.

Kane, R.A., and Kane, R.L. (1981). *Assessing the elderly.* Lexington, MA: Health.

Kanfer, F.H. and Saslow, G. (1965). Behavioral analysis. *Archives of General Psychiatry, 12,* 529-538.

Kaplan, E.F., Goodglass, H., and Weintraub, S. (1983). *The Boston Naming Test.* Philedelphia: Lea and Febiger.

Katz, M.M., and Lyerly, S.B. (1963). Methods for measuring adjustment and social behavior in the community: Rationale, description, discriminative validity and scale development. *Psychological Reports, 13,* 503-535.

Kovar, M.G., and Lawton, M.P. (1994). Functional disability: Activities and instrumental activities of daily living. In M.P. Lawton and J.A. Teresi (Eds.). Annual review of gerontology and geriatrics: Focus on assessment techniques. *Annual Review of Gerontology and Geriatrics, 14,* 57-75. New York: Springer Publishing Co, Inc.

Levin, H.S., High, W.M., Goethe, K.E., Sisson, R.A., Overall, J.E., Rhoades, H.M., Eisenberg, H.M., Kalisky, Z., and Gary, H.E. (1987). Neurobehavioral rating scale: Assessment of the behavioural sequelae of head injury by the clinician. *Journal of Neurology, Neurosurgery, and Psychiatry, 50,* 183-193.

Levin, H.S., O'Donnell, V.M., and Grossman, R.G. (1979). The Galverston Orientation and Amnesia Test. A practical scale to assess cognition after head injury. *Journal of Nervous and Mental Disease, 167,* 675-684.

Lezak, M. (1987). Relationship between personality disorders, social disturbances, and physical disability following traumatic brain injury. *Journal of Head Trauma Rehabilitation, 2,* 51-59.

Lezak, M. (1995). *Neuropsychological Assessment, 3rd ed.* New York: Oxford University Press.

Lodge, M. (1992). Meeting the challenge of atypical agitation in the brain-injured patient: A case study. *Rehabilitation Nursing, 17,* 92-93.

Loewan, S.C., and Anderson, B.A. (1988). Reliability of the Modified Motor Assessment Scale and the Barthel Index. *Physical Therapy, 68,* 1077-1081.

Mahoney, F.I., and Barthel, D.W. (1965). Functional evaluation: The Barthel Index. *Maryland Medical Journal, 14,* 61-65.

Marshall, S.C., Heisel, B., and Grinnell, D. (1999). Validity of the PULSES profile compared with the Functional Independence Measure for measuring disability in a stroke rehabilitation setting. *Archives of Physical Medicine and Rehabilitation, 80,* 760-765.

Mattison, P.G., Aitken, R.C.B., and Prescott, R.J. (1991). Rehabilitation status-The relationship between the Edinburgh Rehabilitation Status Scale (ERSS), Barthel Index, and PULSES profile. *International Disability Studies, 13,* 9-11.

McGlynn, S. (1990). Behavioral approaches to neuropsychological rehabilitation. *Psychological Bulletin, 108(3),* 420-441.

McNeil, J., and Greenwood, R. (1999). The use of disability outcome measures in a neurological rehabilitation unit. *Neuropsychological Rehabilitation, 9,* 321-328.

McPherson, K.M., Pentland, B., Cudmore, S.F., and Prescott, R.J. (1996). An inter-rater reliability study of the Functional Assessment Measure (FIM + FAM). *Disability and Rehabilitation, 18,* 341-347.

McReynolds, P. (1986). History of assessment in clinical educational settings. In R.O. Nelson and S.C. Hayes (Eds.), *Conceptual foundations of behavioral assessment,* pp. 42-80. New York: Guilford Press.

Meyers, J.E., and Meyers, K.R. (1995). *The Meyers Scoring System for the Rey Complex Figure and the Recogntion Trial: Professional Manual.* Odessa, Fl: Psychological Assessment Resources.

Mintzer, J., Lewis, L., Pennypaker, L., Simpson, W., Bachman, D., Wohlreich, G., Meeks, A., Hunt, S., and Sampson, R. (1993). Behavioral intensive care unit (BICU): A new concept in the management of acute agitated behavior in elderly demented patients. *The Gerontologist, 33,* 801-806.

Moskowitz, E., and McCann, C.B. (1957). Classification of disability in the chronically ill and aging. *Journal of Chronic Disease, 5,* 342-346.

Neal, L.J. (1998). Current functional assessment tool. *Home Healthcare Nurse, 16,* 766-772.

Noordsy, D.L., Torrey, W.C., Mead, S. and Brunette, M. (2000). Recovery-oriented psychopharmacology: redefining the goals of antisychotic treatment. *The Journal of Clinical Psychiatry, 61,*22-29.

Overall, J.E. and Gorham, D.R. (1962). The brief psychiatric rating scale. *Psychological Reports, 10,* 799-812.

Pender, N., and Fleminger, S. (1999). Outcome measures on inpatient cognitive and behavioural units: an overview. *Neuropsychological Rehabilitation, 9,* 345-361.

Randoph, C. (1998). *Repeatable Battery for the Assessment of Neuropsychological Status (RBANS).* The Psychological Corporation: Harcourt Brace and Company.

Rappaport, M., Hall, K.M., Hopkins, K., Belleza, T., and Cope, D.N. (1982). Disability Rating Scale for severe head trauma: Coma to community. *Archives of Physical Medicine and Rehabilitation, 63,* 118-123.

Reitan, R.M. and Davison, L.A. (1974). *Clinical Neuropsychology: Current Status and Applications.* Washington, D.C.: V.H. Winston.

Reitan, R.M. and Wolfson, D. (1993). *The Halstead-Reitan Neuropsychological Test Battery: Theory and clinical interpretation.* Tucson, AZ: Neuropsychology Press.

Schwamm, L.H., Van Dyke, C., Kiernan, R.J. et al., (1987). The Neurobehavioral Cognitive Status Examination. *Annals of Internal Medicine, 107,* 485-491.

Spreen, O., and Strauss, E. (1998). *A Compendium of Neuropsychological Tests: Administration, Norms, and Commentary, Second Edition.* New York: Oxford University Press.

Staats, A.W. (1963). *Complex Human Behavior.* New York: Holt, Rinehart and Winston.

Teasdale, G., and Jennett, B. (1974). Assessment of coma and impaired consciousness. *Lancet, ii,* 81-84.

Thomas, D. F. (1984). The construction and validation of the Vocational Adaptivity Scale. *Dissertation Abstracts International. 45(1-B),* 340-341.

Tiffin, J. (1968). *Purdue Pegboard: Examiner Manual.* Chicago: Science Research Associates.

Treadwell, K. and Page, T. (1996). Functional analysis: Identifying the environmental determinants of severe behavior disorders. *Journal of Head Trauma Rehabilitation, 11(1),*62-74.

Turner-Stokes, L. (1999). Outcome measures for inpatient neurorehabilitation settings. *Neuropsychological Rehabilitation, 9,* 329-343.

Uomoto, J., and Brockway, J. (1992). Anger management training for brain injured patients and their family members. *Archives of Physical Medicine Rehabilitation, 73,* 674-679.

Wade, D.T. (1999). Goal planning in stroke rehabilitation: Evidence. *Topics in Stroke Rehabilitation, 6,* 37.

Wechsler, D. (1997). *Wechsler Adult Intelligence Scale - Third Edition Administration and Scoring Manual.* The Psychological Corporation: San Antonio.

Whiteneck, G.G. (1988). A Functional Independence Measure trial in spinal cord injury model systems. [Abstract]. *Proceedings of the American Spinal Injury Association, 14,* 48.

Wilksonsin, G.S. (1993). *WRAT3 Administration Manual.* Delaware: Wide Range.

Woodcock, R.W., and Mather, N. (1989). *Woodcock-Johnson Tests of Achievement.* Allen, TX: DLM Teaching Resources.

Yesavage, J.A., Brink, T.L., Rose, T.L., Lum, O., Huang, V., Adey, M.B., and Leirer, V.O. (1983). Development and validation of a geriatric depression rating scale: A preliminary report. *Journal of Psychiatric Research, 17,* 37-49.

Yip, A.M., Gorman, M.C., Stadnyk, K. and Mills, W.G. (1998). A standardized menu for goal attainment scaling in the care of frail elders. *The Gerontologist, 38,* 735-742.

Yudofsky, S.C., Silver, S.M., Jackson, W., Endicott, J., and Williams, D. (1986). The overt aggression scale for the objective rating of verbal and physical aggression. *Journal of Psychiatry, 143,* 35-39.

In: New Psychological Tests and Testing Research
Editor: Lydia S. Boyar, pp. 157-172

ISBN: 978-1-60021-570-4
© 2007 Nova Science Publishers, Inc.

Chapter 8

NEUROPSYCHOLOGICAL ASSESSMENT IN SPANISH SPEAKING POPULATION

Feggy Ostrosky-Solís and *Asucena Lozano*

Laboratory of Neuropsychology and Psychophysiology,
National Autonomous University of Mexico, Mexico D. F., Mexico

ABSTRACT

Health care professionals are now faced with a growing number of patients from different ethnic groups, and from different socio-economical backgrounds. In the field of neuropsychology there is an increasing need of reliable and culturally fair assessment measures. Spanish is the official language in more than 20 countries and the second most spoken language in the world. The purpose of this article was to describe two tests developed and standardized for Spanish-speaking population and to review the main findings with a variety of clinical and experimental populations. The Brief Neuropsychological Test Battery NEUROPSI briefly assesses a wide spectrum of cognitive functions, including orientation, attention, memory, language, visuoperceptual abilities, and executive functions; normative data were collected from 1614 monolingual Spanish-speaking individuals, ages 16 to 85 years. Four age groups were used: (1) 16 to 30 years, (2) 31 to 50 years, (3) 51 to 65 years, and (4) 66 to 85 years. Data also are analyzed and presented within 4 different educational levels that were represented in this sample: (1) illiterates (zero years of school); (2) 1 to 4 years of school; (3) 5 to 9 years of school; and (4) 10 or more years of formal education. The NEUROPSI Attention and Memory was designed to assess orientation, attention and concentration, executive functions, working memory and immediate and delayed verbal and visual memory. Normative data were obtained from a sample of 950 monolingual Spanish Speaking subjects, aged 6 to 85 years. Educational level ranged from 0 to 22 years of education. These instruments may help fill the need for brief, reliable and objective evaluation of a broad range of cognitive functions in Spanish-speaking people.

---

* Address correspondence to: Feggy Ostrosky-Solis, Laboratory of Neuropsychology and Psychophysiology, National Autonomous University of Mexico. Rivera de Cupia 110-71, Lomas de Reforma, México, D. F., 11930, Mexico. E-mail: feggy @servidor.unam.mx

Keywords: Neuropsychological tests, Normative data, Attention, Memory, Age, Educational level, Culture.

INTRODUCTION

Spanish is the official language in more than 20 countries and the second most spoken language in the world (330 million speakers). When tests developed in other countries are used within Latin America, they are frequently just translated and the norms of other populations are used. This procedure undoubtedly invalidates the results. Furthermore, neuropsychological tests are translated to Spanish literally, with little consideration of cultural relevance. For example, using backward word spelling for the evaluation of attention (such as in the Mini-Mental State Examination; Folstein et al., 1975), naming the fingers to evaluate language or word finding difficulty (as found in the Alzheimer's Disease Assessment Scale; Rosen et al., 1984), or asking for the seasons of the year to assess orientation, as included in several geriatric scales, may be inappropriate in certain countries and some cultural contexts. In many countries, instead of four seasons there are only a rainy and a dry season. In tropical areas, there may be two rainy and two dry seasons. The seasonal changes around the year may be so mild and unnoticed, that the concept of "season" is irrelevant and nonsense. In many world areas the names of the fingers are rarely used, even by highly educated neurologically intact people. The use of visual stimuli that are of high frequency for one culture but infrequent or nonexistent for another (i.e. drawing of a pretzel) is also inappropriate. Since the simple translation, use of inappropriate visual stimuli and use of norms of a foreign instrument does not take into account this kind of cultural differences, errors in diagnosis can be predicted unless items are correctly adapted or developed to assess the new population and new normative data are obtained.

It has also been proposed that in neuropsychological testing, schooling is a more significant variable than age (Ostrosky-Solís et al., 1998). This effect of education has been reported not only for Spanish speaking populations but for English speaking as well; for example, the Mini Mental State Examination Score is affected more by level of education than by age across whites, Hispanics and Afro-American English speaking subjects (Launer et al., 1993, Murden, McRae, Kaner, and Bucknam, 1991). Moreover, the effects of education extend to both verbal and non verbal neuropsychological measures (Rosselli and Ardila, 2003).

Cognitive assessment, of both healthy and pathological populations, requires the use of objective and reliable neuropsychological instruments designed and adapted to appropriately evaluate the populations we are interested in. Moreover, appropriate normative data must be developed in order to establish an accurate clinical picture about the nature of the impairments (Bauer, Tobias, and Valenstein, 1993; Mayes, 1986; Squire and Shimamura, 1996). Therefore, it is important to have neuropsychological tests that are developed and standardized for Spanish-speaking populations. It is not only important to have data collected in Spanish-speaking populations, but also, given the influence that educational factors have on cognitive performance (Ardila, Ostrosky-Solis, Rosselli and Gomez, 2000; Ardila, Rosselli and Ostrosky, 1992; Castro-Caldas, Reis and Guerreiro, 1997; Heaton, Grant and Matthews, 1986; Ostrosky-Solís, Ardila, and Rosselli, 1999; Ostrosky-Solís, Ardila, Rosselli,

López and Mendoza, 1998; Ostrosky-Solís, Arellano and Pérez, 2004; Ostrosky, Canseco, Quintanar, Navarro and Ardila, 1985; Ostrosky, et al., 1986, 2003b), norms for neuropsychological tests should represent persons with different educational levels including illiterates.

Given the current limitations in the neuropsychological assessment of Spanish speakers, two tests were developed and standardized with this population. The purposes of the present article are: 1) to describe and review findings obtained from the Brief Neuropsychological Test Battery NEUROPSI (Ostrosky-Solís et al., 1997) with Spanish-speaking adults; and 2) to describe and review findings obtained from the NEUROPSI Attention and Memory with Spanish-speaking children and adults (Ostrosky-Solís et al., 2003).

BRIEF NEUROPSYCHOLOGICAL TEST BATTERY IN SPANISH: NEUROPSI

Different comprehensive evaluation instruments have been developed to assess cognitive dysfunctions in the neuropsychology domain. Some of these instruments represent extensive neuropsychological test batteries, such as the Halstead–Reitan Neuropsychological Battery (Reitan and Wolfson, 1993), the Luria–Nebraska Neuropsychological Battery (Golden, 1980), and the Scheme of Neuropsychological Assessment (Ardila and Ostrosky, 1991; Ardila et al., 1981). Such comprehensive batteries have two significant limitations: (1) their administration and scoring require many hours making them impractical for use in many clinical settings; and (2) administration and scoring require rather specialized training.

To overcome these difficulties, short mental status questionnaires (e.g., the Mini-Mental Status Exam; Folstein et al., 1975), and behavioral scales (e.g., Blessed Dementia Scale; Blessed et al., 1968) have been developed. They are easy to administer, score, and interpret. These instruments, however, are not completely satisfactory. Some limitations of these short questionnaires are (1) false negatives are high, and they are not sensitive to mild brain impairments (Bertolucci et al., 1994; Dick et al., 1984; Nelson et al., 1986; Schwamm et al., 1987); and (2) they may point to general cognitive impairments, but they are not specific enough. As a potential solution to these difficulties, some short instruments have been proposed such as the instrument of the Consortium to Establish a Registry for Alzheimer's Disease (CERAD; Morris et al., 1989), or the Brief Neuropsychological Cognitive Examination (BNCE; Tonkonogy, 1997).

The NEUROPSI was developed taking into account principles and procedures developed in cognitive neuroscience. Therefore, measures of specific cognitive domains that can be differentially impaired following brain damage are included. This battery has standardized procedures for both administration and scoring. It includes items that are relevant for Spanish speaking individuals, and can be applied to illiterate or subjects from low educational groups. It includes language and picture tests that have high, medium, and low frequency of occurrence in the Spanish language (Aveleyra et al., 1996). Normative data were collected from 1614 monolingual Spanish-speaking individuals, ages 16 to 85 years. Four age groups were used: (1) 16 to 30 years, (2) 31 to 50 years, (3) 51 to 65 years, and (4) 66 to 85 years. Data also are analyzed and presented within 4 different educational levels that were represented in this sample: (1) illiterates (zero years of school); (2) 1 to 4 years of school; (3) 5 to 9 years of school; and (4) 10 or more years of formal education.

The domains covered include Orientation, Attention, Concentration, Language, Memory, Visuo-Motor, Executive Function, Reading, Writing, and Calculation, each having its own subtests. Each area includes assessment of different aspects of that particular cognitive domain. Thus, memory assessment includes immediate and delayed recall of verbal and visual–nonverbal functioning. Retrieval is assessed by independent recall and by different types of cuing (semantic clustering or recognition). Language evaluation includes the assessment of several important parameters such as naming, repetition, comprehension, and fluency. Assessment of attention includes level of alertness, span or efficiency of vigilance–concentration, and selective attention. Executive function includes both problem solving (abstraction and categorization) and several motor programming tasks. Potentially, therefore, the NEUROPSI provides data regarding distinct clinical neuroanatomic syndromes.

Interpretation of NEUROPSI results is twofold: (1) quantitative, in that each item is scored, and can be further compared with normal performance in the general population; and (2) qualitative; different types of errors can be distinguished and specifically analyzed. For example, in addition to an overall memory performance score, the battery provides several memory parameters including rate of decay, primacy and recency effects, rate of acquisition across learning trials, intrusion and perseveration rates, semantic *versus* serial-order clustering and signal detection parameters (discriminability and response bias) of recognition performance.

This battery has been used in a number of research with different types of Spanish speaking populations. One of the first studies was carried out with patients with primary systemic hypertension (Ostrosky-Solís, Mendoza and Ardila, 2001). This condition represents a risk factor for cerebrovascular disease. It has been hypothesized that the chronic hypertension may eventually result in small subcortical infarcts associated with some cognitive impairments. One hundred fourteen patients with primary systemic hypertension (PSH) and 114 matched subjects were selected. PSH patients were further divided in four groups depending upon the hypertension severity. In addition to the medical and laboratory exams, a neuropsychological evaluation was administered. The NEUROPSI neuropsychological test battery was used. An association between level of hypertension and cognitive impairment was observed. Most significant differences were observed in the following domains: reading, executive functioning, constructional abilities and memory recall. No differences were observed in orientation, memory-recognition and language. It was concluded that some neuropsychological functions appeared impaired even in the PSH group with the least risk factors, thus cognitive evaluation may be important in cases of PSH not only to determine early subtle cognitive changes, but also for follow-up purposes, and to assess the efficacy of different therapeutic procedures.

The NEUROPSI has also been used to establish sensitivity and specificity indexes in a group of schizophrenic patients and with a sample of demented and mild cognitive impairment patients.

Cognitive impairment is a prominent feature of schizophrenia that correlates with functional outcome. In the clinical practice and research, there is a need to count on brief, reliable and standardized instruments to evaluate the cognitive profile in psychiatric, geriatric and neurological patients. There are only a few standardized and validated instruments with the Hispanic population, so the adaptation and validation of instruments become a high relevance issue, is a brief neuropsychological battery evaluating a wide spectrum of cognitive functions and standardized with Spanish speaking population according to age and educational level. The purpose of the present study was to determine the sensitivity and specificity of The Brief Neuropsychological Test in Spanish (NEUROPSI) for its clinical use in patients with schizophrenia, as well as in distinct subtypes of schizophrenic patients positive, negative and mixed. A total sample of 60 subjects (30 patients with schizophrenia and 30 matched controls) were assessed. Using the NEUROPSI total score we found 87.5% sensitivity and 92.8% specificity. A discriminant analysis using the 25 subtest scores of the NEUROPSI accurately classified 83.3% of the sample. None of the control subjects was classified as patient. Classification by subtype showed 80% of patients with negative symptoms, 90% of patients with positive symptoms and 70% of patients with mixed symptoms. The results showed that the instrument contributes to an accurate diagnosis of cognitive dysfunction in schizophrenic patients and it could help in management as well as development of more specific pharmacological treatment for each schizophrenic subtype (Picasso and Ostrosky-Solís, 2004)

Regarding dementia, a group of 314 Spanish-speaking elders were classified in 55 participants with mild to moderate dementia, 74 participants with mild cognitive impairment (MCI), and 185 control participants, according to clinical evaluation. Sensitivity, specificity and detection characteristics of frequently cognitive and functional tests were calculated in comparison with the clinical evaluation: Minimental State Examination, Brief Neuropsychological Test Battery (NEUROPSI), Short Blessed Test, Pfeffer Functional Activities Questionnaire and Blessed Dementia Scale. Influence of education on sensitivity and specificity values varied along the tests. For all the cognitive and functional measures, a great number of MCI participants who fulfilled Mayo's clinical criteria (Petersen et al., 1999) were misclassified as controls and a few were misclassified as demented. Level of education plays a very important role in both cognitive and functional assessment. The cognitive tests that are commonly used to screen demented patients may fail to detect MCI particularly in high-functioning individuals as well as those who are well educated (Mejia, Gutierrez, Villa and Ostrosky-Solis, 2004).

The NEUROPSI has also been used to assess the impact of variables such as education and culture in the cognitive profile of adults. Although culture and education are factors that significantly affect cognitive performance, it is often difficult to distinguish between the effects of education and the effects of culture, since the educational level influences the sociocultural status of an individual. Therefore, although it is common to attribute the differences between the performance in neuropsychological tests to both the level of education and culture, frequently the effects of the two variables are confounded. In this study (Ostrosky-Solis, Ramirez, Lozano, Picasso and Velez, 2004) we analysed the influence of education and of culture on the neuropsychological profile of indigenous and a nonindigenous population. We studied a total sample of 44 individuals divided into 4 groups: (1) 7 illiterate indigenous subjects; (2) 7 control subjects with no education; (3) 15 indigenous subjects with 1–4 years of education; and (4) 15 control individuals with 1–4 years of education. Subjects were paired by age and educational level. The indigenous population was Maya, who live in the state of Yucatan in the Mexican Republic. The NEUROPSI (Ostrosky-Solís, Ardila, and Rosselli, 1997, 1999) was individually administered. Results showed differential effects for both variables. Indigenous subjects showed higher scores in visuospatial tasks, and their level of education had significant effects on working and verbal memory. No significant differences were found in other cognitive processes (orientation, comprehension, and some executive functions). Our data showed that culture dictates what it is important for survival and that education could be considered as a type of subculture that facilitates the development of certain skills instead of others. However, the influences of both variables on cognitive skills are different, which should be considered when assessing subjects of different cultures. The interpretation of neuropsychological tests, leading to accurate assessment of cognitive dysfunction, is dependent on both education and cultural skills.

On the other hand, the ability to read and write is important for an individual's success and survival in the contemporary world, therefore understanding the variables associated with illiteracy represents a significant task not only in developing, but also industrialized countries. It is therefore proposed that the neuropsychological profile is related to the learning to read ability. A sample of 497 adults who were learning to read and primary school programs were selected in four different Mexican states. The participants were divided into groups (normal, moderately abnormal, severely abnormal) according to their neuropsychological profile obtained from the total score of the NEUROPSI test battery. Lower scores in the abnormal groups were observed especially in motor, memory and conceptual subtests. In the memory subtests, a significantly increased frequency of intrusions was observed. Lower neuropsychological test performance was additionally associated with deficits in phonological processing. Increased left-handedness was observed in participants with abnormal scores and among those spending a longer time at school. It was concluded that even though illiteracy may be associated with a diversity of factors, two major variables can be distinguished: socioeconomic factors and learning disabilities. It was further concluded that phonological processing could be regarded as a predictor to the learning to read ability and that having the neuropsychological profile could help in avoiding individual frustration while spending many years trying to learn how to read and write before adequate diagnosis is made (Ostrosky-Solís, Ardila, Lozano, Ramírez, Picasso, González-Cantú and Lira-Hereford, 2004).

NEUROPSI ATTENTION AND MEMORY

Appropriate performance and personal adjustment in daily life requires both attention and memory; which, in turn, are indispensable preconditions for suitable functioning of other cognitive domains (Lezak, 1995). The evaluation of these processes is essential in neuropsychological assessment because impairments of these functions are some of the most common symptoms observed following brain damage in children, adolescents and adults (Larrabee and Crook, 1996; Lezak, 1995; Ruff, Light and Quayhagen, 1989; Squire and Shimamura, 1996).

Evidence of multiple attentional and memory systems is provided by experimental, neuropsychological, psychopharmacological and developmental dissociations between performances in a variety of situations. Classification of attention and memory has proved to be heuristically useful for describing specific problems (Tulving, 1987; Van Zomeren and Brouwer, 1994). Components of attention and memory are often related to each other and to other cognitive abilities as well, such as executive functions; yet the specifications and relationships among these components are not consistent, nor fully understood.

Development of attention and memory subfunctions involves a complex pattern of change, with some aspects exhibiting significant change and others exhibiting remarkable stability across the life span (Klenberg, Korkman and Lahti-Nuuttila, 2001; Plude, et al., 1994). The scarcity of developmental studies which include a wide age range, as well as a wide spectrum of attentional and mnemonic subfunctions, restricts the comprehension of development as a continuous and complex process. Therefore, the NEUROPSI Attention and Memory was developed to measure these components across the life span, thus providing objective data for both clinical and experimental assessment.

This test was standardized with a sample of 950 non paid volunteers (Ostrosky-Solís et al., 2003). Sample age ranged from 6 to 85 years, and, in the adult sample (16 to 85 years), educational level ranged from 0 to 22 years of education. The normative sample was gropupes into nine age groups (6 to 7 years, 8 to 9 years, 10 to 11 years, 12 to 13 years, 14 to 15 years, 16 to 30 years, 31 to 55 years, 56 to 64 years and 65 to 85 years); and three educational levels: (zero to 3 years of education, 4 to 9 years of education and 10 to 22 years of formal education). For a detailed description of the sample characteristics, please refer to Ostrosky-Solís et al. (2003)

The NEUROPSI Attention And Memory (Ostrosky-Solis et al., 2003) cover the following domains: orientation, attention and concentration, executive functions, working memory, immediate verbal memory, delayed verbal memory, immediate visual memory and delayed visual memory, each having its own subtests. Each area includes assessment of different aspects of that particular cognitive domain. Thus, assessment of attention includes level of alertness, span or efficiency of vigilance–concentration, and selective attention. Executive function assessment comprises concept formation, flexibility, inhibition and several motor programming tasks. Memory assessment includes immediate and delayed recall of auditory-verbal and visual–nonverbal functioning. Word list learning includes three learning trials of 12 words. Each of the 12 items belonged to one of three high frequency semantic categories in Spanish language (animals, fruits or body parts). Delayed recall includes free and semantic cued recall, as well as a recognition trial, which includes a 24 words list, that does not contain high frequency words within each category.

It is important to point out that items were not simply translated but adapted according to frequency and relevance for Spanish-speaking individuals, for example the battery included language and picture tests that were previously standardized according to high, medium, and low frequency of occurrence in the Spanish language (Aveleyra et al.,1996). Phonological verbal fluency was evaluated using letter *P*. This letter was selected based on the ratio of words in the Spanish language starting with this letter, relative to the total number of words in a Spanish dictionary. According to this analysis, there is a good proportion of high frequency words beginning with this letter in Spanish.

Interpretation of NEUROPSI Attention and Memory follows the same reasoning of the NEUROPSI test Battery. A quantitative approach is obtained from the total score, and qualitative data from each subtest is also available. The subtests included are described in the appendix. In total, 30 different scores are obtained. The Stroop subtest (Stroop, 1935) was not used with adults having fewer than 4 years of education. In children aged 6 to 7 years and in adults having fewer than 4 years of education, the Rey-Osterreith figure (Osterreith, 1944) was replaced by the semicomplex figure (Ostrosky-Solís et al., 1999). Since data of these populations were missing for Stroop and Rey-Osterreith Complex Figure, both tests were excluded of the factor analysis, but descriptive information is presented for the remaining age and education groups.

In order to identify the developmental sequences of attention and memory, a study was carried out with normative data derived from the neuropsychological battery NEUROPSI Attention and Memory. A sample of 521 Spanish-speaking individuals, aged 6 to 85 years, participated in this study. Nine age groups were evaluated: 1) 6-7, 2) 8-9, 3) 10-11, 4) 12-13, 5) 14-15, 6) 16-30, 7) 31-55, 8) 56-64 and 9) 65-85 years. In the adult sample, data were also analyzed within 3 different educational levels: 1) 0-3, 2) 4-9, and 3) 10 or more years of education. Data from subtests measuring orientation, attention and concentration, executive functions, working memory, immediate and delayed verbal memory, immediate and delayed visual memory were included. The developmental staging and clustering of attention and memory subfunctions suggested that although these subfunctions are related, their developmental sequences are separated from one another. The effect of education was uneven: while in some factors it proved to be particularly sensitive, in some others it was unnoticed. The consideration of both the developmental sequence, as well as differential effects of education, can improve the sensitivity and specificity of neuropsychological measures, allowing early diagnosis of cognitive dysfunction and implementation of adequate rehabilitation programs (Gómez and Ostrosky-Solis, In Press)

The NEUROPSI Attention and Memory has also been used to evaluate the effects of hormone therapy (HT). Recent reports suggest that HT with estrogen may have a protective effect on the ageing brain and cognitive function. However, clinical evidence regarding the cognitive effects after 6 months of HT in 30 early postmenopausal women, who were divided into three groups as follows: group 1, Therapy conjugated equine estrogen (ET) CEE 0.625 mg/day (n=10); group II, Estrogen-progestine Therapy (EPT), CEE 0.625 mg/day plus chlormadinone 1mg/day (n=10); and group III, the control group, who did not receive treatment (n=10). The three groups were matched by age and years of education. Exclusion criteria were: central nervous system diseases, severe cardiac disease, and clinical history of cancer and depression. Subjects were tested using a comprehensive battery for the evaluation of attention memory and executive functions, which was standardized and validated in Spanish speaking subjects. The rate of cognitive change was defined by the difference between the measurements at the sixth month minus the baseline score. Mean group differences were assessed with MANOVA, followed by one-way ANOVA considering statistical significance when $p<.05$; the alpha significance level.05 was corrected using the Bonferroni procedure. The EPT group showed higher scores than the control group and ET group in the Total Attention Score and in the copy of the Rey-Osterreith Complex figure. The ET group showed significantly higher scores than the control group and the EPT group in the subtest of spatial backward span and in the immediate face codificaction. The short-term positive effects observed with the HT in this sample could be related to the stimulation of brain receptors and/or neurotrophic factors that are still present at this age (Aveleyra, Carranza-Lira, Ulloa and Ostrosky-Solís, 2005).

CONCLUSION

In Latin America and in Spanish-speaking countries there is a need for brief, reliable, and norm-based neuropsychological instruments to assess cognitive abilities of geriatric, neurological, and general medical populations. Standardized neuropsychological instruments in Spanish are still few. Notably, Spanish is the first language for about 10% of the world population. Interestingly, the United States represents the fifth-largest Spanish speaking country in the world (Mexico, Spain, Colombia, Argentina, and the U.S.) with over 20,000,000 Spanish speakers. The tests reviewed were developed to help fill this need of the Spanish-speaking world, and eventually, it might be adapted to other languages. However, it has to be emphasized that current results were obtained in Mexico. There is, as a consequence, a limitation in generalizability of results to other populations. Furthermore, sensitivity at higher educational level has to be taken with caution, considering the ceiling effect observed in participants with over 10 years of education.

From a clinical point of view, attention and memory impairments represent the most common symptoms observed following brain damage in children, adolescents and adults (Anderson, Northam, Hendy and Wrennall, 2001; Larrabee and Crook, 1996; Lezak, 1995; Ruff, Light and Quayhagen, 1989; Squire and Shimamura, 1996). In order to provide an adequate assessment, differential diagnosis and treatment of these populations, normative developmental data is required. Even more, educative training depends on the knowledge we have about the differential capabilities along the life-span. Assessment of cognitive functions in healthy populations is essential to understand the disabilities reported after brain damage, as well as to plan effective rehabilitation programs.

In summary, the NEUROPSI and the NEUROPSI Attention and Memory may help fill the need for brief, reliable and objective evaluation of a broad range of cognitive functions in Spanish-speaking people. It is the only available Spanish instrument that provides norms across a broad range of ages and educational levels including illiterates, primary school, high school, and professional level.

ACKNOWLEDGMENTS

This research was partially supported by a grant given to the Laboratory of Psychophysiology and Neuropsychology (Dr. Feggy Ostrosky-Solis), National University of Mexico, by the Consejo Nacional de Ciencia y Tecnología and *Programa de Apoyo a Proyectos de Investigación e Innovación Teconlógica*

REFERENCES

Anderson, V. Northam, E., Hendy, J. and Wrennall, J. (2001). *Developmental Neuropsychology*. New York: The Psychology Press.

Ardila, A. and Ostrosky-Solís, F. (1991). *El Diagnostico del Daño Cerebral: Enfoque Neuropsicologico* [Brain damage assessment: A neuropsychological approach]. D.F., Mexico: Trillas.

Ardila, A., Ostrosky-Solís, F., Rosselli, M., and Gómez, C. (2000). Age-related cognitive decline during normal aging: The complex effects of education. *Archives of Clinical Neuropsychology*, 15, 495-513.

Ardila, A., Ostrosky-Solís, F. and Canseco, E. (1981). *Esquema de diagnóstico neuropsicológico* [Scheme of neuropsychological assessment]. Bogotá, Colombia: Pontificia Universidad Javeriana.

Ardila, A., Rosselli, M., and Ostrosky, F. (1992). Sociocultural factors in neuropsychological assessment. In A.E. Puente and R.J. McCaffrey (Eds.), *Handbook of neuropsychological assessment: A biopsychosocial perspective* (pp. 181–192). New York: Plenum Press.

Aveleyra, E., Carranza-Lira, S., Ulloa. A. and Ostrosky-Solís F. (2005). Cognitive Effects of Hormone Therapy in Early Postmenopausal Women. *International Journal of Psychology*, 40 (5) 314-323.

Aveleyra, E., Gómez, C. Ostrosky-Solís, F. Rigalt, C., and Cruz, F. (1996). Adaptación de los estímulos no verbales de Snodgrass y Vanderwart en población hispanohablante: Criterios para la denominación, concordancia de la imagen, familiaridad y complejidad visual [Snodgrass and Vanderwart nonverbal stimuli adaptation to a Spanish-speaking population: Criteria for naming, concordance, familiarity, and visual complexity]. *Revista Mexicana de Psicología*, 13, 5–19.

Bauer, R.M., Tobias, B. and Valenstein, E. (1993). Amnesic disorders. In K.M. Heilman and E. Valenstein (Eds.), *Clinical Neuropsychology* (3rd ed.). New York: Oxford University Press.

Bertolucci, P.H.F., Brucki, S.M.D., Campacci, S.R., and Juliano, Y. (1994). O Mini-Examen do Estado Mental en uma populacao geral [Mini-Mental State Exam in a general population]. *Arquives Neuropsiquiatria*, 52, 1–7.

Blessed, G., Tomlinson, B.E., and Roth, M. (1968). The association between quantitative measures of dementia and of senile changes in the cerebral grey matter of elderly subjects. *British Journal of Psychiatry*, 114, 797–811.

Castro-Caldas, A, Reis. A. and Guerreiro, M. (1997). Neuropsychological aspects of illiteracy. *Neuropsychological rehabilitation*, 7, 327-338.

Dick, J. Guiloff, R., and Stewart, A. (1984). Mini-Mental State Examination in Neurological patients. *Journal of Neurology, Neurosurgery and Psychiatry*, 47 496–499.

Folstein, M.F., Folstein, S.E. and McHugh, P.R. (1975). "Mini-Mental State." A practical method for grading the cognitive state of patients for the clinician. *Journal of Psychiatric Research*, 12, 189-198.

Golden, C.J. (1980). *Manual for the Luria-Nebraska Neuropsychological Battery*. Los Angeles, CA: Western Psychological Services.

Gómez-Pérez, E. and Ostrosky-Solís, F. Attention and memory evaluation across the life span: heterogeneous effects of age and education. *Journal of Clinical and Experimental Neuropsychology, In press.*

Heaton, R.K., Grant, I., and Matthews, C. (1986). Differences in neuropsychological test performance associated with age, education and sex. In I. Grant and K.M. Adams (Eds.), *Neuropsychological assessment in neuropsychiatric disorders* (pp. 108–120). New York: Oxford University Press.

Klenberg, L., Korkman, M. and Lahti-Nuuttila, P. (2001). Differential development of attention and executive functions in 3-to 12- year old Finnish children. *Developmental Neuropsychology*, 20, 407-428.

Larrabee, G.J. and Crook, T.H. III (1996). Computers and memory. In I. Grant and K.M. Adams (Eds.), *Neuropsychological assessment of neuropsychiatric disorders*. (pp. 102-117). New York: Oxford University Press.

Launer, L., Dinkgreve, M.Jonker C, Hooijer C, Lindeboom J. (1993) Are age and education independent correlates of the Mini-Mental State Exam performance of community-dwelling elderly? *Journal of Gerontology*, 48, 138-145.

Lezak, M.D. (1995). *Neuropsychological assessment* (3rd ed.). New York: Oxford University Press.

Mayes, A.R. (1986). Learning and memory disorders and their assessment. *Neuropsychologia*, 24, 25-39.

Mejia, S., Gutierrez, L., Villa, M. and Ostrosky-Solis F. Cognition Functional Status Education and the Diagnosis of dementia and Mild Cognitive impairment in Spanish Speaking Elderly. *Applied Neuropsychology* 11, 4,196-203, 2004.

Morris, J.C., Heyman, A., Mohs, R.C., Hughes, J.P., van Belle, G., Fillenbaum, G., Mellits, E.D., and Clark, C. (1989). The Consortium to Establish a Registry for Alzheimer's Disease (CERAD). Part I. Clinical and neuropsychological assessment of Alzheimer's disease. *Neurology*, *39*, 1159–1165.

Murden, R., Mcrae, T., Kaner, S., and Bucknam, M. (1991). Mini-Mental Status Exam scores with education in blacks and whites. *Journal of American Geriatrics Society*, 39, 149-155.

Nelson, A., Fogel, B., and Faust, D. (1986). Bedside screening instruments: A critical assessment. *Journal of Nervous and Mental Disorder*, *174*, 73–83.

Osterreith, P.A. (1944). Le test de Copie d'une figure complexe. *Archives de Psychologie*, 30, 206-356.

Ostrosky-Solís, F., Ardila, A. and Rosselli, M. (1999). NEUROPSI: A brief neuropsychological test battery in Spanish with norms by age and educational level. *Journal of the International Neuropsychological Society*, 5, 413-433.

Ostrosky-Solís, F., Ardila, A., Rosselli, M., López, G. and Mendoza, V. (1998). Neuropsychological test Performance in illiterates. *Archives of Clinical Neuropsychology*, 13, 645-660.

Ostrosky-Solis, F., Arellano, M., and Perez, M. (2004). Can learning to read and write change your brain anatomy: An eletrophysiological study. *International Journal of Psychology*. 39, 27-35.

Ostrosky, F., Canseco, E., Quintanar, L., Navarro, E., and Ardila, A. (1985). Sociocultural effects in neuropsychological assessment. *International Journal of Neuroscience*, 27, 53–66.

Ostrosky-Solís, F., Gómez, M.E., Matute, E., Rosselli, M., Ardila, A. and Pineda, D. (2003). *NEUROPSI ATENCIÓN Y MEMORIA 6 a 85 años [NEUROPSI ATTENTION AND MEMORY 6 to 85 years]*. Mexico: American Book Store.

Ostrosky-Solís, F., Lozano, A., Ramírez, M., Picasso, H., Gómez, E., Vélez, A., Castillo-Parra, G., Ardila, A., Gonzalez-Cantú, R., and Lira-Hereford, B. (2003b). Estudio neuropsicológico de población mexicana adulta en proceso de alfabetización [Illiteracy in mexican population: a neuropsychological study of adults learning to read]. *Revista Mexicana de Psicología*, 20, 5-17.

Ostrosky-Solís, F. Mendoza V. and Ardila. (2001). A neuropsychological profile of patients with Primary Systemic Hypertension. *International Journal of Neuroscience*, 110,159-172.

Ostrosky, F., Quintanar, L., Canseco, E., Meneses, S., Navarro, E., and Ardila, A. (1986). Habilidades cognoscitivas y nivel sociocultural [Cognitive abilities and sociocultural level]. *Revista de Investigación Clínica*, 38, 37–42.

Ostrosky-Solis, F., Ramirez, M., Lozano, A., Picasso, H. and Velez, A.Culture or Education? Neuropsychological Test Performance of a Maya Indigenous Population. *International Journal of Psychology* 39, 1, 36-46 2004.

Petersen, RC., Smith, GE., Waring, SC., Ivnik, RJ., Tangalos, EG. y Kokmen, E. (1999) Mild Cognitive Impairment. Clinical Characterization and Outcome. *Archives of Neurology*, 56, 303-308.

Picasso, H. and Ostrosky-Solís, F. (2004). Sensibilidad y especificidad de un instrumento neuropsicológico en la evaluación de subtipos de esquizofrenia: un estudio con población hispano-hablante. *Actas Españolas Psiquiátricas*, 32.

Plude, D.J., Enns, J.T. and Brodeur, D. (1994). The development of selective attention: A life-span overview. *Acta Psychologica*, 86, 227-272.

Reitan, R.M. and Wolfson, D. (1993). *The Halsted–Reitan Neuropsychological Test Battery: Theory and clinical interpretation*. Tucson AZ: Neuropsychology Press.

Rosen, W.G., Mohs, R.C. and Davis, K.L. (1984). A new rating scale for Alzheimer's disease. *American Journal of Psychiatry, 141*, 1356-1364.

Rosselli, M and Ardila, A. (2003). The impact of culture and education on non-verbal neuropsychological measurements: A critical review. *Brain and Cognition, 52*, 326-333.

Ruff, R.M., Light, R.H. and Quayhagen, M. (1989). Selective reminding tests: A normative study of verbal learning in adults. *Journal of Clinical and Experimental Neuropsychology, 11*, 539-550.

Schwamm, L., Van Dyke, C., Kierman, R., and Merrin, E. (1987). The neurobehavioral cognitive status examination: Comparison with the cognitive capacity screening examination and the Mini-Mental State Examination in a neurosurgical population. *Annals of Internal Medicine, 107*, 486–491.

Squire, L.R. and Shimamura, A. (1996). The neuropsychology of memory dysfunction and its assessment. In I. Grant and K.M. Adams (Eds.), *Neuropsychological assessment of neuropsychiatric disorders* (pp. 232-262). New York: Oxford University Press.

Stroop, J.R. (1935). Studies of interference in serial verbal reactions. *Journal of Experimental Psychology, 18*, 643-662.

Tonkonogy, J.M. (1997). *Brief Neuropsychological Cognitive Examination*. Los Angeles, CA: Western Psychological Services. Vygotsky, L. (1962). *Thought and language*. Cambridge, MA: Cambridge University Press.

Tulving, E. (1987). Multiple memory systems and consciousness. *Human Neurobiology, 6*, 67-80.

Van Zomeren, A.H. and Brouwer, W.H. (1994). *Clinical Neuropsychology of Attention*. New York: Oxford University Press.

APPENDIX. DESCRIPTION OF THE BRIEF NEUROPSYCHOLOGICAL TEST BATTERY IN SPANISH: NEUROPSI

I. ORIENTATION. *Time* (day, month, and year), *Place* (city and specific place), and *Person* (age or, when were you born). Maximum score 6 points.

II. ATTENTION AND CONCENTRATION (maximum score 27).

Digits Backwards. Up to six digits. Maximum score 6 points. *Visual Detection.* On a sheet that includes 16 different figures, each one repeated 16 times, the respondents are requested to cross out those figures identical to the one presented as a model. The 16 matching figures are equally distributed at the right and at the left visual fields. The test is suspended after 1 min. Two scores are obtained: number of correct responses (maximum score 16), and number of errors. *Serial 3 Substraction* from 20 to 5; maximum score 5.

III. ENCODING (maximum score 18). *Verbal Memory.* Six common nouns corresponding to three different semantic categories (animals, fruits, and body parts), are presented three times. After each presentation, the participant repeats those words that he or she remembers. The score is the average number of words repeated in the three trials (maximum score 6). In addition, intrusions, perseverations, recency and primacy effects are noted. *Copy of a Semicomplex_Figure.* A figure similar to the Rey–Osterrieth Complex Figure, but much simpler, is presented to the participant. The participants are instructed to copy the best they can. A specified scoring system is used, with a maximum score of 12 points.

IV. LANGUAGE (maximum score 26): *Naming.* Eight different line drawing figures are presented to be named. They correspond to animals, musical instruments, body parts and objects. The names used are different from those names included in the Verbal Memory section. If the participant presents visual difficulties, an alternative procedure is used: The patient is required to name body parts and small objects placed in the hand. Maximum score 8. *Repetition.* The participant is asked to repeat one monosyllabic word, one three-syllable word, one phrase with three words, and one seven-word sentence. Successful repetition in each one is scored 1. Maximum score 4. **Comprehension.** On a sheet of paper two circles (small and large) and two squares (small and large) are drawn. Six commands, similar to those used in the Token Test are given to the participant. The easiest one is, "Point to the small square," and the hardest one is "In addition to the circles, point to the small square." Maximum score 6. *Verbal Fluency: Semantic Verbal Fluency (animals).* Two scoring systems are used: the total number of correct words; and an abbreviated 4-point scale. In the latter, 1 point is given to zero to 5 words; 2 points to 6 to 8 words; 3 points to 9 to 14 words; and 4 points to 15 or more words in 1 min. Intrusions and perseverations are noted. For the current analyses, only the first scoring system was used. *Phonological Verbal Fluency* (words beginning with the letter 'F '). Two scoring systems are used: the total number of correct words, and an abbreviated 4-point scale. One point is given to zero to 3 words; 2 points to 4 to 6 words; 3 points to 7 to 9 words; and 4 points to 10 or more words in 1 min. Intrusions and perseverations are noted. For the current analyses, only the first scoring system was used.

V. READING. Participants are asked to read aloud a short paragraph (109 words). Next, three questions about the paragraph are orally presented. The correct answer to each question is scored 1. Maximum score 3. Paralexias are noted.

VI. WRITING. This involves writing a six-word sentence to dictation, and copying a different six-word sentence. Maximum score 2. Paragraphias are noted.

VII. CONCEPTUAL FUNCTIONS (maximum score 5 10). *Similarities.* Three pairs of words (e.g., orange–pear) are presented and participants are asked to report the similarity. An example is provided. Each one is scored as zero (physical similarity: *both are round*), 1 (functional similarity: *both can be eaten*), or 2 (the answer corresponds to the supraordinate word: *fruits*). Maximum score 6. *Calculation Abilities.* Three simple arithmetic problems are presented. Maximum score 3. *Sequences.* The participant is asked to continue a sequence of figures drawn on a paper: one circle, one cross, two circles, two crosses, three circles ("What figure follows?"). Maximum score 1.

VIII. MOTOR FUNCTIONS (maximum score 8). *Changing the Position of the Hand.* Participants are asked to repeat three positions with the hand (right and left). The task is demonstrated by the examiner up to three times. A maximum score of 2 is used for each hand. Maximum score 4. *Alternating Hand Movements.* To alternate the position of the hands (right hand closed, left hand open, and to switch). Maximum score 2. *Opposite Reactions.* If the examiner shows a finger, the respondent must show a fist; if the examiner shows a fist, the subject must show a finger. Maximum score 2.

IX. RECALL (maximum score 30). *Recall of Verbal Information.* Recall of the six words presented in verbal memory. (1) *Spontaneous Recall.* Maximum recall 6. (2) *Cued Recall.* Recall by categories (*animals, fruits,* and *body parts*). Maximum score 6. (3) *Recognition.* The examiner reads 14 different words, and the participant must tell which ones were previously presented. Maximum score 6. *Recall of the Semicomplex Figure.* Maximum score 12.

APPENDIX. DESCRIPTION OF THE NEUROPSI ATTENTION AND MEMORY

I. ORIENTATION. General information regarding subject's orientation in time, place and person. (Maximum score = 7 points).

II. ATTENTION AND CONCENTRATION:

Auditory/verbal: Digit forward span. It consists of pairs of random number sequences that the examiner reads aloud, at the rate of one per second, the subject's task was to repeat each sequence exactly as it was given. (Maximum score = 9 points).

Digit Detection. This vigilance test examines the ability to sustain and focus attention. It involves the sequential presentation of digits over a period of time with instructions for the patient to tap only when the target item 5 was preceded by the item 2. (Maximum score = 10 points).

Mental Control. Requires the subject to count from 1 to 40 by 3's within a time limit. (Maximum score = 3 points).

Visual/nonverbal: Spatial forward span. A board with blocks attached in an irregular arrangement. In the spatial forward span test, each time the examiner taps the blocks in a prearranged sequence, the patient must attempt to copy this tapping pattern exactly as it was given. (Maximum score = 9 points).

Visual Search. This test requires visual selectivity at fast speed on a repetitive motor response task. It consists of rows of figures randomly interspersed with a designated target figure. The subjects were requested to cross out those figures equal to the one presented as a model. Two scores were obtained: total number of correct responses (maximum score = 24), and number of intrusions.

III. MEMORY

Working Memory.

Auditory/verbal: Digit backward span. Pairs of random number sequences that the examiner reads aloud, at the rate of one per second, and the subject's task was to repeat each sequence in an exactly reversed order. (Maximum score = 8).

Visual/nonverbal: Spatial backward span. Board with blocks. Each time the examiner taps the blocks in a prearranged sequence, the patient must attempt to copy the tapping pattern in an exactly reversed order. (Maximum score = 9).

Immediate and 20 minutes delayed recall.

Auditory/verbal: Word List. (Three learning trials of 12 words.) Immediate trials consisted of three presentations with recall of a 12-word list. Each of the 12 items belonged to one of three semantic categories (animals, fruits or body parts). After each presentation, the subject repeated those words that he/she remembered. The total score was the average number of words repeated in the three trials (maximum score = 12). The delayed presentation provided one first free recall on the long term (20 min) (maximum score = 12). The second long term recall trial utilized the item categories as cues, asking the subject for items in each of the three categories (maximum score = 12). A recognition trial, in which the examiner asked the subject to identify as many words as possible from the list, when shown a list of 24 words containing all the items from the list, as well as words that were semantically associated or phonemically similar, was also provided (maximum score = 12 points). In addition, intrusions, perseverations and false positive errors scores were noted.

Verbal Paired Associates. Twelve word pairs, four that were not readily associated (i. e., coche-payaso), four forming phonetic associations (i. e., camión-melón) and four forming semantic associations (i. e., fruta-uva). The list was read three times, with a memory trial following each reading. The words were randomized in each of the three learning trials to prevent positional learning. The total score was the average number of words repeated in the three trials (maximum score = 12). It was provided a 20 min. delayed recall (maximum score = 12). In addition, intrusions, perseverations and errors were noted.

Logical Memory I and II. Prose learning that allows to score thematic recall and factual knowledge. The examiner reads two stories, stopping after each reading for an immediate free recall. Each story contains 16 story units and five thematic units. A delayed recall trial after 20 minutes was also given.

Visual/Nonverbal: Rey-Osterreith Complex Figure / Semicomplex Figure. In the copy administration subjects were shown a nonsense figure which they must copy. A delayed recall was also provided in which subjects were asked to recall what they had drawn on the administration trial. (Maximum scores = 32 in Rey-Osterreith Complex Figure, 12 in Semicomplex figure).

Faces. On the immediate trial subjects were shown two photographs with their respective names. After seeing each of them for five seconds, subjects were asked to repeat the names (maximum score = 4 points). On the delayed recall subjects were asked to remember the names of the persons (maximum score = 8 points) and to identify the previously shown persons among a set of four photographs (maximum score = 2 points). In addition, false positive errors were noted.

IV. EXECUTIVE FUNCTIONS

Category Formation Test. Five visually presented sets, each one containing four figures of common objects. Each set was organized on the basis of different principles. On each set trial the subjects were asked to form as many categories as they could. (Maximum score = 25).

Verbal Fluency. Measures the quantity of words produced within a time limit of one minute and consists of a semantic as well as a phonological trial. On the semantic trial subjects were required to generate items in a category (animals), whereas on the phonological trial subjects were required to generate words according to an initial letter ("P"). Total number of correct words, intrusions, perseverations, clusters and switchings were noted in both tests.

Design Fluency. The subject was instructed to draw different patterns by connecting the dots in each five-dot matrix using four lines. Subjects were given three minutes to perform this test. Total number of correct designs, intrusions and perseverations were noted.

Motor Functions.

Conjugate eye movement. **A pencil was shown to the subject** and he/she has to follow it with his eyes to the left and then to the right. (Maximum score = 4 points).

Conflicting commands. The instruction was: "Tap once, when I tap twice; tap twice when I tap once". (Maximum score = 2 points).

Go/No-Go. The instruction was: "Tap twice, when I tap once, but when I tap twice, don't tap at all". (Maximum score = 2 points).

Luria's Hand sequences. The examiner with his right hand made a fist, then extended his fingers, holding his hand horizontally and finally turned his hand by 90^0 with the extended fingers still pointing forward. After seeing this sequence of movements, subjects with their right hand must repeat it exactly as it was given. In a second trial the examiner repeated the sequence in an exactly reversed order with his left hand and subjects must repeat it with their left hand, exactly as it was given. (Maximum score = 4).

Alternating pattern. Copy of a drawing without lifting the hand from the paper. The test required alternating between peaks and blocks. (Maximum score = 8).

Stroop Test. Subjects were required to read, as fast as they could, a set of color words printed in black ink. On the second trial, subjects were required to call out, as fast as they could, the color names of colored ovals. On the third trial subjects were asked to call out, as fast as they could, printed color names when the print ink was in a different color than the name of the colored word. In the three trials, the total number of correct answers and the time employed to perform each trial were noted (maximum score = 36).

In: New Psychological Tests and Testing Research   ISBN: 978-1-60021-570-4
Editor: Lydia S. Boyar, pp. 173-184   © 2007 Nova Science Publishers, Inc.

Chapter 9

TESTING PATIENTS WITH SUBCORTICAL VASCULAR DEMENTIA: A PROPOSAL FOR A RAPID EVALUATION

Rita Moretti[*], Paola Torre,
Cristina Vilotti and Rodolfo M. Antonello
Università degli Studi di Trieste, Ospedale di Cattinara 34149 Trieste, Italy

ABSTRACT

Vascular dementia is an uncertain nosological entity, in which unevenly distributed patterns of cognitive deficits comprising slowing of cognitive processing, and impairment of executive function occur. Nevertheless, its clinical role in the detection of early dementia and its correlations with other cognitive process is still under investigation. Considering the potential role of subcortical frontal circuits in vascular dementia, executive functions and behaviour should be taken into account for a correct definition of the clinical diagnosis. In conclusion, new neuropsychological criteria, based on study of the natural course of vascular cognitive impairment, that focus on early disease are urgently needed. The Ten-Point Clock test (TPCT) can be used to identify early forms of Alzheimer's disease, because it is a reliable, well accepted, and easily administered at the bedside. The TPCT is a valid well-accepted, cross-cultural executive measure, correlated with verbal and semantic fluency, and with left and right recognition

Whereas Alzheimer's disease is the most common cause of dementia, comprising 50-75% of the total dementia prevalence, other forms of dementia, such as vascular dementia, dementia due to Lewy body disease (DLB), dementia due to Parkinson's disease, and frontotemporal dementia (FTD), also affect many individuals and may rise in prevalence with the aging population. Differential diagnosis among dementias remains challenging; ultimately definitive diagnosis of Alzheimer's disease still depends on histopathologic evidence via autopsy or biopsy.Indeed, some of the boundaries between various forms of dementia, such Alzheimer's disease, Lewy body variant of Alzheimer's disease, DLB, and dementia due to

[*] Please address correspondence to Rita Moretti M.D., Clinica Neurologica, Dipartimento di Medicina Clinica e Neurologia, Università degli Studi di Trieste, Ospedale di Cattinara 34149 Trieste, Italy or e-mail (moretti@univ.trieste.it).

Parkinson's disease remain somewhat unclear. Clinical differentiation of vascular dementia from Alzheimer's disease has also remained difficult. Many works reported the relationship of severity of autopsy-confirmed cerebrovascular disease and autopsy-confirmed degree of Alzheimer's disease pathology to neuropsychological performance. Severity of cerebrovascular disease was not consistently related to dementia, and neuropsychological profiles as interpreted by experts kept naïve to other clinical data were insensitive markers of cerebrovascular pathology. In contrast, these expert ratings showed good sensitivity and specificity to the presence of Alzheimer's disease pathology (with or without concomitant cerebrovascular pathology).

The pathophysiology of acute cerebral ischemia has been described, but the mechanisms leading to the selective vulnerability of some brain regions and the heterogeneity of injury is not yet fully understood. The most vulnerable areas to acute cerebral ischemia include the cerebral cortex, Purkinje cells of the cerebellum, and the CA-1 sector of the hippocampus. Selective injury is also noted in different layers of the cortex with layer 3 the most sensitive, followed by layers 5 and 6. The cortex is more susceptible to injury compared to the deeper structures, such as the brainstem. With cortical injury, seizures and impairment in cognition and memory may be observed. The thalamus and basal ganglia are other structures that are susceptible to injury. Among the myriad functions of the thalamus, it is probably the role in arousal and consciousness that is most critical during the recovery phase from global ischemia. The re-establishment of functional thalamo-cortical processing is vital in coma emergence after cardiac arrest. Injury to the basal ganglia and cerebellum account for subsequent problems with movement and coordination.

Subcortical VaD relates to small vessel disease and hypoperfusion resulting in focal and diffuse ischemic white matter lesions and incomplete ischemic injury (Erkinjuntti, 1997). In patients with subcortical VaD, ischemic lesions are particularly apparent in the prefrontal subcortical circuit, including the prefrontal cortex (Cummings, 1993). This deterioration of the frontal lobe is reflected in the fact that dysexecutive syndrome seems to be the core feature of subcortical VaD (McPherson and Cummings, 1996; Looi and Sachdev, 1999). The concept of Vascular Cognitive Impairment encompasses patients across the entire continuum of cognitive impairment resulting from cerebrovascular disease, ranging from high-risk patients with no frank cognitive deficit (the "brain-at-risk" stage) through vascular dementia.

In the so-called subcortical vascular dementia, three frontal-subcortical circuits are mainly interested. Three potential site of interests have been identified (Miller, 2000). A common feature of all these circuits is their unification of different parts of the frontal cortex with the basal ganglia and the thalamus in closed circuits with open elements that receive input from and project to other regions outside the loops. The hypothesized function of the orbitobasal circuit is the correction of social control as the deficits seen with the selective disruption are disinhibition, impulsiveness, confabulation and antisocial conduct. The dorsolateral net supports attention and alternative programming capacities, as well as working memory (area 46) programs. Its deficit causes poorly focus attention, marked alteration of working memory, poor organization, defective planning capacities, lack of insight, and abnormal expression of empathy and sympathy. The medial frontal circuit might be involved in energy, motivation and selectivity of thoughts, while its disruption may cause apathy, abulia and marked depression.

Within each of the circuits there are two pathways: a direct, which links the striatum with the globus pallidus interna/substantia nigra complex and an indirect pathway, which projects from striatum to globus pallidus externa, to subthalamus, to globus pallidus interna/substantia nigra to thalamus.

A common question in dementia research has been whether there is a clinically observable cognitive distinction between deficits seen in dementias that involve primarily cortical neuropathology (Alzheimer's disease being the prototypic example) versus those associated with subcortical neuropathology (such as Huntington's disease and Parkinson's disease, or vascular dementia.

There are accepted differences in the neuropsychological profile of patients with Alzheimer's disease and vascular dementia. Memory impairment and attentional deficits are apparent in vascular dementia, but patients and carers often experience mood changes such as depression, personality changes and emotional lablilty. In particular, these behavioral symptoms can be a major cause of stress, anxiety and concern for caregivers, and frequently lead to the institutionalization of patients.

In patients with vascular dementia, executive functions that tend to be disproportionately impaired include planning and sequencing, speed of mental processing, performance on unstructured tasks, and attention. Language production may be impaired in patients with vascular deteriorationm but primary language functions otherwise tend to be preserved; these patients also exhibit significantly more perseverations than patients with Alzheimer's. Compared to vascular dementia, patients with Alzheimer Disease may exhibit greater deficits in functions (including memory) mediated by posterior cortical structures, such as the temporal and parietal lobes. AD patients exhibit a faster rate of information decay, reduced ability to benefit from cues to facilitate retrieval, and higher frequency of intrusion errors; in addition, certain aspects of language function, such as naming, may exacerbate deficits on verbal memory tasks. AD tends to affect lexicon while VaD tends to affect syntax. When patients with AD exhibit perseverations, they tend to be elicited by tests of semantic knowledge (Desmond, 2004). Patients with vascular dementia have poor verbal fluency and more perseverative behavior compared with patients with AD. They may even have other signs of executive dysfunction such as cognitive slowing, difficulty in shifting sets, and problems with abstraction. Commonly used mental status tests include the Folstein Mini-Mental State Examination and the Cognitive Abilities Screening Instrument. In patients with extensive deep white matter disease, impairments may be observed in tests of psychomotor speed, dexterity, executive function, and motor aspects of speech (eg, dysarthria, reduced verbal output). A very recent study (Oosterman and Scherder, 2006), was intended to, meta-analytically, review whether the subtests of the Wechsler Adult Intelligence Scale are useful in differentiating between vascular dementia and Alzheimer's disease. The Authors expected the Alzheimer's disease group to outperform the vascular dementia group on those subtests that require executive functions, whereas inferior performance of the Alzheimer's disease patients was expected on memory tests. Two steps in the analysis were undertaken in an attempt to clarify this issue. The first step consisted of including all studies examining Wechsler Adult Intelligence Scale subtest performance in vascular dementia and Alzheimer's disease patients. Secondly, a subcortical vascular dementia subgroup was distinguished and performance of this subgroup was compared to that of the Alzheimer's disease group. Overall, the analyses showed that both the vascular dementia and, more strongly, the subcortical vascular dementia group revealed decreased executive functions on several subtests compared to the Alzheimer's disease group. The Alzheimer's disease group showed inferior performance on a single semantic memory test only compared to both the vascular dementia and the subcortical vascular dementia groups. These results indicate that several subtests of the Wechsler Adult Intelligence Scale can differentiate between these two clinical groups, and that most of these tests reveal more impaired performance in the vascular dementia group (Oosterman and Scherder, 2006).

As reported in a recent study (Looi and Sachdev, 1999), the most frequently involved alteration in cognitive profile of subcortical vascular dementia is the so-called dysexecutive syndrome. This concept seems even more evident when the scores obtained by subcortical vascular dementia patients have been compared with those obtained by AD patients. Executive function refers to cognitive abilities involved in volition, planning, purposive action and effective performance. While these abilities are critical to the daily functioning and maintenance of independence in a complex society, many executive abilities are not adequately assessed by the traditional standardized neuropsychological examinations, as the testing environment and the examiner provide the patient with motivation, goals, planning and structure. In particular, planning involves the capacity to conceptualize change from present circumstances, deal objectively with the environment and with the self in relationship to the environment, weigh and evolve a framework for carrying on a plan (Lezak, 1995).

It is widely believed that the cognitive syndrome in subcortical vascular dementia is distinct from that seen in AD with a predominance of executive deficits due to undercutting of the frontal lobes and disconnection of fronto-striatal loops (Looi and Sachdev, 1999). Clinical experience suggests that such patients are grossly slowed up with poor information retrieval, and problems with tasks that require mental flexibility and shifting of attention (Sachdev, Brodaty, and Looi, 1999). When attention is inappropriately dominated by environmental stimuli, environmental dependency occurs, and is evident in patients with prefrontal or orbitobasal dysfunction, such as in Vascular dementia (Cummings and Trimble, 1995).

Starting from the perspective that the deterioration of the frontal lobe is reflected by the dysexecutive syndrome that seems to be the core feature of subcortical vascular dementia (McPherson and Cummings, 1996; Looi and Sachdev, 1999), our group tried to compare the neuropsychological differences which merge in two homogeneous groups of patients, suffering respectively from subcortical vascular dementia and frontal degenerative dementia (Moretti et al., 2005-B): Both the groups, the FLD and the subcortical vascular dementia, presented a direct involvement of the frontal neural pathways. All patients underwent a standardized baseline assessment that included a detailed history, a physical examination, laboratory test, and psychiatric evaluations. All the patients had undergone a CT of the head and an MRI evaluation. The neuroimages of FLD patients showed clear signs of frontal atrophy, without asymmetric preferences and with relatively little change of the other cortical and subcortical regions. On the other hand, a patient was diagnosed as having subcortical vascular dementia when the CT scan showed moderate to severe ischaemic white matter changes and at least one lacunar infarct (Erkinjuntti, Ketonen, Sulkava, Vuorialho, and Palo, 1987). Patients were divided into two groups of forty, matched for education level, one is composed by patients with frontal lobe dementia, and the other of patients with subcortical vascular dementia.

All patients were followed for 12 months, with periodical neurological and neuropsychological examinations. Global cognitive function was assessed using Mini-Mental State Examination (MMSE) (Folstein, Folstein, and McHugh, 1975) at each visit. In addition, executive and planning function were assessed using the Ten Point Clock Test (Manos, 1997), the Proverbs Test (Gorham, 1956), and the Stroop Test (Stroop, 1935) at each visit.

Behavioral performance was assessed using different tests, reliable and validated, widely known by the Literature: the NeuroPsychiatric Inventory (NPI) (Cummings, Mega, Gray, Rosenberg-Thompson, Carusi, and Gornbein, 1994), the Clinical Insight Rating Scale (CIR) (Ott, Lafleche, Whelihan, Buongiorno, Albert, and Fo, 1996), and the Cornell Scale for Depression in Dementia (Alexopoulos, Abrams, Young, and Shamoian, 1988) at every visit. The Behavioral pathology in Alzheimer's Disease Rating Scale (BEHAVE-AD) (Reisberg, Borenstein, Salob, Ferris, Franssen, and Georgota, 1987; Mendez, Perryman, Miller, and Cummings, 1998) was given at baseline and at 14 months. Caregiver's stress was evaluated at each visit by the Relative Stress Scale (Greene, Smith, Gardiner, and Timburg, 1982). Only 80 patients were involved, and the potential for generalization is seriously limited.

A direct involvement of the cortical (decisional) layers in frontal dementia (Moretti and Torre, 2003), in contrast with the prominent and widespread involvement of the subcortical pathways (refinement and corrections programs), may be the reason for the different cognitive and behavioural profiles of the two groups: the frontal patients we described have more difficulties in abstract reasoning, in focusing attention, and in implementing strategies to solve problems. In contrast, they exhibit more profound behavioural alterations, in personality and social conduct, loss of basic emotions and social embarrassment, selfishness, and disinhibition. The frontal patients showed moderate depression and a total lack of insight in their clinical condition. On the contrary, our patients with subcortical vascular dementia have poor general cognitive functions, a high level of insight, an important depression and apathy as the principal and most salient characteristic of their behavioral conduct. Dys-executive syndrome (which better characterize subcortical vascular dementia; Cannatà, Alberoni, Franceschi, and Mariani, 2002) was not so evident when compared to results obtained by our patients with frontal lobe dementia. Moreover, subcortical vascular dementia encompasses both cognitive impairment, and also a wide range of behaviour disturbances (Cannatà, et al., 2002; Traykov, Baudic, Thibaudet, Rigaud, Smagghe, and Boller, 2002;). A recent study (Aharon-Peretz, Kliot and Tomer, 2000) indicated that patients with mild subcortical VaD are more disturbed on behavioural aspects that are influenced by frontal and subcortical mechanisms than AD patients. This suggests that in addition to neuropsychological assessment, quantification of the personality behaviour disorder is important for standardizing the diagnosis of subcortical vascular dementia and distinguishing it from any other dementias.

Moreover, current criteria for vascular dementia start with a paradigm that first diagnoses dementia on the basis of Alzheimer-type criteria and then superimposes upon this vascular events and risk factors to convert a diagnosis of Alzheimer disease to one of vascular dementia. The neuropsychological features of AD are not the same as those of vascular dementia, and so use of the current criteria will fail to diagnose many cases particularly those in whom memory loss is not prominent (Chui, 2001). In concordance with what previously debated, new neuropsychological evaluations should be considered for the correct diagnosis of subcortical vascular dementia; the battery should comprise a rapidly applicable, but exhaustive, behavioural evaluation and a specific and sensitive test for executive functions. The need for all physicians to be comfortable with cognitive assessments is increasing, and primary care physicians are the most likely to be able to detect early cognitive decline for consideration of treatment and future life planning (e.g., wills, advance directives). Executive cognitive dysfunction can have a significant impact on decision-making capacity, and this condition is particularly challenging to diagnose in someone with a normal MMSE score. Ideally, every physician would have rapid access to a referral centre. However, these scenarios are not the reality of modern medicine. A detailed cognitive assessment in a busy office is often not possible, but the administration of an MMSE and a clock-drawing test to patients with suspected functional decline is possible (Juby et al, 2002).

The clock-drawing test has been shown to be an acceptable, non-threatening assessment that is reliable and effective for diagnosis and longitudinal assessment of cognition and correlates with the MMSE score. Like the MMSE, the clock-drawing test can be education dependent, particularly when a predrawn circle is not provided. Unlike many other tools for measuring cognitive function, the clock-drawing test is independent of ethnic background (Juby et al., 2002).

When the MMSE score is abnormal, the suspicion of cognitive impairment is already raised. Under these circumstances the clock-drawing test score is often abnormal, and it reinforces the suspicion of cognitive impairment. The more difficult cases involve patients with a history of unusual or abnormal function or whose physician has concerns about their higher cognitive functioning (e.g., medication compliance or competency assessment) and whose MMSE score is normal. In such cases the clock-drawing test can be particularly useful to examine cognitive domains not evaluated by the MMSE.

The best method for scoring clock drawings is still being debated, as highlighted by the abundance of scoring methods available. The scoring methods described by Mendez and associates and by Shulman were shown to be superior to others in their ability to diagnose Alzheimer's disease. The method by Mendez and associates requires the use of a 20-point scale; the Shulman method requires the use of a 6-point scale to score subjects' drawn and predrawn circles (Juby et al., 2002).

According to our experience, the Ten-Point Clock test, also called Clock Drawing Test (TPCT) is thought to be related to different aspects of cognition: thus, some authors suggest that the clock test assesses frontotemporal brain functions (Royall, Mulroy, Chiodo, and Polk, 1999; Moore and Wyke, 1984) whereas others suggest that clock drawing is sensitive to semantic memory (Libon, Malamut, Swenson, Prouty Sands, and Cloud, 1996). In fact, when considering a typical test of executive functions, the Ten Point Clock Test, it could be observed the under-reported differences, when tested the general cognitive performances, by MMSE, and the executive functions, by Ten Point Clock Test (Moretti et al., 2005, A). Manos (1999) concluded that the TPCT may prove useful in screening for early stage Alzheimer's disease, though they do not specifically identify Alzheimer's disease. A cross sectional study (Heinik, Solomesh, Shein, and Becker, 2002) showed that scores on the clock test correlated well with the demographic and cognitive variables studied, but this correlation changed with severity of the dementia severity. Another study (Powlishta, von Dras, Stanford, Carr, Tsering, Miller, and Morris, 2002) concluded that although the clock drawing test can be scored reliably and can differentiate cognitively normal older adults from those with at least mild dementia of the AD type, it does not appear to be a useful screening instrument for detecting very mild dementia of the AD type.

We commonly use the Ten Point Clock Drawing Test (Manos and Wu, 1994), as a well accepted, easily administered test with convincing results (Moretti, Torre, Antonello, Cazzato, and Bava, 2002).

We hypothesized (Moretti et al., 2005) that the Ten Point Clock Test could be a reliable tool to evaluate executive frontal function and the perception of peripersonal and extrapersonal space, which may result from the disconnection of fronto-subcortical loops in subcortical vascular dementia (Looi and Sachdev, 1999).

Therefore, we followed 287 patients affected by subcortical vascular dementia, to whom we applied the Ten Point Clock Drawing Test as well as more common battery of neuropsychological tests. The current clinical study involved only subcortical vascular dementia patients, because the inclusion criteria needed to be as clear and unequivocal as possible. CT scans of patients with subcortical vascular dementia show clear evidence of vascular disease in deep white matter and relative preservation of the cerebral cortex. In contrast, patients with multi-infarct dementia (not involved in this study) are not as easily identified.

Study subjects were 146 men and 141 women, mean age 73.24 ± 4.5 years old, with Mini-Mental State Examination (MMSE) scores of at least 14 and satisfying the fourth edition of the Diagnostic and Statistical Manual of Mental Disorders (DSM-IV) for dementia, who attended for the first time the Ambulatory Clinic of Cognitive Disturbances of the Institute of Clinical Neurology of Trieste. They also satisfied the criteria for probable Vascular dementia in accordance with the National Institute of Neurological Disorders and Stroke and the Association Internationale pour la Recherche et l'Enseignement en Neurosciences (NINDS-AIREN) criteria (Erkinjuntti, Ketonen, Sulkava, Vuorialho, and Palo, 1987).

Patients were diagnosed as having subcortical Vascular dementia when the CT scan showed moderate to severe ischaemic white matter changes (Roman, Tatemichi, Erkinjuntti, Cummings, Masdeu, Garcia, Amaducci, Orgogozo, Brun, and Hofman, 1993) and at least one lacunar infarct. Patients were not included in the study if they showed signs of non-lacunar territorial infarcts or radiological signs of normal pressure hydrocephalus. Patients with previous psychiatric illness or central nervous system disorders and alcoholism were excluded.

Cognitive functions were assessed using the MMSE (Folstein, Folstein, and McHugh, 1975), the semantic and phonological Word fluency (WFs and WFp) tests (Wechsler, 1981), and visuospatial skills test. Patients were asked to copy eight given figures, printed in black ink on a white sheet, four on the left side of the paper, four on the right side of the paper.

The score was assigned as follows: 0 if the figures is not complete, or represented with the wrong number of angles; 0.5 if the figure looks like the given, but is imprecise, or it is incomplete for little particulars; 1 point if the figure closely resemble the given image, with a maximum score of 8/8. Patients were evaluated for hetero- and autotopognosia, in order to assess their ability to recognize and denominate right and left in the space. This ability was measured by a non parametric scale, created by us (4= no reverse in the identification of right and left space; 2= alteration in one of the two recognition tasks; 0= no recognition at all).

Patients also responded to the Proverb Interpretation test (Gorham, 1956) and the Ten Point Clock test (Manos and Wu, 1994).

In this latter test, an 11.4 cm diameter circle is traced, using a template, and the patient is asked to put the numbers in the face of a clock and then make the clock say 10 minutes after 11. Instructions for scoring were obtained from a dedicated work (Manos, 1999): a 10 point scoring system was used to quantify the accuracy of the spatial arrangement of the numbers and setting of the hands. To score the test, a line is drawn through the centre of the number 12 and the middle of the circle, dividing the circle in half. In those rare instances when the 12 is missing, its position is assumed to be counter-clockwise from the 1 at a distance equal to the distance between the numbers 1 and 2. A second line is drawn at right angles to the first through the centre of the circle, dividing it into quarters. Two more lines are drawn through the centre of the circle, dividing it into eights. One point each is given for the 1, 2, 5, 7, 8, 10 and 11 if half its area is in the proper eighth of the circle relative to the 12. One point each is given for an obvious long hand pointing at the number 2 and obvious short hand pointing at number 11. No points for hands if their relative lengths are not obvious at glance. No points are given if hands point to other numbers (Manos, 1999).

The Instrumental Activity of Daily Living (IADL) (Lawton and Brody, 1969) was used to assess in particular instrumental activities and it was performed at baseline, 12 months and 24 months.

The scores of TPCT have been compared with that obtained by 250, consecutive ambulatory (for general neurological problems) outpatients (mean age: 71.2 ± 4.1 years old). None of the patients referred cognitive disturbances. Results can be summarized as follows (table 1).

Statistical analyses were performed using the Statistical Package for the Social Sciences (SPSS, version 10.0) using the 2-sample Wilcoxon test. This was done for each efficacy variable, with means, standard deviations and p-values are presented. An ANOVA test has been made to compare TPCT scores and other cognitive variables over time. Spearman's rank correlation analyses were performed between cognitive function and TPCT scores, in each session.

Table 1. A complete synopsis of the results made by sVAD patients during the follow-up

Test	Baseline	Differences 12 months	Differences 24 months
Mini Mental State Examination	21.3 ± 3.9	-2.4 ± 0.15 B	-4.3 ± 0.2 D
Semantic Fluency	20.3 ± 6.8	-3.6 ± 2.10 B	-7.2 ± 0.03 C
Phonological Fluency	12.5 ± 5.3	-4.45 ± 1.1 B	-0.76 ± 0.2 C
Ten Point Clock Test	3.6 ± 1.23	-1.1 ± 0.3 B	-1.43 ± 0.23 D
Proverbs Interpretation	6.1 ± 1.8	-0.67 ± 0.1 NS	-1.34 ± 0.1 C
Visuospatial Tests	3.43 ± 1.12	-0.54 ± 0.1 A	-0.45 ± 0.3 C
Instrumental Activity Daily Living	11.1 ± 1.24	-1.45 ± 0.1 A	-0.8 ± 1.7 C
Topoagnosia	2.78 ± 0.34	-0.56 ± 0.2 A	-0.5 ± 0.6 C

A : $p<0.05$ vs. baseline

B : $p<0.01$ vs. baseline

C : $p<0.05$ vs. 12 months

D : $p<0.01$ vs. 12 months.

Brain CT scans were available for all the patients. 58.7% of patients have MRI scans of the brain, as well. Accuracy and inter-rater reliability were high (94.3%; kappa=0.87) for the two neurologists (R.M. and P.T.) who assessed the scans. All the patients completed the full 24 month study. After twelve months, there was a worsening of general cognitive performances, expressed by a statistical significant decrease of MMSE, fluency, and of TPCT ($p<0.01$, according to a Wilcoxon two-related signed rank test), and of visuospatial perception, topoagnosia, IADL, and NPI (p<0.05). There was no decrease in scores on Proverb's Test task. Twenty-four months after the beginning of the study, there was a decrease in global performance (MMSE score), and in TPCT (p<0.01, according to a Wilcoxon two-related signed rank test). There also were decreases in fluency, visuospatial construction abilities, in Proverbs, in right/left recognition, and in IADL scores (p<0.05). however, there was a nonsignificant increase in behaviour symptoms. There is a significant difference at baseline and at 24 months in TPCT scores in vascular dementia patients (p<0.01). The mean score of TPCT of group B is 7.67 ± 2.1. Spearman's rank correlation analyses showed positive correlations between TPCT and topognosia (p<0.01), visuospatial abilities (p<0.01), fluency (p<0.01) all over 24 months follow-up. Weaker correlations were found between MMSE (p<0.05) and Proverb's test (p<0.05). No significant correlations were found with IADL and NPI scores. Error rates in the different test sessions (baseline, 12 and 24 months) have been compared by using ANOVA one way test. TPCT variations are significant over time (p<0.01 at 12 and 24 months), as well as topoagnosia, visuospatial perception and IADL functions.

We hypothesized that TPCT test could define the planning and executive capabilities of individuals, as well as the abstract reasoning functions. Finally, due to its involvement of visuospatial reasoning, we argued that it might be related to subjects' space perception.

Our results showed that the TPCT correlated not only with visuo-spatial perception, which would be expected, but also to specific frontal functions, which include semantic and phonological abilities, and with recognition of right and left. The correlations obtained were stable over the two-year follow-up.

Particularly, we identified a strong correlation between TPCT scores and perception of right and left in a specific subgroup of patients, suffering from subcortical vascular dementia, and not, as it might be expected with a group of patients suffering from ischemic strategic lesions or watershed infarcts, which might involve visuo-spatial areas.

Surprisingly different and recent studies indicated that the correct right and left perception o space relies on an integrity of "body schema". This internal representation refers to an on-line, real-time diagram of one's own body in space which is derived from sensory input. It provides a three dimensional, dynamic representation of the body in space that articulates with motor systems in the genesis of action (Coslett, 2001) and is related to the visuospatial representation of the human body (Coslett, 1997; Coslett, 1998; Coslett, 2001). The performance of recognition of left and right space, is strongly influenced by the biomechanical properties of the human body as well as the position of the subject at the time of the testing (Parsons, Fox, Downs, Glass, Hirsch, Martin, Jerabek, and Lancaster, 1995).

It is interesting that there is a parallel worsening in TPCT and in left and right perception; in particular, the portrayal of the clocks by patients is quite often characterized by a reversal of right and left hemispace (i.e. 1 o'clock has been written at 11 o'clock, 2 o'clock at 10, and so on) or by an inability to locate hours in a circular dimension. Hours were located in the middle of the template, or disposed casually; when asked to copy a given model, subjects draw the hours correctly, but do not know consciously what is right or what is left.

In contradistinction in Alzheimer's disease, implicit memory, which underlies the capability to read the time, is spared in comparison with subjects who have vascular dementia even in very advanced stages of the illness.

In conclusion, new neuropsychological criteria, based on study of the natural course of vascular cognitive impairment, that focus on early disease are urgently needed. They should focus on executive frontal functions and behavioural alterations; the TPCT is a valid well-accepted, cross-cultural executive measure, correlated with verbal and semantic fluency, and with left and right recognition.

ACKNOWLEDGEMENTS

The Authors express their debt of gratitude for the precious encouragement by Peter J. Manos; (Section of Psychiatry and Psychology, Virginia Mason Medical Center, Seattle Washington).

REFERENCES

Aharon-Peretz J., Kliotd R, Tomer R (2000) Behavioral differences between white matter lacunar domentia and Alzheimer's disease: A comparison of the neuropsychiatric inventory. Dement Geriatr Cogn Disord, 11, 294-298.

Alexopoulos, G.S., Abrams R.C., Young R.C., Shamoian C.A.(1988) Cornell Scale for Depression in Dementia. Biol. Psychiatr., 23: 271-284.

Cannata, AP., Alberoni, M., Franceschi, M., Mariani, C (2002). Frontal impairment in subcortical ischemic vascular dementia in comparison to Alzheimer's Disease. Dementia Geriatric Cognitive Disorders, 13: 101-111.

Chui, H. (2001) Dementia associated with subcortical ischemic vascular disease. American Academy (AAN), Philadelphia, 2FC.005-89-107.

Coslett, H. B. (1997) Neglect in vision and visual imagery: a double dissociation Brain, 120, 1163-1171.

Coslett, H. B. (1998) Evidence for a disturbance of the body schema in neglect. Brain and Cognition, 37, 527-544.

Coslett, H. B. (2001) Body representations: neuropsychology and anatomic bases. American Academy of Neurology (AAN), Philadelphia, 7FC. 00S, 41-50.

CUMMINGS, J. L. Fronto-subcortical circuits and human behaviour. Arch Neurol. 1993; 50: 873–80.

Cummings, J. L, Trimble, M.R. (1995) Concise guide to neuropsychiatric and behavioral neurology. Washington: American Psychiatric Press, Inc.

Cummings, J.L., Mega, M., Gray, K., Rosenberg-Thompson, S., Carusi, D.A., and GORNBEIN, J. (1994) The Neurpsychiatric Inventory: comprehensive assessment of psychopathology in dementia. Neurology, 44, 2308-2314.

Desmond, D.W. The neuropsychology of vascular cognitive impairment: is there a specific cognitive deficit? J Neurol Sci. 2004 Nov 15;226(1-2):3-7.

Englund, E. (1998) Neuropathology of white matter changes in Alzheimer's Disease and vascular dementia. Dem. Ger. Cogn. Disord., 9 (S1), 6-12.

Erkinjuntti, T. (1997) Vascular dementia: challenge of clinical diagnosis. Int Psychogeriatrics 9, 77–83.

Erkinjuntti, T., Ketonen, L, Sulkava, R., Vuorialho, M., and Palo, J. (1987) CT in the differential diagnosis between Alzheimer's disease and vascular dementia. Acta Neurol. Scand., 75, 262-270.

Esiri, M. M, Wilcock, G. K, and Morris, J. H. (1997) Neuropathological assessment of the lesions of significance in vascular dementia. J Neurol. Neurosurg. Psych., 63, 749-753.

Folstein, M., Folstein, S., and McHugh, P. 1975. Mini-Mental state. A practical method for grading the cognitive state of patients for the clinician. J. of Psychiatric Research., 12, 189-198.

Gorham, D. R. 1956. The proverbs test. Psychological Test Specialists, Missoula, Montana.

Greene, JG, Smith, R, Gardiner, M, Timburg, GC.(1982) Measuring behavioural disturbance of elderly demented in patients in the community and its effects on relatives: a factor analytic study. Age Ageing 11: 121–6.

Heinik, J., Solomesh, I., Shein, V., and Becker, D. (2002) Clock drawing test in mild and moderate dementia of the Alzheimer's type: a comparative and correlation study. Int. J. Geriatr. Psychiatry, 17, 480-485.

Juby A, Tench S, Baker R. V (2002) The value of clock drawing in identifying executive cognitive dysfunction in people with a normal Mini-Mental State Examination score CMAJ, 15, (8): 167-178.

Lawton, M.P., Brody, E.M. (1969) Assessment of older people: self-maintaining and instrumental activities of daily living. Gerontologist, 9, 179-189.

Lezak, M. D. (1995) Neuropsychological assessement New York: Oxford University Press.

Libon, D.J., Malamut, B. L. , Swenson, R., Prouty Sands, L., and Cloud, B. S. (1996) Further analysis of clock drawing among demented and non demented older subjects. Archives of Clinical Neuropsychology, 11 (3), 193-205.

Looi, J.C. L., and Sachdev, P.S. (1999) Differentiation of vascular dementia from AD on neuropsychological tests. Neurology, 53, 670-678.

Manos, P. J. (1997) The utility of the ten-point clock test as a screen for cognitive impairment in general hospital patients. Gen.Hosp. Psych,. 8, 469-476.

Manos, P. J. (1998) Monitoring cognitive disturbance in delirium with the ten point clock test. Int. J. Geriatr. Psychiatry, 13, 646-648.

Manos, P. J. (1999) Ten-Point Clock test sensitivity for Alzheimer's disease in patients with MMSE scores greater than 23. Int. J. Geriat. Psychiatry, 14, 454 – 458.

Manos, P.J., and Wu, R. (1994) The ten point clock test: a quick screen and grading method for cognitive impairment in medical and surgical patients. Int. J. Psych. Med. 24 (3): 229-244.

Mckahnn, G., Drachman, D., Folstein, M., Katzman, R., Price, D., Stadlan, E. (1984) Clinical diagnosis of AD: report of the NINCS-ADRDA work group under the auspices of the Department of Health and Human Services Task Force on Alzheimer's Disease. Neurology, 34, 939-944.

McPherson, S. E., and Cummings, J. L. (1996) Neurospychological aspects of vascular dementia. Brain Cogn. 31, 261-282.

Miller Fisher, C. (1965) Lacunes: small deep cerebral infarcts. Neurology, 1965, 15, 774-784.

Moore, V., and Wyke, M. A. (1984) Drawing disability in patients with senile dementia. Psychological Medicine, 14, 97-105.

Moretti, R., Torre, P, Antonello, R. M. , Cazzato, G., and Bava, A. (2002) Ten-point clock test: a correlation analysis with other neuropsychological tests in dementia. Int. J. Geriatr. Psychiatry, 17, 347-353.

Moretti, R, Toppe, P., Antonello, R. M, Cattaruzza, T, Cazzato, G, Bava A. (2005). Frontal lobe dementia and subcortical vascular dementia: a neuropsycological comparison. Perceptual and Motor Skills, 2005; 96: 141-151. (a)

Moretti R, Torre P, Antonello RM, Cazzato G, Bava A, Manos PJ. (2005) Use of the Ten-Point Clock test to compare executive functioning across 24 months in patients with subcortical vascular in vascular dementia. Perceptual and Motor Skills, 2005; 100: 207-216. (b)

Oosterman, J M., Scherder EJ.A. (2006) Distinguishing between Vascular Dementia and Alzheimer's Disease by Means of the WAIS: A Meta-analysis Journal of Clinical and Experimental Neuropsychology, 7: 1158 – 1175

Ott, BR., Lafleche, G., Whelihan, W.M., Buongiorno, GW., Albert, M.S., FO BS (1996). Impaired awareness of deficits in Alzheimer's Disease. Alzheimer Disease Associated Disorders, 10: 68-76.

Parsons, L. M. , Fox, P. T., Downs, J. H., Glass, T., Hirsch, T.B., Martin, C.C., Jerabek, P. A., and Lancaster, J. L. (1995) Use of implicit motor imagery for visual shape discrimination as revealed by PET. Nature , 375, 54-59.

Powlishta, K.K., Von-Dras, D.D., Stanford, A., Carr, D.B., Tsering, C., Miller, J.P., and Morris, J.C. (2002) The clock drawing test is a poor screen for very mild dementia. Neurology 59, 898-903.

Reisberg, B, Borenstein, J, Salob, SP, et al. (1987) Behavioral symptoms in Alzheimer's disease: phenomenology and treatment. J Clin Psychiatr 48(S1): 9–15.

Roman, G. C., Tatemichi, T. K., Eekinjutti, T., Cummings, J. L., Masdeu, J. C., Garcia, J. H., Amaducci, L., Orgogozo, J. M., Brun, A., Hofman, A. (1993) Vascular dementia: Diagnostic criteria for research studies. Report of the NINDS-AIREN International Workshop. Neurology, 43, 250-260.

Royall, D.R., Murloy, A.R., Chiodo, L.K., and Polk, M.J. (1999) Clock drawing is sensitive to executive control: a comparison of six methods. Journal of gerontology, 54(B), 328-333.

Sachdev, P. S., Brodaty, H., Looi, J. C. (1999) Vascular dementia: diagnosis, management and possible prevention. Med J Australia, 170, 81–5.

Wexhsler, D. 1981. Wechsler adult intelligence scale-R-Manual. New York, NY: Psychological Corp.

In: New Psychological Tests and Testing Research
Editor: Lydia S. Boyar, pp. 185-202

ISBN: 978-1-60021-570-4
© 2007 Nova Science Publishers, Inc.

Chapter 10

ADAPTATION AND VALIDATION OF THE PERSONALITY ASSESSMENT QUESTIONNAIRE ON 12-YEAR-OLD CHILDREN IN SRI LANKA

Piyanjali de Zoysa[1], Lalini Rajapakse[2] and Peter A. Newcombe[3]

[1] Department of Psychological Medicine, Faculty of Medicine, University of Colombo, Kynsey Road, Colombo 8, Sri Lanka
[2] Department of Community Medicine, Faculty of Medicine, University of Colombo, Kynsey Road, Colombo 8, Sri Lanka
[3] School of Social Work and Applied Human Sciences, University of Queensland, Brisbane, Australia 4072

ABSTRACT

The objective of this study was to adapt and validate the child version of the Personality Assessment Questionnaire with 12-year-old Sinhala speaking school children in Sri Lanka. Content and consensual validity was determined by the Delphi Process. Criterion validity was determined by the degree of consensus between a clinical psychologist's assessment and respondent's total score on the instrument. Test-retest and internal consistency reliability were determined in two ways - a large group administration and a small group administration. The instrument showed satisfactory content and consensual validity. The cut-off score for the Sinhala version of the Child PAQ was determined as 89, at a sensitivity of 71.1% and specificity of 69.4% (95% confidence interval). The validated version's full scale test-retest and internal consistency reliability were satisfactory. The instrument is best administered in small rather than in large groups of respondents.

INTRODUCTION

An essential aspect of using an instrument in a culture different to that of its origin, is to ensure that the concepts measured by the instrument are equivalent or similar in both cultural groups [Browner, Ortiz de Montellano and Rubel, 1988; Flaherty et al., 1988; International Test Commission, 2001]. The dearth of culturally valid psychological instruments has been a tremendous drawback in the development of psychological services in many countries. Within this context, the present paper investigates the adaptation and validation of the Child version of the Personality Assessment Questionnaire [PAQ: Rohner, 1999] in Sri Lanka. The availability of such culturally adapted and validated instruments is important in furthering psychological services in Sri Lanka, where psychology is still in its infancy [De Zoysa and Ismail, 2002]. Therefore, the objectives of the study were: to translate the Child PAQ to the Sinhala language (Sinhala is the official language of the country); to asses the content, consensual and criterion validity of the Sinhala version; to determine the Sri Lankan cut-off score for deducing psychological (mal)adjustment in 12-year-old Sinhala-speaking school children; and to determine the test re-test and internal consistency reliability of the instrument.

In the domain of psychological (mal)adjustment in children, several instruments have been developed [e.g., Child PAQ: Rohner, 1999; Child Behavior Checklist: Achenbach, 1991; Multidimensional Anxiety Scale for Children: March, 1999]. Most of these instruments have been developed and validated in western cultures, although some of these, such as the PAQ, have been subsequently used in non-western communities [e.g., Rohner, Kean, and Cournoyer, 1991]. The PAQ is a self-administered instrument designed to assess an individual's perception of him/her self (or of his/her child) with respect to seven behavioral dispositions [Rohner, 1999]. They are: hostility and aggression; dependency; negative self-esteem; negative self-adequacy; emotional unresponsiveness; emotional instability; and negative world view. Three versions of the PAQ have been developed: one asks adults to reflect on their behavioral dispositions (Adult PAQ); a second asks children to reflect on their behavioral dispositions (Child PAQ); and, a third asks mothers (or other caretakers, such as teachers) to reflect on a child's behavioral depositions (Mother PAQ). The Child PAQ, the version validated in this study, is intended to be used with children aged seven to 12 years.

The Child PAQ has 42 items with six items for each of the seven behavioral dispositions (scales). All items are arranged in a cyclical order. Higher scores on a scale relate to greater levels of maladjustment as measured by that scale. In order to minimize response acquiescence, 13 of the 42 items are phrased in a manner such that the respondent's responses to them are reverse scored when summing the scores for the full instrument or its scales. By summing the scores of each of the seven scales, an overall assessment of the level of psychological (mal)adjustment of the respondent can be made. Higher total scores reflect greater emotional/behavioral impairment. Scores on the instrument can range from 42 to 168. Scores at or above 105 are reported to indicate problems in psychological adjustment [R. Rohner, personal communication, September 17, 2002]. The Child PAQ, as in the other two versions, asks respondents to reflect on their true, rather than ideal or wished for feelings about themselves. The response options available are: (1) almost always true of me; (2) sometimes true of me; (3) rarely true of me; and (4) almost never true of me. The child is asked to indicate how s/he really feels in response to each of the items and to tick the appropriate response option.

The Child PAQ has been developed to be used cross-culturally [Rohner, 1999]. In designing it, evidence that the dimensions measured in the PAQ manifest in humans everywhere in varying degrees, was taken in to consideration [Rohner, 1975]. Further, classes of items which had common international referents were chosen to be included in the instrument by utilizing a cross-cultural survey conducted on a world sample of 101 societies [Rohner, 1975].

Concurrent validity of the Child PAQ has been assessed by correlating the scales with others that measure the same or similar constructs. Such concurrent validation has indicated, with the exception of the negative self-adequacy scale, that the remaining six scales correlated significantly with their validation instruments [Rohner, 1999]. Rohner claimed that the poor validation of the negative self-adequacy scale might have been a result of a validation instrument that was only an approximate to the conceptual criterion.

Cronbach's coefficient alpha was used as the principal measure of the instrument's reliability. In a study assessing the alpha for the Child PAQ's scales, the instrument was administered to 220, nine to eleven-year-olds. Estimates for the seven scales ranged from 0.46 to 0.74 (median alpha = 0.63) [Rohner, 1999]. Though the scale alphas in this study were not ideal, a recent meta-analysis of the instrument [Khaleque and Rohner, 2002] involving nine studies revealed a full-scale mean alpha of 0.83, allowing for the full-scale's confident use in research, clinical, and applied settings.

METHOD

Participants

The Child PAQ was adapted and validated on 12-year-old Sinhala speaking school children. In Sri Lanka, by the age of 12 years, school children are familiar with self-administered questionnaires as it is a common examination paper format they come across. Younger school children, however, are generally unfamiliar with self-administered questionnaires.

Instruments

The instruments used in the study were the original version of the Child PAQ, its Sinhala translation, a Focus Group Interview Schedule, and two Structured Interview Schedules. The interview schedules were developed specifically for this study.

Consequent to obtaining permission from the author of the PAQ [Rohner, 1999] for adapting and validating the instrument in Sri Lanka, a professional translator who is a native speaker of Sinhala and who is also proficient in English translated the original Child PAQ to Sinhala. This Sinhala translation was then translated back into English by a second translator who was also a native speaker of Sinhala as well as being proficient in English. This method of back translation was in keeping with international guidelines [ITC, 2001; Neuman, 1997].

To ascertain the conceptual equivalency of the translations, the instrument's original version and the back translated (from Sinhala to) English version were presented for comparison to a bilingual (in Sinhala and English) professional from the behavioral sciences. Discrepancies in the two versions were identified and the necessary modifications in the Sinhala version were made. Thus, the process of translating and back translating was carried out independently by persons who were proficient in both Sinhala and English.

Subsequent to the translation, the Sinhala version of the instrument was pre-tested twice. A conveniently located co-educational school which has children from diverse socio-economic classes in the Gampaha District of the Western Province of Sri Lanka was chosen for conducting both pre-tests. The first pre-test was in the form of a structured exploratory interview (based on a Structured Interview Schedule) with five Sinhala speaking, 12-year-old children (two boys and three girls). The teacher in charge of Grade seven chose students belonging to both genders and different socio-economic classes for this structured interview. The children were interviewed separately. At the interview, the children were presented with each item in the instrument and asked the item was difficult to understand (and if so, how), whether the concept intended to be conveyed by the item was correctly understood, whether any discomfort was felt when answering the items (and if so, what), and whether the instrument was too long. The feedback given by the children together with observations of the interviewer were used to revise the wording of the instrument. Once revised, the instrument was pre-tested a second time on a group of 10 children (four boys and six girls) who were selected as in the first pre-test. After completing the instrument, the children took part in a focus group discussion (based on a Focus Group Interview Schedule). They were asked for feed-back on the appropriateness of the length of the instrument, difficulty level of the items, clarity of the written instructions, clarity of the response alternatives, and their views on the formatting style of the instrument. These comments as well as the observations of the focus group moderator were used to further revise the wording of the instrument, the instructions, and the formatting style.

Procedure

Validity: Content-, Consensual- and Criterion-Related Validation

Content-related validation (judgment of whether the conceptual definition of a scale/item has been appropriately translated into operational terms) and consensual-related validation (judgment of the appropriateness to use a scale/item) of the Child PAQ was determined by the Delphi Process [Jones and Hunter, 1995]. Whilst content-related validation was a judgment on the operational aspects of the conceptual definition of a scale/item, consensual-related validation assessed the extent of agreement about the (cultural) appropriateness of a scale/item [Abramson and Abramson, 1999]. Consensus methods [Fink, Kosecoff, Chassin and Brook, 1984; Jones and Hunter, 1995] such as the Delphi Process are useful in determining the extent to which a panel of judges (either experts or lay people) agrees about a given issue.

A group of six experts from the social and behavioral disciplines served as the judges for content- and consensual-related validation of the instrument. In terms of content-related validation, the judges were asked to rate, on a scale from zero (total disagreement) to nine (total agreement), whether each item in a scale was an appropriate indicator of that scale, and if the composite of six items in each scale was an adequate measure of the concept measured by that particular scale. In terms of consensual-related validation, the judges rated, again on a scale of zero to nine, whether each item was appropriate to be used with 12-year-old Sinhala speaking school children. They were also asked to judge whether the conceptual meaning of the original item had been retained after its translation to Sinhala and whether each item was culturally relevant to Sri Lanka. The judges' ratings for content- and consensual-related validation were collated and presented for a second round of the Delphi Process. At this point, the judges re-rated their agreement with each item/scale and were given the opportunity to change their rating by considering the ratings given by the other judges. These re-ratings were summarized and assessed for degree of consensus [Jones and Hunter, 1995].

The best and most obvious way of appraising validity of an instrument is to find a criterion that is known or believed to be closest to the truth and to compare the results generated by the instrument with this criterion [Abramson and Abramson, 1999]. Such a comparable test was not available in Sri Lanka. Thus for the present study an interview by a clinical psychologist was used as the reference for criterion-related validation of the instrument. Each such interview (based on a Structured Interview Schedule) lasted approximately 10 minutes. After each interview, the clinical psychologist determined the presence or absence of psychological (mal)adjustment in the child with consideration to the seven behavioral dispositions measured by the instrument. The instrument was also administered to the children who were so interviewed. Criterion-related validation thus involved comparing a child's total score on the PAQ with that of the independent assessment by the clinical psychologist. The sample size required for the criterion-related validation was estimated by using the formula [Hulley and Cummings, 1988]:

$$N = \frac{4 \, z \, \alpha^2 \, P \, (1\text{-}P)}{W^2}$$

[where, $z\alpha^2$ = the standard normal deviate for a two tailed test α where $(1\text{-}\alpha)$ is the confidence level (i.e., since $\alpha = 0.05$ for a 95% confidence level, $z\alpha = 1.96$); P = expected proportion of true positives; W = total width of confidence interval] (see below for use of this formula).

In order to determine the cut-off score of the Sinhala version of the Child PAQ, it was necessary that an appropriate sensitivity and specificity level be chosen. The sensitivity of an instrument is the proportion of respondents who have the condition that is being tested and for whom a positive result on the instrument is obtained (i.e., a true positive or "hit" rate). This indicates how good an instrument is at identifying those with the condition. The specificity of an instrument is the proportion of respondents who do not have the condition that is being tested for and for whom a negative result on the instrument is obtained (i.e., true negative rate). This indicates how good an instrument is at identifying those without the condition. For the present study, a sensitivity of 85% and a specificity of 90% were targeted. The number of respondents that need to be identified as psychologically maladjusted for the instrument's sensitivity to be 0.85 ± 0.05 (95% confidence interval) was calculated by the above formula, where, P = 0.15 (as 0.85 is greater than half, the sample size was estimated from the proportion expected to have negative results - that is, 0.15), W = 0.15, and confidence interval = 95%. The number of respondents that needed to be so identified to obtain a sensitivity of

85% was (a minimum of) calculated as 87. The number of respondents to be identified as psychologically adjusted, for the instrument's specificity to be 0.90 ± 0.05 (95% confidence interval), was calculated in the same manner as that for sensitivity. However the expected proportion, P, was 0.10 and the total width, W = 0.10. Therefore, the number of respondents that needed to be identified as psychologically adjusted to obtain a specificity of 90% was (a minimum of) 138.

A convenience sample of 306 (142 girls and 164 boys) Sinhala speaking 12-year-old school children, from diverse socio-economic classes, took part in the criterion-related validation. The schools so chosen were different to those in which the pre-tests were conducted. The children's scores on the instrument were compared to their level of psychological (mal)adjustment as assessed by the clinical psychologist. The sensitivity and specificity of the instrument at different cut-off scores was studied, and a cut-off score for the Sinhala version of the Child PAQ was determined using the Receiver Operator Characteristic curve [ROC: Hulley and Cummings, 1998]. ROC curve is a graphic way of portraying the trade-offs involved between improving either a test's sensitivity or specificity. Several cut-offs are selected, and the sensitivity and specificity at each point is determined. The sensitivity is then graphed as a function of 1-specificity. The best cut-off point in this graph is chosen and this is usually where the ROC curve "turns the corner" [Hulley and Cummings, 1998].

Reliability

The reliability of the Child PAQ was determined using both test-retest and internal consistency measures. Test-retest reliability of the study was assessed over a 14-day interval (Time 1 - Time 2). The internal consistency reliability was computed based on the data at Time 1 and Time 2 administration of the instrument. All 12-year-old children who attended class on Time 1 were invited to take part in a second administration. The data of those children absent at Time 2 was not included in test-retest analyses.

To determine the method most appropriate for administering the PAQ to 12-year-old school children in Sri Lanka, two different modes of administration were evaluated. In the first method, the Child PAQ was administered to large groups of approximately 40 children, and in the second method, the instrument was administered to smaller groups of approximately 20 children. The large and small group administrations were conducted in different schools (and these were also different from the pre-test and criterion-related validation study schools). In the large group administration, 119 12-year-olds (61 boys and 58 girls) from a co-educational school in the Gampaha District participated. With eight students giving incomplete records, the final sample for the large group administration was 111 children. In the small group administration, 111 12-year-olds (54 boys and 57 girls) from two schools (a boys and a girls school), also in the Gampaha District, participated. All children in the small group administration returned completed questionnaires.

In the large group administration, the children completed the instrument in their classroom, in the absence of a teacher. The test administrator remained with the children until its completion. Often, teachers and the principal came in to the classroom during the administration and some even looked at the respondent's answers (though they were repeatedly asked not to do so by the test administrator). Further, it was observed that the children were distracted, possibly because of the cramped conditions in classrooms (some classrooms had up to 50 children sitting side by side). On the other hand, the small group situation was an environment removed from the classrooms (e.g., an empty hall), though within the school itself. The test administrator observed the children to be more relaxed and task oriented.

Judges and children were assured of confidentiality and anonymity. It was explained that there would be no direct benefit to them from the study and that the information provided would be useful when planning services for Sri Lankan children. All respondents were informed that they were free to withdraw from the study at any time should they wish to do so. Governmental approval for the study was obtained from the relevant Ministry. Ethical approval was obtained from the Faculty of Medicine, Colombo. Verbal consent of the participants was obtained.

RESULTS

Translation

During the back translation and the consensual-related validation (of the dimension of conceptual equivalency between the original and the translated version) process, a number of items in the original instrument had to be modified for the Sinhala version. For example, "I feel bad or get angry when I try to do something and cannot do it" from the original Child PAQ was difficult to translate perfectly as there is no conceptually equivalent term for "feel bad" in Sinhala. Similarly, the item "I feel that life is nice" was also difficult to be translated, as there is no equivalent word for "nice" in Sinhala. Therefore, the concepts of "feel bad" and "nice" had to be conveyed by the words "feel sad" and "beautiful", respectively. These words were conceptually somewhat different to that in the original items. Similarly, the item "I am in a bad mood and grouchy without any reason" also posed difficulties. In Sinhala, "bad mood" and "grouchy" do not have conceptually equivalent terms. Therefore, the resultant Sinhala words of, "angry" and "unpleasant" was used though conceptually narrower to that intended by the original item. The item, "when I meet someone I do not know, I think he is better than me" could not be translated to Sinhala in a way that the meaning of "better than me" could be wholly retained in the translated version. So the resultant translation was conceptually narrower than in the original and only conveyed "cleverer than me". Similarly, the item "I like to be given encouragement when I have trouble with something" posed a difficulty. The term "encouragement" cannot be perfectly translated to Sinhala and thus the resultant Sinhala translation conveyed "to help" rather than the broader concept of "encouragement". The items "I get upset when things go wrong", "I like my mother to give me a lot of attention", "I am cheerful and happy one minute and gloomy and unhappy the next" and "I get unhappy with myself" also posed certain difficulties. The concepts of "get upset", "give attention", "gloomy" and "unhappy with myself", respectively, are concepts not used in the Sinhala language. Therefore, these concepts had to be explained using many words rather than indicated by a specific term or word. Thus, in these four items, the original meaning was retained to a large extent, yet there was not a perfect conceptual translation.

Validity

Content-and Consensual-Related Validation

Results of the content- and consensual-related validation are presented in table 1. They provide a summary of the judge's ratings after the second round of the Delphi Process. Data was analyzed in predetermined three-point categories: 0-3, 4-6, and 7-9 [Scott and Black, 1991]. For the first and second round of the Delphi Process, the decision of which items/scales of the original instrument were to be retained in the Sinhala version was based on the following criteria: (a) if 70% or more of the ratings of an item (or scale) was in the category 0-3, if in the second round, that item/scale was to be omitted from the Sinhala version (or, if in the first round, that item was reworded to make it more acceptable in the event the wording was the reason for the low rating), or (b) if 70% or more of the ratings for a particular item/scale was in categories 4-6 and 7-9, then that item/scale was to be retained in the Sinhala version.

In content-related validation other than four items (see table 1), ratings for all others were in the acceptable categories of 4-6 and 7-9. As table 1 shows, the four items which had a rating in the 0-3 category had been so rated by only one judge whilst the remaining five judges had rated these items in the acceptable categories of 4-6 or 7-9. In consensual-related validation all item ratings were in the acceptable categories of 4-6 and 7-9 (see table 1).

In consensus methods such as the Delphi Process, it is not necessary that all judges give the same high rating of consensus and so a certain level of divergence is the norm [Scott and Black, 1991]. Due to divergence in ratings, studies using consensus methods have adopted their own criteria for determining consensus [e.g., Jones and Hunter, 1995; Scott and Black, 1991]. The three-point range adopted for determining consensus in this study was that used by Scott and Black [1991]. It operates on the premise that if there is at least one rating in 0-3 and one rating in the 7-9 category, the rating(s) which are furthest from the median be discarded before assessing consensus. In content-related validation (see table 1), there were four items that had at least one rating in the 0-3 and at least one rating in the 7-9 category. The outliers furthest away from the median in all of these items were the ratings in the 0-3 category. In keeping with the suggestion of Scott and Black [1991] these outliers were eliminated. Subsequent assessment of consensus of these four items revealed that that they could be retained in the Sinhala version as it was within the acceptable category of agreement. Results for consensual-related validation (see table 1) did not have items with rating on both the 0-3 and 7-9 categories as all items were rated in the acceptable categories of 4-6 or 7-9. Therefore, consensual-related validity of the Sinhala version of the instrument was satisfactory.

Criterion-Related Validation

The criterion-related validation of the Child PAQ involved assessing the consensus between an assessment of a clinical psychologist and the respondent's total score on the instrument. The sensitivity and specificity for different values of the total score was calculated and a cut-off score of 89 for the Sinhala version of the instrument was determined by a ROC curve. The sensitivity and specificity at this cut-off score is 71.1% and 69.4%, respectively (at 95% confidence interval).

Table 1. Summary of re-ratings (by percentages) by the 6 judges for content- and consensual-related validation of items/scales in the Sinhala version of the Child PAQ

Child PAQ Scale/Item	Content-related validation ratings						Consensual-related validation ratings								
	Appropriateness of item (%)			Items assess the concept (%)			Appropriateness with 12-year-old children (%)			Retains the conceptual meaning (%)			Cultural relevance to the Sri Lankan context (%)		
	0-3	4-6	7-9	0-3	4-6	7-9	0-3	4-6	7-9	0-3	4-6	7-9	0-3	4-6	7-9
HOSTILITY AND AGGRESSION					83	17									
I think about fighting or being mean			100					17	83		17	83		17	83
I want to hit something or someone			100					33	67		33	67		33	67
I get so mad I throw or break things			100					33	67		67	33		33	67
I make fun of people who do dumb things			100					17	83		17	83		17	83
I pout or sulk when I get mad	17	17	67					17	83		17	83		17	83
I have trouble controlling my temper			100					17	83			100		17	83
DEPENDENCY					50	50									
I like my mother to feel sorry for me when I feel sick		17	83					17	83		17	83		83	17
I like my parents to give me a lot of love		17	67						100		50	50			100
When I am unhappy I like to work out my problems by myself		17	83					67	33		67	33		33	67
I like my mother to give me a lot of attention	33		67					17	83		33	67		17	83

Table 1. (Continued).

Child PAQ Scale/Item	Content-related validation ratings						Consensual-related validation ratings								
	Appropriateness of item (%)			Items assess the concept (%)			Appropriateness with 12-year-old children (%)			Retains the conceptual meaning (%)			Cultural relevance to the Sri Lankan context (%)		
	0-3	4-6	7-9	0-3	4-6	7-9	0-3	4-6	7-9	0-3	4-6	7-9	0-3	4-6	7-9
I like to be given encouragement when I have trouble with something	17	33	50					17	83		17	83		17	83
I like my parents to make a fuss over me when I am hurt or sick		50	50					17	83		67	33		17	83
NEGATIVE SELF-ESTEEM					33	67									
I like myself		33	67					17	83		17	83		67	33
I feel I am no good and I never will be any good		17	83					17	83		67	33		17	83
When I meet someone I do not know, I think he is better than me		17	83					33	67		50	50		33	67
I think I am a good person and other people should think so too		33	67					50	50		67	33		33	67
I feel pretty good about myself		17	83					33	67		50	50		33	67
I get unhappy with my self		33	67						100		50	50		50	50
NEGATIVE SELF-ADEQUACY					50	50									
I feel I can do the things I want as well as most people		17	83						100		17	83		17	83
I feel I cannot do things well			100					17	83		67	33		17	83

Table 1. (Continued).

Child PAQ Scale/Item	Content-related validation ratings						Consensual-related validation ratings								
	Appropriateness of item (%)			Items assess the concept (%)			Appropriateness with 12-year-old children (%)			Retains the conceptual meaning (%)			Cultural relevance to the Sri Lankan context (%)		
	0-3	4-6	7-9	0-3	4-6	7-9	0-3	4-6	7-9	0-3	4-6	7-9	0-3	4-6	7-9
I can compete successfully for things I want		17	83					33	67		33	67		17	83
I think I am a failure		17	83					17	83		33	67		17	83
I feel I cannot do many of the things I try to do		17	83					17	83		17	83		17	83
I feel I am a success in the things I do			100					33	67		50	50		67	33
EMOTIONAL UNRESPONSIVENESS					50	50									
I have trouble showing people how I feel		17	83					33	67		17	83		17	83
It is easy for me to be loving with my parents		33	67					17	83		50	50		33	67
I feel I have trouble making and keeping friends		33	67					17	83		50	50		33	67
It is easy for me to show my family that I love them		17	83					17	83		50	50		17	83
It is hard for me when I try to show the way I really feel to someone I like		17	83					67	33		67	33		67	33
It is easy to show my friends I really like them			100					17	83		50	50		17	83
EMOTIONAL INSTABILITY					33	67									
I feel bad or get angry when I try to do something and cannot do it		17	83					17	83		17	83			100

Table 1. (Continued).

Child PAQ Scale/Item	Content-related validation ratings						Consensual-related validation ratings								
	Appropriateness of item (%)			Items assess the concept (%)			Appropriateness with 12-year-old children (%)			Retains the conceptual meaning (%)			Cultural relevance to the Sri Lankan context (%)		
	0-3	4-6	7-9	0-3	4-6	7-9	0-3	4-6	7-9	0-3	4-6	7-9	0-3	4-6	7-9
I am in a bad mood and grouchy without any reason			100					33	67		67	33		50	50
I get upset when things go wrong		33	67						100		50	50		33	67
I am cheerful and happy one minute and gloomy and unhappy the next		17	83					67	33		33	67		17	83
It is unusual for me to get angry or upset		33	67					17	83		33	67		33	67
I get upset easily when I meet hard problems		33	67					33	67		50	50		17	83
NEGATIVE WORLD VIEW						100		33	67			100		33	67
I feel that life is nice			100												
I see life as full of dangers		33	67					33	67		17	83		50	50
I think the world is a good, happy place			100					17	83		17	83		17	83
For me the world is an unhappy place		17	83					33	67		50	50			100
I see the world as a dangerous place			100					17	83		33	67		33	67
Life for me is a good thing			100					67	33		33	67		50	50

There was agreement between the clinical psychologist and the PAQ cut-off scores on 70% of the cases (215 of 306). Of the 97 children classed as psychologically maladjusted by the clinical psychologist, 70 (72%) were also categorized in this group following completion of the Child PAQ. For the children classed as psychologically adjusted by the clinician, 69% were similarly grouped according to their responses on the Child PAQ. The Kappa value for the agreement between the clinician's rating and PAQ was 0.37 (p<0.001), which shows there is significant agreement between the two.

Reliability

Test-Retest Reliability

The test-retest reliability for the Sinhala version of the full scale, for the large and small group administration, was an Inter-Class Correlation Coefficient (ICC) of 0.70 and 0.84, respectively (see table 2). Both these values exceeded the minimum acceptable criterion of 0.70 [De Vaus, 1991] for test re-test, indicating confident use of the full instrument in research, clinical, and applied settings. The test-retest reliabilities of the seven scales ranged from 0.40 to 0.71 (large group administration) and 0.59 to 0.81 (small group administration). Other than Dependency and Negative Self-Adequacy, all other scales in the small group showed ICC's in the acceptable criterion of 0.70 or greater. However, this was not so in the large group administration.

Table 2. Reliability estimates of the Sinhala-version of the PAQ scales and full scale for the large and small group administration

Child PAQ Scale	Internal Consistency (alpha)		Internal Consistency (alpha)	Test-Retest (ICC)	
	Sinhala version		Original version	Sinhala version	
	Large group Time 2 (Time 1)	Small group Time 2 (Time 1)		Large group	Small group
Hostility and aggression	0.62 (0.62)	0.62 (0.64)	0.66	0.48*	0.81*
Dependency	0.44 (0.44)	0.47 (0.32)	0.47	0.40*	0.59*
Negative self-esteem	0.41 (0.41)	0.42 (0.47)	0.66	0.67*	0.73*
Negative self-adequacy	0.55 (0.55)	0.63 (0.60)	0.63	0.61*	0.62*
Emotional unresponsiveness	0.52 (0.51)	0.57 (0.50)	0.46	0.57*	0.70*
Emotional instability	0.28 (0.24)	0.55 (0.51)	0.52	0.44*	0.74*
Negative world view	0.75 (0.75)	0.65 (0.70)	0.74	0.71*	0.76*
Full Scale	0.79 (0.79)	0.82 (0.84)	0.83	0.70*	0.84*

* p<.001.

Internal Consistency Reliability

The internal consistency reliabilities for the full scale and for each of the seven scales were estimated using Cronbach's alpha. Table 2 shows the alphas for Time 1 and Time 2 administration and it shows that the values are consistent with each other. For purposes of uniformity and ease of discussion, only Time 2 alphas would be used in further discussions on internal consistency. This is because the same group of children who participated in test-retest reliability was also included in Time 2 internal consistency estimates.

The internal consistency reliability of the full instrument, for the large and small group administration, was 0.79 and 0.82, respectively. For the seven scales, internal consistency reliabilities ranged from 0.28 to 0.75 (median 0.52: large group administration) and 0.42 to 0.65 (median 0.57: small group administration). In the original version, the alpha for the full scale was a mean of 0.83 [from a meta analysis of nine studies: Khaleque and Rohner, 2002] and a range of 0.46 to 0.74 (median 0.63) for its seven scales (see table 2). The scale alphas in the original version and in this study were not ideal. However, the full instrument alpha in the original version [Khaleque and Rohner, 2002] and in the small group administration of this study exceeded the minimum criterion of 0.60 (De Vaus, 1991; Tran and Aroian, 2000), indicating the full-scale's confident use in research, clinical and applied settings. Thus, the internal consistency reliabilities for the full scale and the seven scales are consistent in the original meta analysis and the Sinhala version.

DISCUSSION

The objective of this study was to adapt and validate the Child version of the PAQ on 12-year-old Sinhala speaking school children in Sri Lanka. Translating the Child PAQ to the Sinhala language posed certain difficulties. Such problems in translating instruments have been highlighted in the Introduction of the Linguistic Evaluation Protocol devised by the World Health Organisation [1997]. As suggested by Guilliman, Bombardier, and Beaton [1993], the translation process in the present study involved more than one individual to minimize such difficulties. Therefore, following the initial back translation process [ITC, 2001; Neuman, 1997], experts from the social and behavioral professions assessed the degree of conceptual equivalence of the original Child PAQ to its Sinhala version. This two-way process - back translation and consensual-related validation - assisted in making the Sinhala version conceptually equivalent as possible to the original version. However, there were instances in which perfect conceptual and literal equivalence could not be achieved. Terms in the original child PAQ were difficult to translate into Sinhala; the original meaning of an item had to be modified during translation because only a part of the original meaning was present in Sinhala; and some of the associations in the original version were lost making the translated item much narrower in the Sinhala version. These difficulties have been found to commonly occur when translating instruments [World Health Organisation, 1997].

Content- and consensual-related validation of the instrument involved the Delphi Process [Jones and Hunter, 1995]. Content-related validation involved two dimensions: each item in a scale was rated on the extent it was an appropriate indicator of that scale, and the composite of six items in each scale was rated on the extent it measured the concept assessed by that scale. Consensual-related validation involved three dimensions: whether each item was appropriate for use with 12-year-old Sri Lankan school children; whether the conceptual meaning of the item was retained after back translation to Sinhala; and whether each item was culturally relevant to Sri Lanka. For each item and scale, an acceptable level of content- and consensual-related validity was deemed reached if the item/scale received a minimum of 70% agreement among the judges. As indicated in table 1, such a minimum of 70% agreement was obtained with the result that the Sinhala version of the Child PAQ demonstrated satisfactory content and consensual validity.

Criterion-related validity of the Child PAQ was also determined. The criterion used in this study was an independent assessment of the children by a clinical psychologist. A ROC curve was used to determine the cut-off score for the Sinhala version of the Child PAQ. This was determined to be 89 with a sensitivity of 71.1% and a specificity of 69.4%. This indicates that at the cut-off score of 89, the Sinhala version of the child PAQ could detect those who are psychologically maladjusted 71.1% of the time and those who are not maladjusted 69.4% of the time. Although a sensitivity of 85% and a specificity of 90% was targeted at the time of determining the sample size for criterion-related validation, the cut-off score for the Sinhala version was determined to be at 89 as this was the point at which the ROC curve "turned the corner" [Hulley and Cummings, 1988]. This cut-off score for the Sinhala version is lower than that of the original Child PAQ (set at 105). The difference in the cut-off scores may suggest cultural differences between Sri Lanka and the USA where child behaviors that may be considered normative in the latter may be considered maladaptive in Sri Lanka. Such a change in the cut-off score of the original version of an instrument to suit the culture to which it is being adapted and validated on, has also been reported in validating other psychometric instruments [e.g., Diareme, Tsiantis, and Tsitoura, 1997; Raven, Court, and Raven, 1993].

The test-retest reliability of the full instrument and its seven scales was determined in two ways - firstly through a large group administration and then with a small group administration. The test-retest reliability for the full instrument and the scales were higher in the small group than in the large group administration (see table 2). According to De Vaus [1991], a "rule of thumb" acceptability of an instrument's test-retest reliability is an ICC value greater than 0.70. The ICC values for the full instrument and its scales in the small group administration shows that all ICC's except Dependency (ICC=0.59) and Negative self-Adequacy (ICC=0.62) were acceptable (see table 2). However, the ICC values for the large group administration indicate that other than that of the full instrument and the Negative world view scale, all other values were not acceptable.

As in test-retest reliability, the internal consistency reliability of the Sinhala version of the instrument was also computed for the large and small group administrations. The full instrument alpha was 0.79 and 0.82 for the large and small group administrations, respectively (see table 2). As the large and small group administration's full scale alpha exceeded the minimum acceptable criterion of 0.60 [Tran and Aroian, 2000; De Vaus, 1991], the full instrument could be confidently used in research, clinical and applied settings in Sri Lanka. However, some of the scale alphas (see table 2) of both the large and small group administration were not ideal though they were consistent with values reported for the original instrument [scale alphas ranging from 0.46 to 0.7; median alpha=0.63: Rohner, 1999].

The reliability results indicate that there is more variability in responses in large groups than in small groups - both for the full instrument and the scales. Therefore, small group administration may be the best choice when administering self-report instruments, such as the Child PAQ, to Sri Lankan children. This method would yield more consistent and reliable results than would a large group. It may be that as children in large groups seemed distracted from the task at hand (as observed by the test administrator) they may not have provided accurate and consistent data. The physical environment of the testing situation may also have contributed to the difference in results obtained in the large and small group administration.

In the large group administration, the children completed the instrument in their classroom where teachers and the principal often came in to the classrooms. Though corporal punishment and other forms of punitive disciplinary strategies are legally banned in Sri Lankan schools, it still occurs frequently. Thus, in such a seemingly punitive environment, the children may not have felt comfortable to engage in the task at hand - especially as the Child PAQ probes into information of themselves. On the other hand, the small group administration was in an environment away from the classrooms (e.g., an empty hall), though within the school itself and the children were observed by the test administrator to be more relaxed and task oriented. Therefore, many factors may have contributed to the differences in the reliability results with in the large and small group administration.

CONCLUSION

The aim of the present study was to adapt and validate the Child PAQ to be used in Sri Lanka. The instrument indicated good content, consensual validity and criterion validity and test-retest and internal consistency reliability in the Sri Lankan context. Though the original Child PAQ was used with large groups of children [Rohner, 1999], its Sinhala version showed stronger psychometric properties when administered in small groups (20 children). Thus, the Child PAQ full instrument could be confidently used in research and applied settings with 12-year-old Sinhala speaking government school children - provided it is done so in small groups. The availability of such culturally adapted and validated instruments is important in furthering psychological services in Sri Lanka, where psychology is still in its infancy [De Zoysa and Ismail, 2002]. However, as some scale alphas and ICC values were below the minimum acceptable criteria [De Vaus, 1991], these scales if used, should be interpreted with caution.

A limitation of this study was that the instrument was validated only on 12-year-old Sinhala speaking school children. As such, this instrument and its cut-off score may not be appropriate to be used with illiterate children (as it is self-administered), children of other ages, non-Sinhala speaking children, or, with non-school-going (though literate) children in Sri Lanka. Therefore, future research would need to explore the possibility of expanding the use of the Child PAQ to such diverse populations in Sri Lanka. Further, the present study assessed only some types of validity of the Child PAQ. There are many other methods of validation [Anastasi, 1988] which, if undertaken, would further improve the psychometric value of the instrument. The Sinhala version's full instrument test-retest and internal consistency reliability provides satisfactory evidence for its consistency and stability over time - provided it is used in its entirety and in small groups. In considering future research, those scales that indicated low test-retest and internal consistency reliability values need to be further studied in order to establish the reasons for this finding.

ACKNOWLEDGEMENTS

The authors wish to thank the children who participated in this study as well as the principals and teachers who provided the opportunity for the study to be conducted in their schools. The study was funded by a grant from the Save the Children Fund (SCF) - UK and Norway. The authors wish to thank SCF for their financial assistance.

REFERENCES

Abramson, J. H., and Abramson, Z. H. (1999). *Survey methods in community medicine. Epidemiological research program evaluation. Clinical trials* (5th Ed.). Churchill Livingstone: Harcourt Brace and Company Limited.

Achenbach, T. M. (1991). *Manual for the Child Behavior Checklist and Teacher's Report Form.* Burlington, Vermont: University of Vermont, Department of Psychiatry.

Browner, C. H., Ortiz de Montellano, B. R., and Rubel, A. J. (1988). A methodology for cross cultural ethnomedical research. *Current Anthropology, 29(5),* 681-702.

Cannino, G., Bird, H., Rubo-Stipe, M., and Bravo, M. (1997). The epidemiology of mental disorders in adult population in Puerto Rico. *Puerto Rico Health Science Journal, 16(2),* 117-124.

De Vaus, D. A. (1991). *Surveys in social research* (3rd ed.) Sydney, NSW: Allen and Unwin Pty Ltd.

De Zoysa, P., and Ismail, C. (2002). Psychology in an Asian country: A report from Sri Lanka. *International Journal of Psychology, 37(2),* 110-111.

Diareme, S., Tsiantis, J., and Tsitoura, S. (1997). Cross-cultural validation of the Child Abuse Potential Inventory in Greece: A preliminary study. *Child Abuse and Neglect, 21 (11),* 1067-1079.

Fink, A., Kosecoff, J., Chassin, M., and Brook, R. H. (1984). Consensus methods: Characteristics and guidelines for use. *American Journal of Public Health, 74,* 979-983.

Flaherty, J. A., Gariria, F. M., Pathak, D., Mitchell, T., Wintrob, R., Richman, J. A., and Birz, B. S. (1988). Developing instruments for cross-cultural research. *Journal of Nervous and Mental Diseases, 178(5),* 257-263.

Guilliman, F., Bombardier, C., and Beaton, D. (1993). Cross cultural adaptation of health related quality of life measures: Literature review of proposed guidelines. *Journal of Clinical Epidemiology, 46(12),* 1417-1432.

Hamby, S. L., and Finkelhor, D. (2001). Choosing and using child victimisation questionnaires. *Juvenile Justice Bulletin* (pp. 13-16). Washington DC: US Department of Justice.

Hui, H. C., and Triandis, H.C. (1985). Measurement in cross-cultural psychology: A review and comparison of strategies. *Journal of Cross-Cultural Psychology, 16,* 131-152.

Hulley, S. B., and Cummings, S. R. (1988). *Designing clinical research: An epidemiological approach.* Baltimore, MD: Williams and Wilkins.

International Test Commission (2001). ITC Guidelines on Adapting Tests. Retrieved February 24th 2005 from http://www.intestcom.org/itc_projects.htm#Translations of the Test Use Guidelines

Jones, J., and Hunter, D. (1995). Consensus methods for medical and health services research. *British Medical Journal, 311*, 376-380.

Khaleque, A., and Rohner, R. P. (2002). Reliability of measures assessing the pancultural association between perceived parental acceptance-rejection and psychological maladjustment. *Journal of Cross-Cultural Psychology, 33, 86-98.*

Kleinman, A. M. (1977). Depression, somatisation and the new cross-cultural psychiatry. *Social Science and Medicine, 11*, 3-10.

March, J. S. (1999). *Multidimensional anxiety scale for children.* New York: Multi-Helath Systems Inc.

Neuman, W. L. (1997). *Social research methods: Qualitative and quantitative approaches* (3rd Ed.). Boston, MA: Viacom Company.

Raven, J. C., Court, J. H., and Raven, J. (1993*). Manual for Ravens Progressive Matrices and Vocabulary Scales.* Oxford, England: Oxford Psychologists Press Ltd.

Rohner, R. P. (1975). Parental acceptance-rejection and personality development. A universalist approach to behavior science. In R. W. Brislin, S. Bochner, and W. J. Lohner (Eds.), *Cross-cultural perspectives in learning* (pp. 251-269). Beverly Hills: Sage Publications.

Rohner, R. P. (1999). *Handbook for the study of parental acceptance and rejection.* USA: Rohner Research.

Rohner, P., Kean, K. J., and Cournoyer, D. E. (1991). Effects of corporal punishment, perceived caretaker warmth, and cultural beliefs on the psychological adjustment of children in St. Kitts, Wets Indies. *Journal of Marriage and the Family,* 53, 681-693.

Scott, E. A., and Black, N. (1991). When does consensus exist in expert panels. *Journal of Public Health*, 13, 35-39.

Sumathipala, A., and Murray, J. (2000). New approach to translating instruments for cross-cultural research: a combined qualitative and quantitative approach for translation and consensus generation. *International Journal of Methods in Psychiatric Research*, 9, 87-95.

Tran, T. V. T., and Aroian, K. J. (2000). Developing cross cultural research instruments. *Journal of Social Work Research and Evaluation*, 1(1), 35-48.

World Health Organization. (1997). *International Classification of Impairments, Disabilities and Handicap (ICIDH). Field trial protocol for linguistic analysis.* Geneva: World Health Organization.

In: New Psychological Tests and Testing Research
Editor: Lydia S. Boyar, pp. 203-213

ISBN: 978-1-60021-570-4
© 2007 Nova Science Publishers, Inc.

Chapter 11

DEVELOPING AND VALIDATING PSYCHOMETRIC TESTS FOR USE IN HIGH PERFORMANCE SETTINGS

Andrew M. Lane

School of Sport, Performing Arts and Leisure
University of Wolverhampton

ABSTRACT

Identifying factors associated with human performance could provide evidence on which to develop intervention strategies designed to enhance performance. A prospective research methodology that is sensitive to the range of psychological states experienced by individuals performing under stress needs to be developed for such a purpose. Collecting data intrudes on the typical preparation of individuals in such situations. The act of completing a psychological inventory can make participants aware of how they feel. For example, asking a soccer penalty taker how anxious he/she feels before shooting could raise anxiety as the researcher has made the participant sensitive to how anxious they are feeling. What could follow from this is the player, who is likely to have experienced anxiety previously, will make self-regulatory efforts to reduce anxiety. Theoretically, researchers do not wish to change the construct they are seeking to assess, and if such research has damaging effects to participants beyond the benefits of conducting the research, then the study is unethical. Research teams need to consider the research skills of data collectors. The aim of the present chapter is to evaluate issues relevant to selecting psychometric measures used in research that seeks to assess relationships between psychological constructs and performance. The chapter outlines an approach for developing measures that participants are more likely to complete and suggestions for future research.

Key words: Measurement, ethics, high-performance, emotions, and validity.

INTRODUCTION

The English soccer team were knocked out of the 2006 World Cup on penalties after defeat to Portugal. Public uproar and upset followed with questions as 'why can't the England players take penalties in major competition?' and 'Do English penalty takers have the nerve for major competition?' being asked. The English soccer team has lost their last three penalty shoot-outs in major competitions. What follows are anecdotal reports about why English players cannot score from penalties. Players discuss the value of taking penalties in training. One side of the argument is that you cannot simulate the stress of competition and so practice is meaningless. The other side of the argument is that it is better to practice penalties and therefore not have the excuse that the team should have practised. Why is this relevant to psychological testing? Clearly what is needed to answer the question on why the English players fail to score is carefully conducted and controlled research that identifies the factors associated with success and failure under stressful situations.

Consider the difficulties in trying to do this type of study. Would the players complete self-report measures shortly before taking a penalty? If this was in a real game, the answer is no they would not. The players would see this as an intrusion and the coaches and management team would simply not permit such research to take place. Would the players complete a self-report measure before taking a penalty in a practice game? The answer is a reserved yes, and some studies have used such a design. In the study by Cushion and Lane (1997), we asked 30 players to rate how confident they were on scoring immediately before taking the penalty. Players volunteered to take part in the project and the penalties were taken in training. Dr Cushion was the coach and so could add a sense of realism and importance to the penalty-taking experiment. However, a question that could be pointed at the study by Cushion and Lane, and many studies that seek to assess psychological states such as confidence and emotion in experimental type studies is 'how valid are the results?' At least two issues are relevant to answering this question. First, did the athletes present a true and honest depiction of their psychological states? Researchers need some insight on how participants complete measures, for example, do participants overestimate or underestimate the psychological state under investigation. Self-efficacy reports tend to be inflated (Bandura, 1997) whereas emotional states of dejection and depression tend to be low. Lane and Terry (2000) argued that the typical score is zero when athletes complete a measure an hour before competition. Second, does completing such a test raise awareness of the construct the researcher was trying to measure? The act of completing a mood questionnaire or rating self-efficacy to succeed could, at least, for the time it takes to complete the questionnaire, turn the focus of the individual to how they are feeling at that time. For example, if asked to rate your confidence to succeed on a scale from 1 to 100 shortly before taking the task, this should raise self-awareness of confidence. If you rated yourself only 30 out of 100 for self-efficacy to succeed, recognition of this low confidence could change how you approached the task and thereby the researcher has changed the construct he/she is trying to assess.

Few studies have been conducted to assess psychological states during performance. The typical research design is to assess psychological states approximately one hour before competition (see Lane and Terry, 2000; Lane, 2001; Martens, Vealey, Burton, Bump, and Smith, 1990). In applied sport psychology, Terry (1995) recommended assessing mood states the night before competition as this allows time for processing measures and possible interventions. In seeking to predict academic performance, Lane, Whyte, Terry, and Nevill (2005) assessed mood states immediately before an examination. Students completed mood measures as they sat at a desk waiting to start the examination. Lane (2006a) pointed out that the aim of such research is to study the relationship between psychological states and performance with the assumption that assessments taken before performance are associated with psychological states during performance. Conducting research in situations such as before competition or before an examination, where the participants are principally interested in how they will perform, rather than completing psychometric questionnaires requires sensitivity on the behalf of the researcher.

The aim of this chapter is to evaluate issues relevant to selecting psychometric measures used in research that seeks to assess relationships between psychological constructs and performance. As performance refers to a range of behaviours, some clarification is needed. In the present chapter, performance relates to a set of behaviours designed to bring about success. Further, goal attainment has considerable personal meaning to the individual. The types of situations in which this could be relevant are diverse. They could range from athletes successfully achieving his/her goals, to foreign exchange dealers in banks dealing with large sums of money, and to the key decisions by company bosses. Tasks also include ones of critical importance such as a surgeon, pilot or military personnel performing life saving tasks. I argue that in all of the above examples the key issue for the researcher is that the participant will devote only a short amount of time to completing the measure. The research is less important to the participant, and if not correctly managed, could be detrimental to performance. An acknowledged limitation of this chapter is that many of the examples are drawn from sport research. However, through an in-depth discussion of factors that influence the research process, it is hoped that the reader can draw parallels to their own area of interest. In the present chapter three factors are examined:

1. Comprehensibility of items;
2. Developing measures grounded in the experience of participants;
3. The number of items needed to assess a construct.

COMPREHENSIBILITY OF ITEMS

A key question that the research team should ask is 'how will the potential participants react to completing the measures designed to assess the target construct?' Our strategy is to spend a great deal of time developing and validating measures so that they are fit for purpose. For example, to assess mood states in situations where brevity was important we developed The Brunel Mood Scale (BRUMS: Terry, Lane, Lane, and Keohane, 1999; Terry, Lane, and Fogarty, 2003). The BRUMS was validated with the explicit intention of developing a scale that participants would find easy to complete. In the case of the BRUMS, reduced completion time was addressed by having items that participants could easily understand (see figure 1). The intention was to develop a measure that could be used in situations where participants complete the measure with little prior notice. Terry and colleagues achieved this by using adolescents as the starting population to validate the inventory. The assumption was that if adolescents could understand the meaning of items, then so should adults. Items that participants find difficult to understand will be problematic. Terry et al. (1999) developed an alternative word list for items that were difficult to understand so that such issues could be addressed in a standardised way. However, it should be noted that reviews of their work (Lane, 2004) report that the alternative word list is rarely used. As figure 1 indicates, the use of a single item to assess an indicator of a construct should be quicker than having to read a sentence.

Below is a list of words that describe feelings people have. Please read each one carefully. Then tick the answer which best describes **HOW YOU FEEL RIGHT NOW**. Make sure you respond to every word.

	Not at all	A little	Moderately	Quite a bit	Extremely
Panicky	0	1	2	3	4
Lively	0	1	2	3	4
Confused	0	1	2	3	4
Worn out	0	1	2	3	4
Depressed	0	1	2	3	4

Figure 1. Selected items and instructional response timeframe for using the Brunel Mood Scale.

When using self-report measures, the researcher assumes the items means one thing, but if participants assume it means something different, this can lead to problems with interpretation. Researchers interested in assessing anxiety before competition typically used the Competitive State Anxiety Inventory-2 (CSAI-2: Martens et al., 1990). What developed from studies that used the CSAI-2 was the notion that individuals interpret anxiety symptoms as positive of performance whilst others perceived anxiety negatively (Jones, 1995). A scale and instructional set was developed (see figure 2) to assess directional perceptions of anxiety. A limitation of this measure is that some participants struggle with the dual question and pose the question back to the researcher on how they should complete the directional aspect of the measure. Indeed, advocates of the CSAI-2 encourage researchers to train participants on how to complete the measure (Thomas, Hanton, and Jones, 2002). In this instance, participants are provided with a copy of the measure and have the opportunity to discuss the meaning of items not easily understood. Participants should understand the intended meaning of items following training. However, it is important to distinguish studies in which participants received training from studies where participants were presented the measure to athletes for the first time shortly before competition. The need for a standardised training programmes could preclude using the measure to assess anxiety in large groups of individuals before competition. It could be argued that if a training programme is required to produce a valid assessment, then given the increased demands in time to conduct the research, that a qualitative approach should be used to assess anxiety.

Although the BRUMS was designed for ease of administration, a limitation with the BRUMS is the excessive negative orientation. Participants typically report zero for all 20 unpleasant mood items. There are only 24-items on the scale and therefore, the majority of items are scored as zero, a finding that could be interpreted as meaning 'not relevant'. It is questionable whether the questionnaire has assessed meaningful constructs for athletes. Quick completion time could be a function of athletes finding it easy to complete, but also athletes getting into a pattern of scoring zero for unpleasant mood states. It is conceivable that the measure could take longer to complete if items assessed mood states were more meaningful to athletes.

Directions: A number of statements that athletes have used to describe their feelings before competition are given below. The questionnaire is divided into two sections. In section 1 please read each statement and then circle the appropriate number to the right of the statement to indicate *how you would feel if you were highly anxious and about to take part in the most important competition of the season.* There are no right or wrong answers. Do not spend too much time on any one statement, but choose the answer which describes your feelings *if you were highly anxious and about to take part in the most important competition of the season.*

In addition in section 2 please indicate whether you regard this thought/feeling as negative (debilitative) or positive (facilitative) in relation to performance in your sport. N.B. if you have scored '1' (Not at all) on the fourth item then you respond on this scale as if you had *no* self-doubts. If you respond '4' (very much so) to item 4 then you respond on this scale as if you had *a great deal* of self-doubt.

Section 1: Please read each statement and then circle the appropriate number to the right of the statement to indicate *how you would feel if you were highly anxious and about to take part in the most important competition of the season.*				Section 2: Please indicate whether you regard this thought/feeling as negative (debilitative) or positive (facilitative) in relation to performance in your sport						
	Not at all	Somewhat	Moderately so	Very Much so	Very debilitative			Neutral			Very Facilitative
1) I am concerned about this competition	1	2	3	4	-3	-2	-1	0	+1	+2	+3
2) I feel nervous	1	2	3	4	-3	-2	-1	0	+1	+2	+3
3) I feel at ease	1	2	3	4	-3	-2	-1	0	+1	+2	+3
4) I have self-doubts	1	2	3	4	-3	-2	-1	0	+1	+2	+3
5) I feel jittery	1	2	3	4	-3	-2	-1	0	+1	+2	+3
6) I feel comfortable	1	2	3	4	-3	-2	-1	0	+1	+2	+3

Figure 2. Selected items from the Competitive State Anxiety Inventory-2 with directional scale.

A strategy for developing measures that participants will be able to understand and are meaningful is to use qualitative techniques in the initial stages of development. Although some measures use participants from the target group to develop items, it is not considered an obligatory stage in validation. The qualitative stages used to develop the Sport Emotion Questionnaire represent an example of good practice (SEQ: Jones, Lane, Bray, Uphill, and Catlin, 2005). The first stage developed a set of suitable items that reflected each of the five emotional constructs that participants could easily understand. Two-hundred and sixty-four athletes reported adjectives and phrases that best described the emotions that they had experienced when competing in sport. A key feature of this stage of the process was the large sample size used. Rarely do qualitative aspects of research use large sample sizes due to limitations regarding data analysis. Jones et al. (2005) found 548 separate adjectives and phrases. Frequency analysis indicated that 52 of the adjectives accounted for 73.3% of the total number of adjectives listed, therefore the 52 adjectives would appear to be emotions commonly experienced by athletes.

Please think of how you typically feel immediately before competition. Below is a list of words that describe feelings people have. Please read each one carefully. Then circle the answer which best describes *how you typically feel before playing an important game*.

	Not at all	A little	Moderately	Quite a bit	Extremely
Upset	0	1	2	3	4
Exhilarated	0	1	2	3	4
Uneasy	0	1	2	3	4
Tense	0	1	2	3	4
Sad	0	1	2	3	4

Figure 3. Items from The Sport Emotion Questionnaire and Instructional Set.

Recent research into self-efficacy theory has developed measures that assess confidence to perform behaviours or personal qualities needed to deliver success (Devonport and Lane, 2006; McConville and Lane, 2006; Lane, Devonport, and Horrell, 2004; Lane, Hall, and Lane, 2002, 2004; Lane, Lane, and Kyprianou, 2004; Lane, Lane, and Cockerton, 2003; Lane, Jones, and Stevens, 2002; Lane and Lane, 2001, 2002). Lane, Hall, and Lane (2002) used qualitative methods to develop a 39-item self-efficacy scale to assess student confidence to deliver success in a statistics course. The procedure used was to provide participants with an open-ended questionnaire on which they indicate factors that are relevant to performance. In a competitive setting, Lane, Jones and Stevens (2002) developed a 6-item self-efficacy questionnaire to assess self-efficacy in tennis. The process used in these studies should increase the likelihood of developing contextually valid measures principally as the target group who are to be used assist in the development of the scale to be used. A limitation of this approach is that it is incumbent on researchers to develop a scale for each study which could be unnecessarily time constraining. Secondly, each scale is different and therefore comparisons between studies are difficult. Even among samples from the same population, Lane and colleagues have found that each sample produced specific items and the extent to which these items generalise to the population of interest is questionable.

Devonport and Lane (2006) developed a scale to assess self-efficacy estimates toward passing Level 1 of an undergraduate degree course. In their study, Level 2 students were asked to describe the competencies required to complete level one of an undergraduate degree course using a similar procedure to that reported by Lane et al. (2002). Devonport and Lane (2006) argued that students who recently passed the course would have a better understanding of the requirements than students about to start the course. Importantly, it is argued that students who recently passed the course will be able to identify the difficulties involved having recently experienced them. Although lecturers set the assignments, they might underestimate difficulties of the tasks or fail to consider the competencies deemed important by students (e.g., availability of computers, book, library opening times, how to manage time). The key point is that it is important to use people with knowledge of the difficulties of the task to develop the competencies on which to assess self-efficacy estimates. It is argued that such people will be similar in skill and experience to the target population, but who have, and importantly, recently completed the task.

It is proposed that the first stage in questionnaire development should be to administer open-ended questionnaires and then use experts to modify the items. The modified items should be re-presented to a sample from the target population, a method used by Jones et al. (2005). This approach should lead to the development of questions that are both contextually and theoretically valid.

In summary, it is important to develop items that participants find interesting and meaningful. I argue researchers should conduct a qualitative study of the meaningfulness of items as the first stage of the research process. Mood researchers (Terry et al., 1999, 2003) used participants in the development stage to produce a measure that is easily understood by participants. However, the limitation of the BRUMS is the negative orientation of factors and therefore it is possible that the BRUMS does not assess meaningful mood states, a limitation that Jones et al. (2005) addressed so comprehensively in the SEQ. Anxiety researchers using the CSAI-2 with directional scale are encouraged to use a training period. However, it is argued that qualitative research to explore how athletes complete the scale might offer meaningful insight into how participants approach completing the directional scale. I argue that the approach to developing self-efficacy scales represents the best strategy for developing meaningful scales as it is participant-driven. Further, each of the self-efficacy studies cited included a validation stage of the research

LENGTH OF A CONSTRUCT

An important research decision in the development of a questionnaire is the number of items to include in each factor. Psychometric theory postulates that there is a universe of items and therefore researchers should seek to select a representative sample of items. Logically, each item represents a part of the construct and therefore the more items assessed, the greater the chance that the construct will be accurately assessed. Practically, using a large number of items is difficult and could be counter-productive in research domains where participants have limited time.

In terms of findings from the literature, Jackson and Marsh (1996) argued that the optimum number of items needed to describe a construct in a short questionnaire is four. Further, Bollen (1989) cautioned against reducing the number of items in a factor to less than three. From a statistical perspective, Watson and Clark (1997) reported that factors with less than four items typically fail to yield an internal consistency (alpha) coefficient (Cronbach, 1951) above the generally accepted criterion value of 0.70 (Tabachnick and Fidell, 1996). However, I argue that reliance on alpha coefficients for factors designed for brevity is problematic and could be counter-productive. It is commonly known that alpha coefficients are influenced by the size of correlations between items and the number of items being assessed. The size of correlations and the number of items being assessed are related. The more items assessed, the smaller the average inter-item correlation needs to be to achieve the .70 standard.

Researchers developing short questionnaires who seek to obtain an alpha over .70 will tend to select three items which are similar to each other. The BRUMS (Terry et al., 1999) offers an example where alpha coefficients are over .70 but where items are similar. For example, depressed, downhearted, unhappy and miserable assess the depression scale. It is argued that all four items represent terms to express intense depressed feelings with terms such as sad and gloomy being removed during the validation process as they showed weaker relationships. Indeed, Lane, Soos, Leibinger, Karsai, and Hamar (2007) further reduced the BRUMS to 3-items per factor and Lane (2006b) has used two-items from each subscale. As BRUMS items are closely associated together, it is possible that each item adds little additional information. It is possible that research that assesses psychological states such as emotion should use direct indicators of the construct rather than attempt to develop factors. Single-item assessments are clearly prone to possible distortion, but if researchers are to use as few as four indicators of a construct, and where those items are similar in nature, that equally valid results could be attained. Suggestion on how to resolve this issue are made in the next section that calls for future research.

FUTURE RESEARCH

Despite the volume of research that has looked at the validity of developing self-report measures for use in performance domains, I found no published studies that investigated the opinions and perceptions of participants who took part in such studies. The absence of any published evidence should not be surprising as such a line of investigation is unlikely to capture the interest of research students. However, I argue that future research is needed to explore what participants in research that asked for completion of measures before performance thought of the measures used. Two studies are suggested.

The first study I suggest is to evaluate commonly used methods. Participants complete a measure of the target construct as close to performance as possible (see Martens et al., 1990). It is argued that this type of research could be explored in one of two ways. After the performance has been completed, the researcher should contact participants to see if they would take part in either focus group or one to one interviews. The aim of the interviews is explore the extent to which taking part in the study affected their psychological preparation and to explore the validity of the measures used with a specific view to ascertain if participants reported honest responses at the time when they were tested. For example, if participants reported a score of 3 on the BRUMS for the items 'Nervous' which equates to feeling *moderately* nervous, did the act of acknowledging being nervous affect subsequent preparation. Equally, if participants reported to feeling 2 for the item Nervous, did this raise self-awareness. There is a need to identify the extent to which the completion of self-report scales raises self-awareness and further, to identify the levels at which people start becoming aware of their feelings.

One approach to conduct this study would be to assess a large sample of participants and select a subsection for interviews. The second approach would be for a relatively small sample of participants to complete multiple measures before a number of different competitions. The advantage of the first approach is that it is possible to obtain a large amount of data and the diversity of responses would be desirable. A limitation of the approach is that participants may not hold strong views on the process and thus provide less valuable data. An advantage of the second approach is that participants will develop insight into the strengths and weaknesses of the measure and over time, learn which items are personally problematic. The relatively small sample size used would be a limitation of this approach.

A second approach would be to administer the measure and ask participants to complete the measure retrospectively remembering an important performance. A benefit of such an approach is that it could identify possible issues before they arise in a prospective research. It is possible that this type of research would expose ethical issues such as being made aware of feeling depressed or low in confidence before the research is conducted prospectively. Arguably, researchers should explore ethical issues before the measure is used with participants. From an ethical perspective, I have found no studies that have sought to identify the potential harm of completing measures such as the BRUMS (Terry et al., 1999) or the CSAI-2 (Martens et al., 1990) and given the usage of these measures, such studies are needed.

CONCLUSIONS

Research to investigate factors that predict human performance under stressful conditions remains a key line of investigation. Despite the volume of research, difficulties remain regarding the validity of the measures used. It is suggested that researchers seek to develop measures that were validated for the situation that are to be used, and importantly, to ensure that the act of completing the inventory does not overly affect the very construct the researcher is seeking to assess. Research is needed to explore issues related to the act of completing measures in stressful conditions and such research should be exploratory, and therefore is likely to use a qualitative methodology. It is suggested that researchers develop contextually valid scales with the Sport Emotion Scale (Jones et al., 2005) and the self-efficacy scales reported (see Lane et al., 2002) representing good examples. The procedure used to develop the SES and the one followed in self-efficacy research, which uses the views of participants as central to the validation process is one that is worth considering. Future research is needed to tease out potential ethical issues surrounding such research, for despite the volume of research; few studies exist that have tackled this issue.

REFERENCES

Bandura, A. (1997). *Self-efficacy: The exercise of control*. New York: W.H. Freeman.

Bollen, K.A. (1989). *Structural Equations with Latent Variables*. New York: Wiley.

Cronbach, L. J. (1951). Coefficient alpha and internal structure of tests. *Psychometrika, 16*, 297-334.

Cushion, C., and Lane, A. M. (1997). Self-efficacy and penalty taking performance. *British Association of Sport and Exercise Sciences Student Conference*, Roehampton, London, March 13-15th 1997.

Devonport, T. J., and Lane, A. M. (2006). Relationships between self-efficacy, coping and student retention. *Journal of Social Behavior and Personality, 34*, 127-138.

Jackson, S.A., and Marsh, H.W. (1996). Development and validation of a scale to measure optimal experience: The flow state scale. *Journal of Sport and Exercise Psychology, 18*, 17-35.

Jones, J. G. (1995). More than just a game: research developments and issues in competitive anxiety in sport. *British Journal of Psychology, 85*, 449-478.

Jones, M. V., Lane, A. M., Bray, S. R., Uphill, M., and Catlin, J. (2005). Development of the Sport Emotions Questionnaire. *Journal of Sport and Exercise Psychology, 27*, 407-431.

Lane, A. M. (2001). Relationships between perceptions of performance expectations and mood among distance runners; the moderating effect of depressed mood. *Journal of Science and Medicine in Sport, 4*, 235-249.

Lane, A. M. (2004). Measures of emotions and coping in sport. *In Coping and Emotion in Sport*. Pp255-271. Editors Lavallee, D., Thatcher, J., and Jones, M. Nova Science, NY.

Lane, A. M. (2006a). Mood-Performance Relationships with a Focus on Depression: A review of Lane and Terry's model. Mood and human performance: Conceptual, measurement, and applied issues. In Lane, A. M. *Mood and human performance: Conceptual, measurement, and applied issues.* Nova Science Publishers.

Lane, A. M. (2006b). Psychological preparation for the Marathon Des Sable. From Education to Application. British Association of Sport and Exercise Sciences Conference, University of Wolverhampton. September 11-13th 2006

Lane, A. M., and Terry, P. C. (2000). The nature of mood: Development of a conceptual model with a focus on depression. *Journal of Applied Sport Psychology, 12*, 16-33.

Lane, A. M., Devonport, T. J., and Horrell, A. (2004). Self-efficacy and research methods. *Journal of Hospitality, Leisure, Sport and Tourism Education, 3*, 25-37.

Lane, A. M., Hall, R., and Lane, J. (2002). Development of a measure of self-efficacy specific to statistic courses in sport. *Journal of Hospitality, Leisure, Sport and Tourism Education, 1*, 47-56.

Lane, A. M., Hall, R., and Lane, J. (2004). Self-efficacy and statistics performance among Sport Studies Students. *Teaching in Higher Education, 9*, 435-448.

Lane, A. M., Jones, L., and Stevens, M. (2002). Coping with failure: The effects of self-esteem and coping on changes in self-efficacy. *Journal of Sport Behavior, 25*, 331-345.

Lane, A. M., Soos, I., Leibinger, E., Karsai, I., and Hamar, P. (2007). Validity of the Brunel Mood Scale for use with UK, Italian and Hungarian athletes. In A.M. Lane (ed.), *Mood and human performance: Conceptual, measurement, and applied issues* (pp 119-130). Hauppauge, NY: Nova Science.

Lane, A. M., Whyte, G. P., Terry, P. C., and Nevill, A. M (2005). Mood and examination performance. *Personality and Individual Differences, 39*, 143-153.

Lane, J., and Lane, A. M. (2001). Self-efficacy and academic performance. *Social Behavior and Personality, 29*, 687-694.

Lane, J., and Lane, A. M. (2002). Predictive validity of variables used to select students onto post-graduate courses. *Psychological Reports, 90*, 1239-1247.

Lane, J., Lane, A. M., and Cockerton, T. (2003). Prediction of academic performance from self-efficacy and performance accomplishments among master's degree students. *Journal of Hospitality, Leisure, Sport and Tourism Education, 2*, 113-118.

Lane, J., Lane, A. M., and Kyprianou, A. (2004). Self-efficacy, self-esteem and their impact on academic performance. *Social Behavior and Personality, 32*, 247-256.

Lazarus, R. S. (2000). How emotions influence performance in competitive sports. *The Sport Psychologist, 14*, 229-252.

Martens, R., Vealey, R. S., Burton, D., Bump, L., and Smith, D. E. (1990). Development and validation of the Competitive Sports Anxiety Inventory-2. In R. Martens, R. S. Vealey, and D. Burton (Eds.), *Competitive anxiety in sport.* (pp. 117-178). Champaign, IL: Human Kinetics.

McConville, S. A., and Lane, A. M. (2006). Using on-line video clips to enhance self-efficacy toward dealing with difficult situations among nursing students. *Nurse Education Today, 26*, 200-208.

Tabachnick, B. G., and Fidell, L. S. (1996). *Using multivariate statistics.* New York, NY: Harper and Row.

Terry, P. C. (1995). The efficacy of mood state profiling among elite competitors: a review and synthesis. *The Sport Psychologist, 9*, 309-324.

Terry, P. C., Lane, A. M., and Fogarty, G. (2003). Construct validity of the Profile of Mood States-A for use with adults. *Psychology of Sport and Exercise, 4*, 125-139.

Terry, P. C., Lane, A. M., Lane, H. J., and Keohane, L. (1999). Development and validation of a mood measure for adolescents: POMS-A. *Journal of Sports Sciences, 17*, 861-872.

Thomas, O., Hanton, S.M., and Jones, G. (2002). An Alternative Approach to Short-Form Self-Report Assessment of Competitive Anxiety. *International Journal of Sport Psychology, 33*, 325-336.

Watson, D., and Clark, L. A. (1997). Measurement and mismeasurement of Mood: Recurrent and emergent issues. *Journal of Personality Assessment, 68*, 267-296.

In: New Psychological Tests and Testing Research
Editor: Lydia S. Boyar, pp. 215-229

ISBN: 978-1-60021-570-4
© 2007 Nova Science Publishers, Inc.

Chapter 12

THE RELATIONSHIP BETWEEN ACCURACY, CONSISTENCY, AND CONFIDENCE IN VISUAL RECOGNITION MEMORY OVER WEEKS IN AGING

Anders M. Fjell*, Kristine B. Walhovd
and Ivar Reinvang
Institute of Psychology, University of Oslo

ABSTRACT

The effects of age on accuracy, consistency, and confidence of visual recognition memory were tested with the Continuous Visual Memory Test (CVMT) in an adult life-span sample (20-88 yrs, n = 83). CVMT delayed recognition was without warning again administered by mail after a mean retention interval of 10 weeks. The participants were also asked to rate how confident they were in each of their judgments at the 10 weeks test. Statistical analyses were done for each of the seven sets of CVMT target items separately and for the total scores. It was demonstrated that older participants are less confident in their memory judgments than younger, independently of memory performance. Further, the analyses revealed that the different target items of CVMT had non-identical psychometric characteristics. In predicting memory performance, an interaction between retention interval and target items from CVMT was found, and memory consistency turned out as a trait associated with type of item, not age group or retention interval.

Keywords: visual memory, CVMT, age, recognition, consistency, confidence.

* Address correspondence to: Anders M. Fjell, University of Oslo, Department of Psychology, POB 1094 Blindern, 0317 Oslo, Norway; phone: +47 22 84 51 29; fax: +47 22 84 50 01; e-mail: andersmf@psykologi.uio.no

INTRODUCTION

Higher age usually brings with it a subjective experience of reduced memory capabilities. This experience may be caused by actual decrease in memory-related intellectual abilities, less stable memory skills, and, in addition, a lesser degree of confidence in ones memory judgments. The present paper is targeted at disentangling the effect of accuracy, consistency, and confidence in a visual recognition memory test, the Continuous Visual memory Test (CVMT; Trahan and Larrabee, 1988) in an adult life-span sample.

Consistency of Memory

Consistency of memory, defined as the ability to form representations of learned material which can be *reliably* retrieved, is a little applied concept in clinical neuropsychological practice. However, the stability of memory is crucial in everyday life, and recall consistency has also been investigated in patient groups with different types of memory disorders (e.g. Delis et al., 1991). The concept of consistency should preferably be defined in a way that makes it potentially partly independent of accuracy in memory. In a study of age effects on the California Verbal learning Test (CVLT; Delis et al., 1987) over an extended time period, Walhovd, Fjell, and Reinvang (manuscript submitted for publication) employed a measure of consistency or intra-subject variability assessed retrospectively: To what extent was an item recalled at a later point also recalled at the previous occasion? Thus, if a person tends to remember information at an extended memory test that was not remembered at a previous test, then this person has low consistency of memory. This way, low consistency means that the probability that a recognized target item was also recognized at the previous test is low, while high consistency means that the probability is high. For tests with multiple memory trials, this definition makes it possible to have a reasonable accuracy score, that is, to ultimately recall or recognize a large proportion of the material to be remembered, while at the same time have a lower score on consistency. Of course, memory consistency will ultimately be related to learning skills. Still, by the operationalization described above, the concepts should be partly non-overlapping, and memory consistency may contribute to the often-observed decline in memory function with higher age. Walhovd et al. (2004) found evidence for increased intra-subject variability in recall with age, but were not able to identify a significant interaction between variability and retention interval. The authors suggested that both increased rate of forgetting and increased intra-subject-variability in elderly are due to retrieval deficits. Walhovd et al.'s results fit with other reports indicating that increased intra-subject variability may be a feature of normal aging (e.g. Anstey, 1999; Shammi et al., 1998) as well as clinical conditions (e.g. Hetherington et al., 1996).

The question of memory consistency in aging has implications for the discussion of encoding, consolidation, and storage vs. retrieval in aging. If elderly people show less consistency, that is, more frequently fail to identify an item on one occasion, but still successfully identify the same item after a prolonged interval, retrieval deficits seems to be a more appropriate candidate explanation for declining memory in aging than encoding deficits or loss from long term store. Some studies have concluded that elderly have a steeper rate of forgetting of acquired material over time than younger (Harwood and Naylor, 1969; Huppert and Kopelman, 1989; Ivnik et al., 1990; Rybarczyk et al., 1987; Spikman et al., 1995; Tsang et al, 1991; Tombaugh and Scmidt, 1992; Woodruff-Pak and Finkbiner, 1995; Tombaugh and Hubley, 2001; Wheeler, 2000), while others have found no such effect when acquisition differences are controlled for (Fjell et al., 2005; Geffen et al., 1990; Haaland et al., 1983; Measso et al., 1990; Mitrushina and Satz, 1989; Mitrushina et al., 1991; Paolo et al., 1997; Slamecka and McElree, 1983; Trahan and Larrabee, 1992; Youngjohn and Crook, 1993). The concept of consistency or intra-individual variability may contribute to shed light on the importance of consolidation and storage vs. retrieval in successful memory performance in such comparative studies. Further, the question of intra-subject variability in older compared to younger persons also has implications for the reliability and clinical validity of memory assessment for different age groups. Since everyday memory function requires storage and retrieval of information over much longer time intervals than those normally used in neuropsychological assessment, it may be appropriate to extend retention intervals beyond 30 minutes. In the present study, an additional retention interval of several weeks was employed. This gave us the opportunity to study consistency over longer time periods, which may be necessary to disentangle age effects. We employed the Continuous Visual Memory test (CVMT; Trahan and Larrabee, 1988), which has a visual recognition format with no semantic load on memory. It is known that performance on recognition tests shows less difference between age groups than recall formats, which place more demands on retrieval processes susceptible to age effects. Thus, it is not evident that results from recall tests, as used in the Walhovd et al. (2004) study reviewed above, are applicable to recognition memory tests. In addition, the CVLT has a high verbal semantic load, contrary to the pure non-semantic visual stimuli in the CVMT.

Confidence in Memory

To be able to benefit from successful memory in daily life, it is vital that one is able to trust ones true memories. Touron and Herztog (2004) found that older adults were more reluctant than younger to rely on memory retrieval in a skill acquisition task, related to metacognitive reports of memory confidence. The authors concluded that low confidence in ones memory abilities may hinder or slow acquisition of new skills. Touron and Herztog (2004) further found that older adults' retrieval reluctance is not exclusively determined by low memory ability. Marquité and Huet (2000), however, found that elderly did not differ from younger in confidence level. Thus, consensus is still not reached about the relationship between age and confidence level in memory performance. This question is important, however. If older adults are less confident in the accuracy of their memories than younger, it is possible that this tendency will be elevated when the retention interval is greatly increased, demanding higher load on metacognitive abilities, and generally increasing task difficulty.

Rationale for the Present Study

The aim of the present study was to do detailed analyses of three variables of visual recognition memory; accuracy, consistency, and confidence in memory at different retention intervals and to explore how these different parameters relate to age. CVMT was divided into to its composite variables, the seven different sets of target items, which for many analyses will be used instead of the total test scores. The reason for this is that we wanted to explore effects of the target items in isolation. Since the nature of the items vary, it is important to know how these may differ in terms of accuracy over an extended time period, load on general visuocognitive abilities, consistency, and subjective experience of confidence, and whether an interaction with age exists.

Three general research questions were investigated:

1. Is the different target items of the CVMT differentially related to age at different test times? The analyses of the relationships between the CVMT sub-variables will also include tests of their relationships with two measures of general visuocognitive ability. Since the seven sets of CVMT items are quite different, it is probable that the accuracy of recognition will vary across item sets. Further, it is possible that general visual abilities will affect the accuracy of recognition differently for different variables. Finally, the items that are hardest to encode at shorter time intervals (30 minutes) will probably be even harder to identify correctly after an extended retention interval (10 weeks).
2. Is memory consistency related to age? This will be explored both across different CVMT items and at different test times. In accordance with some previous reports reviewed above, it is reason to expect less consistency with higher age. However, as mentioned, the present study uses a non-semantic visual recognition test, which may serve to diminish age-differences in memory-related variables.
3. Is confidence rating related to age? This will be explored in relation to recognition performance level. We expect older participants to be less confident in their memory judgments, and that this effect will be larger at extended retention intervals than at shorter.

The sample in the present study is almost identical to the sample described in Fjell et al. (2005). That paper investigated, among other things, the effect of age on CVMT total scores at learning, 30 minutes, and 10 weeks recall. The main conclusion was that even though there were age differences in memory, no significant effect of age group X retention interval was identified. In contrast to Fjell et al. (2005), the present paper includes the variables confidence ratings and consistency, in addition to accuracy at the level of individual classes of CVMT stimuli, none of which was the topic of the former paper. In addition, a large overlap with the sample used in Walhovd et al.'s (2004) study of CVLT exists.

METHODS

Sample

Participants were recruited by newspaper adverts or based on participation in a longitudinal research project in Oslo on cognitive aging (see Walhovd and Fjell, 2003, and Fjell et al. (2005) for more details). The original sample consisted of 94 participants, aged 21-88 years, screened for general health problems that could interact with central nervous system function (e.g. hypothyroidism, stroke, diabetes, alcohol problems, medications, etc.), psychiatric disorders (e.g. depression), or cognitive dysfunction (e.g. dementia). For these purposes we used a self-report inventory about physical and mental health, Beck Depression Inventory (Beck, 1987), Wechsler Abbreviated Scale of Intelligence (WASI, Wechsler, 1999), and the Mini Mental Status Exam (Folstein et al., 1975). Participants were required to have a MMS score of at least 26, a Beck score of maximum 15 and an IQ score of at least 85. All participants underwent a broad neuropsychological examination, a two-hour neurophysiological examination (EEG and ERP, which will not be reported here), and an MRI scan. 11 persons were excluded before, during, or after the examination, due to failure to satisfy the inclusion criteria. Of these, 70 completed the extended memory tests. Thus, for analyses involving CVMT learning scores and scores at the 30 minutes recognition test, the sample counts 83, while for analyses involving the 10 week recognition test, the sample counts 70. For some analyses, the sample was divided into three different age groups; 20-41 years, 42-66 years, and 67-88 years. Further sample characteristics are reported in table 1.

Table 1. Sample characteristics

	Young group (n = 27)	Middle-aged group (n = 28)	Old group (n = 28)
Age	27.3 (20-41)	56.3 (43-66)	74.6 (67-88)
Gender	19 f/ 8 m	14 f/ 14 m	14 f/ 14 m
Education (yrs)	15.8 (12.5-18.0)	15.8 (9-20)	14.1 (7-19)
IQ	113.6 (102-128)	115.1 (93-129)	112.5 (85-134)
Beck DI	2.9 (0-10)	3.2 (0-11)	6.5 (1-14)
MMS	29.2 (28-30)	29.1 (28-30)	28.4 (26-30)
CVMT learning	82.6 (64-93)	78.9 (61-90)	74.1 (58-82)
CVMT 30 min	5.3 (3-7)	4.9 (2-7)	3.6 (0-7)
CVMT 10 wks	5.0 (3-7)	3.4 (0-7)	2.4 (0-4)

Memory Test: Continuous Visual Memory Test (CVMT)

The CVMT (Trahan and Larrabee, 1988) is comprised of 112 items, which are complex, ambiguous drawings (e.g., 12-point polygons, etc.) and irregular nonsense figures. The drawings are printed on 5 x 8 inch white cards and organized in 7 blocks of 16 stimuli. The items are presented successively to the subject and exposed for 2-4 s each. Stimuli in the first block by definition are new and different and represent the input stimuli. Seven of these items appear once in each of the remaining six blocks and are "old" items whenever they reappear (see figure 1). The other nine items in each block are entirely new stimuli that never reappear in the task. However, seven of the "new" items in each of the last six blocks have stimulus characteristics designed to be similar (e.g., 12-point polygons, 7-point polygons, etc.) to the "old" items, one from each category. These drawings are perceptually quite similar to the corresponding "old" drawings. The other two "new" stimuli in each block belong to other stimulus classes. Because no "old" stimuli are presented in the first block, analysis of performance is based on responses given in the last six blocks, which together contain 42 "old" and 54 "new" items. Scores employed in the current study included a learning score (number of hits + 54 – number of false alarms), and a delayed multiple choice recognition memory score administered at 30 minutes and after a delayed mean interval of 10 weeks (this came as a surprise for the participants, and were administered by mail). At the 10 weeks retention interval, participants were also asked to judge how certain they were of each of their judgments on a 3-points scale (with 3 representing "almost certain" of the memory judgment, 2 representing "I have a feeling that this is the right one", and 1 representing "just guessing"). In addition to the total scores, scores were calculated for each of the 7 target item separately. That is, for the learning session, the number of hits on a certain target item (maximum 6) is calculated. For the recognition tests, each of the target variables were scores as either 0 (miss) or 1 (hit). For some analyses, each of these 7 target items is treated separately.

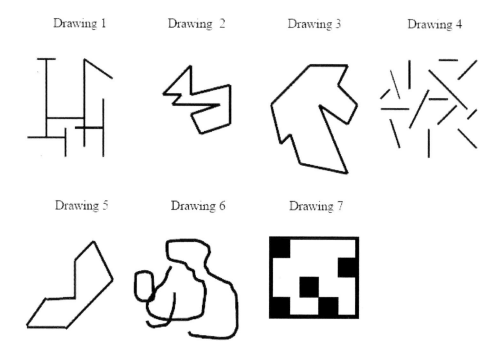

Figure 1. A reproduction of the seven target drawings from CVMT. Due to copyright issues, we have constructed versions of each of the 7 target drawings from CVMT. These are not identical to the originals, but they have some resemblance, and would probably be recognized by those familiar with the test.

Statistics

ANOVA with 2 test times (30 minutes, 10 weeks) X 7 target items X 3 age groups was performed for number of hits (accuracy) to determine if the different target items of the CVMT are differentially related to age at different test times. Further Cronbach's alpha was calculated to get a measure of scale reliability of the CVMT at 30 minutes and 10 weeks, and to explore whether any individual drawing deviates from the rest. The corrected item to total correlations were then compared to the correlations with performance abilities, to assess whether the most deviant of the stimuli were more or less related to general visuocognitive abilities. Further, correlations were computed to assess whether it is the same individuals that obtain high and low scores at different test intervals.

For consistency in memory scores, ANOVA with 7 target items at each of the two delayed test times X 3 age groups were computed. As mentioned, consistency is defined as the ability to retrieve an item at a later occasion than one failed to retrieve at the previous occasion. Thus, if a participant remember 7 CVMT items at one test, and remembered none at the previous occasion, this represents the lowest possible memory consistency (consistency = 0). An optimal consistency score (consistency = 7) can be obtained by perfect memory (full score on both tests), or by the worst possible score at the second test (then the score at the previous test will not affect the consistency score). Thus, it is obvious that learning and memory consistency are different concepts. Next, an ANOVA with 7 target items X 3 age groups for 30 minutes and 10 weeks recognition separately were performed. These analyses would give us a hint about whether consistency is a matter of age, a matter of time, or a matter of target item type.

Finally, we investigated the effects of confidence ratings by correlating degree of confidence in memory judgments at the 10 weeks recognition test with memory performance, both for the total score and for the individual drawings. To assess the influence of age, an ANOVA with confidence ratings for 7 drawings X 3 age groups were computed, in turn controlling for the CVMT learning performance level and the 10 weeks recognition performance level.

RESULTS

Accuracy

Mean and range for CVMT learning score, 30 minutes recognition and 10 weeks recognition for each age group are presented in table 1. ANOVA with 2 test times (30 minutes, 10 weeks) X 7 target items X 3 age groups yielded significant main effects of time $(F [1, 65] = 18.000, p < .001)$, target item $(F [5.284, 343.477] = 23.159, p < .001)$, and age group $(F [2, 65] = 16.348, p < .001)$, in addition to an interaction effect of time X target item $(F [5.530, 359.453] = 9.275, p < .001)$. Thus, in addition to age, time and target item type exerted an influence on the probability of a correct recognition response, and the effect of item interacted by time. If, however, CVMT learning score was used as a covariate, all effects but that of age $(F [2, 64] = 6.725, p < .01)$ group ceased to be significant.

Since item type had both a main effect and an interaction effect with time, we wanted to check in greater detail the characteristics of the different sets of items. Thus, we conducted an inter-item reliability analysis for the 7 target items at the 30 minutes recognition condition and the 10 week recognition condition separately. For the 30 minutes recognition items, Cronbach's alpha was .66, and the corrected item-total correlations ranged from .25 to .58, with a median r of .36. No variables stood out as deviant from the rest, and the alphas if the item had been deleted ranged between .56 and .66. For the 10 weeks recognition items, the results were quite similar, with a Cronbach's alpha of .63, with corrected item-total correlations between .23 and .42, with a median r of .35. The alpha if item deleted values ranged from .57 to .63. Thus, the scale reliabilities were very similar at the two test times.

Also, no single item lowered the Cronbach's alpha substantially. However, the alpha was not especially high, and several of the corrected item-total correlations were around .30. Thus, the variance in performance to the different drawings overlapped only to a modest extent.

Because of this, we wanted to check whether any of the target items were more related to a measure of more general visuospatial ability. Thus, we correlated the 7 items and the total recognition scores at the two test times with a composite score of the two performance subtests from WASI (matrixes and block design). This composite performance score was estimated by transforming the scores of each person on each of the two tests to a t-score relative to the sample. Thus, the composite score has a sample mean of 50 and a standard deviation of 10, and is not corrected for age. First, we correlated the we correlated the total score for 30 minutes and 10 weeks recognition with performance abilities, and found almost identical coefficients of moderate strength (r = .59 and .54, p < .0001, respectively). We repeated these analyses with the sample split in two equal halves based on the median age (56 years), and found that the relationship between the total score and performance abilities seem invariant across age, r = .52 and .35 for the youngest half, and r = .51 and .20 for the oldest, respectively. As expected, when t-tests on the Fisher z-transformed coefficients were performed, no statistically significant differences were found.

The next step was to repeat the analyses with the separate drawings instead of the total scores. The two sets of correlations are presented in figure 2, along with their corrected item-total correlation. As can be seen, the different target items exhibit different relationships with performance abilities, especially for the 30 minutes relationships. As a formal statistical test of the difference between the correlation coefficients, William's (1959) test for a significant difference between dependent correlations was performed (using Crawford et al.s [1996] computer implementation). Even though this test may be somewhat strict, five of the 30 minutes coefficients were significantly different when tested pairwise (6 with 1, 3, 4, and 5, and 5 with 7). Even more important, however, is that for the 30 minutes relationships, the items with the highest corrected item-total correlations are also those correlating highest with performance abilities. However, this pattern was not so clear at 10 weeks. Thus, it may be that performance after 10 weeks is a measure of visual memory with less influence from more general visuocognitive abilities. Contrary to this hypothesis are the almost identical correlations with performance abilities found for the total score for 30 minutes and 10 weeks recognition.

To test whether the individual scores are stable across test times, correlations between learning score, 30 minutes recognition score, and 10 weeks recognition score were calculated. CVMT learning score correlated r = .58 (p < .001) and .54 (p < .001) with 30 minutes and 10 weeks recall, respectively, while the latter two correlated .53 (p < .001). If these coefficients were corrected for the influence of age, the resulting coefficients dropped somewhat, r = .48, .38, and .40, respectively, but all were still significant (p < .001).

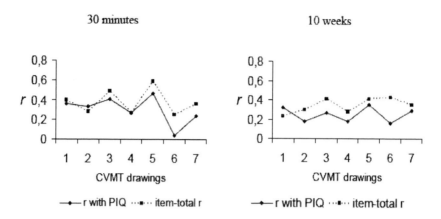

Figure 2. Correlations between probability of hit for each of the seven CVMT target items at 30 minutes (left) and 10 weeks (right) and performance abilities (PIQ) and the total scale (corrected for the influence of the item itself).

Consistency

ANOVA with 3 age groups X consistency at two time points (learning and 10 weeks) yielded no significant effects (main effect of time: $F [1, 66] = 2.927$, n.s., main effect of age group: $F [1, 66] = 1.779$, n.s., age group X time: $F [2,000] = 0.353$, n.s.). This is illustrated in figure 3. Next, ANOVAs with 7 target items X 3 age groups for learning consistency and 10 weeks consistency were calculated separately. For learning, the only significant result was the main effect of item ($F [5.177] = 7.114$, $p < .001$), and the results for the extended consistency mimicked this ($F [4.446] = 5.484$, $p < .001$). This is illustrated in figure 4. Thus, consistency does not seem to be a trait of individuals at different ages, but rather a characteristic of the different target items themselves.

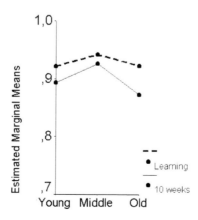

Figure 3. Consistency (defined as the probability that a recognized target item was also recognized at the previous test) over time as a function of age group.

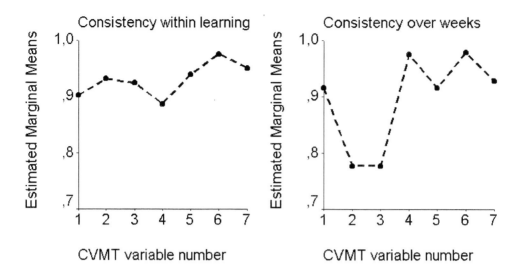

Figure 4. Consistency (defined as the probability than a recognized item was also recognized at the previous test) for each of the seven target items (within learning and across weeks – not separated by age since no significant age effects were found). ANOVA confirmed that the effect of drawing was significant (p < .05) for both retention intervals.

Confidence

A correlation between mean confidence rating and number of recognized items in the 10 weeks recognition test of r = .36 (p < .01) was found. When age was controlled for, the correlation dropped to .18, and was no longer significant. The effect of confidence on individual target items was checked by further correlation analyses. Three of the seven correlations were significant, ranging from .29 to .46 (p < .05). Controlling for age rendered all the correlations insignificant except for one (r = .40, p < .05). Thus, the relationship between confidence and accuracy is weak at best.

To investigate age effects on confidence ratings, an ANOVA with 3 age groups X 7 confidence rated variables yielded a main effect of item (F [5.136] = 17.088, p < .001) and age group (F [2, 65] = 6.770, p < .01), and an interaction effect of age X item (F [10.272] = 2.610, p < .01). The effect of age is illustrated in figure 5, and the effect of item in figure 6. When learning score was used as a covariate, the effect of item became insignificant, while both the main effect of age (F [2, 64] = 3.467, p < .05) and the age group X item interaction remained significant (F [10.298] = 2.050, p < .05). When the 10 weeks recognition memory score was used as covariate, the effect of age group was marginally insignificant (F [2, 63] = 2.977, p = .058), while the interaction still remained (F [10.209] = 1.924, p < .05). Thus, participants at different ages differ in their confidence ratings, also when level of performance is corrected for. Older participants are less confident about their judgments, and this holds even when level of performance is corrected for.

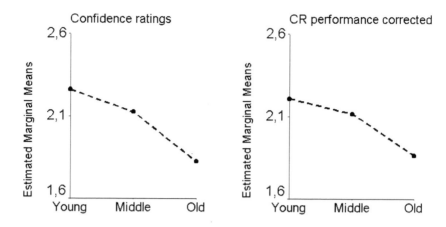

Figure 5. Confidence ratings (CR) across 7 target items, not corrected for CVMT total learning score. The effect of variable is significant only as long as level of learning performance is not corrected for.

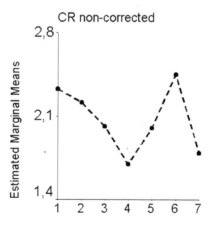

Figure 6. Confidence ratings (CR) across 3 age groups, raw scores (left) and corrected for CVMT total learning score (right). 3 represent "almost certain" of the memory judgments, 2 represents "I have a feeling that this is the right one", and 1 represents "just guessing". The effect of age group is significant both when level of confidence is corrected and non-corrected for learning score.

DISCUSSION

Accuracy

The present study demonstrates age effects on several variables related to different aspects of visual recognition memory performance. Further, differential effects of the CVMT target items clearly manifest themselves. A main effect of item on accuracy was found, indicating that some of the drawings are clearly harder to encode and recognize than others. Further, items interacted with time and age. For some items, the accuracy increased at 10 weeks in comparison to 30 minutes, while most of the items showed the opposite pattern. Also, some items were relatively easier to remember for participants in one age group than in others. E.g. item number 2 was the one with the next highest accuracy in the young group, but only the 6th best in the two older groups. Thus, as indicated by the identified interactions, the different sets of items are not uniform with respect to psychometric characteristics, at least not in a life-span sample. As shown by the inter-item reliability analysis, Cronbach's alpha was not very high, thus indicating that the different items only to a moderate extent are related to the same construct. Still, none of the variables stood out as having a large detrimental effect on Cronbach's alpha. Interestingly, for the 30 minutes interval, the items correlating the most with the total scale (corrected for the influence of the item itself) were the drawings that also correlated highest with general visuocognitive abilities. Thus, it may be that the recognition performance at 30 minutes is still related to non-memory abilities. Larrabee, Trahan, and Curtiss (1992) found that the CVMT recognition score at 30 minutes was relatively uncontaminated by influence from general visuocognitive abilitites. The present results indicate that the items may be related to general visuocognitive abilitites to different degrees and that the more they tap visuocognitive abilities, the closer they are related to the rest of the items in the scale. However, after 10 weeks, this pattern was substantially weaker. Thus, it is possible that the influence from performance abilities on the CVMT scores diminish gradually from the learning session to the 30 minutes recognition test, and further to the 10 week recognition task. However, as noted above, the correlations between performance ability and the total recognition memory scores did not differ between 30 minutes and 10 weeks, thus weakening the hypothesis that the contribution from memory abilities increases and the contribution from more general performance ability decreases over time.

It is remarkable that the correlation between learning and recognition at 30 minutes is almost identical to the correlation between learning and recognition at 10 weeks. The learning test and the recognition tests are assumed to tap partially different concepts, and correlations exceeding .50 must be regarded as quite robust. Further, a correlation exceeding .50 between recognition at 30 minutes and at 10 weeks is also quite high, indicating both between-subjects stability of visual non-semantic memory and a certain reliability of test scores. However, the finding that the correlation between learning and recognition is as high after 10 weeks as after 30 minutes is more surprising. Thus, it seems from our data that visual recognition memory is as stable in terms of inter-individual variation between 30 minutes and 10 weeks as between learning and 30 minutes.

Consistency

Analyzes of consistency of responses within the learning session and between 30 minutes and 10 weeks showed that type of item was the single significant predictor. Consistency was neither related to age nor time. This indicates that consistency of responses, at least in the CVMT, is a trait more descriptive of specific items than of individuals. In light of previous reports of less consistent memory in aging, the present results may be taken to mean that the non-semantic visual recognition format may suppress individual variation in inconsistent responding.

Confidence

A moderate relationship between confidence ratings and number of recognized items at the 10 week recognition test was identified. This relationship was weakened to the degree of insignificance when age was controlled for. However, as shown by the later ANOVA, an interaction between age and target item confidence ratings exists. Thus, controlling for age in a partial correlation analysis may be inappropriate. The present data indicate that a relationship between participants' confidence in their memory judgments and their actual performance exists, but this relationship is not strong. Thus, a person's belief in his or her accuracy in identifying a specific item is not a good predictor for actual accuracy.

Of most interest, however, were the significant effects of age. Age influenced level of confidence even when learning performance was controlled for. Older participants are less confident in their own memory judgments, and differences in performance level are not sufficient to explain this. Thus, an aspect of older peoples' experience of memory difficulties seems to be lack of confidence. In addition to the effect of age, level of confidence was influenced by the actual stimuli in question. Which stimuli gave rise to the highest and lowest memory ratings were dependent upon age group.

CONCLUSION

Most neuropsychologists are sensitive to the possibility of non-identical psychometric characteristics of different memory tests. The present data point to differential psychometric characteristics of same-level items also within a widely used memory test, the CVMT, and indicate that item-specific effects exist for this test. Interaction effects with retention time and age were found for accuracy, consistency, and confidence ratings. Memory consistency, at least in CVMT performance, seems associated with type of item, not age group or retention interval. The present data also show that older participants are less confident in their memory judgments than younger, independently of memory performance, and this may be part of the often-reported subjective age decrease in memory ability.

REFERENCES

Anstey, K. (1999). Sensorimotor variables and forced expiratory volume as correlates of speed, accuracy and variability in reaction time performance in late adulthood. *Aging, Neuropsychology, and Cognition, 6*, 84–95.

Beck, A. T. (1987). *Beck Depression Inventory*. San Antonio, TX: The Psychological Corporation.

Crawford, J. R., Mychalkiw, B., Johnson, D. A. and Moore, J.W. (1996). WAIS-R short-forms: Criterion validity in healthy and clinical samples. *British Journal of Clinical Psychology, 35*, 638-640.

Delis, D. C., Kramer, J.H., Kaplan, E., Ober, B.A.(1987). *California Verbal Learning Test*. San Antonio, TX: The Psychological Corporation.

Delis, D. C., Massman, P. J., Butters, N., Salmon, D. P., Cermak, L. S., and Kramer, J. H. (1991). Profiles of Demented and Amnesic Patients on the California Verbal Learning Test: Implications for the Assessment of Memory Disorders. *Psychological Assessment, 3*, 19-26.

Fjell, A.M., Walhovd, K. B., Reinvang, I., Lundervold, A., Dale, A. M., Quinn, B. T., Makris, N., Fischl, B. (2005). Age does not increase rate of forgetting over weeks – neuroanatomical volumes and visual memory across the adult life-span. *Journal of the International Neuropsychological Society, 63*, 1193-1197.

Folstein, M. F., Folstein, S. E., and McHugh, P. R. (1975). "Mini-mental state". *Journal of Psychiatric Research, 12*, 189-198.

Geffen, G. Moar, K. J., O'Hanlon, A. P., Clark C. R., and Geffen, L.B. (1990). Performance measures of 16 to 86-year-old males and females on the Auditory Verbal Learning Test. *The Clinical Neuropsychologist, 4*, 45-63.

Haaland, K.Y., Linn, R. T., Hunt, W. C., and Goodwin, J. S. (1983). A normative study of Russell's variant of the Wechsler Memory Scale in a healthy elderly population. *Journal of Consulting and Clinical Psychology, 51*, 878-881.

Harwood, E. and Naylor, G. F. K. (1969). Recall and recognition in elderly and young subjects. *Australian Journal of Psychology, 21*, 251-257.

Hetherington, C.R., Stuss, D.T., Finlayson, M.A.J. (1996). Reaction time and variability 5 and 10 years after traumatic brain injury. *Brain Injury 10*, 473–486.

Huppert, F. A. and Kopelman, M. D. (1989). Rates of forgetting in normal ageing: A comparison with dementia. *Neuropsychologia, 27*, 385-390.

Ivnik, R. J., Tangalos E. G., Petersen, R. C., Kokmen, E., and Kurland, L. T. (1990). The Auditory-Verbal Learning Test (AVLT): Norms for ages 55 years and older. *Psychological Assessment: A Journal of Consulting and Clinical Psychology, 2*, 304-312.

Larrabee, G. J., Trahan, D. E., and Curtiss, G. (1992). Construct validi6ty of the Continuous Visual Memory Test. *Archives of Clinical Neuropsychology, 7*, 395-405.

Marquié, J., C., and Huet, N. (2000). Age differences in feeling-of-knowing and confidence judgments as a function of knowledge domain. *Psychology and Aging, 15*, 451-461.

Measso, G. Romani, L., Martini, S, and Zappala, G. (1990). Preliminary analysis of effects of "normal" aging on different memory processes and abilities. *Perceptual and Motor Skills, 71*, 395-401.

Mitrushina, M., and Satz, P. (1989). Differential decline of specific memory components in normal aging. *Brain Dysfunction, 2*, 330-335.

Mitrushina, M., Satz, P., Chervinsky, A., and D'Elia, L. (1991). Performance of four age groups of normal elderly on the Rey Auditory-Verbal Learning Test. *Journal of Clinical Psychology, 47*, 351-357.

Paolo, A. M., Tröster, A.I., and Ryan, J. J. (1997). California Verbal Learning Test: Normative data for the elderly. *Journal of Clinical and Experimental Neuropsychology, 19*, 220-234.

Rybarczyk, B. D., Hart, R. P., and Harkins, S. W. (1987). Age and forgetting rate with pictorial stimuli. *Psychology and Aging, 2*, 404-406.

Shammi, P., Bosman, E., and Stuss, D.T., 1998. Aging and variability of performance. *Aging, Neuropsychology and Cognition 5*, 1–13.

Slamecka, N. J., and McElree, B. (1983). Normal forgetting of verbal lists as a function of the degree of learning. *Journal of Experimental Psychology: Learning, Memory and Cognition, 9*, 384-397.

Spikman, J. M., Berg, I. J., and Deelman, B. G. (1995). Spared recognition capacity in elderly and closed-head injury subjects with clinical memory deficits. *Journal of Clinical and Experimental Neuropsychology, 17*, 29-34.

Tombaugh, T. N., and Scmidt, J. P. (1992). The learning and memory battery: Development and standardization. *Psychological Assessment, 4*, 193-206.

Tombaugh, T. N., and Hubley, A. M. (2001). Rates of forgetting on three measures of verbal learning using retention intervals ranging from 20 min to 62 days. *Journal of the International Neuropsychological Society 7*, 79-91.

Touron, D. R. and Hertzog, C. (2004). Strategy shift affordance and strategy choice in young and older adults. *Memory and Cognition, 32*, 298 - 310.

Trahan, D. E. and Larrabee, G. J. (1988). *Continuous Visual Memory Test*. Odessa, FL: Psychological Assessment Resources.

Trahan, D. E., and Larrabee, G. J. (1992). Effect of normal aging on rate of forgetting. *Neuropsychology, 6*, 115-122.

Tsang, M. H., Aronson, H., and Hayslip, B. (1991). Standardization of a learning and retention task with community residing older adults. *The Clinical Neuropsychologist, 5*, 67-77.

Walhovd, K. B., Fjell, A. M., Reinvang, I, Lundervold A, Fischl, B, Quinn, B. T., and Dale, A. M. (2004). Size does matter in the long run - Hippocampal and cortical volume predict recall across weeks. *Neurology, 63*, 1193-1197.

Walhovd, K.- B. and Fjell, A. M. (2003). The relationship between P3 and neuropsychological function in an adult life span sample. *Biological Psychology, 62*, 65-87.

Wechsler, D. (1999). *Wechsler Abbreviated Scale of Intelligence*. San Antonio, TX: The Psychological Corporation.

Williams, E. J. (1959). The comparison of regression variables. *Journals of the Royal Statistical Society (Series B), 21*, 396-399.

Woodruff-Pak, D. S., and Finkbiner, R. G. (1995). Larger non-declarative than declarative deficits in learning and memory in human aging. *Psychology and Aging, 10*, 416-426.

Wheeler, M. A. (2000). A comparison of forgetting rates in older and younger adults. *Aging, Neuropsychology, and Cognition, 7*, 179-193.

Youngjohn, J. R. and Crook, T. H. (1993). Learning, forgetting and retrieval of everyday material across the adult lifespan. *Journal of Clinical and Experimental Neuropsychology, 15*, 447-460.

In: New Psychological Tests and Testing Research
Editor: Lydia S. Boyar, pp. 231-241

ISBN: 978-1-60021-570-4
© 2007 Nova Science Publishers, Inc.

Chapter 13

THE EFFECTS OF EXPERTISE LEVEL AND MOTOR SKILL CHARACTERISTICS ON MENTAL ROTATION

Aymeric Guillot[*], Magali Louis,
Patrice Thiriet and Christian Collet

Université Lyon 1, Université de Lyon, EA 647, Centre de Recherche et d'Innovation sur le Sport, 27-29 Boulevard du 11 Novembre 1918, 69622 Villeurbanne Cedex, France.

ABSTRACT

This study investigated the effect of sport expertise level and motor skill requirements on mental rotation ability, by comparing athletes with non-athletes abilities using a well-established mental rotation questionnaire. A total of 496 students (404 athletes and 92 non-athletes), aged from 17 to 32 years, participated in the study and completed the Mental Rotation Test (Vandenberg and Kuse, 1978). The results confirmed the well-established gender effect, men scoring higher than women. However, the results showed that athletes did not score better than non-athletes and they challenged the hypothesis stating that athletes, who usually have to perform spatial body rotations may have greater mental rotation ability than those whose sporting activities do not require a modification of the body's postural organization. There was, therefore, a lack of evidence of any transfer between the ability to perform physical rotations during sporting situations to mental rotations of non-body objects. Finally, no effect related to expertise level was found, suggesting that the general mental rotation ability did not depend on expertise level, by contrast to the motor imagery ability.

Keywords: Mental rotation, Motor performance, Open/Closed skills.

---

[*] Correspondence: Aymeric Guillot, Centre de Recherche et d'Innovation sur le Sport, Université Claude Bernard Lyon I, 27-29 Boulevard du 11 Novembre 1918, 69622 Villeurbanne cedex, France. Tél.: 33 4 72 43 16 25 Fax: 33 4 72 43 28 46; e-mail: aymeric.guillot@univ-lyon1.fr

INTRODUCTION

The effects of motor imagery to improve motor task performance are well-established in the sport's literature (Feltz and Landers, 1983; Driskell, Copper and Moran, 1994). Data collected in population of expert athletes, or in athletes with high motor imagery abilities, have provided evidence that they form mental representations of movements more easily than intermediate or novices athletes with poorer motor imagery abilities. Altogether, when considering the preservation of temporal characteristics of actual movement during motor imagery, the timing of the expert athletes of mentally simulated actions has been found to closely approximate the actual movement times, while the timing of the non-athletes is inconsistent (for review, see Guillot and Collet, 2005). This may be explained, at least partially, by the perceived difficulty of the task, but also by the amount of knowledge of how to perform and the degree of movement automation (Reed, 2002). Similarly, non-expert athletes have been found to have greater difficulty in using kinesthetic imagery (*i.e.* perceiving the movement through muscles and articulations cues) than visual imagery (Guillot, Collet and Dittmar, 2004), since kinesthetic imagery is beneficial only with an adequate degree of expertise (Hardy and Callow, 1999).

Among the various components of motor imagery, athletes may form mental images of motor acts including rotations of the whole body or of a body part. For example, gymnasts usually imagine a series of complex skills including acrobatics, such as tucked or stretched saltos. Hence, motor imagery accuracy will depend on image vividness and preservation of the temporal organization of the movements, but also on the abilities of the athletes to rotate their body mentally. Mental rotation (MR), therefore, requires cognitive manipulation and spatial transformation of an imagined object. MR ability has been found to be useful in spatial reasoning and problem-solving, such as with spatial orientations and mental navigation tasks using map displays (Gunzelmann and Anderson, 2004). Initially, behavioral experiments were conducted to investigate the processes of MR and typical experimental designs requested subjects to judge whether pairs of visual 3D stimuli, presented from different angles, were identical or not (*e.g.* the Shepard and Metzler test, 1971). Results suggested that subjects formed a visual image of the object and rotated this image, until equivalence with the reference was reached. In recent years, both object and body MR have been investigated through neuroimaging techniques to determine the neural foundations of MR (*e.g.* Parsons, 2003; Vingerhoets, De Lange, Vandemaele, Debmaere and Achten, 2002; Wexler, Kosslyn and Berthoz, 1998; Wraga, Shephard, Church, Inati and Kosslyn, 2005; Zacks, Rypma, Gabrieli, Tversky and Glover, 1999). The main structures to be activated were the frontal and prefrontal cortical areas, associated with parietal and temporal cortices, as well as extrastriate visual regions. Although, the main parts of the cerebral cortex were involved, differences being shown to be task-dependent. However, only a few studies were devised to examine the effects of "sport expertise" on MR ability. Overby (1990) has shown that experienced dancers significantly differed from novices on their spatial abilities. Dror, Kosslyn and Waag (1993) have further hypothesized that US air-force pilots had higher MR ability than non-pilots, as they frequently found themselves in orientations requiring them to use imagery and to rotate objects back to their upright relative positions. Although they were not better than non-pilots at scanning visual mental images or at encoding the kind of spatial relations that were used to note the relative positions of the segment, they were found to mentally rotate objects faster than non-pilots. Similarly, Naito (1994) has reported that athletes performed better than non-athletes in a MR task. More recently, Ozel, Larue and Molinaro (2004) have hypothesized that open-skill athletes ought to be quicker than closed-skill athletes in the encoding, discrimination and execution phases of motor response, but that they shouldn't be any different in the MR phase. They also have provided evidence that non-athletes took longer to discriminate and rotate the objects mentally. However, the authors did not find any effect when they compared the open-skills to the closed-skills athletes. This latter result remains difficult to interpret, as athletes engaged in specific motor skills requiring several body rotations (such as gymnastics or trampoline) may be expected to have better MR abilities and therefore to perform MR more easily than athletes who never experienced physical rotations. Moreover, the sample size used by Ozel et al. (2004) may have been too small to elicit differences between open- and closed-skill athletes, as only 36 athletes (3 groups of 12 subjects) took part in their experiment. Finally, the authors did not take into consideration the expertise levels of the athletes (all participants trained 10 hours a week). Based on these findings, the current study was devised to re-examine the effects of both expertise level and motor skill requirements on MR ability. Athletes who usually perform physical rotations were expected to score better than athletes engaged in motor skills that do not require body rotations. Furthermore, it was hypothesized that the expertise level may increase the ability to perform MR.

MATERIALS AND METHODS

Participants

A total of 496 students (327 men and 169 women, mean age 19.9 years, range 17–32 years, SD=2.9) took part in the experiment, after providing their informed consent. The non-athlete group comprised 32 men and 60 women, aged from 18 to 32 years (mean age 23.25 years, SD=3.1). All were students enrolled for a literature course and/or agronomics lectures at the University of Lyon (France) and they did not practice any regular sports activities. The participants of the athletes' group (295 men and 109 women, mean age 19.13 years, range 17–28 years, SD=1.3) were students enrolled for a course in sport at Claude Bernard University (Lyon, France). Experimental procedures were approved by the local research ethics board. Participants had normal or corrected-to-normal vision, and none had any specific experience in the field of spatial cognition. The students were not aware of the purpose or hypotheses of the experiment until after the test was completed. The athletes came from various sports and had different expertise levels (table 1).

Table 1. Sport categories and expertise level of athletes. Each athlete fell into one of the three categories: team sport (group 1), sports requiring athletes to perform physical rotations (group 2) and individual sporting activities which do not (group 3). Three levels of expertise were distinguished (novices, regional and national)

	Level 1 - novices		Level 2 - Régional	Level 3 - National		Total	Sport Category (group)
	Novices	Intermediate	Regional	National	International		
Archery				1		1	3
Badminton	4	4	3	1		12	3
Basketball		19	22	4	2	47	1
Climbing	5	3			2	10	3
Cycling		1	6	1	1	9	3
Dancing	6	1		3		10	2
Equestrian sports		4	3	1		8	3
Football				1		1	1
Gymnastics		1	4	12		17	2
Handball		5	6	7		18	1
Horse-ball				1		1	1
Ice Hockey				1		1	1
Judo	3	3	6	4		16	2
Kayak	1		1	4		6	3
Martial arts	1	3	9	6		19	2
Pétanque				1	1	2	3
Powerlifting	2		2			4	3
Rhythmic gymnastics			1	4		5	2
Rink-hockey			1			1	1
Rowing				3		3	3
Rugby	1	2	12	10	2	27	1
Sailing	2			3		2	3

Table 1. (Continued).

	Level 1 - novices		Level 2 - Régional	Level 3 - National		Total	Sport Category (group)
	Novices	Intermediate	Regional	National	International		
Skating	1			1		2	3
Ski	2	2	2	2		8	3
Snowboard	1					1	2
Soccer	4	40	48	1		93	1
Subaquatic diving	1					1	2
Swimming	3	2	4	4		13	3
Table tennis		6	4			10	3
Tennis		20	8			28	3
Track and field	1	3	5	3	1	13	3
Trampolin				1		1	2
Volleyball	2	8	3			13	1
Waterpolo				1		1	1
Total	*40*	*127*	*150*	*78*	*9*	*404*	

Procedure

The participants completed the Vandenberg and Kuse (1978) Mental Rotation Test (MRT). Particular sessions were scheduled on campus, in order for the test to be simultaneously conducted in a quiet room with a group of around 30 students. The MRT was constructed from the 3D items used in the chronometric study by Shepard and Metzler (1971). A reference item was presented on the left, while 4 other figures were placed on the right of the page. Two figures among the 4 presented were systematically similar to the reference, albeit rotated around one axis in increments of 20° (Hochberg and Gellman, 1977). Participants were asked to find and cross the two 3D objects, which were identical to the reference. They were told to rotate figures mentally, in order to match them to the reference whenever possible. The test was made up of 24 items and the reference figure changed on each line. The trials were completed within a 6-minute period. Participants were discouraged from using a strategy that would lead to a decrease in response times at the expense of the correct number of responses.

Data Analysis

The MRT score was the dependent variable, while the independent variables were the characteristics of the population (athletes *vs.* non-athletes), the type of sport (open-skills *vs.* closed-skills), as well as the gender and the expertise level (novices, regional and national). As in the study by Peters et al. (1995), the MRT scoring method that discouraged guessing was used, 1 single point being given, if and only if, both stimuli were correctly identified. This method was favored by Vandenberg and Kuse (1978). MRT Scores thus, ranged for each individual from 0 to 24. MRT scores were then compared for each condition by using an analysis of variance. The significant threshold for all analyses was set at $p < .05$.

RESULTS

The mean MRT score for the whole population (athlete and non-athlete groups) was 8.94 (SD = 4). Men scored significantly better than women ($F_{1,494} = 49.76$, $p < .001$), mean scores being 9.81 (SD = 3.9) and 7.26 (SD = 3.6) respectively. The mean non-athletes MRT score was 7.71 (SD = 4.1), the lowest and highest scores being 0 and 21. Men were found to score significantly higher than women ($F_{1,90} = 4.5$, $p < .05$), mean scores being 8.94 (SD = 4.1) and 7.05 (SD = 4.1) respectively. Further, the mean athletes MRT score was 9.23 (SD = 3.9), the lowest and highest scores being 1 and 22. Men were also found to score significantly better than women ($F_{1,402} = 35.35$, $p < .001$), mean scores being 9.89 (SD = 3.9) and 7.38 (SD = 3.3) respectively.

To analyze the effects of the requirements of sporting activities, athletes were divided into different groups. First, three expertise levels were distinguished (novices, regional or national/international athletes), and athletes were also divided into 3 groups according to the characteristics of their sporting activity: *i)* team sports (*e.g.* soccer, basketball or rugby – Group 1), *ii)* sports requiring athletes to perform physical rotations (*e.g.* gymnastics, trampoline – Group 2) and *iii)* other individual sporting activities (*e.g.* cycling, racket sports, sailing, archery – Group 3). A 3 x 3 (expertise level x sporting activity group) analysis of variance showed that the difference did not reach a significant level ($F_{2,399}$ = 2.03, p = .09). More generally, athletes scored better than non-athletes ($F_{2,494}$ = 11.9, p < .001). However, as there was a strong effect of gender, and as the distribution of men and women was strongly different across the groups, comparisons between men and women within the 4 groups (3 athlete groups and 1 non-athlete group) were conducted. A 4 x 2 (sport groups x gender) analysis of variance confirmed the strong effect of gender in favor of males ($F_{1,488}$ = 34.7, p < .001), but did not show a significant effect of the sport category ($F_{3,488}$ = .8, p > .05) or an interaction of sport group x gender ($F_{3,488}$ = .22, p > .05). Whatever the gender, athletes were therefore not found to score better than non-athletes.

Second, results were compared between athletes performing individual sporting activities and team sport athletes, with the different levels of expertise taken into consideration. Although individual sport athletes scored lower than team sport athletes, the 3 x 2 (expertise level x individual/team sport) analysis of variance did not show a significant interaction ($F_{2,399}$ = 1.36, p > .05), mean scores being 8.69 (SD = 4.1) and 9.63 (SD = 3.9) respectively.

Finally, the specific effect of open *vs.* closed skills was investigated by comparing results obtained by athletes for their respective types of sports, using a 3 x 2 (expertise level x open/closed skills) analysis of variance. Open-skills athletes were found to score lower than closed-skills athletes, but no significant difference was shown between the 2 groups, with regard to their expertise levels ($F_{2,399}$ = .11, p > .05), mean score being 8.89 (SD = 3.9) and 9.30 (SD = 3.9) respectively. These results are summarized in Figure 1.

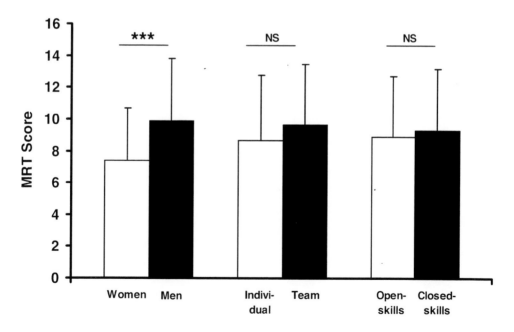

Figure 1. Effect of gender and sport affiliations on the Mental Rotation Test (MRT) in athletes. Men were found to score significantly better than women. The difference did not reach significance when considering sport affiliations. ***: p<0.001, NS: non-significant.

CONCLUSION

The aim of the study was to test the hypothesis of transferring MR ability of 3D objects according to three factors: performing a sport's activity or not, the sport's level practiced and gender. The athletes engaged in closed skills and who usually perform physical body rotations were expected to have greater MR ability than those engaged in other types of sports. The expertise level was also expected to influence the MRT scores, as high-level athletes are supposed to have greater MR abilities than non-expert athletes. Previous work by Ozel et al. (2004) challenged this hypothesis as their results showed that open-skill athletes did not perform better than closed-skill athletes in a MR task. However, the authors did not take into consideration the expertise level, and the sample size may have been too small to elicit significant differences among groups. First, the current results did not provide evidence that the athletes scored better than non-athletes in a MR task in spatial abilities and on both discrimination and rotation times, as suggested by Overby (1990), Naito (1994) and Ozel et al. (2004). Indeed, the difference in performance between the two groups was dependent on gender. Second, although a larger sample was used in our study, the MRT scores did not depend on the type of sport or the expertise level of athletes. In sum, athletes who usually perform physical body rotations did not have greater abilities in rotating 3D objects. The athletes, who usually have specific motor imagery training, did not transfer their ability to form accurate mental images of body movements to a MR task of 3D objects. This finding supports the hypothesis stated by Heil, Roesler, Link and Bajric (1998), hence suggesting that MR skills may only be transferred to an identical condition. However, experimental data showed that motor activation elicited by MR of body parts (Zacks et al., 1999) could be transferred implicitly across different MR tasks of non-body objects, even without specific instructions (Wraga, Thompson, Alpert and Kosslyn, 2003), although researchers have consistently found faster and more accurate performances during imagined self-rotations than during MR of an object (*e.g.* Amorim and Stucchi, 1997; Wraga, Creem and Proffitt, 2000). At this time, the degree of specificity of the implicit transfer, therefore, remains unclear, as a body-centered egocentric reference frame may not map onto an object-relative reference frame as readily as does a hand-centered frame (Wraga et al., 2003). This may explain the lack of transfer between the ability to perform physical rotations during sport's situations to MR of non-body objects observed in the current study.

Furthermore, Wraga et al. (2005) and Zacks et al. (2005) have reported that MR of a body part and of non-body objects activates distinct neural mechanisms as low-level motor areas were specifically activated during object rotation tasks. Finally, studies with brain-damaged patients have also provided evidence of a dissociation between deficits in egocentric and externally based-object MR tasks (Rumiati, Tomasino, Vorano, Umiltà and De Luca, 2001; Sirigu and Duhamel, 2001; Tomasino, Toraldo and Rumiati, 2003). When considering these results, it may be hypothesized that even though the practice of a sporting activity requiring some body rotation may be expected to be linked to a general MR ability, there is no evidence of a specific effect of open-skills *vs.* closed-skills or of the expertise level, *i.e.* no transfer between MR of a 3D object to MR of a body part.

Although this study did not focus specifically on differences between males and females, strong gender effects were found. These results support the well-established gender differences in MR, men scoring higher than women (Jones, Braithwaite and Healy, 2003;

Guillot, Champely, Batier, Thiriet and Collet, 2006). Women have generally been found to encounter greater difficulties in generating and manipulating mental images of 3D objects due to their lower spatial ability's potential, whereas men and women are supposed to use similar motor strategies during egocentric MR (Seurinck, Vingerhoetz, De Lange and Achten, 2004). However, the advantage of males in spatial ability still remains unclear and could be explained by multifaceted factors, including socio-cultural differences, task complexity, biological factors (hormonal influences and brain organization) or time taken to perform MR (Parsons et al., 2004; Peters, 1995).

To summarize, although a potential positive transfer between a neutral MR task involving 3D objects and another MR task of the body (or a body part), may be of interest in sporting activities, current findings did not lead to this conclusion. Especially, as in the study by Ozel et al. (2004), there was no relationship between MRT scores and both expertise level and types of sport. Moreover, these results did not replicate the difference between athletes and non-athletes, challenging the hypothesis of Ozel et al. (2004), who suggested a positive effect of regular sport practice on MR ability. However, these authors reported that there was an effect of sport practice when considering both the discrimination and rotation times. Such factors were not investigated in this particular study, as we only focused on the number of correct responses in the MR test. Finally, the relationship between sport practice and MR may reach significance if MR tests would specifically require subjects to perform MR of body segments, as they usually perform them during physical exercise, instead of 3D objects. Especially, Amorim, Isableu and Jarraya (2006) have recently reported that providing 3D cubes with body characteristics (*e.g.* by adding a head to the cubes to evoke a posture) may facilitate the mapping of the cognitive coordinate system of one's body onto the abstract shape. However, this hypothesis still remains an ongoing assumption awaiting further experimental investigation.

REFERENCES

Amorim, M. A. and Stucchi, N. (1997). Viewer- and object-centered mental explorations of an imagined environment are not equivalent. *Cognitive Brain Research, 5,* 229-239.

Amorim, M. A., Isableu, B. and Jarraya M. (2006). Embodied spatial transformations: "body analogy" for the mental rotation of objects. *Journal of Experimental Psychology: General, 135,* 327-347.

Driskell, J. E., Copper, C. and Moran, A. (1994). Does mental practice enhance performance? *Journal of Applied Psychology, 79,* 481-492.

Dror, I. E., Kosslyn, S. M. and Waag, W. L. (1993). Visual-spatial abilities of pilots. *Journal of Applied Psychology, 78,* 763-773.

Feltz, D. L. and Landers, D. M. (1983) The effects of mental practice on motor skill learning and performance: a meta-analysis. *Journal of Psychology, 5,* 25-57.

Guillot, A., Collet, C. and Dittmar, A. (2004). Relationship between visual *vs* kinesthetic imagery, field dependence-independence and complex motor skills. *Journal of Psychophysiology, 18* 190-199.

Guillot, A. and Collet, C. (2005). Duration of mentally simulated movement: a review. *Journal of Motor Behavior, 37* 10-20.

Guillot, A., Champely, S., Batier, C., Thiriet, P. and Collet, C. (2006). Relationship between spatial abilities, mental rotation and functional anatomy learning. *Advances in Health Sciences Education*, in press, DOI: 10.1007/s10459-006-9021-7.

Gunzelmann, G. and Anderson, J. R. (2004). *Spatial orientation using map displays: a model of the influence of target location*. Proceedings of the 26th Annual Conference of the Cognitive Science Society, August 4-7 (pp .517-522), Chicago, USA.

Hardy, L. Callow, N. 1999. Efficacy of external and internal visual imagery perspectives for the enhancement of performance on tasks in which form is important. *Journal of Sport and Exercise Psychology, 21*, 95-112.

Heil, M., Roesler, F., Link, M. and Bajric, J. (1998). What is improved if a mental rotation task is repeated - The efficiency of memory access, or the speed of a transformation routine? *Psychological Research, 61*, 99-106.

Jones, C. M., Braithwaite, V. A. and Healy, S. D. (2003). The evolution of sex differences in spatial ability. *Behavioural Neuroscience, 117*, 403-411.

Naito, E. (1994). Controllability of motor imagery and transformation of visual imagery. *Perceptual and Motor Skills, 78*, 479-487.

Overby, L. Y. (1990). A comparison of novices and experienced dancers' imagery ability. *Journal of mental imagery, 14*, 173-184.

Ozel, S., Larue, J. and Molinaro, C. (2004). Relation between sport and spatial imagery: comparison of three groups of participants. *Journal of Psychology 138*, 49-63.

Parsons, T. D., Larson, P., Kratz, K., Thiebaux, M., Bluestein, B., Buckwalter, J. G. and Rizzo, A. A. (2004). Sex differences in mental rotation and spatial rotation in a virtual environment. *Neuropsychologia, 42*, 555-562.

Parsons, L. M. (2003). Superior parietal cortices and varieties of mental rotation. *Trends in Cognitive Neurosciences, 7*, 515-517.

Peters, M. (2005). Sex differences and the factor of time in solving Vandenberg and Kuse mental rotation problems. *Brain and Cognition, 57*, 176-184.

Reed, C. L. (2002). Chronometric comparisons of imagery to action: visualizing versus physically performing springboard dives. *Memory and Cognition, 30*, 1169-1178.

Rumiati, R. I., Tomasino, B., Vorano, L., Umiltà, C. and De Luca, G. (2001). Selective deficit of imagining finger configurations. *Cortex, 37*, 730-733.

Seurinck, R., Vingerhoetz, G., De Lange, F. P. and Achten, E. (2004). Does egocentric mental rotation elicit sex differences? *Neuroimage, 23*, 1440-1449.

Shepard, R. N. and Metzler, J. (1971). Mental rotation of three dimensional objects. *Science 171*, 701–703.

Sirigu, A. and Duhamel, J. R. (2001). Motor and visual imagery as two complementary but neurally dissociable processes. *Journal of Cognitive Neuroscience, 13*, 910-919.

Tomasino, B., Toraldo, A. and Rumiati, R. I. (2003). Dissociation between the mental rotation of visual images and motor images in unilateral brain-damaged patients. *Brain and Cognition, 51*, 368-371.

Vandenberg, S. and Kuse, A. (1978). Mental rotation, a group test of 3-D spatial visualization. *Perceptual and Motor Skills, 47*, 599-604.

Vingerhoets, G., De Lange, F. P., Vandemaele, P., Debmaere, K. and Achten, E. (2002). Motor imagery in mental rotation: an fMRI study. *Neuroimage, 17*, 1623-1633.

Wexler, M., Kosslyn, S. M. and Berthoz, A. (1998). Motor processes in mental rotation. *Cognition, 68*, 77-94.

Wraga, M., Creem, S. H. and Proffitt, D.R. (2000). Updating displays after imagined object and viewer rotations. *Journal of Experimental Psychology: Learning, Memory and Cognition, 26*, 153-168.

Wraga, M., Thompson, W. L., Alpert, N. M. and Kosslyn, S. M. (2003). Implicit transfer of motor strategies in mental rotation. Brain and Cognition, 52, 135-143.

Wraga, M., Shephard, J. M., Church, J. A., Inati, S. and Kosslyn, S. M. (2005). Imaging rotation of self versus objects: an fMRI study. *Neuropychologia, 43*, 1351-1361.

Zacks, J., Rypma, B., Gabrieli, J. D. E., Tversky B. and Glover, G. H. (1999). Imagined transformations of bodies: an fMRI investigation. *Neuropsychologia, 37*, 1029-1040.

INDEX

B

C

F

O

N

P

Q

R

T

U

V

W